Markets in the Name of Socialism

Markets in the Name of Socialism

The Left-Wing Origins of Neoliberalism

Johanna Bockman

Stanford University Press

Stanford, California

Stanford University Press
Stanford, California

Printed on acid-free, archival-quality paper

Printed and bound in Great Britain by
Marston Book Services Ltd, Oxfordshire

Library of Congress Cataloging-in-Publication Data

Bockman, Johanna, author.
    Markets in the name of socialism : the left-wing origins of neoliberalism /
Johanna Bockman.
        pages cm
    Includes bibliographical references and index.
    ISBN 978-0-8047-7566-3 (cloth : alk. paper)
    ISBN 978-0-8047-8859-5 (pbk. : alk. paper)
    1. Neoliberalism—History.   2. Neoclassical school of economics—History.
3. Marxian economics—History.   4. Socialism—History.   I. Title.
    HB95.B63 2011
    320.51—dc22

                                                            2010045298

Typeset by Thompson Type in 11/13.5 Adobe Garamond

Contents

Preface

IN FALL 1988, I ARRIVED IN BUDAPEST, Hungary as an exchange student through the University of California's Education Abroad Program. I fell into a situation that I did not understand but that would send my life in a new direction. Through the year, at the Karl Marx University of Economics, we exchange students studied with Hungarian scholars, who provided us new ways to understand the world, even in such courses as American literature. We took part in large protests, visits to Roma villages, evenings in underground punk clubs, panicked discussions with our Education Abroad Program directors, and the general social life of young college students, who happened to arrive in a place of historic change.

The language of our professors, who talked positively about markets, democracy, and freedom, surprised me. The American right wing had done so much to politicize these words and done such evil in Central America and elsewhere in their name. Our professors in the Karl Marx University of Economics sounded like Reagan robots. After returning to the United States and entering graduate school, I found myself drawn to trying to understand what I had experienced. What was socialism? What was capitalism? What had happened in 1989? This book is my current answer to these questions.

During my dissertation research, I discovered that Hungarians had been calling for both markets and socialism since the 1950s. For those familiar with Hungary, such a discovery was not a surprise. Yet, in the 1990s, scholars already assumed that socialism had been, and would likely always be, the centrally planned, state socialism exemplified by the Soviet Union. In this environment, a reminder of Hungary's market socialist past was important. At the same time, I found that some Hungarian econo-mists had studied in the United States and elsewhere, exposing themselves to mainstream neoclassical economics. In the 1990s, it was important to recognize that Hungarians were not entirely isolated from the rest of the world. In my dissertation, I had assumed that this exposure to American neoclassical economics, in particular, had made Hungarian economists capitalist.

Yet I felt that I still did not understand what happened in 1989. As a postdoctoral fellow at Harvard University's Davis Center for Russian Studies, I began interviewing American economists who had worked with Hungarians and other Eastern Europeans during the Cold War. The econo-mists involved in these East–West discussions were not peripheral but rather central figures in the field. How did these Americans indoctrinate Eastern European economists into capitalism? To understand the indoc-trination process, I had to understand professional economists' theories and models. What were they exporting abroad? Following their connec-tions with other economists took me to Italy and the former Yugoslavia. It also introduced me to an economics dialogue that extended throughout the first, second, and third worlds. Through years of interviews, I realized that American economists did not export neoclassical economics as an American model but rather that neoclassical economics since its begin-nings offered a language that economists around the world used to talk about markets and planning, economic freedom and efficiency, capitalism and socialism.

I would not have understood economists' ideas without sitting with many of them for hours over many years. These economists often found my interviews confusing and disorienting. What did I want to know? I wanted to understand their ideas, their training, their motivations, their politics, and their lives in general. I found all of this essential to under-standing their ideas. These economists gave me much of their time be-cause, I believe, they wanted some answers too.

Economists' voices are not directly quoted in this manuscript for several reasons. From the start, I sensed that tape recording and signing Human Subjects Review forms raised suspicions among my interviewees worldwide. One economist told me that, if I recorded our discussion, he would not tell me anything. I quickly turned to taking notes by hand and no longer thought about Human Subjects Review. Instead, I decided to use these interviews as a springboard for research, to direct me to archives and published materials. These interviews also became more like conversations. It was extremely difficult to understand what the economists were trying to tell me, both technically and politically. I slowly began to understand them and tried out my interpretations on other economists to get their feedback. Therefore, economists became more like conversation partners than interviewees.

At the same time, it is disappointing not to have a verbatim written or audio record of my interviews with these economists. Many of them have since passed away. However, I had long ago decided to interview economists as part of a process of making sense of their worlds. I felt driven to write this book because many, though by no means all, of these economists were connected in so many ways to people who had fought to change the world in liberating ways. As I wrote about Italian economics, such a potentially bland topic, my mind was full of the connections of its practitioners with Second World War antifascist partisans, with their colleagues who had lost their lives in the Soviet Union under Stalin, with Third World allies, and with official and dissident socialists worldwide. To tap into and document part of this flow of energy and experience has been exhilarating. It has also helped me to understand 1989 and socialism for myself. I thank all the economists and other individuals who spoke with me. The interpretations advanced and any errors are my responsibility alone.

List of Interviewees

The affiliations listed are those at the time of the interviews.

Economists

Luca Anselmi, University of Pisa, 2004

Kenneth Arrow, Stanford University, 2007

Abram Bergson, Harvard University, 2000

Joseph Berliner, Harvard University, 2001

Ivo Bićanić, University of Zagreb, 2008

Ferruccio Bresolin, Ca' Foscari University, Venice, 2004

András Bródy, Institute of Economics, Budapest, 1995 and 1996

Giorgio Brosio, University of Turin, 2004

Andrzej Brzeski, University of California, Davis, 2004

Anne Carter, Brandeis University, 2000 and 2001

Božidar Cerović, University of Belgrade, 2008

Janet Chapman, formerly Harvard University, 2001

Alberto Chilosi, University of Pisa, 2004

Richard Cooper, Harvard University, 2001

Béla Csikós-Nagy, Hungarian Economic Association, 2002

Bruno Dallago, University of Trento, 2004

Robert Dorfman, Harvard University, 2000

Božo Drašković, Institute of Economic Sciences, Belgrade, 2008

Ivo Družić, University of Zagreb, 2008

Dinko Dubravčić, Institute of Economics, Zagreb, 2008

John T. Dunlop, Harvard University, 2000

Dejan Erić, Institute of Economic Sciences, Belgrade, 2008

Mario Ferrero, University of Eastern Piedmont, 2004
Murray Feshbach, Woodrow Wilson Center, 2002
Vojmir Franičević, University of Zagreb, 2008
Marshall Goldman, Harvard University, 2000
Gregory Grossman, University of California, Berkeley, 2001 and 2004
Hans Heymann, formerly Central Intelligence Agency, 2001
Branko Hvastija, Center for International Cooperation & Development, Ljubljana, 2008
Peter de Janosi, formerly Ford Foundation, 2001
Dale Jorgenson, Harvard University, 2001
Milena Jovičić, University of Belgrade, 2008
Peter T. Knight, formerly Ford Foundation and World Bank, 2007
János Kornai, Harvard University and Collegium Budapest, 2000
Oskar Kovač, Megatrend University, 2008
Roger Levien, formerly RAND, 2001
Aladár Madarász, Institute of Economics, Budapest, 1996
Ljubomir Madžar, "Braća Karić" University, Belgrade, 2008
Stephen Marglin, Harvard University, 2000
Jože Mencinger, University of Ljubljana, 2008
Mieke Meurs, American University, 2007
Branko Milanović, World Bank, 2008
Milić Milovanović, University of Belgrade, 2008
Jim Millar, George Washington University, 2002.
Peter Miovic, World Bank, 2008
J. Michael Montias, Yale University, 2000 and 2001
John H. Moore, Grove City College, 2001
András Nagy, Institute of Economics, Budapest, 1995.
D. Mario Nuti, University of Rome "La Sapienza," 2004
Časlav Ocić, formerly Institute of Economic Sciences, Belgrade, 2008
Merton J. Peck, Yale University, 2001
Pavle Petrović, University of Belgrade, 2008
Janez Prašnikar, University of Ljubljana, 2008
Howard Raiffa, Harvard University, 2000
Ivan Ribnikar, University of Ljubljana, 2008
Gianni Salvini, University of Pavia, 2004 and 2005
Thomas Schelling, University of Maryland, 2001
Gertrude Schroeder, formerly Central Intelligence Agency, 2001.
Michael Schwarz, Harvard University, 2001

Marjan Senjur, University of Ljubljana, 2008
Jan Svejnar, University of Michigan, 2008
László Szamuely, Kopint-Datorg, Institute for Economic and Market Research
    and Informatics, Budapest, 1998
Maks Tajnikar, University of Ljubljana, 2008
Vladimir Treml, Duke University 2001
Aleš Vahčič, University of Ljubljana, 2008
Vittorio Valli, University of Turin, 2004
Milan Vodopivec, World Bank, 2008
Gordana Vukotić-Cotič, Institute of Economic Sciences, Belgrade, 2008
Benjamin Ward, formerly University of California, Berkeley, 2007
Martin Weitzman, Harvard University, 2001

Others Interviewed

Francesco Leoncini, Ca' Foscari University, Venice, 2005
Carlo Lottieri, Bruno Leoni Institute, Turin, 2004
Bianca Mieli, Milan, 2004
Leonardo Morlino, University of Florence, 2004
Igor Pavlin, International Center for Promotion of Enterprises, Ljubljana, 2008
Yale Richmond, formerly U.S. State Department, 2001
Duško Sekulić, University of Zagreb, 2008
Priyadarshi Thakur, International Center for Promotion of Enterprises,
    Ljubljana, 2008
Anton Vratuša, International Center for Promotion of Enterprises, Ljubljana,
    2008

Acknowledgments

A BOOK OF THIS SCALE accumulates many debts. My most important debt is to Andrew Zimmerman. I could not have completed this book without his scholarly and personal support. Our continuous discussions and lively debates made the book much better than it would otherwise have been. He has also read the book countless times. The benefits of such a shared intellectual life are endless.

A second important debt is to the Library of Congress, especially the European Reading Room and the John F. Kluge Center. While my research took me around the world, the Library of Congress is just down the street from my house and has one of the greatest collections of books, journals, and manuscripts. The European Reading Room provides a beautiful space in which to read these wonderful works, as well as to drink tea on Friday afternoons. As a fellow at the John F. Kluge Center, I benefited immensely from the intellectual life created by Caroline Brown, Marcy Dinius, Monica Dominguez Torres, Agnes Kefeli, Kelly Pemberton, Mary Lou Reker, Zachary Schrag, and Vidhya Swaminathan. I am very lucky to live near such a national treasure.

Research and writing for this book was generously supported by the American Council for Learned Societies (ACLS); the Center for Global Studies and the Office of the Provost at George Mason University; the Davis Center for Russian Studies at Harvard University; the Institute for European, Russian, and Eurasian Studies at the George Washington University; the International Research and Exchanges Board (IREX); the John W. Kluge Center at the Library of Congress; and the Woodrow Wilson International Center for Scholars. I am grateful to these institutions for their support. I would also like to thank the archives for giving me access to their papers and an enjoyable environment in which to work: the Archives of Serbia and Montenegro, the Confindustria Archives, the Ford Foundation Archives, the archives of Harvard University, the Hoover Institution Archives, the archives of the Hungarian Academy of Sciences, the Hungarian Communist Party Institute Archive, Hungarian Communist Party Institute Archive, the archive of the Budapest University of Economic Science, the Hungarian National Archive, the Library of Congress's Manuscript Room, the Oral History Archives, and the Yale University archives.

Many individuals read parts of this book, made important comments and criticisms, and generously shared their knowledge and views with me. I mentioned in the preface the economists who helped me to make sense of their field. I want to give special thanks to Kenneth Arrow, Branko Milanović, Gianni Salvini, and Howard Wachtel for their comments on chapters of this book or my related articles. Gil Eyal, Dietrich Rueschemeyer, and Yuval Yonay, as well as several anonymous reviewers, read the entire manuscript and have made substantial contributions to the logic and strength of the manuscript. Many thanks also to Michael Bernstein, András Bródy, Ellen Comisso, Martha Lampland, Ákos Róna-Tas, and Steven Shapin for reading earlier parts of this book. I learned much from my coauthors Michael Bernstein and Gil Eyal. Margo Beth Crouppen and Jessica Walsh at Stanford University Press, as well as my copy editor Margaret Pinette, have been a joy to work with. I also wish to thank James Cook for his kind support of my manuscript.

As a postdoctoral fellow at Harvard University's Davis Center for Russian Studies, I had the great opportunity to participate in various working groups. I would like to thank David Engerman, Ethan Pollock, Sheila Jasanoff, and the participants in her Science Studies Research Seminar. I would also like to thank Volker Berghahn and Timothy Mitchell for their continuous support. Timothy Mitchell invited me to New York University to a formative workshop on "How Neoliberalism Became a Transnational Movement."

I feel lucky to be a part of George Mason University. Our provost Peter Stearns has been supportive of me since the first day I arrived. Faculty in my department greatly influence my work. I thank especially Amy Best, John Dale, Hugh Gusterson, Nancy Hanrahan, Mark Jacobs, Karen Rosenblum, Tony Samara, Susan Trencher, and Steve Vallas, as well as

Terrence Lyons, Peter Mandaville, Agnieszka Paczyńska, and Paul Smith in other departments.

Finally, I would like to thank my family, friends, and neighbors. My father, sisters, brother, aunts, uncles, cousins, nieces, nephews, and family friends have been endlessly supportive and interested in my work. The world of DC provides an exciting environment—full of wildly social people, local politics and activism that matters, endless political conversation, and opportunities to have a motorcade slow down your day—in which to develop such ideas deviously outside the Washington Consensus.

Markets in the Name of Socialism

Introduction
Economists and Socialism

ONE OF THE MOST DRAMATIC EVENTS of the past fifty years has been the worldwide embrace of neoliberalism, an economic and political ideology that glorifies the market and condemns the state, socialism, and even collective ideals, such as social justice. The Reagan and Thatcher governments epitomized these trends by attacking the welfare state, rejecting state regulation, privatizing state companies, and turning over state functions to market actors. Observers soon found that many Eastern Europeans also had a seemingly Reaganite or Thatcherite obsession with free markets. As an exchange student in Budapest, Hungary, in fall 1988 and spring 1989, I also was bewildered by the supposed socialists who taught us at the Karl Marx University of Economics and sounded more like Reagan Republicans than socialists. The fall of the Soviet Union in 1991 seemed to affirm the global victory of neoliberal capitalism, leading to the further dismantling of state socialism and the implementation of market and democratic reforms around the world. Neoliberalism fundamentally changed the world. This book suggests that, far from a hegemonic juggernaut, neoliberal capitalism was a parasitic growth on the very socialist alternatives it attacked.

An enormous literature explores the rise of neoliberalism and its profound effects on economies, polities, cultures, and societies. A new literature investigates whether neoliberalism is now on the decline.[1] In this book, I study the central role of professional economists in the development and spread of neoliberal ideas and policies. Economists create many of the images and the language that policy makers and laypeople use to discuss the economy. Through their influence on political and other elites, they also change the world to better fit their theories and abstract models.[2] Even "the economy" itself as a distinct sphere and an object of social science and government policy resulted from the professional work of economists collaborating with governments and other organizations (Mitchell 2002: ch. 3).

In general, scholars have presented three accounts of how economists developed and spread neoliberalism. Each assumes that economists have always taken a side either for the state or for the market and thus that every economist can be located on a state–market axis. The first account focuses on individual right-wing economists, most significantly Milton Friedman and Friedrich von Hayek, who developed radical free market ideas that form the core of neoliberalism. A strategic network of right-wing think tanks, associations like the Mont Pelerin Society, and foundations like that of the Scaife family packaged these neoliberal ideas and used them worldwide to attack any state role in the economy, from regulation to Keynesianism to central planning (Bourdieu and Wacquant 1999; Campbell 1998; Centeno 1998; Cockett 1995; Hartwell 1995; Harvey 2005; Kelly 1997; Klein 2007; Mirowski and Plehwe 2009; Smith 1993; Valdés 1995; Yergin and Stanislaw 1998).[3] In her *Shock Doctrine*, Naomi Klein (2007) argues that Milton Friedman and other neoclassical economists took advantage of economic crises to realize this radical free market package as shock therapy, which produced "disaster capitalism" worldwide.

A second type of account suggests that neoclassical economics, with its free market models, acts as a kind of neoliberal Trojan horse (Aligica and Evans 2009; Biglaiser 2002; Kogut and Macpherson 2007).[4] In his *A Brief History of Neoliberalism*, David Harvey (2005) brilliantly describes neoliberalism as a political project to restore the power of economic elites after the successes of the left in 1960s, but he conflates neoliberalism and neoclassical economics.[5] Ronald Reagan and Margaret Thatcher came to power with a mandate to realize this political project, bringing it together with a separate "utopian project" to realize right-wing economists' vision of free market capitalism that masked the political project. According to many authors, this neoliberal vision is based on neoclassical economics, in opposition to Marxism. Harvey writes:

The neoliberal label signaled their [these economists'] adherence to those free market principles of neoclassical economics that had emerged in the second half of the nineteenth century (thanks to the work of Alfred Marshall, William Stanley Jevons, and Leon Walras) to displace the classical theories of Adam Smith, David Ricardo, and, of course, Karl Marx. (2005: 20)

Harvey finds the core of neoliberalism in neoclassical economics with its "free market principles." Sociologists Campbell and Pedersen similarly argue that "a deep, taken-for-granted belief in neoclassical economics" forms the core of neoliberalism (2001: 5). Scott Sernau represents a more generally held view:

Many nations around the world were discovering the ideas of free trade and free markets. The intellectual basis for this approach comes from neoclassical economics. This approach is sometimes termed neoliberalism . . . Thus neoliberalism is the economic philosophy of American political conservatives . . . On the international level, the IMF and the World Bank champion their own form of neoclassical economics. (2010: 39–40)

Neoclassical economics, many observers agree, has played a fundamental role in the rise of neoliberalism worldwide. The conversion of much of the world to neoclassical economic thinking, according to these accounts, led to support for neoliberalism and thus undermined socialism, which did indeed suffer a cataclysmic decline from the late 1980s.

The third type of account points to economists with American neo- classical training who gained powerful positions in international financial institutions, such as the World Bank and the IMF, which impose neoliberal ideas on countries around the globe and support the formation of neoliberal advocates worldwide (Babb 2001; Dezalay and Garth 2002; Henisz, Zelner, and Guillén 2005; Orenstein 2008).[6] Economists within these institutions and their worldwide network of advocates successfully replaced state-led development with neoliberal free market policies. These three arguments work nicely together to demonstrate how economists' ideological project worked in parallel with business elites' political project to reorganize capitalism and reestablish their own power (Blyth 2002; Harvey 2005; Klein 2007).

This manuscript builds on, but also criticizes, these three types of accounts by revealing the socialist origins of neoliberalism. The right-wing, capitalist origins of neoliberalism have been clearly demonstrated. Observers have noted that not only right-wing leaders, such as Pinochet in Chile and Fujimori in Peru, but also socialists, such as those in Western Europe and Latin America, implemented neoliberal policies (Bourdieu and

Grass 2002; Mudge 2008; Sader 2008). To understand this, I argue that we should not conflate neoliberalism and neoclassical economics, we should not assume that neoclassical economics is a capitalist science or ideology, and, most importantly, we should go beyond the state–market axis.

I define *neoliberalism* as a set of ideas about how to organize markets, states, enterprises, and populations, which shape government policies.[7] These policies include deregulation, liberalization of trade and capital flows, anti-inflationary stabilization, and privatization of state enterprises. My understanding of the debates in Eastern Europe and about Eastern Europe in the early 1990s informs this definition.[8] The most striking characteristic of neoliberalism has been its advocacy of free, unfettered competitive markets, or in the words of Joseph Stiglitz its "market fundamentalism" (2003: 74).[9] According to neoliberal ideology, competitive markets and prices, free from political intervention or bureaucratic interests, could and should take over state functions. Competitive market prices could guide governance more effectively and more justly than the state could. At the same time, neoliberals call for a strong or even authoritarian state to protect private property, as well as to create private property and markets.[10] Neoliberalism also privileges the power of managers and owners and attacks the rights or potential rights of employees (Harvey 2005). There is a distinct lack of concern among neoliberals about the inefficiencies and concentrations of power within large corporations (Mirowski 2009: 438). Finally, Milton Friedman, Friedrich von Hayek, and other neoliberals also had a commitment to capitalism, a kind of capitalism with the qualities listed above: free markets, authoritarian yet small states, and hierarchical firms controlled by managers and owners, rather than by workers. In sum, neoliberalism avidly supports all of the following:

1. competitive markets

2. smaller, authoritarian states

3. hierarchical firms, management, and owners

4. capitalism

Someone who supports only one of these elements, even competitive markets but not the others, is not necessarily neoliberal.

This fourfold definition avoids the common assumption that economists are either pro-state or promarket. As Timothy Mitchell (1990) argues, elites "enframe" the world into dichotomies, constructing a seemingly dualistic world—Soviet socialism versus Western free market capitalism, for instance—to bolster their own authority. The state–market dichotomy obscures the nature of economics and elite power. This dichotomy easily blurs into other dichotomies: between socialism and capitalism, between central planning and the market, between Keynesianism and monetarism, between Latin American structuralist economics and American neoliberalism, and between Marxism and neoclassical economics. As a result, arguments about the state almost effortlessly become a mishmash of arguments about socialism, central planning, Keynesianism, Latin American economic structuralism, and neoclassical economics. In contrast, I have found that neoclassical economists, in their professional writing, do not focus on whether they are for or against the competitive market; rather, they use markets, central planning, socialism, and neoclassical economics simultaneously as analytical tools and sometimes as normative models. They have also been more concerned about another axis altogether: hierarchy and democracy. For example, some neoclassical economists advocated markets and rejected state planning in the name of economic democracy and communism. Thus, these economists criticized state socialism and state capitalism, as well as corporations, with the goal of ending worker exploitation and creating a new form of socialism. Another set of neoclassical economists also advocated markets but assumed hierarchical firms and an authoritarian state. The state–market axis used in public discourse hides a very different conversation going on within professional economics.

My approach complements, but also deviates from, Foucauldian Foucault studies of neoliberalism. In his lectures at the Collège de France in 1978 and 1979, Michel Foucault (2008) discussed neoliberalism as a form of governmentality. Those following Foucault understand neoliberal governmentality as seeking to manage populations by shaping individuals as governable, self-disciplined, enterprising subjectivities—thus engineering their souls—and by governing them from a distance, not though direct intervention by state agents, but by calculation, guidance, and incentives (Ong 2006; Rose 1996, 1999). Using this approach in his study of Czechoslovak technocrats, Gil Eyal (2003) has demonstrated that neoliberalism also emerged independently from capitalism and out of Eastern European socialism. Eyal has suggested that neoliberalism is not necessarily capitalist but rather is an art of governance possible under a variety of economic systems. By highlighting the ways that state, market, and expert power were fused in a new neoliberal configuration during socialism, Eyal productively avoids assuming that economists have always taken a side either for the state or for the market. Yet, while the Foucauldian approach has produced many insights into neoliberalism, it collapses alternatives to neoliberalism, including socialisms, into neoliberalism as simply other examples of engineering the soul. To understand the views of neoclassical economists more generally, one must move beyond the state–market axis to recognize the variety of socialisms that neoclassical economists have explored since the nineteenth century.

In the United States and now around the world, neoclassical economics represents the mainstream of the economics discipline. Neoclassical economics differs from heterodox economics, including Marxism, evolutionary economics, and the Austrian School after the Second World War, which this book only briefly discusses. Keynesians, libertarian and monetarist Chicago School economists like Milton Friedman, and many Eastern European socialists all practiced this neoclassical economics, while Friedrich von Hayek and the Austrian School abandoned this practice after the Second World War. Neoclassical pioneer and Keynesian Paul Samuelson acknowledged this view: "Economists do agree on much in any situation" (1983: 5). For example, in regards to Milton Friedman, Samuelson continued, "I could disagree 180° with his policy conclusion and yet concur in diagnosis of the empirical observations and inferred probabilities" (1983: 5–6).[11] Therefore, to understand neoliberalism, we must separate neoliberalism and neoclassical economics and leave behind the common assumption that neoclassical economics is a science of capitalism.

William Stanley Jevons in England, Carl Menger in Austria, and Léon Walras in Switzerland are generally credited with simultaneously discovering neoclassical economics in the 1870s.[12] Neoclassical economists moved beyond the classical view that the value of goods is based on the *objective* costs of their production (the labor theory of value) to the neoclassical view that value is *subjective* or *perceived*, that the individual agent—an individual or a firm—judges the utility or usefulness of certain goods or services. This shift to a subjective understanding of value and prices in the 1870s created what became known as the Marginalist Revolution because neoclassical economists began to study individual agents' behavior at the margins, such as the additional satisfaction a consumer gains from each extra (or marginal) unit of consumption. This is why neoclassical economics is often referred to as "marginalism."[13] While not all neoclassical economists used mathematics, such marginalist understandings of economic behavior allowed economists to apply calculus, theorems, and metaphors from physics to the field of economics, which seemed to promise a new scientific foundation based on the regularities of the mechanical world (Mirowski 1989).[14] Neoclassical economists also studied how markets coordinate agents in some regular way, thus allowing economists to describe and predict collective action. These economists assumed that markets (individually and collectively) have at least one equilibrium state in which prices encourage the most efficient production, distribution, and consumption. Neoclassical economics was not immediately popular among economists but became the mainstream by the Second World War (Bernstein 2001; Howey 1989; Yonay 1998). In sum, neoclassical economics is characterized by the study of individual agents, subjective values and prices, marginal calculation, collective action through markets, and market equilibrium.[15]

Neoliberalism can be said to have socialist origins for three reasons: Economists use socialist models to create new knowledge; these socialist models allowed for a professional dialogue among neoclassical economists in the socialist East and the capitalist West; and neoliberalism incorporates the knowledge created in this transnational dialogue about socialism. I explain each of these points in the following paragraphs.

First, while the language of individuals, markets, and prices suggests a capitalist perspective on the economy, socialism in fact plays a foundational role in neoclassical economics. Because some neoclassical economists have played a central role in promoting and implementing neoliberal polices, this suggests that neoliberalism has socialist origins. Neoclassical founders created mathematical models of the entire economy and showed that freely competitive markets produced optimal results in production, distribution, and consumption. Unexpectedly, by the 1890s, neoclassical economists also discovered that the competitive market economy was mathematically identical to the centrally planning economy. An economist could, therefore, take the mathematical models of the market and, rather than predicting how a free market might act, the economist could solve the equations and figure out the best prices and quantities without a market. Economists developed models of a "socialist state" with a central planner and state ownership of the means of production to develop new neoclassical theories and tools. As a result, both the pure competitive market and centrally planned socialism sit together at the center of neoclassical economics, no matter the politics of an economist. The methodological centrality of socialism to neoclassical economics informs neoliberalism.

Today, neoclassical economists still regularly use models of a socialist state to develop their theories. Former head of the China division at the International Monetary Fund and current advisor to the Indian government Eswar Prasad recently stated, "We economists think that a benevolent dictator—a benevolent dictator with a heart in the right place—could actually do a lot of good" (Kestenbaum 2010). Prasad does not voice some eccentric view. A benevolent dictator, more usually called "the social planner," appears throughout mainstream economic writing. The Chicago School (for example, Becker, Murphy, and Grossman 2006) and the rational expectations school (Hansen and Sargent [1994] 1996; Kydland and Prescott 1982; Lucas 1972; Lucas and Prescott 1971),[16] as well as the more left-leaning market failure school (Dasgupta and Stiglitz 1980a,b), base their models on a hypothesized social planner.[17] According to economists, the social planner is an imaginary benevolent representative for all of society. This planner has complete information about costs and preferences.[18] With perfect knowledge and certainty, the social planner chooses, for example, production activities to maximize consumption. In this way, the social planner seeks to maximize social welfare for all members of society. The economist then evaluates the results of a new policy or institution in comparison with the results obtained by the social planner, which serve as a benchmark. As this book shows, the social planner is the socialist state as imagined in the 1890s. Mainstream economists, no matter their political persuasion, mobilized state socialist models to study all economic systems and policies.

Neoliberalism appears as disembedded liberalism, as a commitment to unfettered markets (Blyth 2002), when, in fact, institutions are always the object of debate. If we understand institutions as taken for granted social patterns, then markets and planning should also be considered institutions, but I have found that neoclassical economists think about markets and planning differently from other institutions. On the surface, some economists present a narrow interpretation of neoclassical economics that markets and any necessary institutions would spring up like mushrooms when the state retreated from the economy. Alternatively, Eastern European conservatives also offered a narrow view of neoclassical economics, which instead argued that central planning and any necessary institutions would spring up like mushrooms when markets disappeared. Markets and a centrally planned socialist state exist at the core of neoclassical economics and thus embody these narrow views. However, narrow interpretations merely take the existing institutions as given (Horvat 1961, 2). Neoclassical economists continually talk about institutions required for the successful functioning of these core elements, the market or the centrally planned socialist state.

Neoclassical economists claim that both competitive markets and central planning require either (1) hierarchical, authoritarian institutions or (2) decentralized, egalitarian, democratic institutions. For example, economists David Lipton and Jeffrey Sachs argued for the necessity of hierarchical institutions, such as large (often foreign) corporations that have the funds to buy state-owned firms, for the eradication of worker self-management and ownership due to their supposed inefficiencies, and for a strong state to enforce massive redistribution of resources. In contrast, some socialist economists in Germany and England in the early part of the twentieth century optimistically thought that socialist institutions would make the economy actually resemble the ideal neoclassical models of the free market. These institutions included state or social ownership of certain parts of the economy, worker ownership of firms, workers' self-management, cooperative ownership, and various forms of democracy, as well as antimonopoly laws and company autonomy, that would make free markets, as well as efficient and just socialism, possible. Thus, an economist like Joseph Stiglitz has been equally committed to competitive markets and to economic democracy. In the eyes of neoclassical economists, this was not a mix of systems, a little bit of socialism mixed with a little bit of capitalism, like some image of Keynesianism. Rather, these economists sought a fully competitive market and socialism. The fact that neoclassical economists speak so positively about markets confuses outsiders into thinking that they are necessarily neoliberal.

Second, the methodological centrality of socialism to neoclassical economics allowed for a decades-long conversation about socialism and markets among economists, no matter their political commitments, in the socialist East and the capitalist West. The centrality of socialism to neoclassical economics meant that a wide variety of socialisms were relevant to neoclassical economics—abstract models of centralized and decentralized planning, real experiments in market socialism, abstract models of worker self-management socialism, real experiments in worker self-management socialism, cooperatives, and so on—and that neoclassical economics was relevant to socialism. After the death of Joseph Stalin in 1953 and the end of McCarthyism, the relaxation of Cold War tensions allowed the flourishing of new liminal spaces and liminal individuals, who criticized both Soviet socialism and Western capitalism. Douglas (1966) and Turner (1967, [1969] 1995) theorize that individuals "betwixt and between" statuses are seen as polluting and thus dangerous, as well as charismatic, due to their access to inaccessible and potentially corrupting knowledge of the realms they are between. Although examining rituals, Douglas's and Turner's concepts help illuminate the emergence of transnationally connected liminal spaces within Eastern Europe, Western Europe, and the United States. Within these liminal spaces, transnational dialogue among heterogeneous networks created new neoclassical knowledge and new knowledge about socialism that did not and could not exist before.[19] Within these liminal spaces, small, though soon expanding, numbers of economists from East and West discussed neoclassical economics and socialism.

This book explores two Eastern European experiments in decentralized socialism, Yugoslav worker self-management socialism and Hungarian market socialism. Because an abstract model of one form of socialism, central planning, existed at the center of neoclassical models, neoclassical economists found all kinds of abstract and concrete models of socialism helpful for developing new knowledge. This transnational conversation involved the leading members of the economics discipline and made fundamental contributions to neoclassical economics, which, in turn, informed neoliberalism.

Third, neoliberalism incorporated the transnational discussion about socialism in support of competitive markets but replaced the socialist calls for political and economic democracy with capitalist demands for hierarchical institutions. Eastern European economists' apparent mass conversion to free markets supported the triumphalist view of the post-1989 right. Yet, as has been briefly discussed, neoclassical economists agreed that markets could be integrated into socialism and, in fact, that socialism might provide the best conditions for markets. Groups of socialists worldwide had long criticized state control of the economy and advocated markets, while at the same time calling for economic and political democracy, worker or cooperative ownership of the means of production, and other socialist institutions. Many, though by no means all, neoclassical economists took part in this discussion in the hopes of creating democratic and

TABLE I.1   Comparison of socialisms and neoliberalism. Terms are italicized to emphasize the similarities across economic systems.

Soviet socialism	Hungarian socialism[a]	Yugoslav socialism[b]	Neoliberalism
Pro-state	Pro-state and antistate	*Antistate*	*Antistate*
Antimarket	*Promarket*	*Promarket*	*Promarket*
State ownership of the means of production	State ownership of the means of production	Nonstate ownership (social property)	Private ownership
Large monopolistic firms	Competitive firms	Competitive firms	Large monopolistic firms
Hierarchical management	Hierarchical and workers' self-management	Workers' self-management	Hierarchical management
Socialist	Socialist	Socialist	Capitalist

[a] This is the Hungarian model envisioned in the New Economic Mechanism reforms.

[b] This is the model promoted by leading Yugoslav economic experts in the 1950s and 1960s.

prosperous economies and replacing the often hierarchical and repressive structures equally characteristic of both Soviet state socialism and Western monopoly capitalism.

These new forms of socialism appeared neoliberal because outside observers often assumed that Soviet state socialism was the only form of socialism and that markets were necessarily capitalist. Outside observers often could not distinguish neoliberalism from the new forms of socialism. In the accompanying table, we can see how Yugoslav socialism differs from Soviet socialism but also how Yugoslav socialism, particularly as envisioned in the 1950s and 1960s, resembles neoliberalism in some of its ideals. Yugoslav socialism and neoliberalism share a distrust of the state and an embrace of the market (see Table I.1).

However, Yugoslav socialism and neoliberalism greatly differ on the institutions required for a functioning market. While they agree on economic means, their political ends and fundamental values are diametrically opposed. If one viewed Eastern European economic debates through the binary of market versus planning, then one would easily conflate neoliberalism with the new forms of socialism.

International and domestic political elites created a package of neoliberal ideas to take advantage of the changing political situation around 1989. These elites, as well as right-wing economists and activists, co-opted critical, transnational socialist discussions and presented them, along with a narrow version of neoclassical economics, as calls for private property, hierarchy, and markets within capitalism.[20] In doing so, they distorted the neoclassical economic discussion of socialism and markets into neoliberal ideology. Neoliberalism thus, despite the intentions of its proponents and the worst fears of its opponents, still contains, at least in potential, decades of radical democratic and socialist experiments.

A libertarian economist or a monetarist might now stand up and say, "See, we were right! Those Keynesians were a bunch of socialists!" Many observers assume that there is a capitalist economics that is fundamentally different from a socialist economics. They might argue that current-day Austrian School economics is capitalist, while Marxist political economy is socialist. In the eyes of many neoclassical economists, however, Marxist political economy was not, in fact, an economics of socialist planning but rather a critical economics of capitalism. The nineteenth-century Austrian School, paradoxically, presented an economics of socialism, as discussed in Chapter 1 of this book.

Scholars have not recognized these aspects of neoclassical economics because they often have not read the professional writings of a broad swath of neoclassical economists carefully enough and have instead assumed that economists' professional work, what they publish in their professional journals, reflected neoliberal capitalist principles. Economists themselves have often obscured the nature of their own professional work. Some of the most popular works by economists like Milton Friedman in his *Capitalism and Freedom* (1962a) and Friedrich von Hayek in *Road to Serfdom* (1944) bolster the view that economists write primarily political or ideological tracts. Scholars and journalists also often focus on a small group of celebrity economists—such as Jeffrey Sachs or Milton Friedman and people close to them—and assume that all mainstream economists share their ideas (for example, Harvey 2005; Klein 2007). Some economists might be angry about this misperception, though most economists do not seem aware of the problem. I once asked an economist why he and other economists continued to let the public think that they were conservative right-wingers. He immediately criticized me for thinking that economists were conservative right-wingers. All the economists he knew were left wing. Although I tried to say that I did not actually think this but rather wanted to know why economists allowed this common misperception, he continued to fume at me about my ridiculous assumptions. It seemed as if he did not know that people in general assumed this about economists as a group. Yes, professional work is always ideological, but not necessarily in the way it first seems. Analysts have not taken the time to study economists' professional writings and clarify what economists actually do.

Scholars have also often privileged the agency of Western economists and right-wing activist networks, considering Eastern European, as well as African, Asian, and Latin American, economists as naïve or passive recipients of knowledge. It has generally been assumed that Eastern European economists did not know about supposedly capitalist neoclassical economics (Aligica and Evans 2009; Grosfeld 1990) and that they either followed only Marxist-Leninist political economy or created a new ad hoc economics based on "learning by doing" (Kovács 1990: 224). After observing socialist economists speaking like free market capitalists in Hungary in 1988 and 1989, I began to question the relation of "Western" capitalist and "Eastern" socialist economic knowledge. In Hungary, I interviewed economists and conducted research in the archives of the Communist Party, the state, the Academy of Sciences, and the Karl Marx University of Economics. Without knowing it at the time, I had embarked on a long journey following the transnational connections of socialist economists supposedly isolated from capitalist neoclassical economics. What I found in Hungary led me to conduct interviews with these economists' colleagues in the United States. This research then directed me to a think tank in Italy and to further archives and interviews in the former Yugoslavia. Finally, these findings prompted research into the Yugoslav economists' colleagues in the Third World.

The advantages of conducting research in many locations are twofold. First, most scholars study economists and their ideas in a single country, so that, even when many studies of individual cases are put together, these national disciplines are studied separately (Fourcade 2009; Kaase, Sparschuh, and Wenninger 2002; Milenkovitch 1971; Wagener 1998). The scholarship has been comparative but not transnational. Economists may, in fact, share more in common with colleagues abroad than with their colleagues at home (Babb 2001; Coats 1996; Fourcade 2006; Valdés 1995). Second, by using a variety of languages, the scholar can gain access to works not deemed worthy of translation and works containing items of interest primarily to the local economist, such as book reviews, conference reports, reports on new professional developments, and so on. In this book, I use texts written originally in French, German, Italian, Hungarian, Russian, and Serbo-Croatian, which, unless otherwise stated, I translated myself and which provide insight into local trends and debates. In addition, one can potentially read works that more ideological economists refer to and reinterpret, and thus one can investigate the original texts and local interpretations. This is particularly important within the ideological context of the Cold War and post–Cold War triumphalism, when the histories of socialism were rewritten to appear to lead inexorably to the neoliberal, capitalist present.

We can see right-wing activists as a reactive force that exploited the creative struggles occupying and defining Cold War liminal spaces.[21] Many institutions brought together individuals interested in convergence between East and West, South and North to talk about socialism, human rights, social justice, and many other topics. Through these discussions, people sought to understand not only capitalism but also what socialism might become if it was not necessarily Soviet socialism. The knowledge about socialism and capitalism that developed out of liminality now appears as nothing more than neoliberal ideology but only because "the narrow window of the neoliberal imagination" makes invisible the liminal discussion and the alternatives, leaving only hegemony in view (Mitchell 1999: 32). I seek to reconstruct the liminal spaces that have since been divided into dichotomies by a dualistic world of power, to reconnect the history of neoliberalism with that which it has excluded from its own history: socialism, Eastern Europe, and the transnational left.[22] Those in transnationally connected liminal spaces again seek to understand the post-1989 convergence, what post-state-socialism is, what neoliberal capitalism is, and what socialism might become.[23]

Chapter 1 of this book examines the emergence of neoclassical economics from the 1870s to the 1950s, laying the foundation for the rest of the text. This chapter explores not only the historical origins of neoclassical economics in Western Europe and how socialism became an analytical tool with which to develop neoclassical economics but also its parallel development in the Soviet Union as a tool with which to improve socialism. The death of Stalin in 1953, the end of McCarthyism, and a thaw in the Cold War allowed economists to begin a direct, though difficult, East–West dialogue based on neoclassical economics, which Chapter 2 explores. Chapter 3 turns to Yugoslavia, which was expelled from the Soviet bloc and became a widely admired global economic model with its antistate, pro-market, worker self-management socialism. Chapter 4 focuses on Hungarian "goulash communism," Hungary's own form of market socialism. In Chapter 5, I turn to Western Europe, examining a think tank in Milan, Italy, the Center for the Study of Economic and Social Problems (CESES), which was, to all appearances, a right-wing institution controlled by transnational right-wing activists, but, in fact, depended on left-wing scholars thinking about critical Marxism and far-left alternatives to both state socialism and Western capitalism. In Chapter 6, I reinterpret the Eastern European revolutions of 1989, not as an embrace of free market capitalism but rather as an attempt to realize democratic market socialism. In the final chapter, Chapter 7, I seek to explain how the goal of transition transformed from realizing democratic market socialism to destroying socialism and creating capitalism, as well as how neoclassical economics was mobilized to support neoliberalism. However, socialism remains latent within the very methods and theories of neoclassical economists, including those of Milton Friedman and the Chicago School, those of Joseph Stiglitz and his market failure colleagues, and those of economists living in socialist and postsocialist Eastern Europe.

1

Neoclassical Economics and Socialism
From the Beginnings to 1953

> Like most teachers of economic theory, I have found it quite worth
> while to spend some time studying any particular problem in hand
> from the standpoint of a socialist state.
>
> Fred M. Taylor, Presidential Address to the 1928 annual meeting
> of the American Economic Association (1929: 1)

THE SCHOLARLY AND POPULAR LITERATURE has generally assumed that neoclassical economics lends ideological support to capitalism and seeks to discredit socialism. On the surface, neoclassical economics—the mainstream economics practiced in the United States and around the world, founded on the view that markets, free from outside intervention, are the most efficient way to allocate resources—certainly appears pro-capitalist and antisocialist. In fact, however, models of socialism, as well as of markets, lie at the core of neoclassical economics.

This chapter charts the development of neoclassical economics from its nineteenth-century origins in Western Europe, through its use in the Soviet Union, and up to the changes it underwent in the Cold War 1950s. Histories of economic thought do not usually recognize the role of socialism and socialists in neoclassical economics but rather relegate socialist economic thought to separate chapters or sections (for example, Ekelund and Hébert 1990; Niehans 1994). One exception to this treatment is the so-called socialist calculation debate. According to the standard narrative, in the early 1920s Austrian economist Ludwig von Mises published a devastating critique of socialism, arguing that an economy without money, markets, or prices would not allow rational economic calculation and therefore that socialism was impossible (for example, Ekelund and Hébert 1990: 575–577). In 1936, in this account, Oskar Lange responded to Mises with a neoclassical model of socialism, in which planners set prices and subsequently allow markets to adjust these prices. To Lange, this system allowed

17

rational economic calculation and suggested the possibility of socialism. In response to Lange, Friedrich von Hayek then altered Mises's argument: A socialist economy would be inefficient, not impossible.[1] Over the decades, different authors have claimed victory for each side (for example, Bergson 1948: 447; Lavoie 1985).

Hayek

The fact that Lange first responded sixteen years after Mises made his initial salvo raises some questions about the nature of this "debate." Time, and potentially significant historical events, play almost no role in the conventional narrative about the debate. The standard narrative presents free market advocates challenging those who support central planning, a dichotomy that blends together the Soviet Union, socialism, central planning, Keynesianism, and almost any form of government intervention in the economy into an amorphous object opposed to the equally amorphous object of the free market capitalism somehow allied with (non-Marxist) economists.[2] Right-wing activists have to this day used the "socialist calculation debate" to make broad ideological claims about socialism, capitalism, and the discipline of economics itself. Economists on both sides of the debate—including members of the Austrian School at the time and later the Chicago School—used neoclassical economics based, as we shall see, on socialist models. To better understand neoclassical economics, I have intentionally removed the "socialist calculation debate" and Keynesianism from their usual place at the center of the history of economics, a center that blinds most scholars to the fundamental importance of socialism to neoclassical economics as practiced from Chicago to Moscow, from Cambridge, Massachusetts, to Belgrade.[3]

∑·

This chapter documents how a variety of socialisms became intertwined at the center of neoclassical economics. At first, the founders of neoclassical economics in the 1870s built their science on the assumption that pure competitive markets provided optimal results in production, exchange, and consumption. By the 1890s, neoclassical economists had developed the idea that the pure competitive market model and the centrally planned socialist model were mathematically equivalent. Both of these models lie at the center of neoclassical economics. Therefore, analyzing a centrally planned socialist economy provided new insights into neoclassical economics and markets and vice versa. The words of the American Economic Association president, Fred M. Taylor, quoted at the beginning of this chapter reflect this neoclassical methodological discovery. Using socialism as an analytical tool to develop neoclassical economics, however, did not necessarily mean that economists considered themselves socialists. In fact, many rejected or were quite critical of socialism.

While it might seem that economics in the socialist East and economics in the capitalist West were quite different, economists in the East and West both developed neoclassical economics within discussions of socialism. The formal, mathematical identity between competitive markets and centrally planned socialism suggested that actually existing socialism in the new Soviet Union would be relevant to neoclassical economics and neoclassical economics would be relevant to Soviet socialism. However, as Soviet state socialism became ever more hierarchical and authoritarian, economists with more democratic, egalitarian, and decentralized inclinations created abstract decentralized market socialist models and incorporated them into the core of neoclassical economics. These market socialist models were not some mixed economy like Keynesianism but rather assumed a pure competitive market. At the same time, neoclassical economists began to explore the institutions required for the competitive market. Some socialists suggested that nonhierarchical socialist institutions provided the ideal environment for the neoclassical competitive market. Neoclassical economists in East and West thus developed their professional knowledge in parallel based on a common disciplinary past. This chapter ends in 1953, when Joseph Stalin's death, the end of the McCarthy trials, and the relaxation of Cold War tensions allowed a revival of a transnational neoclassical dialogue and the realization of neoclassical socialist ideas.

The Emergence of Neoclassical Economics

As discussed in the introduction, it is generally recognized that William Stanley Jevons in England, Carl Menger in Austria, and Léon Walras in Switzerland simultaneously discovered neoclassical economics in the 1870s.[4] The novelty of neoclassical economics was its rejection of the labor theory of value, used by both classical economists and Marxists, which was replaced by neoclassical subjective or perceived value.

Economists had long written prolifically and often quite negatively about socialism and communism. Most economic handbooks and manuals contained extensive criticisms of socialism (Gide 1904; Pareto 1896; Sidgwick 1887; Taussig 1911). Economists primarily described the First International; the newly published works of Karl Marx, whose first volume of *Das Kapital* had just been published in 1867; and various communist experiments—including those of Owen, Saint-Simon, Blanc, and Fourier, who were judged as failures. Economists, no matter their politics, deemed these experiments and socialist movements relevant enough to economics to be included in basic manuals.

Socialists often wrote quite negatively about marginalism and about economics more broadly. In contrast to Marx, economists of the classical school generally rejected socialism and advocated laissez faire capitalism, showing that socialist and other forms of economic intervention worked against "natural laws" and thus resulted, unintentionally, in reducing the welfare of society. Economists with laissez faire liberal and antisocialist views were some of the first to embrace neoclassical economics (Mornati 2001: 5). Thus, socialists also viewed neoclassical economists and their tools with great suspicion (Kurz 1995; Lerner 1934b; Michelini 2001: lxviii).[5] It was commonly believed that economics and socialism were antithetical (Mason 1980).

According to nineteenth-century socialist views, socialism would function without capitalist economic categories—such as money, prices, interest, profits, and rent—and thus would function according to laws other than those described by current economic science. While some socialists recognized the need for money and prices at least during the transition from capitalism to socialism, socialists more commonly believed that the socialist economy would soon administratively mobilize the economy in physical units without the use of prices or money (Brus 1972).

However, because the doctrines of both neoclassical economics and socialism were changing, neoclassical economists gradually developed new ideas about socialism. As British economist Henry Sidgwick wrote of socialist and neoclassical economics:

It is obvious that two systems or modes of thought, so close in their subject-matter—for the aim of both, so far as Political Economy has a practical aim, is to establish the production and distribution of wealth on a right basis—can hardly have lived side by side for a century without exercising an important influence on each other. (1895: 336)[6]

British economist John Stuart Mill symbolized the shift in political economy to include the study of wealth and income distribution: "The laws and conditions of the production of wealth, partake of the character of physical truths. . . . It is not so with the Distribution of Wealth. That is a matter of human institution solely" ([1848] 1917: 199–200). In response to socialist condemnations of social inequalities, many economists began to question their own profession's traditional support of laissez faire.[7] At this time, many younger economists turned to neoclassical economics and yet also became politically sympathetic to socialism. This turn to the distribution of wealth and income, which would include issues of property and potential redistribution mechanisms, met with severe criticisms from conservative economists.[8]

While they may have been politically sympathetic to socialism, neoclassical economists could not agree intellectually with Marxism, primarily because of Marx's commitment to the labor theory of value (Faucci and Perri 1995; Howey 1989; Mason 1980). Neoclassical economists had built their theory and their identity on a critique of classical economics and its labor theory of value (Howey 1989). The first volume of Marx's *Capital* appeared in 1867, while the second (1885) and third (1894) volumes appeared only after Marx's death in 1883. Some neoclassical economists hoped that Marx would have seen the light by the third volume and rejected the labor theory of value.[9] Therefore, even while they may have been politically sympathetic, many economists remained intellectually at odds with socialism.

However, for some, socialism and neoclassical economics could go hand in hand. One of the founders of neoclassical economics, Léon Walras, was a great supporter of both socialism and free competition:

I call myself democratic socialist because I see in slavery, servitude and in the proletariat three empirical phases of one and the same question, namely that of property and taxation, or the distribution of social wealth among men in society. ([1896] 1969: 144)[10]

While declaring himself a socialist since at least 1861, though a rather idiosyncratic one (Baranzini 2001; Cirillo 1980; Landauer 1959, 1623), Walras also continuously argued for "free competition" because "production in a market ruled by free competition is an operation by which services can be combined and converted into products of such a nature and in such quantities as will give the greatest possible satisfaction of wants," maximum utility at minimum cost ([1874] 1984: 255). Like other neoclassical economists, he continually criticized Marxist socialism and its labor theory of value. To explain why perfect competition provided maximum social utility, Walras created one of the most important neoclassical tools, his general equilibrium model. The general equilibrium model describes an entire economy with a series of mathematical equations, showing how this economy reaches and functions at equilibrium, the point where supply and demand are optimally balanced. In a freely competitive economy, companies or individuals move toward an equilibrium price that balances supply and demand, a process Walras called *tâtonnement* or "groping." Interestingly and importantly for this analysis, Walras imagined an auctioneer mediating this process, announcing prices and changing these prices to balance supply and demand. Ideally, in Walras's model, large numbers of companies would compete and would be forced to accept equilibrium prices from the market (or the auctioneer) as given and to make profit-oriented production decisions based on lowest possible costs (marginal costs). As a result, these companies would maximize society's satisfaction and minimize the costs involved.

For Walras, socialism would provide the necessary institutions for free competition and social justice. Socialism, in Walras's view, entailed state ownership of land and natural resources and the abolition of income taxes.[11] As owner of land and natural resources, the state could then lease these resources to many individuals and groups, which would eliminate monopolies and thus enable free competition. The leasing of land and natural resources would also provide enough state revenue to make income taxes unnecessary, allowing a worker to invest his savings and become "an owner or capitalist at the same time that he remains a worker."[12] The socialist institutions advocated by Walras, which did not include state intervention in economic activities, would thus allow the realization of free competition idealized by neoclassical economics. Mathematical neoclassical economics helped to explain this competitive economy and suggested necessary reforms to realize it (Baranzini 2001: 48). To Walras, perfect competition, socialism, neoclassical economics, and mathematics did not just complement each other but, in fact, made each other possible.[13] Walras understood the free market as necessary for socialism and socialism as necessary for the free market.

Surprisingly, however, many innovations in the neoclassical economics of socialism came from economists critical of socialism.[14] Neoclassical economists understood their discipline as applicable and necessary to any economic system, including socialism (Landauer 1959: 1619–1635). These critics in particular pointed out that socialists, especially those following Karl Marx, did not discuss the nature of a future socialist economy (Mises [1920] 1938, 87–88).[15] As a result, socialists incorrectly predicted that a socialist economy would be liberated from economic categories—including prices, money, supply and demand, and profit—and economic laws. Neoclassical economists who supported laissez-faire policies and criticized Marxist socialism argued that both capitalist and socialist economies would share the same economic laws and economic rationality and thus that attempts to avoid these laws would lead only to disappointment (Böhm-Bawerk [1889, 1891] 1971; Wieser [1893] 1989). For example, Dutch economist N. G. Pierson wrote, "I hope to show that it is a mistake to believe . . . that the efforts of theoretical economics are unnecessary. This branch of knowledge can never be neglected—not even in the event of socialism being carried into practice" ([1902] 1938: 43). These critics implied that, if one truly understood economic laws, one would not be a socialist. To these critics, neoclassical economics was universally applicable to all economic systems.

At the same time, socialist models helped to develop neoclassical economics. Major innovations in neoclassical economics came from those critical of socialism, who, at the same time, used one particular socialist model, an abstract model of a socialist state, as a methodological tool (Hayek [1935] 1938a: 24; Landauer 1959: 1624; Lavoie 1985: 80; Maksimović 1958: ch. 2). Hayek recognized this: "And up to a certain point from the very beginning the problems of a centrally directed economy found a prominent place in the expositions of modern economics" ([1935] 1938a: 24). To build his theories about value, Austrian School neoclassical economist and critic of socialism Friedrich von Wieser used a "communist state": "We shall think of the communist state as the perfect state . . . Natural value shall be that which would be recognized by a completely organic and most highly rational community" ([1893] 1989: 60). Wieser considered this communist state

an excellent aid in realizing what would remain of our present economy if we could think away private property, as well as the troubles which are a consequence of human imperfection. Most theorists, particularly those of the classical school, have tacitly made similar abstractions. In particular, that point of view from which price becomes a social judgment of value, really amounts to a disregard of all the individual differences which emerge in purchasing power, and which separate price from natural value. A great many theorists have thus written the value theory of communism without being aware of it. (ibid.: 61)

In this idealized economy without private property or income inequality, commodities would have their "natural value," and prices would equal their natural value. Like other neoclassical economists, Wieser considered value calculation identical in capitalism and socialism (Heimann 1939: 89). In a related way, another Austrian School economist, Eugen von Böhm-Bawerk ([1889, 1891] 1971) spent the first hundred pages of his book on capital theory discussing a community with "one single economy, guided by one individual will" (113). In the mind of the neoclassical economist, the centrally planned economy—an economy "guided by one individual will" and without private property—provided knowledge applicable to a freely competitive economy. While these economists often objected to socialism as a practical goal of economic policy, they used socialism in the form of a socialist or communist state as a tool to develop neoclassical economics.[16]

In 1893, Vilfredo Pareto took over Léon Walras's chair in political economy at the University of Lausanne in Switzerland.[17] Pareto created three of the most important neoclassical tools, which would later be called the "social planner," the "social welfare function," and "Pareto optimality." In his 1896–1897 political economy textbook, Pareto followed Walras and described the entire economy as a set of equations about supply and demand, market prices, and so on. He also followed the neoclassical tradition of equating the competitive market economy and the socialist state: "That is to say that both systems are not different in form, and they lead to the same point. This result is extremely remarkable" (ibid.: 59). Throughout the textbook, Pareto used a "socialist State" to theorize about neoclassical economics more generally. According to Pareto, a socialist state arranges all production, has collective ownership of the means of production, and seeks to maximize well-being—or utility—for each individual in society.[18] Any movement away from the arrangement that maximizes social utility and thus is Pareto optimal might make someone better off but would also make someone else worse off.[19] Pareto replaced Walras's auctioneer with an imagined "Ministry of Production," which would solve the equations that Walras used to describe a perfectly competitive market economy, figure out equilibrium prices, and then use these prices to maximize social welfare. The social planner used by neoclassical economists today is this Ministry of Production maximizing social welfare. According to Pareto, however, some people would not benefit from this optimal production, so the socialist state should then redistribute funds to the losers in this process—through a lump-sum tax or dividends—to obtain maximum well-being or utility for *all* its citizens. Pareto thus created the now standard macroeconomic tools of the social planner, social welfare function, and Pareto optimality. Furthermore, Pareto recognized that actually solving the set of equations describing the economy would present immense practical difficulties, but, according to neoclassical economics, such a socialist system was at least theoretically possible (1896: 321).[20]

In 1908, Pareto's colleague at Lausanne, Enrico Barone, also made several fundamental contributions to neoclassical economics and socialism. Barone described how the imagined Ministry of Production's equations could be solved mathematically.[21] In a manner similar to other neoclassical economists, Barone declared, "the system of the equations of the collectivist equilibrium is no other than that of the free competition" ([1908] 1938: 274). For the socialist system to work, producers would have to follow two rules from the purely competitive economy: Minimize the (average) costs of production, and equate prices with the (marginal) costs of production (ibid.: 289). Barone then developed two innovative models of a socialist economy: a centralized one where the state organizes production without the input of consumers and a decentralized one where citizens choose their consumption and occupation. Barone, however, warned that, while central planning using neoclassical methods was "not an *impossibility*," solving the equations would be difficult if not practically impossible (ibid.: 287–290). Instead, he suggested that the equations be solved "experimentally" on "a very large scale," suggesting some way of combining markets and socialism (ibid.: 288). For decades to come, neoclassical economists would follow Barone's assumptions and rules to develop the decentralized market socialist model Barone suggested.

Neoclassical economists held that a socialist state could, at least theoretically, produce the same results as the competitive market. Rather than contrasting the market with a centrally planned socialist state, neoclassical economists used models of both the market and central planning as methodological tools to develop their professional knowledge, whatever their political intentions. They also happened to develop tools for future socialists.

The Bolshevik Revolution and Neoclassical Economics

World events shifted the discussion. The 1917 Bolshevik Revolution, as well as the interwar socialist governments in Austria and Germany, made the possibility of socialism more real than ever. In conventional accounts,

Ludwig von Mises of the Austrian School at this point initiated the social-ist calculation debate to demonstrate that socialism was not possible (or efficient) (Caldwell 1997; Lavoie 1985). In fact, in the face of real social-isms emerging in Europe, Mises claimed that neoclassical economics and markets were not universal but rather purely capitalist, rejecting his own discipline's core assumptions. In contrast to Mises, many other neoclassical economists continued to assume the universality of their discipline and came to realize that their methodological tools could become blueprints for socialism.[22]

Otto Neurath, a student of Austrian School neoclassical economists and German Historical School leader Gustav Schmoller, took this path. By the end of 1918, the Austrian and Weimar German governments set up "socialization" (*Sozialisierungs*) commissions (Uebel 2004: 40). Econo-mists debated what socialization of the economy might entail (Chaloupek 1990). Neurath had already spent several years developing "war econom-ics," which he believed would create international socialism (Uebel 2004: 26–33). In 1919, he presented to the short-lived Bavarian Soviet his "full socialization" model, a completely centralized, moneyless, planned so-cialist economy (Mitchell 1965: 293). Neurath argued that this economy would function without money or markets and thus would be adminis-tratively planned in kind. This model, in fact, closely resembled Austrian School economist Friedrich von Wieser's "communist state." The Bavarian Soviet hired Neurath to implement his plan, but the Soviet ended before he could fully do so (Mitchell 1965; Uebel 2004: 40). Arriving in Vienna in 1919 after his participation in the People's Commissariat of Social Pro-duction in the Hungarian Soviet Republic (Dale 2009: 126), Karl Polanyi similarly recognized that only neoclassical economics provided a model for a marketless, planned economy:

Marx had admittedly created a theory of the capitalist economy, it however always deliberately avoided touching on the theory of socialist economy. The only theory of a marketless economy, which we have at our disposal, stems from the marginal school and admittedly as a theory of a closed economy. A communist managed economy could, so paradoxical it must sound in many ears, only turn to this school, to lay the foundation on its particular theoretical economic doctrine. (1922: 379–380)

Neurath transformed the marginalist communist state from a method-ological tool into a blueprint for socialism.[23] While popular with worker's councils in Bavaria, his model provoked general criticism by both socialist and antisocialist economists.

German and Austrian socialists, including Karl Kautsky and many others, criticized Neurath's model (Chaloupek 1990: 662). In general, Kautsky and other social democrats rejected state authority because the state was, after all, an instrument of class oppression (Zimmerman 2010: 96–98). Many socialist economists shared this perspective and developed nonauthoritarian models, thus moving beyond simplistic market or planning policy options.

These economists called for socialized property and democratically run associations and, later, markets. According to Eduard Heimann in 1921, proponents of socialization sought to overcome "the antagonism of the producers and consumers . . . by entrusting representatives of the producers and of the consumers commonly with the management of the economy and especially with the setting of prices. . . . only Neurath is an exception" (Landauer 1959: 1787). Polanyi (1922) argued that producers' associations and consumers' associations, rather than the state, should make production and price decisions. As can be seen also in *The Great Transformation*, Polanyi did not criticize neoclassical (marginalist) economics, but rather "economic liberals" like Mises and Hayek ([1944] 1957: ch. 13). In contrast to Marxism, Polanyi sought a "positive economic doctrine" of socialism with a "market" and developed a "type of socialist transition economy" (1922: 380, 413). Polanyi did not support state intervention in the market or a mixed economy in the spirit of Keynesianism, but rather he advocated competitive markets along with decentralized democratic worker's institutions, a popular neoclassical view.[24] By the early 1930s, "market socialists" suggested that socialist enterprises might compete on free markets (Heimann 1932; Landauer 1931; Landauer 1959: 1643–1650).[25] Franz Oppenheimer similarly called for economic communes that would compete on a free market (Heimann 1944: 38). As a result, market socialists created a new neoclassical model of socialism, market socialism, that moved beyond an authoritarian central state to a model that better fit social democracy with radical economic and political institutions.

These market socialists had realized that they could use the neoclassical models of Walras, Pareto, Barone, Wieser, and Böhm-Bawerk as a blueprint for a new socialist society. At that time, the newly published work of Swedish economist and socialist critic Gustav Cassel (1923) seemed to provide an ideal socialist plan based on neoclassical economics. According to one of these market socialists, Eduard Heimann, "Cassel's doctrine, like Wieser's, is much closer to socialism than to capitalism"

(1939: 92). Like other neoclassical economists, Cassel criticized the labor theory of value and the ideas of socialists more generally (1923: 290). After describing his model of the economy, Cassel then asserted:

These principles would remain unchanged in any community which took over the control of production and reserved to itself the ownership of the material means of production. Such a community we call "Socialistic." The name indicates a self-contained exchange economy in which the entire production is conducted by and for the community itself through officials appointed for the purpose, and all the material means of production are the property of the community; but in which there is still freedom of work and consumption to the extent to which it is essential to an exchange economy. This definition does not, of course, apply to every economic order that has been described as "Socialist." It represents the theoretically simplest Socialist economy, a pure type. (ibid.: 129)[26]

Cassel, like other neoclassical economists, found the socialist model "useful and profitable" for economics more generally because the model was so simple and provided insight into the universal, essential elements of all exchange economies (ibid.: 129–130). Cassel's work contributed to the new innovations in neoclassical price theory and many other areas. Market socialists found that neoclassical economics helped socialism and socialism helped neoclassical economics.

Most conventional accounts of the socialist calculation debate rely on Hayek's 1935 recounting of the debate in Austria and Germany (for example, Hodgson 1999: 33–36; Lavoie 1985). Hayek made Mises the center of the debate, when in fact he was just one important participant among many. Most socialists by the late nineteenth and early twentieth centuries assumed that a socialist society would use money at least for consumer items (Landauer 1959: 1639). Neoclassical economists had long assumed the need for prices in a socialist economy, so Mises made no revelations here. His most controversial claims were about neoclassical economics and markets. Instead of arguing that capitalism and socialism shared common economic laws that could not be avoided, as other neoclassical economists had before, Mises declared that "socialism is the abolition of rational economy" ([1920] 1938: 110). Therefore, neoclassical economics could apply only to capitalism.

In agreement with Neurath, Mises understood the socialist economy as the eradication of private property and market prices, which would be replaced by centrally planned exchange in kind. To Mises (1922), Neurath did not understand the difficulties involved. Without markets, private property, and market prices, it would be impossible to decide rationally how to act in the economy. He thus also considered socialism and markets as mutually exclusive categories.[27] Therefore, according to Mises, socialism—understood as a centrally planned economy—was impossible. As Carl Landauer recognized, Mises rejected not only socialism but also neoclassical economics: "If either Mises's or Hayek's argument is correct, then Walras, Pareto, Wieser, and Barone had no right to draw their curves and establish their equations" (1959: 164on134). His rejection of universality represented a break with neoclassical economics as much as a critique of socialism.

Mises' Critique of neoclassical economics

    Mises (1920, 1922) directed his criticisms against Marxists who understood socialism as central planning and state ownership of the means of production. At the same time, according to a later Austrian School economist Don Lavoie (1985), Mises thought that the market socialists, with their use of neoclassical economics and criticisms of Marxist central planning, were his allies "against the threat of resurgent classical value theory in the form of Marxism" (3).[28] To Mises and other Austrian School economists, "One will have to admit that today there is only *one* economics," which was marginalist (Mises cited in Kurz 1995: 68–69). Mises and the market socialists shared their neoclassical economics but disagreed politically—especially regarding Mises's advocacy of private property and capitalism—and professionally.[29] Mises did not realize until later that he shared more with the Marxists than with market socialists because Marxists also understood capitalism and socialism as fundamentally different (Lavoie 1985). Mises would soon turn away from neoclassical economics and toward philosophical questions.[30]

The New Socialism in England

    By the 1930s, a "new socialism" based on neoclassical economics had also become immensely popular in England and in the United States (Hutt 1940). This neoclassically based socialism flowered at the London School of Economics (LSE), founded in 1895 by Fabian socialists.[31] The Fabian socialists had long criticized orthodox classical economics and supported alternative economic schools. By the 1890s, Fabian socialists already embraced neoclassical economics, as Friedrich Engels noted: "The Jevons-Mengerians prevail awfully in the Fabian Society and look down on the long out of date

Marx with contempt."[32] Arriving as a faculty member in 1926, John Hicks helped set off a revival of Walrasian and Paretian neoclassical economics.[33] In 1929 and 1930, respectively, Lionel Robbins and Arnold Plant, both critics of socialism and advocates of Austrian neoclassical economics, began teaching at LSE. They brought the ideas of Mises and the Austrian and German neoclassical debates about socialism with them.

Socialist students and lecturers—like Evan Durbin, Abba Lerner, and Oskar Lange—studied with these antisocialists to learn the most cutting-edge work in neoclassical economics, which they themselves used to create models for market socialism (Lerner 1934b; Lange 1936, 1937). The LSE was one of the leading centers creating the new mathematical neoclassical economics. As Yonay (1998) discovered, in the United States of the 1930s institutionalism and "old-fashioned" nonmathematical neoclassical economics of the Austrian School were defeated "by a new approach, which first appeared as a major force in the 1930s and skyrocketed soon after the Second World War. This new winner was mathematical economics" (Yonay 1998: 184). The revival of the general equilibrium theory of Walras, Pareto, and Barone at the LSE brought new tools.[34] Students, including those interested in socialism, eagerly took courses, especially in price theory.[35] Cassel's work was particularly important because he explained how one could use neoclassical economics to set prices in a socialist state. These young socialists explored the neoclassical models of the critics of socialism—Wieser, Böhm-Bawerk, Pareto, and Cassel— both as exciting, new analytical tools and as blueprints for a new socialist society. While taking part in the revolution in neoclassical economics, these LSE students and lecturers also mobilized markets and neoclassical economics for socialism.

Also at the London School of Economics in 1930, future Nobel Laureate in economics and future Chicago School economist Ronald Coase sat in his first course on price theory, which introduced him to neoclassical economics and its advocacy of free market competition (Coase 1997a,b). His professor Arnold Plant opposed any kind of planning and understood the market pricing system as the optimal coordinating mechanism. Remembering that at that time he had been a "socialist," Coase much later wrote, "One may ask how I reconciled my socialist sympathies with acceptance of Plant's approach. The short answer is that I never felt the need to reconcile them" (1991: 39). During a research year in the United States, he realized that a firm was a "little planned society" (1997a: 3). Coase asked himself: If his professors were correct that a competitive market economy required only prices to function, why did firms exist with their nonmarket authoritarian hierarchies? He remembered,

The same problem presented itself to me at that time in another guise. The Russian Revolution had taken place only fourteen years earlier. We knew then very little about how planning would actually be carried out in a communist system. Lenin had said that the economic system in Russia would be run as one big factory. However, many economists in the West maintained that this was an impossibility. And yet there were factories in the West and some of them were extremely large. How did one reconcile the views expressed by economists on the role of the pricing system and the impossibility of successful central economic planning with the existence of management and of these apparently planned societies, firms, operating within our own economy? (ibid.: 2)

Coase applied neoclassical analysis to the black box of the firm. He thus envisioned neoclassical analysis as a tool for studying socialism and hierarchical central planning within a firm. Coase saw the parallels between the firm as a planned society and the planned national economy as a giant firm or factory. Knowledge about planning on a national scale might help planning on a firm level, and vice versa.

In 1931, leading member of the Austrian School of neoclassical economics Friedrich von Hayek arrived at LSE and, according to Peter Boettke (2004), was "blindsided" by the students at LSE. Emerging from the debates in Vienna about centralized planning versus the market, Hayek found the socialist students at LSE espousing free markets and socialism, which sounded familiar to the contemporary German market socialists (Heimann 1932; Landauer 1931). In response to their embrace of market socialism, Hayek ([1935] 1938a,b) repackaged older Central European debates for his new audience in a volume of readings on "Collectivist Economic Planning." In the process, Hayek created the socialist calculation debate from the scattered writings of Mises, Lange, and other earlier authors and thus provided a strategy for right-wing and libertarian groups for decades to come. In the volume, he published criticisms of socialism by Ludwig von Mises from 1920, N. G. Pierson from 1902, George Halm ([1935] 1938), and himself ([1935] 1938), as well as Enrico Barone's mathematical model of socialism from 1908. By putting together these works from different periods in the socialist debate, Hayek took these works out of their historical context and the historical debates from which they emerged. He thus dehistoricized socialism and narrowed its definition to mean only state ownership and central planning of all material productive resources (1938a: 18–19; see also Michelini 2001).[36] Hayek thus embraced Mises's sharp distinction between socialism and the market, which Mises himself had recently reiterated: "Thus the alternative is still either Socialism or a market economy" (1936: 142). This, in fact, was at odds with neoclassical economics.

To support his presentation of socialism as central planning completely separate from markets, Hayek mobilized the idea of the Soviet Union in several ways. On the one hand, Hayek argued that the Soviet Union was run arbitrarily and thus did not have central planning, which meant it "gives us no help towards an answer to the intellectual problem which the desire for a rational reconstruction of society raises" (1938b: 207). On the other hand, according to Hayek, the failure of the Soviet Union to realize higher standards of living than capitalist countries proved that socialism did not work. He, importantly, based his claims on the similar findings of a Russian, Boris Brutzkus, that socialism could not succeed:

although they [Brutzkus's 1920 findings] arose out of the study of the concrete problems which Russia had to face at that time, and although they were written at a time when their author, cut off from all communication with the outside world, could not have known of the similar efforts of the Austrian and German scholars. (1938a: 35)

Thus, Hayek used writers from the Soviet Union as isolated, naïve witnesses to support his case.[37] In his response to the LSE neoclassical socialists, Hayek mobilized antisocialist writings from a range of historical periods and the testimony of supposedly isolated witnesses of the Soviet system to bolster his claim that socialism was always centrally planned and doomed to failure, in contrast to market economies.

At this time, Polish economist and socialist Oskar Lange visited London and published his famous neoclassical model of market socialism (Lange 1936, 1937). Soon afterward, Lange moved to the United States and began work at the University of Chicago, where he continued to teach neoclassical economics. After the Second World War, on the request of Joseph Stalin, he returned to Poland to teach and advise the government (Kowalik 1965).

Socialism, according to Lange, was superior to existing monopolistic capitalism because socialism did away with the private ownership of the means of production and thus removed the obstacles to free competition (1937: 132).[38] Lange brought together decades of neoclassical theorizing about the socialist state, new ideas about market socialism, and innovations in neoclassical economics to create what quickly became the standard theoretical model of market socialism. In this model, Lange followed neoclassical conventions, especially those laid out by Barone. This form of socialism had state ownership of the means of production.[39] Individuals freely chose their occupation and consumer goods, which were sold on a "genuine market" (Lange 1936: 60). Lange rejected centralized state control because of "the undemocratic character of such a system and its incompatibility with the ideals of the socialist movement" (ibid.: 70). In addition to their income, employees would receive a "social dividend," "the individual's share in the income derived from the capital and the natural resources owned by society" (ibid.: 61). There would be no market in producer goods or capital; rather the Central Planning Board would fix prices and interest by trial and error, just as, according to Lange, the competitive market corrected itself. The Central Planning Board would thus act like the Walrasian auctioneer, setting an initial arbitrary price and then altering the price in response to excess supply or demand. Firms would not maximize profit but would follow the two rules discussed by Barone: They must minimize the (average) costs of production and equate prices with the (marginal) costs of production. Lange's model of market socialism would remain a reference point for socialist and neoclassical discussions for decades to come.

During the 1930s, many neoclassical economists came to the conclusion that socialism in fact provided the necessary institutions for the realization of perfect market competition as envisioned by neoclassical economists. British socialist and economist H. D. Dickinson wrote, "The beautiful systems of economic equilibrium described by Böhm-Bawerk, Wieser, Marshall, and Cassel are not descriptions of society as it is, but prophetic visions of a socialist economy of the future" (1939: 205). In his "A Cautious Case for Socialism," Kenneth Arrow, future Nobel Laureate and American neoclassical economist, remembered his time at Columbia University in the early 1940s, "Socialism was the way in which the ideal market was to be achieved. This doctrine was held by many" (1978: 476).[40] Socialist economists in Austria, England, Germany, and the United States at this time agreed that socialist institutions could make economic reality approximate neoclassical models.

Marxist economists—such as Paul Baran, Maurice Dobb, and Paul Sweezy—also wrote about socialism, though in a very different manner. In fact, Marxist economists understood Marxism as essentially the economics of capitalism, while neoclassical economics was the economics of socialism (Leontief 1938; Sweezy 1935). Other neoclassical economists, such as Oskar Lange, would also call themselves Marxists and did not necessarily see a contradiction between Marxism and neoclassical economics. Lange wrote that neoclassical economics "offers more for the current administration of the economic system of Soviet Russia than Marxian economics does" (1935: 191).[41] According to fellow student Ronald Coase, once former LSE student Abba Lerner learned about neoclassical economics, he soon traveled to Mexico City to convince Leon Trotsky that this new neoclassically based market socialism would help the Soviet Union (1988: 8).

From the nineteenth century, neoclassical economists had assumed that competitive markets provided optimal results, but they soon proved that a central planner could provide the same optimal results. Neoclassical economists began to use a socialist state as a methodological tool to develop their professional knowledge. The new socialist governments in Austria, Germany, and the Soviet Union caused some neoclassical economists to rethink their methodological tools as blueprints for socialism. In response, the leader of the Austrian School, Ludwig von Mises, argued that a socialist state could not conduct rational calculation, and thus neoclassical economics did not apply to a socialist state, a radical shift in neoclassical thinking. Mises advocated instead private property and capitalism. Social democratic economists then developed a new neoclassical model of market socialism, which included workers' democracy and a competitive market. These ideas traveled to England and the United States in the 1930s. Over that decade, Mises, Hayek, and other conservative Austrian School economists began to reject neoclassical economics for, at least in part, its support of markets and socialism, and they turned to philosophical discussions.[42] At the same time, various socialisms—real and theoretical—provided economists with the means with which to develop their theories and methods, and neoclassical economics provided socialists models for socialism. It was unclear, however, whether economists in the actually existing socialist economy of the Soviet Union would take part in this dialogue.

Neoclassical Economics in the Soviet Union

Neoclassical economists also worked in tsarist Russia and the Soviet Union.[43] The leaders of the Soviet Communist Party, such as Nikolai Bukharin, recognized the importance of neoclassical economics to socialist debates. In the Russian preface to his *Economic Theory of the Leisure Class*, Bukharin ([1919] 1927) recounted his years spent in exile studying neoclassical economics:

I went to Vienna after succeeding in making my escape from Siberia; I there attended the lectures of Professor Böhm-Bawerk (1851–1914), of the University of Vienna. In the library of the University of Vienna, I went through the literature of the Austrian theorists. I was not permitted, however, to finish this work in Vienna, since the Austrian Government had me imprisoned in a fortress . . . In Switzerland, to which I repaired after my deportation from Austria, I had an opportunity to study the Lausanne School (Walras), as well as the older economists, at the library of the University of Lausanne, and thus to trace the theory of marginal utility to its roots. At Lausanne, I also made an exhaustive study of the Anglo-American economists . . . after reaching the United States, I was enabled to study the American economic literature even more thoroughly in the New York Public Library.

Bukharin studied neoclassical economics so closely because it provided some of the most important models and tools for socialism, to which he planned "a systematic criticism." He specifically rejected the Austrian marginalist school as "bourgeois" and "the most powerful opponent of Marxism" (ibid.).

In the first years of the Soviet Union, Communist Party leaders argued that economics did not have a place at all in the Soviet Union because economists studied commodity exchange relations, which would wither away under socialism. As Bukharin himself, along with Preobrazhensky, argued, direct exchange in kind would soon replace commodity exchange relations, and banks would function merely as "central counting houses," using simple bookkeeping methods ([1919] 1966: 333). Therefore, the "law of value"—market-based prices and exchange—would no longer regulate the economy. In some sense, the national economy would function like a single factory (Sutela 1991: 10).[44] In such a system, as Bukharin and others argued, economists' knowledge would no longer applicable, an argument similar to that made by Mises (Smolinski 1971: 138). In place of economists, engineers took over the field of planning (Ellman 1973).

If one views neoclassical economics as an ideology of the bourgeoisie, it would be logical that neoclassical economics would have no role in the Soviet Union. It is true that, as Pollock remarks, in the Soviet Union, "economists had essentially subordinated analysis of the economy to blind praise for political decisions" (2006: 171). Soviet planning was a rather ad hoc system with a small number of officials attempting to make millions of planning decisions. Both Lange and Hayek agreed that the Soviet central planning system was inefficient, that market-based alternatives were necessary, and that neoclassical economics could improve the Soviet economy. As Hayek and others assumed, economists in the Soviet Union, like Boris Brutzkus in 1920, were "cut off from all communication with the outside world" and had to realize independently the same conclusions already discovered by Western economists ([1935] 1938a: 35).

In contrast to Hayek's assumptions, the early Soviet economists were not isolated. In 1921, the Soviet government implemented the New Economic Policy (NEP), which sought to combine markets and private enterprise with a state-run economy (Bandera 1963). The excitement of the market and planning experiments of the NEP and the highly developed work in mathematics gave rise to innovative mathematical economics in the Soviet Union. Rather than being isolated, "Soviet economists of the twenties mixed into a fruitful combination pre-revolutionary Russian economics and statistics, European Marxism and closely observed American empirical research," which led to much innovation and new knowledge about economics of socialism (Sutela 1991: 28). Within the new economic environment of the Soviet Union, many economists found the existing economic tools inadequate, and many altered Western methods and Marxist theory to create new tools (Katsenelinboigen 1980: 11).[45] Existing general equilibrium models were static, which did not fit the dynamic revolutionary changes in the transition to socialism. Economists and political leaders had an intense ideological controversy over this, which resulted in a new official interpretation of a moving or dynamic economic equilibrium (Chossudowsky 1939). While fundamentally different from the neoclassical mainstream notion of equilibrium, the Soviet concept resonated with new developments in the neoclassical mainstream. Several prominent economists applied neoclassical methods to the Soviet economy, including A. A. Konius (who worked on prices and consumer demand) and Stanislav Strumilin (who made the first neoclassical approach to planning right after the revolution).[46] Vasili Nemchinov, Leonid Kantorovich, and

Viktor Novozhilov developed a wide range of pathbreaking mathematical economic methods.

Joseph Stalin's rise to power in the late 1920s soon shut down these economic discussions. Soviet officials openly attacked mathematical economics as "the most reactionary brand of bourgeois economics."[47] Many prominent mathematical and nonmathematical economists were arrested, imprisoned, exiled, and executed (Ellman 1973; Jasny 1972; Katsenelinboigen 1980; Sutela 1991: 29). The Soviet regime sought to control the flow of publications, ideas, and people. As a result, according to Gregory Grossman, "In the great debate on the 'economics of socialism' of the 'thirties and 'forties one voice was conspicuously silent, the voice of Soviet economists" (1963: 211). In fact, the practice of economics did not disappear in the Soviet Union, but it did change in fundamental ways during the 1930s.

Instead of using markets or economists to regulate the economy, Soviet party leaders expanded the role of "controllers," those who monitored and disciplined state and party institutions (Boim et al. 1966; Lampert 1985; Rees 1987). In tsarist times, controllers had conducted financial audits of government agencies. With the nationalization of the economy in the Soviet Union, controllers' work expanded to monitoring the entire economy. Controllers were closely connected with Stalin, particularly because he had headed the State Control Agency in the 1920s. Stalin introduced new tasks for controllers. According to him, controllers should eradicate bureaucratism and "official local patriotism," improve work discipline, and create a new socialist work morality (Káldor 1949: 471).[48] Bureaucratism and "local patriotism," or local interests, blocked the uniform and effective implementation of Party and government policies. For controllers, economic problems resulted from a lack of work discipline, inattention to the economical use of materials, self-serving attitudes, illegal activities, sabotage, corruption, and the underestimation of resources. Controllers examined state institutions, punished those responsible, and "educated" employees about problems that were discovered. Controllers formed a relatively direct link between policy makers and the objects of policy. For controllers, there was no separation of economics and politics; they monitored all state institutions.

In contrast to this "active" work, the work of political economists, according to one scholar of the Soviet Union, was a "vapid ecclesiastical catechism, characterized by sterility and sycophancy" (Judy 1971: 223).

In the Soviet hierarchy of economic work, Party leaders decided policy and the overall national economic plan.[49] Other occupations, especially engineers, worked out the details of the plans. Controllers monitored the plan. The majority of economists worked as political economists not making decisions but providing theoretical support to Party decisions. Marxist-Leninist economics consisted of the political economy of capitalism, the political economy of socialism, and a variety of applied branch studies, such as planning, agriculture, accounting, and trade. The applied branches sought to teach the technical aspects of these areas, but most people learned technical skills on the job. In general, the applied branches provided Marxist-Leninist justifications for the specific techniques used by Party-state agencies. The two fields of political economy—along with courses in the history of the Soviet Communist Party and Marxist-Leninist philosophy—were part of the Communist "worldview curriculum," the group of classes that Party leaders saw as necessary for gaining the official socialist perspective. With the appropriate perspective or worldview, they hoped Party or state employees would make everyday decisions that followed correctly from the Party's policies. This curriculum was seen as necessary ideological training for leaders and employees within Party-state agencies.[50]

The political economy of capitalism involved the Marxist-Leninist criticism of the different phases of capitalism and capitalist economic ideas. Based primarily on the works of Marx and Engels, this field presented capitalism as inherently exploitative, tending toward monopolies and crisis, profit oriented, and unable to consciously use economic laws in planning. Education in this field started with a study of the method of Marxist political economy and then presented different aspects of capitalism, such as capitalist surplus value, average profit, and the general crisis of capitalism.

The political economy of socialism essentially laid out a blueprint for socialism based on the experience of the Soviet Union, Stalin's ideas about the next necessary steps to communism, and quotations from Marx, Engels, Lenin, and Stalin. In schools, many more class hours were devoted to this field than to the study of capitalism. Political economists explained the blueprint for socialism and described how Party policies fit into this blueprint. They also sought to differentiate socialist economics from capitalist economics, thus maintaining the doctrinal purity of socialism. Political economists defined socialist wages, work structures, commodities, accounting, trade, and banks, in opposition to those in capitalism, which were only similar in form, not in content.[51]

By the mid-1930s, very little was known about the existing Soviet economy, as opposed to about the ideal socialist economy or the existing capitalist economy, and fear stopped economists from talking about what little they did know.[52] Russian economist Stanislav Strumilin was reported to have said, "It is better to stand for high rates than to sit in prison for low ones" (Katsenelinboigen 1980: 140–141). Economists and other instructors of the political economy of socialism did not have a textbook. With the declaration of the Soviet Union as a socialist state in the new 1936 constitution, the Soviet Communist Party commissioned a textbook on this topic, which resulted in seventeen years of discussion among hundreds of economists and most of the Communist Party leadership (Pollock 2006). The fear of making a mistake or even making a claim at all about the economics of socialism meant that not much was known about actually existing socialism in the Soviet Union.[53] Of course, the Soviet economy had significantly changed since the nineteenth-century writings of Marx and Engels, as well as since 1917 and the creation of a planning system. Economists had not kept up with these changes but rather had chosen to avoid them at all costs, and they looked to Soviet leaders for answers. The intellectual result of these discussions was the declaration that "the law of value" still functioned in the Soviet Union, though it functioned in a different way than in capitalist countries (ibid.: 173). However, economists in fear and confusion continued to turn to Stalin himself for direction in economics. A textbook was published only in 1954, eighteen months after Stalin's death (ibid.: 211)

While Russian economists may have been silent internationally during the socialist calculation debate, at home they worked on problems directly related to mathematical neoclassical economics behind the scenes in the Soviet Union (Katsenelinboigen 1980: 28; Schumpeter [1954] 1966).[54] When Stalin took power in 1929, he sought to separate and isolate the emerging Soviet sciences from their disciplinary counterparts in the rest of the world.[55] The Soviet Party-state restricted the communication of Russian scientists with those outside of the Soviet Union and their travel outside the Soviet Union. This isolation reached its peak between the end of the Second World War and the death of Stalin. As a result of the isolation, few scientists could communicate across the Cold War border, and thus scientists had a monologue about the science practiced on the other side.

For example, in 1939, almost at the same time as the socialist calculation debate, a Russian unknown to his Western European counterparts, Leonid Kantorovich, showed that neoclassical methods could be used to calculate optimal prices in a centrally planned economy (Gardner 1990: 644). Kantorovich had already gained worldwide fame through his work in mathematics.[56] In 1939, he presented a work that would much later win him a Nobel Prize in economics.[57] Without mentioning Barone or any other economist, he equated the pure competitive system and the central planning system, as other neoclassical economists also did. He used the case of choosing the optimal mix of machines in a plywood factory and discovered a way to mathematically solve Walras's set of equations to calculate the equilibrium or shadow price, which promised to make planning more systematic and easier (Gardner 1990: 644). With his mathematical discovery, Kantorovich made a significant contribution to neoclassical economics, though his work would not be known outside of the Soviet Union until later.

Kantorovich developed his ideas within the Stalinist state and found particular support and protection within the Soviet military. Given that neoclassical economists equated the pure competitive model and the centrally planned socialist model, the military support of neoclassical economics is not surprising. The decidedly nonmarket military supported neoclassical economics as a means to provide some exactness in planning and logistics (Katsenelinboigen 1978–1979). While scholars have argued that Kantorovich's work was ignored until the late 1950s, Kantorovich in fact presented his results in various venues.[58] In 1949, he also won the Stalin Prize. At the same time, his work also came under public attack as bourgeois (Ellman 1973; Josephson 1997: 221; Katsenelinboigen 1978–1979). When his methods helped to reduce scrap at a railroad-car plant, Kantorovich was summoned to the Leningrad Regional Party headquarters on charges of complicity—he had inadvertently reduced scrap required by other industries—but the charges were dropped because Kantorovich also worked on the priority area of atomic energy (Katsenelinboigen 1978–1979: 134).

The influence of state interests, the demands of the military, and the fear of making political mistakes encouraged a narrow neoclassical economics that focused on just one part of the core of neoclassical economics—the centrally planned socialist state—and did not mention any institutions that might improve planning. According to one of his pupils, Kantorovich "thought much and intensively" about these institutions, though he did not publish his ideas (Sutela 1991: 31). As a result of fear and many different pressures, only a small number of economists practiced neoclassical economics and did so in a narrow sense.

In the 1940s, there were small signs of change in the Soviet Union, which evoked great interest among American economists. In 1944, the *New York Times* published a series of articles discussing a Russian news story titled "Teaching of Economics in the Soviet Union."[59] "The ado is indeed extraordinary," remarked Marxist economist Paul Baran (1944: 862). Why was there such excitement about a seemingly insignificant text? Raya Dunayevskaya (1944), long-time anti-Stalinist and dissident Trotskyist living in the United States, had translated the Soviet article into English and interpreted it as signaling a fundamental change in Soviet economics. The article announced that the political economy of socialism in the Soviet Union had changed and explained how economic laws functioned in socialism. The *American Economic Review* published the entire Soviet article, responses by a number of economists, and a rebuttal by Dunayevskaya herself.

In the *American Economic Review*, the American neoclassical commentators understood their Soviet counterparts as returning to the long tradition of neoclassically based socialism. Carl Landauer, one of the earliest market socialists in Germany and by then a resident of the United States, argued that "the road on which the authors of the statement have started leads from the Marxian camp into that of Jevons, Walras, and Menger" (1944: 342). Oskar Lange (1945) also noted the "considerable comment" that this Soviet article had evoked, but he argued that the article did not signal a fundamental change in Marxist economics; rather, it marked a return to Marxist economics and a recognition of the existence of economic laws and "converges to the view held by the Western students of socialist economics" like Lange himself (ibid.: 127–128, 131). However, the convergence was not yet complete because Soviet economists still assumed the labor theory of value. In contrast to this, in his opinion, inferior tool, Lange called for the only possible answer, the "incorporation into Soviet economics of the methods and techniques of marginal analysis" (ibid.: 133). Landauer agreed:

The revision of the value theory taught in Russia may facilitate a fruitful discussion between Western and Russian economists, who will from now on talk more nearly the same language, although of course many of the Western economists have not explicitly adopted a utility value theory. Even more important, the abandonment of the labor value theory—in fact if not in terms—will free price analysis in Soviet planning from a severe handicap and is therefore likely to result in increasing the advantages of the Soviet planned economy. (1944: 344)[60]

These economists in the United States predicted that Soviet economists would soon adopt neoclassical tools ideally suited, in their minds, for socialism, but any fruitful discussion between them and their Soviet counterparts could not be realized during Stalin's lifetime.

Beginning in 1948, the Soviet Union sought to spread the Soviet system in Eastern Europe. The political economy of socialism formed an important part of the Soviet model because it laid out a blueprint for socialism based on the experience of the Soviet Union, Stalin's ideas about the next necessary steps to communism, and quotations from Marx, Engels, Lenin, and Stalin. However, Soviet state interests, military requirements, and fear stalled the Marxist study of actually existing socialism. Small groups of economists did develop neoclassical economics in the secret world of the Soviet state and accepted the existing hierarchical institutions as given. The political economy of socialism and neoclassical economics of socialism were thus still in flux. After Stalin's death in 1953, the neoclassical economists would create a renaissance of mathematical neoclassical economics in the Soviet Union and reenter the transnational dialogue they had left after the Bolshevik Revolution.

Neoclassical Study of the Soviet Union

The Soviet Union was the first nationwide socialist experiment and thus was of immense interest around the world. However, it was unclear what role the Soviet Union would play in neoclassical economics. In his "A Short View of Russia," Keynes himself did not see that "Russian Communism has made any contribution to our economic problems of intellectual interest or scientific value" ([1925] 1963: 297).[61] In part, this was due to the fact that very little was known about how the Soviet planning system worked, particularly in the 1930s and 1940s (Chossudowsky 1939: 138). Abram Bergson, soon to become an economics professor at Columbia University and a researcher in the Office of Strategic Services (OSS) and RAND, however, reinterpreted Soviet state socialism within the language of mathematical neoclassical economics, welfare economics, and comparative economic systems. As a result, American neoclassical economists deemed knowledge about the Soviet Union directly relevant to their own theories and methods.

Bergson was instrumental in the 1930s rebirth of mathematization and the general equilibrium theory of Walras, Pareto, and Barone in neoclassical economics. In the 1935–1936 academic year as a Harvard graduate student, Bergson took a "Price Theory and Price Analysis" course, which introduced him to the new mathematical neoclassical economics and the economics of socialism.[62] Bergson's professor for this course was Wassily Leontief, who had grown up and completed his university education in the Soviet Union.[63] After the course, Bergson immediately published a foundational neoclassical article on marginal utility measurement (Bergson 1936) and another foundational article on neoclassical welfare economics (Bergson 1938) in major economics journals. In his 1938 piece, Bergson created his "social welfare function" on neoclassical assumptions and mathematical equations from Walras, Pareto, and Barone, as well as other more recent economists, which abstractly described how a social planner could maximize social welfare at a Pareto-optimal equilibrium point. Any losers in a shift to maximize social welfare could be compensated by a portion of the national dividend distributed by lump-sum transfers. By using the social welfare function and Pareto optimality, economists, acting as a kind of social planner, could thus evaluate different alternatives, whether policy alternatives or even alternative economic systems.

Bergson remembered that he turned "rather abruptly" from his theoretical neoclassical work to the study of the Soviet economy and presented himself as working "extra-curricularly" in economic theory (1992: 61–62). While working on these theoretical issues, Bergson started to study the Soviet Union, learned Russian, and conducted research in the Soviet Union in the summer of 1937 (ibid.: 62). He, however, did not break from his earlier work but perceived socialism, the Soviet Union, and neoclassical economics as interconnected. As Bergson remembered, "In the mixed-up world of the time, how socialist planning functioned in the one country where it was being applied on any scale seemed a rather momentous matter" (ibid.: 62). In addition, "remarkably little serious, scholarly work" had been done on the Soviet economy (ibid.). Bergson was drawn simultaneously to both the study of the Soviet system and the discipline of neoclassical economics.

In the Soviet Union in 1937, Bergson found it very difficult to conduct research or talk with potential colleagues because of the repressive political environment. After several attempts to visit ministries, he ended up visiting the Lenin Library on his own and ordered books there. After obtaining an interview with an official in the Komissariat of Heavy Industry, he was also allowed to use the Komissariat library. In the library, he found many books about the inequality of labor earnings in the Soviet Union. After this trip, he decided to write his PhD dissertation on Soviet wage distribution.

In his published dissertation, Bergson ([1944] 1946) claimed that Soviet wages followed the general assumptions of neoclassical economics set out by Lange, Lerner, Dickinson, and Bergson himself:

> The principles of socialist wages stated in this section are the same as those advanced by O. Lange . . . and which Dickinson supports . . . The argument is stated more exactly, with respect to the general problem of attaining an optimum utilization of all resources, in my "Reformulation of . . . Welfare Economics," *Quarterly Journal of Economics*, February 1938. (15) [64]

In building his model of Soviet wages, Bergson borrowed assumptions from Lange's model of market socialism. First, Bergson assumed that workers had the freedom to choose their occupations. Second, Bergson recognized that the Soviet Union and the United States had similar inequalities in wages, thus suggesting that supply and demand worked in both systems. The Soviet wage data showed, remarkably, that Soviet wage distribution was not egalitarian, but, in fact, was very similar to the American wage distribution. Bergson realized that he could apply neoclassical economics to the Soviet Union. While socialism had always been at the core of neoclassical economics as an abstract socialist state, Bergson, for the first time, incorporated actually existing socialism into neoclassical economics. Bergson felt he could do this because the Soviet Union was socialist—"first, the ownership and administration of the bulk of the community's industrial resources by the government; second, the direction and integration of this sector . . . by a system of planning; and finally, the differential wage system" ([1944] 1946: 6–7)—and *not* communist or egalitarian. He thought that a socialist economy, in transition to communism, would likely still function according to capitalist principles, which was also the official view in the Soviet Union (Chossudowsky 1939).[65] Third, Bergson assumed that labor prices would tend to equal marginal costs. Finally, following the neoclassical model, Bergson speculated that a dividend or lump-sum tax might redistribute income and thus allow for maximum utility for each individual in society. In a strange way, Bergson equated the Soviet Union and Lange's market socialist model. For Bergson and those he influenced, the Soviet Union, Lange's market socialist model, and the pure competitive market became interchangeable elements at the core of neoclassical economics.

While the particulars of Soviet Union obviously interested Bergson, he and others decided to study the Soviet Union primarily because it further proved the universal applicability of neoclassical economics (Millar 2005: 294). Knowledge about Soviet state socialism also helped to develop neoclassical theory. Economists like Bergson working on the Soviet Union and socialism created cutting edge work in the new neoclassical economics. As Abba Lerner (1934b: 1944) wrote his famous works on socialist economics, he also published neoclassical works on the elasticity of demand and international trade costs in the top economics journals (1933, 1934a). Similarly, while writing on market socialism, Oskar Lange also published articles in leading economic journals on the utility function (1934) and welfare economics more generally (1942). Such economists made significant advances in the mathematics behind general equilibrium theory in the major journals in their field, where they also published articles on socialist economics.

By 1948, socialist economics was considered an essential subfield of neoclassical economics. In that year, the American Economic Association published *A Survey of Contemporary Economics*, with articles by leading economists, including John Kenneth Galbraith, Wassily Leontief, and Paul Samuelson, on recent developments in the main subfields of economics for "the qualified layman, the beginning graduate student, and the public servant" (Ellis 1948: v). The editors considered socialist economics to be sufficiently well defined to be included as one of the thirteen surveys in the volume (Bergson 1948).

Bergson successfully argued for the centrality of the Soviet Union to neoclassical economics. Bergson thus added Soviet state socialism to the different forms of socialism at the contradictory and yet mutually reinforcing core of neoclassical economics. The interconnection between mathematical neoclassical economics, socialism, markets, and the Soviet Union has several important consequences. Because Bergson viewed the Soviet Union through Lange's neoclassical model, neoclassical economists could move seamlessly between neoclassical models and the actual case of the Soviet Union, as if they were interchangeable. As the following chapters discuss, economists in the Soviet Union and other socialist countries would also use neoclassical economics to reform their own economies. Furthermore, for economists, later economic crises in the socialist Eastern Bloc would bring into question not only socialism but also neoclassical economics itself, as later chapters show.

Postwar Neoclassical Economics

By the 1950s, the Soviet Union had become a hierarchical, authoritarian society. In the United States, American governmental and business elites also supported hierarchical institutions, especially the military-industrial state and large-scale corporations. While Chapter 2 explores this theme in more detail, here I want to touch on a central battle within American neoclassical economics.

During the Second World War, Bergson took over the Soviet economic subsection of the Office of Strategic Services (OSS), the predecessor to the CIA, where economists calculated Soviet economic growth. After the war, he became a faculty member at Columbia University and a consultant for RAND, where he organized a group constructing measures of Soviet economic growth (Hardt 2004: 38). In his "Socialist Economics" survey, Bergson stated, "There hardly can be any room for debate: of course, socialism can work. On this, Lange certainly is convincing . . . After all, the Soviet planned economy has been operating for thirty years" (1948: 447). For Bergson, the debate now turned on whether socialism or capitalism was more efficient: "As we see it, it is now the only issue outstanding" (ibid.). The Soviet Union, socialism, and neoclassical economics were tied together.

Neoclassical economists understood markets and planning as formally identical, which provided important methodological tools. In a rather confusing way, neoclassical economists also were interested in the differences and similarities between socialism and capitalism. The field of comparative economic systems emerged out of the neoclassical core of interchangeable elements. Bergson became known as the father of comparative economic systems (Gregory and Goldman 2005: 239). He trained the top economists in the United States, including Jeffrey Sachs, as well as economists from around the world (Goldman et al., 2005; Millar 1980). Comparative economic systems explored the institutions involved with different economic systems, as well as evaluating these systems, thus providing a more comprehensive form of neoclassical economics.

The American military and state more generally encouraged a narrow form of neoclassical economics—best exemplified by the Arrow-Debreu model—that presented markets free of political intervention and other institutions but could by default assume the existing hierarchical institutions of American society. In December 1952, Kenneth Arrow and Gerard Debreu presented a famous paper, later published as "Existence of an Equilibrium for a Competitive Economy," at a meeting of the Econometric Society (Arrow and Debreu 1954: 265). Arrow and Debreu mathematically proved that general equilibrium existed for a competitive economy. Economists have long considered this mathematical proof and the conditions necessary for competitive equilibrium they laid out as a fundamental contribution to economics. This became known as the Arrow-Debreu model.

Similar to Kantorovich and Bergson, Arrow and Debreu had developed their competitive model within the distinctly nonmarket realm of the military. The Office of Naval Research had given Arrow and Debreu several contracts to fund this research. They had also worked at RAND. As we know from this chapter, economists considered the competitive model and the central planning model formally identical. Therefore, knowledge about the free market was also knowledge about central planning and vice versa. In addition, knowledge about socialism provided the basis for neoclassical knowledge about markets. The military in both the United States and the socialist East encouraged neoclassical economics but of a narrow sort, without the institutions, often socialist, that economists found necessary for competitive markets and central planning. In both the West and the East, more authoritarian political and military elites found that a narrow form of neoclassical economics bolstered their own power.

At the same time that Arrow and Debreu developed their very narrow neoclassical model, Arrow (1951) published his equally famous *Social Choice and Individual Values*. Bergson assumed that the preferences of individuals could be ordered and then somehow compiled with others' ordered preferences into a society-wide ordering of preferences or social welfare function. Preferences might be for certain commodities, for freedom, for a particular economic system, and so on. While the social welfare function could be calculated, Bergson and others did not explicitly state how the preferences would be recognized and ordered. Arrow examined this problem. For a capitalist democracy, according to Arrow, there were only two mechanisms for making social choices, voting or the market. He thus argued against the dictatorship of the social planner. He, however, found that the market mechanism did not create rational social choices because there was no mechanism for reaching consensus (ibid.: 59), and voting could not create rational social choices under the conditions he had established. Arrow's "impossibility theorem" thus pointed to the insufficiency of the new welfare economics as a basis for social choice (ibid.: 37). While some have argued that Arrow made a case for dictatorship or against democratic voting, we can instead understand Arrow as arguing for proper institutional design, for certain institutions that might allow voting and markets to function optimally and democratically. Thus, in response to the narrowing of neoclassical economics around hierarchical institutions, Arrow called for markets, voting, and institutions to enable their functioning, a democratic, decentralizing notion of neoclassical economics in the face of narrowing pressures.

Conclusions

Nicely put

I have removed the "socialist calculation debate" and Keynesian policy from their usual central place in the history of economic ideas because both obscure the role of socialism in neoclassical economics behind an unwieldy dichotomy of planning versus market. As we have seen, neoclassical economics, from its beginnings in the 1870s, assumed that pure competitive markets provide optimal results. By the 1890s, neoclassical economists had realized that the pure competitive market and central planning were mathematically identical. As a result, the market and the socialist state sat together at the center of neoclassical theorizing. Therefore, when, as mentioned at the beginning of this chapter, the president of the American Economic Association, Fred M. Taylor, stated, "Like most teachers of economic theory, I have found it quite worth while to spend some time studying any particular problem in hand from the standpoint of a socialist state" (1929: 1), he expressed the practice of using the socialist state to develop neoclassical economics. Related socialist themes, including the concrete case of the Soviet Union and abstract models of decentralized market socialism, became associated with this core. Neoclassical economists differed over the need for particular institutions—either hierarchical or decentralizing and democratic—to enable markets or central planning to function. By decentering the "socialist calculation debate" and Keynesianism, the role of socialism in neoclassical economics comes into focus.

Small groups of economists in the Soviet Union also developed neoclassical methods and shared a language with their counterparts in the United States and elsewhere. These economists in the East and the West developed a new economics based on mathematics and neoclassical assumptions in part because of similar state needs and therefore with substantial state support. Economists thus laid the groundwork for future dialogues, once the political situation allowed for them. Yet, during the Stalinist period, in the military, and, as is discussed in Chapter 2, in the McCarthy period, economists in the socialist East and the capitalist West experienced criticism and threats to their careers for the political implications of the new neoclassical economics they developed. In response to such threats, they narrowed their understanding of neoclassical economics, avoiding discussions of the institutions required to implement competitive markets and central planning. Yet, once it became possible, economists would challenge the narrowing of neoclassical economics that state elites demanded, looking to new visions of neoclassical socialism in the years to come. The "thaw" in the Cold War after the death of Joseph Stalin in 1953 and the end of McCarthyism would provide this opportunity.

2

A New Transnational Discussion among Economists in the 1950s

THE FIRST CHAPTER EXPLORED THE SURPRISING FACT that economists in the socialist East and capitalist West independently developed mathematical neoclassical economics based on thinking about both competitive markets and central planning. Findings about markets thus functioned as findings about socialism and vice versa. In spite of these shared professional interests, before the early 1950s economists in the East and in the West could not communicate directly with each other and thus did not consider themselves as part of a common economics profession.[1] When Stalin took power in 1929, the Soviet Party-state severely restricted the communication of scientists with those outside of the Soviet Union and the travel of scientists outside the Soviet Union. The United States later also restricted Americans' access to the Soviet Union and to information about it. As a result of this isolation, economists in the emerging Soviet Bloc developed a profession separate from, though in many ways parallel to, that of the United States. Economists on both sides of the Iron Curtain used similar tools and experienced similar professional and political obstacles.

After 1953, however, economists' professional lives changed dramatically. With the death of the Soviet leader Joseph Stalin in March 1953, the 1954 censure of Joseph McCarthy, and the changing diplomatic relations between the Soviet Union and the United States, economists could begin a direct, if difficult, East–West dialogue. Economists could take part in academic exchanges, visiting, studying, teaching, and researching across the Iron Curtain for periods ranging from several weeks to several years. They also corresponded with each other and exchanged books and journals. Even more often, they met each other at international economic conferences. Economists thus resumed the transnational neoclassical discussion that had existed before Stalinism and McCarthyism. As a result, the Soviet Union and Eastern Europe ceased to be isolated places, cut off from professional interaction.

In this chapter, I examine the experiences of American economists as part of a broader group of American Sovietologists, leaving a discussion of Eastern Europeans' experiences to the following chapters. Sovietology was the interdisciplinary study of the Soviet Union and socialist Eastern Europe, which expanded during the Second World War and immediately afterward but seemed to disappear with the end of the Soviet Union and socialist regimes.[2] Sovietologists included economists, political scientists, sociologists, historians, and literature and language specialists. In seeking to understand the Cold War enemy, these scholars entered a kind of liminal space between American capitalism and Soviet state socialism. People generally consider liminal spaces as dangerous and polluting, as well as exciting and full of potential for new phenomena and new knowledge.[3] Sovietologists worked in a highly uncertain and relatively dangerous world. Even before 1953, Sovietologists had to establish scientific credibility both shaped and threatened by their close association with the American state, military, and intelligence agencies. The international political shift and the international reorganization of science after 1953 created the possibility for a common economics profession and forced Sovietologists to consider their counterparts across the Iron Curtain as colleagues. This shift brought new scientific credibility claims, professional disputes, priority controversies, and even espionage cases, as well as new scientific approaches and new economic knowledge. This chapter explores the beginning of this shift.

Separate Dialogues

Like their Soviet counterparts discussed in Chapter 1, American economists found unprecedented opportunities and resources within the wartime and Cold War state, which employed neoclassical economic methods for economic and military planning (Bernstein 1995: 2001; Mirowski 2002). During the 1930s, states around the globe came to base their legitimacy on economic growth. To attain economic and later, during the Second World War, military goals, states worldwide encouraged the growth and organization of the economics profession.[4] Michael Bernstein has observed:

> It is one of the great ironies of this history that a discipline renowned for its systematic portrayals of the benefits of unfettered, competitive markets would first demonstrate its unique operability in the completely regulated and controlled economy of total war. (2001: 89)[5]

Worldwide, state bureaucracies increasingly hired economists to make, implement, and evaluate policy in a wide range of areas (Coats 1981; Fourcade 2009).

The nonmarket realm of the military in particular supported neoclassical economic research because the military perceived its use for logistical planning. Given that neoclassical economists freely interchanged the pure market model and the centrally planned socialist model, the centrally planned military was indeed a relevant venue for neoclassical economics. Military research institutes such as RAND hired neoclassical economists, including many future Nobel Laureates, such as Kenneth Arrow and Tjalling Koopmans, and funded conferences to develop neoclassical mathematical tools.[6] These conferences created such classics in the field as *Activity Analysis of Production and Allocation* (Koopmans 1951). With military and broader state support, American neoclassical economists could develop their highly mathematical and formalistic kind of economics and become the mainstream of American economics profession. The influence of military funding and requirements, as well as concerns about appearing socialist in McCarthy-era America, encouraged a narrow neoclassical economics in which the institutions necessary for neoclassically based markets or planning could not be discussed.

Some neoclassical economists joined scholars from other disciplines studying the Soviet Union in U.S. intelligence services. While a few Americans and Western Europeans had studied Russia and the Soviet Union earlier, the field of Sovietology emerged during the Second World War in the Office of Strategic Services (OSS), the predecessor of the CIA (Byrnes 1976: 10–20). During World War II, experts from a number of disciplines conducted research on the Soviet Union in the OSS. These included important neoclassical economists, such as Abram Bergson and Wassily Leontief, who calculated the Soviet national income. After the war, several foundations sought to replicate this interdisciplinary area studies research by creating the Russian Institute at Columbia University in 1946 and the Russian Research Center at Harvard University in 1948. The Russian Research Center in particular had close, informal ties with the CIA because its faculty and staff worked on projects supported by the CIA, military intelligence, and other government agencies (Engerman 2009: 47–48).[7]

During the Stalinist years, economists found that they could communicate very little with their colleagues across Cold War borders. The organizers of the Russian Institute, for example, had always assumed that their students would be exposed to visiting Soviet scholars and would conduct their own research in the Soviet Union, just as their professors had done in the 1920s and 1930s (Byrnes 1976: 23).[8] In 1947, on a trip organized by the Soviet Embassy, however, Russian Institute Professor Ernest Simmons failed to establish academic exchange programs and found himself attacked by both the Soviet press (*Izvestia*) and the *New York World Telegram* (ibid.: 33).[9] American economists created knowledge about the Soviet Union without contact with those in the Soviet Union.

As a result of the closed nature of both the Soviet Union and the United States, Sovietologists were quite innovative in their methods of study: "Specialists on the Soviet Union area, most of whom were unable to visit the country after World War II, could easily liken themselves to astronomers and the object of their study to some distant planet for all practical purposes inaccessible to earth-bound men" (Reshetar 1955: 3). From the wartime OSS, they adopted anthropological approaches to the study of enemies, where one could not do fieldwork but could do "remote research" (ibid.: 14–15).[10] Economists such as Joseph Berliner, as well as other social scientists, used interviews with former Soviet citizens living in Germany. The employees at the American Embassy in Moscow also provided economists with data, in particular lists of prices obtained by walking through shops and markets.[11] At the Russian Institute and the Russian Research Center, émigrés or exiles working as faculty or traveling through town often gave talks and offered new information, though faculty and others found the information provided by many of these individuals problematic.[12] Others searched for clues to Soviet culture in newspapers, folk literature, proverbs, contemporary fiction, memoirs, and movies (Reshetar 1955: 15).

The CIA and other intelligence agencies also provided Soviet publications and other information to scholars. Those with security clearances or friends with intelligence connections could get some information or even translated articles, which gave them an advantage within their professions. For example, in 1949, Merrill Flood, a RAND researcher, gave a lecture at RAND. During the discussion, "a mathematician whose duties included the reading of Russian technical literature," Max Shiffman, mentioned that Flood's results reminded him of an abstract he had just read summarizing a 1942 article by Soviet economist Leonid Kantorovich.[13] Flood later told Tjalling Koopmans about the 1942 article. Another mathematical economist, W. W. Cooper, wrote in a letter to someone at RAND, "I know the Novozhilov paper through a CIA translation which I saw some years back. It deals with proposals for applying Kantorovich's method to the Russian economy. I also know something of Kantorovich's reputation."[14] Colleagues without security clearances or intelligence connections could not obtain these usually unpublished translations. A broad range of scientific topics, including mathematical economics, was considered relevant to U.S. national security and thus could not be published in professional journals. Many published works were printed for small lists of readers with security clearances.[15] Secrecy was more important than publication. Involvement with the military and intelligence agencies thus broke down the communication within the American and the Soviet economics professions. At the same time, intelligence connections did create some form of an "East–West dialogue," though economists did not speak directly to each other, and only certain people could take part in this "dialogue."[16]

In spite of their connection with the CIA and other government agencies, Sovietologists still experienced McCarthyist attacks. From 1945 to the mid-1950s, American social scientists more broadly experienced what Lazarsfeld and Thielens (1958) called "the Difficult Years" (see also Caute 1978; Haney 2008; Schrecker 1986). After 1945, conservatives attacked many academics as communists and communist sympathizers, which intensified when, in 1950, Senator Joseph McCarthy publicly claimed to have located a domestic communist threat in distinguished American colleges (Lazarsfeld and Thielens 1958: 166–167). Based on their interviews with over 2,000 social scientists in American academia, Lazarsfeld and Thielens found that almost half of the sample reported that a member of their faculty had been accused of "being a subversive or of engaging in any un-American activities in the past few years."[17] In addition, a third of the sample had been visited by an FBI representative three or more times in the past year. Lazarsfeld and Thielens found that "in this period an individual could be called a Communist for almost any kind of behavior, or for holding almost any kind of attitude" (ibid.: 57).[18]

Sovietologists experienced increased difficulty obtaining materials from the Soviet Union. In their responses to Lazarsfeld and Thielens's survey, academics complained that they could not get access to Communist or allegedly Communist materials for research or teaching. Lazarsfeld and Thielens reported:

Leading the list [of difficult to obtain materials], of course, are books and pamphlets dealing with Russia and Communism which cannot be obtained or are considered too risky to use. But *Pravda* and *Izvestia*, the *Daily Worker*, and other outright Communist literature by no means completed the inventory, for many "leftist" and "liberal" books and periodicals were also mentioned. (1958: 219–220)

The Russian Research Center staff felt that "an understanding with the FBI" was necessary before obtaining books from Communist bookshops in New York City (O'Connell 1990: 131).[19]

The FBI paid special attention to Soviet specialists. As O'Connell has shown, the FBI closely surveiled the Russian Research Center at Harvard (1990: 133–138). Almost immediately the FBI declared that the center had "almost been taken over by Communists or Communist Party sympathizers" and advised that an investigation be initiated of individuals in the center by the FBI's Espionage Section.[20] At the same time, the U.S. military, the CIA, and the U.S. State Department paid the center to conduct work on the Soviet Union, which pushed the center to conduct research on particular topics and neglect other topics and nonstate perspectives and protected the center from criticism of those topics that the state encouraged (ibid.). Thus, Sovietologists developed their field within the dual pressures of FBI surveillance and coercive CIA encouragement.

While conservatives inspired by McCarthy did not pose as deadly a threat to American economists as Stalinists did to their Soviet counterparts, political harassment did alter the professional life of economists in the United States. Conservative political leaders criticized economists as Keynesians, New Deal liberals, and red agents (Solberg and Tomilson 1997). Some academic economists lost their jobs or could not find jobs due to political pressure (Fourcade 2009: 88–90).[21] Conservatives focused on those studying the Soviet Union or socialist economics. Given that the

Soviet Union and socialist economics were central to neoclassical economics, these attacks caused problems for neoclassical economists more generally. One economist remembered:

I taught a course in Soviet economics. My opinions traveled widely through the college and were reported back to me from teachers and administrators, not always correctly. Members of the administration sat in on the course—a charming idea! Good course, they said afterwards. I was never actually criticized, never anything wrong with my teaching. There was something wrong with the course—it didn't damn Communism enough. The president suggested to me that it wasn't advisable to have the course just now. It didn't look nice in the catalogue. It was dropped. (Lazarsfeld and Thielens 1958: 252)[22]

In response to such attacks, many social scientists did not teach controversial topics, did not assign readings on Soviet topics, slanted their presentations to be more critical of Soviet phenomena, and chose those textbooks considered acceptable to conservative authorities (Lazarsfeld and Thielens 1958).

The consequences of these attacks are particularly evident in the case of one of the neoclassical pioneers, Paul Samuelson. According to Samuelson (1997), as he began to write his famous neoclassical *Economics* textbook in 1947, another economics textbook, *The Elements of Economics* by Lorie Tarshis, appeared. By 1948, individuals "then considered extremely on the right" viciously criticized Tarshis politically and personally as a "Keynesian-Marxist" and "almost killed" his textbook (Samuelson 1997: 158). With the publication of his famous neoclassical *Economics* textbook, Samuelson too came under assault. In his 1951 *God and Man at Yale*, conservative pundit William F. Buckley attacked Yale's economics department, calling the professors "thoroughly collectivistic" and at least one faculty member an "outspoken socialist" (Buckley 1951: 46, 87). Samuelson remembered this period:

One of your local department-store owners went around the country lecturing to Rotary audiences on my dangerous doctrines; William Buckley received his first baptism of success in his book, *God and Man at Yale*, under the first heading of which the New Haven chaplain came in for a lot of criticism and under the second heading of which I received my due. It all sounds funny in retrospect; and as far as I personally was concerned no real trauma or anguish was involved. But if you were a teacher at many a school around the country and the Board of Regents of your university was on your neck for using subversive textbooks, it was no laughing matter . . . Make no mistake about it, intimidation often did work in the short run. (1972: 21–22)

Samuelson went on to describe how such intimidation "did have an effect upon my formulations" (ibid.: 22). In 1947, Samuelson's *Foundations of Economic Analysis* appeared, a rigorous, highly mathematical text oriented toward the economics graduate student or professor, unlike his 1948 *Economics* undergraduate textbook. His *Foundations of Economic Analysis*, primarily written in 1937 (Samuelson 1947: vii), continuously and openly acknowledged the centrality of socialism to neoclassical economics (for example, Chapter 8), but the index had no entry for "socialism." In the undergraduate *Economics* textbook, "socialism" had an entry in the index, but Samuelson severed the overt ties between neoclassical economics and socialism. He ([1948] 1951) relegated socialism in the textbook to an "Alternative Economic Systems" epilogue.

In contrast to many accounts that assume Sovietologists were politically conservative, Engerman (2009) has shown that they had a wide range of political commitments.[23] Regardless of the range of their politics, neoclassical economists all responded to McCarthyist attacks and military and intelligence demands by making their work more abstract and mathematical. Young scholars, such as Kenneth Arrow and Paul Samuelson, who had turned from mathematics to economics as an exciting area in which to apply their excellent mathematical skills, became rising stars in the postwar period. As discussed in the previous chapter, in 1952, Kenneth Arrow and Gerard Debreu presented their now famous mathematical model of general equilibrium, later known as the Arrow-Debreu model. They developed this highly mathematical model within the military and at RAND. At the same time as the development of the Arrow-Debreu model, Arrow published his equally famous *Social Choice and Individual Values* (1951), in which in very abstract and obscure language he rejected authoritarian planning and argued for institutions that might allow voting and markets to function optimally and democratically. This was not the time to discuss institutions, such as worker control or economic democracy, potentially necessary for competitive markets and central planning. In both the West and the East, more authoritarian political and military elites supported a narrow form of neoclassical economics that assumed existing hierarchical institutions and bolstered their own power.[24]

Economists still developed their neoclassical discipline through models of socialism, though very narrowly. The economist H. Smith in

1955 recognized that, while mainstream economics developed from the study of a socialist state, the socialist nature of the discipline had been separated from it:

Some twenty-five years ago I suspect that nearly every young economist had a pricing system for factors and products in a socialist state tucked away in his desk. Analytical fragments were torn bleeding from the carcase [sic] of the economic systems they were contrived to explain, and sewn together with great skill. (418)

Ironically, neoclassical economists now assumed the highly centralized institutions of the military, the state, and corporations, equally applicable to the Soviet economy. By not speaking overtly about necessary institutions, according to Smith (1955) again, economists presented an authoritarian system without socialist worker control and economic democracy. These economists instead presented a society where "workers are paid the value of their marginal products, in the interests of maximising output, adjusted to allow for the labour-supply curves which slope backwards" (ibid.: 418). Why would workers follow neoclassical models, and why would they want to? Smith complained that "it is not probable that in such a society the ordinary man will be conscious of economic freedom, of the enjoyment of the 'full product of his labour': that he will fulfill the socialist ideal" (ibid.: 419). In the face of pressures by the military and intelligence services, neoclassical economists assumed obedient workers and did not overtly discuss what would be required for the market or central planning to function ideally.

McCarthy-era attacks also shaped Sovietological methodology. State officials required Sovietologists to take a stand against the Soviet Union (Gleason 1995; Meyer 1993). According to Motyl, "Although outward neutrality is generally the visage most scholars prefer to assume, it is unavailable to Sovietologists because of the nature of the beast they study" (1993: 81). Because they studied the "enemy" and thus evoked suspicion, Sovietologists worked hard to maintain trust and credibility. Sovietologists turned to totalitarian theory as a solid moral basis.[25] By arguing that Nazi Germany and the Soviet Union were equally evil, Sovietologists allowed themselves to move beyond these moral claims (Gleason 1995). As a result, it was easy to criticize the Soviet Union but difficult to discuss its positive aspects, while it was also difficult to criticize the United States (Meyer 1993: 169). In the hopes of avoiding ideological attacks, many Sovietologists also turned to empiricism and avoided theory, claiming to let the facts to speak for themselves, rather than having scholars speak out (Motyl 1993: 83).[26]

Economists in each Cold War camp took part in separate dialogues. At the same time, they did continue to practice neoclassical economics, and some learned about each others' work through various channels: older colleagues, exiles and émigrés, economic data from the embassies, newspapers, and articles obtained through intelligence agencies. Furthermore, economists worked on common topics with an at least potentially shared language. In addition, they experienced political attacks, which changed the way they used neoclassical economics and gave them a common motivation to seek allies abroad. Such allies might allow them to bolster their professional claims and protect themselves from devastating, or even potentially deadly, politically motivated attacks.

The New Transnational Economics Discussion

After years of being unable to travel to the East Bloc, in the spring of 1954, American scholars and students found that they could now visit. In August 1954, four graduate students at Columbia University's Russian Institute traveled to Moscow, Leningrad, and Central Asia for one month.[27] As one of the students reported in his alumni newsletter:

We saw cities that only one other American has seen in the last ten years. We wandered about without guides, interpreters, or shadows, talking to hundreds of Russians of all classes about the most sensitive topics from Trotsky to Beria. We took pictures and movies everywhere, and managed to get half of them out of the country. We were arrested sixteen times, but none of us ever disappeared permanently. (Randall 1955: 2)[28]

Sovietology's founders could finally realize their plans. Direct interaction between the United States and the Soviet Union would change not only the education of students but also the organization of science worldwide. When the social worlds of socialism and capitalism collided, Sovietology would also change.

After Joseph Stalin's death in 1953, Soviet policy changed. Communist Party leaders and many committed Communist Party members, like many Soviet citizens, developed a critical consciousness about the Stalinist era, calling for a return to original socialist and communist tenets.[29] Most famously, the new leader of the Soviet Union, Nikita Khrushchev, officially criticized Stalin in 1956 and opened the door to reevaluating the Soviet past and future. Similarly, in the United States, new social movements, such as the civil rights movement, also developed a critical attitude toward the status quo and called for the realization of professed American values of freedom, equality, and democracy. More broadly, these new interactions expanded a liminal space between and beyond the Cold War dichotomy of Soviet state socialism and American market capitalism. Liminal spaces opened up for a discourse critical of both Soviet and American politics and society.

Economists participating in the new East–West dialogues contributed to these liminal spaces. New institutions brought together people with politics outside the usual Cold War dichotomies—including former Communists, anti-Soviet socialists, libertarians, Eastern European reformers, and Eastern European émigrés—to discuss the nature of socialism, both actually existing and possible future socialisms. In the Cold War, they had dangerous access to Cold War enemies in a world entering the 1960s and 1970s. This access produced new forms of knowledge. The perceived danger and charisma of liminality also led to accusations of espionage by individuals and organizations in the United States and the Soviet Union.

Barghoorn (1960) and Raymond (1972: 120) have suggested that Soviet successes in the "indoctrination" of foreign Communists in the Soviet Union, especially immediately after the Second World War, may have prompted the United States to expand its own international student exchange programs. The Soviet Union conducted academic exchange programs in its Comintern schools for Communist Party political elites from other countries. After the death of Joseph Stalin in early 1953, the Soviet leadership quickly started what Americans called a "cultural offensive," "a campaign designed to spread Soviet influence and to undo the harmful effects on the Soviet international position caused by the excesses of Stalinist rudeness, secrecy, bluster, and violence" (Barghoorn 1960: 18).[30] The Soviet leadership also sought to establish connections with the West, including the United States, and supported new exchange programs in part to gain new scientific and technical knowledge (ibid.; Richmond 1987: 5; Richmond 2003: 10).[31] By 1955, the Soviet government had started serious educational training of foreign students in regular universities and in specialty schools (Barghoorn 1964).[32] The Soviet government's 1954 welcome of the four Russian Institute students was part of its opening to the United States and other nonsocialist countries.

In mid-1956, the U.S. National Security Council implemented a new policy toward the Soviet Union and Eastern Europe, NSC 5607, which supported academic exchanges (Richmond 1987: 133–139). Through academic exchanges, the U.S. State Department sought to undermine socialism by exposing those countries to Western influences and by supporting individuals and trends that undermined the monopoly of the Soviet Union and the national Communist Parties. The Statement of Policy asserted that the U.S. policy is "designed to weaken International Communism," by stimulating nationalism, promoting "a courageous policy of defiance of Moscow," and stimulating a "desire for more consumer's goods" (ibid.: 136–137). The State Department actively sought to implement this policy:

Our foreign policies are necessarily *defensive*, so far as the use of force is concerned. But they can be *offensive* in terms of promoting a desire for greater individual freedom, well-being and security within the Soviet Union, and greater independence within the satellites. In other words, East–West exchanges should be an implementation of positive United States foreign policy. (ibid.: 136)

Educational exchanges with the Soviet Union and Eastern Europe formed an important part of U.S. foreign policy, which set about to undermine socialism.

In contrast to the East Bloc, which privileged the technical sciences, the U.S. State Department emphasized the social sciences and humanities.[33] The main objective of the U.S. government was to open the Soviet Union to Western influences and thus to change its foreign and domestic policies (Richmond 1987: 6). To U.S. government officials, Western influences could best be transmitted through educating Eastern European scholars in American social sciences and humanities. These officials also considered American scholars in the social sciences and humanities as best able to collect intelligence information because they often understood the languages and cultures of the region. Furthermore, many natural and physical scientists did not want to go to the East Bloc because they thought they would not gain much professionally from these exchanges.

Previously, students who wished to attend universities abroad or faculty who wished to visit foreign universities just communicated directly with universities, rather than going through their governments. The Cold War relationship between the Soviet Union and the United States made formal intergovernmental agreements and new institutions necessary to allow for contact between their citizens.[34] States began to use academic exchanges as diplomatic instruments, as Merritt recognized: "What gives

exchange programs an aura of importance previously unknown is a recognition (or at least the belief) that they facilitate the implementation of a
nation-state's foreign policy" (1972: 65). Exchanges took on a new level of
importance at the nation-state level.

Before 1953, there were no institutions in the U.S. government or
at universities to organize such exchanges and to allow transnational dialogue, but this would soon change. In 1956, American university faculty
came together to form the Inter-University Committee for Travel Grants
(IUCTG) to provide administrative and financial support for faculty
and students seeking to travel to the Soviet Union. The IUCTG used
one-month tourist visas to send American scholars and students. The Soviet Union and the United States signed a major cultural agreement in
1958, the Lacy-Zarubin agreement, which allowed for regular academic
exchanges and a series of "rights" involved with the agreement. Between
1958 and 1988, about 5,000 Americans and a similar number of Soviet
graduate students, scholars, and teachers visited each others' countries
through the IUCTG and its later replacement, the International Research
and Exchanges Board (IREX) (Richmond 2003: 24).

Exchanges between the United States and Eastern Europe were much
easier than Soviet–American exchanges, but institutions were still required
to mediate these new interactions. In 1951, the Yugoslav government requested a formal academic exchange agreement, and the first Yugoslavs and
Americans took part in an exchange in 1955. In 1956, the Polish government approached the Ford Foundation, seeking connections with American
universities (Byrnes 1976). The Ford and Rockefeller Foundations began
exchange programs in Poland in 1957 and in Yugoslavia in the following
year (Richmond 1987: 114–116). Hungary began its exchanges with the
United States in 1963. The Ford Foundation adopted the State Department
stance on educational exchanges: "It would seem important to help increase
their [Eastern European countries'] contacts with the West and thereby
penetrate these East European areas with Western democratic influences."[35]

The U.S. government and the Ford Foundation gave precedence
to exchanges of economists, and especially mathematical economists, in
Eastern Europe. These organizations wanted to have an impact on approaching economic reforms throughout the region:

Experts inside and outside the State Department believe the process of change in
Eastern Europe is quickening and that the time is auspicious for an extension of the
Foundation's program in Eastern Europe.[36]

A Ford Foundation official declared that "the economists are a strategic group to be given emphasis in the Foundation's exchange program."[37] In the case of Hungary, the Ford Foundation chose economists who would have the most impact on the New Economic Mechanism reform and the Hungarian economics profession: (1) economists who ran important institutes and thus had an influence on younger scholars, (2) economists who were prominent in their fields of economics or promised to become prominent, and (3) economists who worked in fields considered important by the Ford Foundation, such as finance or international economics. One interviewer thought that a specific Hungarian economist would be influential in economic management and suggested that he be put in a "first-class" MBA program.[38] Foundation officials focused on young intellectuals, but they also brought older established professionals because "these are the ones who could obstruct or promote the influence of the young people."[39] Through educational exchanges, officials at the U.S. State Department and the Ford Foundation sought to influence economic reforms.[40]

Those working with the Ford Foundation saw mathematical economics as a gateway science, a science that could lead to broader economic and political discussions. The American Embassy in Budapest told the Foundation that social scientists and humanists were an important force for "liberalization" in Hungary, in contrast to the situation in Bulgaria, where technocrats played this role.[41] An American economist who often provided information to the Ford Foundation referred to mathematical economics as "an important field bridging the ideologies of East and West."[42] Another economist, who initiated the Ford Foundation exchanges with Hungary, remarked:

I thought that I would send you these notes, to get your reactions on the possibility of a "trial attempt or possibility" of some type of unit which would attract "East World" economists to study "West World" methods. Acceptance of "method" [sic] might eventually lead to acceptance of broader economic concepts.[43]

This same economist later wrote that economists more generally might extend their economic ideas to the political sphere:

I emphasize the need for an ample number of well-trained economists simply because of the potential for change in economic systems and planning which considers the preference of individuals (hoping that consideration of individual preference in markets and prices eventually can lead to similar attention to individual preferences in political selection, etc.).[44]

Economists, particularly in Hungary, were thus seen as playing a special role in importing American political values to Eastern Europe.

Another form of connection between economists in the East and West was made through book and journal exchanges. There were public and private book exchanges. Publicly, the Soviet Union and the United States had had book and journal exchange agreements since the 1920s, which the Second World War temporarily interrupted (Richmond 2003: 143–146).[45] Privately, universities, including Harvard and Columbia, exchanged thousands of books with university libraries in the Soviet Union (Byrnes 1976: 226). Russian economist and politician Yegor Gaidar remembered that the library at Moscow State University "opened up enormous opportunities for self-education—Ricardo, Mill, Bohm-Bawerk, Jevons, Marshall, Pigou, Keynes, Schumpeter, Galbraith, Friedman, and many more."[46]

Economists also individually exchanged books with their counterparts across the Iron Curtain. For example, Tjalling Koopmans sent some of his works to Leonid Kantorovich in 1956 and received works in return.[47] The CIA took book orders from American scholars and sent the books to scholars in the Soviet Union and Eastern Europe with the Americans' return addresses. Wassily Leontief, a Russian economist who had emigrated to the United States and taught at Harvard University, asked his secretary in 1962, "Please call Mr. Gilbert (?)—CIA—and ask him whether I could have a new appropriation of some $100 for books for the Soviet Economists and Statisticians—I have a number of requests which should—I think—be satisfied."[48] By 1963, a new supposedly nongovernmental organization, the International Advisory Council, also provided this service, as well as providing requested books to American scholars traveling in the East Bloc.[49] On learning of the council, Leontief immediately ordered books from it, stating, "I receive constantly requests for books, direct and implied, from prominent Soviet scholars and would be able to give you many more names and titles."[50]

In addition to academic exchanges, economists and other scholars could also meet at international conferences. While these conferences usually began by including Western Europeans and Americans, Russian and Eastern Europeans began attending these conferences by the late 1950s. Many intellectuals in Western Europe and the United States sought contacts with each other and those in the Soviet bloc in the hopes that discussions and friendships would overcome wartime divisions and make another world war more difficult.[51] They also had intellectual interests in a broader East–West discussion. Many perceived that all industrialized countries had common problems, and thus these individuals were interested in how those across the Iron Curtain had solved these problems. Conversations at these conferences led to new ideas about the possible convergence of East and West. Finally, these economists in East and West often shared neoclassical economic practices that further enabled their conversation.

Wassily Leontief organized some of the most successful East–West meetings. He initiated the first International Conference on Input-Output Techniques in the Netherlands in 1950. By the 1961 conference, 240 participants came from forty-one countries, including the East Bloc (Barna 1963: 2). And by 1970, the congress in Novosibirsk in the Soviet Union brought together thousands of participants. As shown by his long participation in the Pugwash conferences and disarmament talks, Leontief very much believed in international dialogue as a means to avoid war and particularly supported East–West dialogue.[52] Input-output methods provided a common neoclassical language for this dialogue that had developed in the socialist East and the capitalist West.[53] At the 1961 conference, the Soviet economist V. S. Nemchinov remarked:

An interindustry table of production and distribution was already incorporated in the Soviet national accounts for 1923–24. Leontief's input-output analysis represents the application of a similar method to the United States census data for 1919, 1929 and 1939. In 1925 he had published a detailed review of the first Soviet national balance. (Barna 1963: 177)

Nemchinov recognized that Leontief and others outside the Soviet Union had further developed these ideas and that the Soviets had only recently returned to these ideas.[54] Leontief's colleague Tibor Barna saw that the conference participants "represented an international fraternity of economists and statisticians, trying to talk a common language and trying to learn from each other irrespective of political divisions" (1963: 2).[55] The postwar period created the conditions for the worldwide spread of input-output modeling because states sought the means to evaluate their destroyed economies and estimate the effects of different policies. Input-output tables provided governments with an overview of their economies and a way to test how various policies might help or hurt. Such international conferences organized by Leontief thus provided an important venue for the return to a transnational neoclassical economic discussion.

After the Second World War, UNESCO had founded a range of international social scientific associations, including the International Economic Association (IEA). The first international congress of the IEA was held in Rome in 1956. As early as 1958, Russians and Eastern Europeans participated in an IEA conference in Turkey (Kaser and Robinson 1992). In 1964, IEA organized one of the first East–West conferences in the East Bloc in Bulgaria. Out of the many participants at these conferences, American economists John T. Dunlop, Clark Kerr, Abram Bergson, and others participated in the IEA to meet Soviet experts and to learn how the Soviet government organized industrial production. The Soviets agreed to participate in the meetings because they were interested in planning, so the Americans invited experts from large corporations like IBM, which used planning methods internally, and experts of input-output analysis. These conferences led to study visits—such as the trip by Dunlop, Kerr, Walter Galenson, and their families to Yugoslavia, Czechoslovakia, Hungary, and Poland in the early 1960s—and edited volumes with chapters by those from East and West (Dunlop and Diatchenko 1964; Dunlop and Fedorenko 1969).[56]

Thus, scholars, with the assistance of their governments and various nongovernmental organizations, built an institutional structure to start a transnational discussion. Americans were surprised by their interactions with Soviet citizens. For instance, in 1966 and 1967, Frederick C. Barghoorn and Ellen Mickiewicz (1972) conducted a survey of scholars and others who had recently visited the Soviet Union. From their survey, Barghoorn and Mickiewicz found, "In an almost bewildering variety of ways, 116 [out of the 179] participants reported that Soviet people were human beings" (ibid.: 152).[57] They further noted, "A distinguished biologist wrote that 'intellectual community and sympathy turn into affection in case after case; maybe the cause is the wonderful qualities of Russians as Russians, but surely one factor is the shock of revelation of community against a larger background of estrangement'" (ibid.: 154). Such a "revelation of community" in a Cold War world opened up the possibility not only of a human community but also of a common professional community.

Earlier, economists on both sides of the Cold War divide could assume that their colleagues on the other side of the Iron Curtain practiced a fundamentally different form of economics. It was often thought that Soviet economists toiled in ideological disputes about Marxist-Leninist political economy, while American economists created and advocated models of free markets. Once they came into direct contact, many economists found that they, in fact, shared similar professional tools and methods. Soviet economist Leonid Kantorovich and American economist Tjalling Koopmans, who would jointly won the Nobel Prize in Economics in 1975 for their innovations in linear programming, exemplify these changes.[58]

Koopmans had earlier heard brief references to Kantorovich's work but had not communicated with Kantorovich until 1956. Both Kantorovich and Koopmans contributed to linear programming, a mathematical method for determining optimal outcomes, such as maximum profit or minimum cost. Economists developed linear programming not only for planning within the military and the state more broadly but also within the hierarchical, planned environment of corporations. In 1956, Koopmans made the bold move of writing Kantorovich directly:

Recently I had the opportunity to see a copy of your article, "On the Translocation of Masses," in the Comptes Rendus of the Academy of Sciences of the U.S.S.R. of 1942. It became immediately clear to me that you have in part paralleled but in greater part anticipated a development of transportation theory in the United States which has stretched out over the period from 1941 to the present and is still continuing.[59]

Koopmans sent Kantorovich offprints of some articles and a list of the most important works in linear programming, as well as the names of relevant journals. He also requested offprints of Kantorovich's articles, inquired where he published, and asked for further indication of the practical uses or theoretical developments of his research. He ended his letter expressing the hope "that this letter may lead to an exchange of information between us."[60] Surprisingly, Kantorovich soon wrote back, sending a list of his writings. He then sent another package with his 1939 work *Mathematical Methods of Organizing and Planning Production.* After having this Russian work translated into English, Koopmans wrote, "The contents of the paper are simply amazing."[61]

The communication between Kantorovich and Koopmans signaled a change. Learning that they shared cutting-edge methods, Soviet and American economists began to realize that they could consider each other colleagues. Their professional circle expanded enormously. This change took place not only in economics but throughout the sciences. This expansion also brought new norms and practices. For example, Soviet and American economists had previously made dismissive comments about each other's work because they did not expect any response. Now economists responded to each other. This meant that they also had to consider the scientific priority of a new set of colleagues.

"There is a little storm blowing up in the Kantorovich teapot," wrote Koopmans to his friend and colleague Herbert Scarf in 1960.[62] The new connection between Koopmans and Kantorovich resulted in a scientific priority debate: Who had discovered linear programming first? In general, scientists strive for originality, but this priority debate revealed surprising aspects about the 1950s "thaw" in the Cold War and the similarities between capitalism and socialism.

The controversy around the priority in linear programming focused on what Kantorovich had actually discovered and whether it was the same as that which Koopmans and another linear programming pioneer, George B. Dantzig, had discovered.[63] Both Kantorovich and Koopmans developed their ideas out of specific practical problems, reflecting the specificities of the contexts in which they worked. Kantorovich generalized his ideas from the specific case of maximizing the use of wood in the plywood industry of the Soviet planned economy. Koopmans developed his methods from his wartime research on optimizing allied shipping capacity to move troops and materiel among and between the various theaters of military operations. Were Kantorovich and Koopmans talking about the same concepts and same mathematical methods? The priority debate became very heated. An economist involved referred to it as a "brawl."[64] At one point, Kantorovich wrote privately to an American journal editor about an article criticizing his work, "In the thirty years of my scientific activity, I have never encountered a mathematical work written with such lack of restraint as this one."[65]

The contentious nature of the priority debate reflected the changing nature of professional behavior.[66] Soviet and American scientists found themselves forced to treat their counterparts across the Iron Curtain as colleagues in part because their counterparts could now make themselves heard. In his short preface to an article by Kantorovich published in *Management Science*, Abraham Charnes (1958) stated that Kantorovich "is one of the most distinguished of Russian mathematicians," but he did not identify him as an economist. Charnes provided some reasons why readers of *Management Science* might want to read the article. He warned, however, that "an effective method of actually acquiring the solution to a specific problem is *not* solved in this paper. In the category of development of such methods we seem to be, currently, ahead of the Russians" (1). In response, Kantorovich complained directly to Tjalling Koopmans that the method was, in fact, provided in the paper. When Koopmans told the editor of *Management Science* about Kantorovich's complaint, the editor agreed with Kantorovich, "I should have caught this myself, but I read Charnes' statement out of context and therefore allowed it to get into the Journal."[67] The editor read it out of context because earlier it was perfectly acceptable to write negative and competitive comments about Russian scientists. With the possibility of direct responses by Russian and American economists to each other's publications, economists had to think twice about their published comments and act in a collegial manner.

With the new East–West interactions, economists also changed their publishing practices. Economists found it difficult to determine priority because many of their writings were not public. Earlier, scientists on both sides of the Cold War divide had restrictions on their publications. A broad range of scientific topics, including mathematical economics, were considered relevant to national security and thus could not be made public. In addition, the majority of mathematical economists in both the United States and the Soviet Union worked in some way, either directly or through grants, with the military. Many published works were printed for small lists of readers with security clearances. For example, wartime security restrictions prevented Koopmans from publishing his 1943 discussion of linear programming until 1947, and even then this publication only summarized his findings and contained no equations. Due to restrictions, many economists were thus left out of the cutting-edge professional discussions happening within the military and military intelligence. With the new East–West communication, scientists sought to declassify their work and published it in professional journals, so that their work would be recognized more widely.

It was also difficult to determine priority because many economists' writings were untranslated. In the early Cold War and the new field of Sovietology, economists with Russian translation skills were in short supply and great demand. Many scholars relied on translators who had little knowledge of their fields or on experts with large backlogs of translations. Adding to these difficulties, translators were not often credited, which made their reliability unclear. For example, W. H. Marlow, the translator and collector of Kantorovich's work for the Office of Naval Research, had received a copy of an article by Kantorovich and a colleague, which he was told was acquired in Europe by a private citizen who had no information concerning the translator.[68] With the opening conversations among Soviet and American economists, Marlow found out that an American academic economist had made the translation. Marlow was relieved because he did not have to retranslate this article that was translated by a trusted colleague.

Translations remained problematic even apart from these linguistic issues because American economists sought to translate across economic systems. Given the changes in the Cold War context, which allowed for the communication between Kantorovich and Koopmans and the potential formation of a common economics profession, translation of Kantorovich's text from Stalinist Russian to the McCarthy era and post–McCarthy era American context required further historical interpretation and evaluation. Are the concepts used in the Soviet Union the same as those in the United States? How do you separate a translation from an innovation? Furthermore, U.S. knowledge about the Soviet Union was also in flux, as the Soviet system itself changed. The United States was also changing. What would be an accurate translation? A good translation could change both the cultures involved because translation allows for the coming together of previously separated people and for them to change their points of view (Ives 2006). In the Cold War, translation could be dangerous.

Economists also had to recognize, in at least a minimal way, the intellectual property of their supposed Cold War enemies. Earlier, American economists had never asked—nor could they have asked—Kantorovich or other Soviet scholars whether they wanted to have their works published and how they might want them published. However, reflecting the change, Koopmans corresponded at length with Kantorovich about the publication of his article, discussing the translation and editing on numerous occasions. Koopmans also asked his colleague A. W. Tucker how he and his coauthor, Harold Kuhn, felt when their edited book was translated and published in Russian without their knowledge. Tucker responded:

Harold and I have not been especially upset by the fact that the translation was made without our knowledge. This seems to be quite standard. Mr. Bailey, the Director of the Princeton University Press, is surprised [sic] that we were sent copies of the translation so promptly. I explained that this was due to you.[69]

During the earlier period, both sides of the Cold War border published each other's work without any concern for intellectual property rights, but the emerging conversation between American and Russian scientists rapidly changed this practice.[70]

While Sovietologists had earlier worked closely with U.S. intelligence and other governmental agencies, they now found that this work had become a professional liability. When traveling in the East Bloc, they had to present themselves as scholars independent of the American government. Such independence, especially of American intelligence agencies, was required to obtain foreign visas, establish contacts, and visit colleagues. Social scientists in general experienced these difficulties abroad. In 1967, one political scientist wrote:

This anxiety is aroused particularly by social science research financed by United States government departments and military services. By and large, foreigners assume that the Department of Defense or the U.S. Army or the CIA supports research only for purposes that are, at least potentially, hostile to the countries in which the research is carried on. The highly publicized instances involving American University, Michigan State University, and M.I.T. have served to blur the distinction both between the private scholars and the servant of government and between private research funds and public funds . . . Under these circumstances, it is not surprising that scholars, universities, and foundations are suspected of serving the CIA or other government agencies. (Knorr 1967: 466)

Sovietologists, throughout the socialist period and afterward, found Eastern European and Soviet governments extremely suspicious of them and willing to harass them in many ways. As a result, American Sovietologists sought to maintain a boundary against being perceived as spies for either the Soviet Union or the United States.[71]

During this time, the United States had also changed. According to Johnson (1989), starting in 1961, with the Bay of Pigs crisis and continuing with the increasing U.S. involvement in Vietnam, the universities became increasingly critical of the government and foreign policy. The 1960s opened the door to criticism of Sovietology's close relationship to the state. For example, in 1973, one Sovietologist, Alexander Dallin said:

Especially in regard to assumptions implicit in government-sponsored information, there has often resulted a symbiotic relationship which at worst has been parasitic and at best has stimulated a vicious circle in which government-sponsored research helps shape the work of private scholars, which in turn serves to reinforce the conceptions and biases of official agencies. (O'Connell 1990: 4–5)

Sovietologists began to understand that scientific work was possible only if they did not have direct connections with intelligence work. Sovietologists found it necessary to "prove" to the American public, to Soviet colleagues, and to the Soviet government that they were not too committed to the United States, that they were independent scholars. The American academic community became more critical of people who had connections to espionage for the United States, especially after the outrage over Project Camelot and with the growing the anti–Vietnam War movement.[72] In anthropology in particular, these revelations about Projects Camelot and Phoenix led to a discussion about the need to protect informants and anthropologists and to the formation of the first ethical code for the discipline of anthropology (Pels 1999). The unclear boundary between international science and espionage both expanded and made uncertain the professional lives of academics.

East–West interactions remained very difficult. The participants continually had to cope with diplomatic difficulties and professional misunderstandings. For example, the organizer of the IUCTG program, Robert Byrnes, known as rather fanatical and "moralistic," demanded that the U.S. government play no role in the exchanges so that scholars would not be considered as spies. He also demanded that graduate students follow a strict moral code. If there was evidence that the American exchange students living in the Soviet Union were drinking too much or having sexual relationships with Russians, they were immediately sent home. Byrnes and others believed that exchange students who acted in immoral ways could be blackmailed by the Soviet government and used as spies.[73]

Soviet and East European authorities accused several Sovietologists of espionage and, in a few cases, even arrested them. *The New York Times* reported that in 1963 a Professor Joseph T. Shaw of the University of Wisconsin was accused and possibly arrested for seeking to recruit a Russian for the American intelligence service and for taking photographs of "secret objects." In the same year, the Soviet secret police arrested Yale political science professor Frederick Barghoorn in Moscow as a spy and detained him for sixteen days.[74] In 1966, Yale economist and Eastern European expert John Michael Montias was expelled from Hungary for spying. The Hungarian government did not allow him to return to Hungary until 1989. As his Hungarian colleague, János Kornai, remembered, "His Hungarian adventure rather dampened Montias's enthusiasm for 'Sovietology' and he turned to the more safe topic of seventeenth-century Dutch painting" (Kornai 2006: 172–176).

To cope with similar difficulties, economists in the East and West also began to support their counterparts abroad as international allies. These connections provided economists access to data, relevant books and articles, and letters of support for travel and funding. American and Western European economists supported Russian economists' very difficult attempts to take part in the new East–West institutions. For example, organizers found that it was relatively easy to invite Eastern Europeans to international conferences, but it was very difficult to invite their counterparts from the Soviet Union. As Hendrik S. Houthakker, organizer of the World Congress of the Econometrics Society in Rome in 1965, wrote,

As I see it, the main arguments in favor of soliciting Russian participation are that it agrees with the international character of this meeting and may present a unique opportunity of increasing Russian membership of the Society. The arguments against are first, that no other country needs this kind of special treatment; second, that we may only get some party hacks who give propaganda speeches rather than serious contributions; third, that even if some contributions are obtained the speakers may not turn up at the last moment, thus disrupting the program. There is ample precedent for these last two developments . . . Perhaps it is already clear from this summary that I am rather sceptical about a major effort to attract Russian contributors.[75]

The attempts by the Econometrics Society reflect the general problems with inviting Soviet economists.

A year before the 1965 World Congress, the organizers decided to formally invite Soviet economists, which American economist Robert Solow did through the Soviet Academy of Sciences. Tjalling Koopmans was particularly interested in inviting his colleague (and future Nobel Prize cowinner) Leonid Kantorovich, but "the invitation to Kantorovich is awaiting a high-level approach by Solow to the Academy of Sciences in Moscow."[76] Leontief then wrote a separate letter to a high-level economist in the Soviet Union, but received no response.[77] By March 1965, about six months before the conference, the Russians had still not replied: "Solow still has not had any reply from Russia. . . . Tjalling Koopmans is leaving shortly for Poland and Russia and will try to explore the matter further."[78]

Finally, in mid-May, Leontief received word that the Russians had accepted the invitation to the World Congress: "This obviously is the result of the long talk I had four weeks ago in Venice with Academician Mil-lionschechikov, Vice-president of the Soviet Academy of Sciences and of my handwritten memorandum which he took to Moscow."[79] Houthakker wrote to Leontief, "I want to congratulate you on this success in scientific diplomacy."[80]

In spite of these difficulties, these dialogues provoked theoretical and methodological changes. These dialogues, along with Soviet criticisms of Stalinism from the highest levels, brought into doubt older perspectives, such as the totalitarian model, which presented the Soviet Union as an unchanging and all-controlling system. By 1960, as discussed in Chapter 5, Sovietologists in the United States and elsewhere had begun a revolution in their own field, rejecting the totalitarian framework that dominated Sovietology and calling for new approaches. Furthermore, in the new East–West institutions, economists realized that societies around the world experienced similar problems and thus might in the search for solutions converge. Sovietologists also found that they could now travel to the East Bloc and apply more conventional research methods there. By the 1960s, according to Engerman, "As the field of economics came to value technical expertise over nation-specific knowledge, a whole group of area specialists and comparative economists found their place in the profession shrinking" (2009: 127). At the same time, neoclassical economists with their technical expertise found the new socialist models, as discussed in the following chapters, increasingly interesting and relevant to their work.

Conclusions

In the early 1950s, the Soviet, Eastern European, and American governments established new institutions that would allow economists to begin to form a transnational scholarly community. Economists came into contact through academic exchanges, international conferences, and their written work. These transnational discussions among economists and other scholars opened up new opportunities and new difficulties within the shifting international terrain of the Cold War. New institutions and dialogues expanded liminal spaces critical of both Soviet state socialism and American free-market capitalism. With the expansion of the professional community of economists worldwide, many economists began to treat their counterparts across the Iron Curtain as colleagues. They also learned from these interactions, creating innovative approaches and new forms of knowledge, as the next chapters on Yugoslav worker self-management socialism and Hungarian market socialism demonstrate. At the same time, these interactions were not easy. A shared notion of "the economy" and a shared economics profession would slowly emerge from these East–West, as well as from South–North, dialogues among economists. Yugoslavia would be the earliest and most open to this dialogue.

3

Neoclassical Economics and Yugoslav Socialism

AFTER THE SECOND WORLD WAR, the Yugoslav Communist Party led by Marshall Josip Broz Tito took control of the Yugoslav state and began building a Soviet-style socialist system, nationalizing companies and replacing markets with centralized planning.[1] As Ramet has noted, "The Yugoslavs worked hard at being Stalin's 'best comrades'" (2006: 176).[2] As in the rest of the East Bloc, the Communist Party declared neoclassical economics "bourgeois" as opposed to proletarian Marxist political economy, removed existing economics professors from their jobs, and created a new cadre of Marxist-trained economists to replace them. Yugoslavia was a solid member of the East Bloc, clearly following the Soviet path to socialism. In just a few short years, however, the Yugoslavs would reject the Soviet model and embark on a socialist experiment that would find enthusiastic followers around the world.

In 1948, the Soviet leadership dramatically expelled Yugoslavia from the Cominform, the Soviet-dominated organization uniting the Communist Parties of Eastern and Western Europe, which set Yugoslavia on a new path.[3] While Yugoslavs had many grievances with the Soviet Union—including the Soviet Union's infiltration of the Yugoslav Communist Party—the main tension emerged from the fact that Tito sought to be a politically autonomous ally with, rather than a subordinate to, the Soviet Union (Ramet 2006: 176). The expulsion from the Cominform came as a great surprise to Yugoslav leaders, who hoped that the Soviets might soon readmit them. In response to what they soon realized was a permanent expulsion, heightened military aggression from the East Bloc countries, and the resulting trade embargo with the entire East Bloc, Yugoslavia rejected the Soviet system and developed a new kind of socialism. This new form of socialism brought together the decentralization of the state and the economy, worker-based economic democracy, a move away from state ownership of the means of production, and an expanded role for the market. With this new type of socialism, Yugoslavia and Tito himself stepped onto a very receptive international stage.

The new socialist system in Yugoslavia provided economists there with the opportunity to develop a new economics of socialism. This chapter starts with a description of this new kind of socialism and then turns to the work of economists within it. It is true that many Yugoslav economists continued to practice Marxist-Leninist political economy, and others pursued a nontheoretical economics, but, in the new socialist system, groups of Yugoslav economists began to mobilize neoclassical economics—seemingly so Western and capitalist—as a tool to help build a new non-Soviet socialism. Through academic study trips, exchanges of literature, and international conferences, these Yugoslav economists quickly joined the emerging transnational neoclassical dialogue discussed in the previous chapters. Economists in the United States in dialogue with those in Yugoslavia reinterpreted the Yugoslav system and placed it within the core of neoclassical economics. Through the nonaligned movement, the World Bank, and other transnational networks, the Yugoslav model itself became a global model for development.[4] For decades, the Yugoslav economy had some of the highest growth rates in the world. Even when, in 1980, the economy went into crisis and it became apparent that the Yugoslav model had not been fully realized in its place of origin, an abstract version of this model remained central to neoclassical economics and socialist thought.

Yugoslav Socialism

Soon after their expulsion from Cominform, the Yugoslavs found themselves in a dire situation. As enemies of both the Soviet Union and the United States, Yugoslavia had few trading partners and even faced an approaching famine.[5] Both the Cold War superpowers also militarily threatened Yugoslavia. In response, the leaders of the Yugoslav Party-state—Tito, Edvard Kardelj, Milovan Djilas, and the main economic policy maker

Boris Kidrič—began criticizing the Soviet Union and developed a new Yugoslav model (Campbell 1967; Comisso 1979; Hoffman and Neal 1962; Milenkovitch 1971; Obradović and Dunn 1978; Prout 1985).[6] By 1949, Edvard Kardelj rethought the idea of the "transition" from capitalism to communism (Milenkovitch 1971: 65). While Soviet leaders had earlier forced newly socialist countries to follow the Soviet model with its central planning, its state ownership of the means of production, and its strongly hierarchical relations, Kardelj argued that this state socialism was just the first stage of the transition and that Yugoslavia had begun to move to the next stage of socialism through the withering away of the state long predicted by Marxist theory (ibid.).[7] Yugoslav leaders understood both the state socialism of the Soviet Union and the state capitalism of the United States as hopelessly bureaucratic and monopolistic. By encouraging the withering away of the state, Yugoslavia would, in their minds, move closer to communism.[8]

The Yugoslav model aimed to decentralize the state and the economy, create worker-based economic democracy, move away from state ownership of the means of production to its "social" ownership, and expand the role of the market in the economy (Milenkovitch 1971; Rusinow 1977). One long-time observer of Yugoslavia called the system "laissez-faire socialism" (Rusinow 1977: 231).[9]

The Yugoslav leadership sought to decentralize and dismantle the state by devolving state tasks to the republic level and to the enterprise level (Montias 1959: 295). First, the individual republics took over many administrative tasks from the central government, such as the supervision of electric power, mines, agriculture, forestry, light industry, and public works (Ramet 2006: 190). Second, in place of the state intervention in enterprises, workers' councils were supposed to take control of the factories and realize economic democracy within the workplace, which was called worker self-management. Milovan Djilas remembered:

One day—it must have been the spring of 1950—it occurred to me that we Yugoslav Communists were now in a position to start creating Marx's free association of producers. The factories would be left in their [the workers in that factory] hands, with the sole proviso that they should pay a tax . . . [When they presented their plan to Tito, the] most important part of our case was that this would be the beginning of democracy, something that socialism had not yet achieved; further, it could be plainly seen by the world and the international workers' movement as a radical departure from Stalinism. Tito paced up and down, as though completely wrapped in his own thoughts. Suddenly he stopped an exclaimed: "Factories belonging to the workers—something that has never yet been achieved!" (1969: 219–222)[10]

In late 1949 on an experimental basis, and in mid-1950 officially, workers' councils were introduced to manage all enterprises with fifteen or more employees (Ward 1956a).[11] Leaders intended worker self-management to bring about "socialist democracy" and to make the state unnecessary (Kidrič [1950] 1979: 84).[12]

Yugoslav Party-state leaders also encouraged the withering away of the state by transforming state ownership of the means of production into "general people's ownership" (Kidrič ([1950] 1979: 84). They defined capitalism as the private ownership of the means of production and socialism as the social ownership of the means of production (ibid.: 80). The lowest form of social ownership was state ownership, as in the Soviet Union, which would eventually take on "the character of state capitalism of a pure type (without ownership by middle classes, but with an all-powerful parasitic bureaucracy of a capitalist character)" (ibid.: 84). According to Kidrič, the implementation of worker self-management and its control over individual enterprises had transformed state ownership into general people's ownership. Over time, Yugoslavs referred to this kind of ownership as "social ownership," neither individual private ownership nor state ownership.

In addition to decentralization, worker self-management, and social ownership, Party-state leaders considered markets essential to the Yugoslav model. Conventionally, Marxists and Soviet leaders had viewed markets and planning as mutually exclusive economic methods, an "either-or" perspective (Milenkovitch 1971: 7). Yet, during the Soviet Union's New Economic Program introduced in 1921, important Bolshevik leaders supported markets and prices as necessary parts of the transition to socialism and communism. By the late 1920s, the Soviet leader Joseph Stalin ended the NEP and reasserted the dichotomy of markets versus the plan. The Yugoslav leadership took seriously the ideas of early Soviet thinkers, such as Leon Trotsky, who criticized centrally planned war communism and argued that "only through the interaction of three elements: state planning, the market, and Soviet democracy, can the economy be correctly controlled in the transition epoch."[13] Kidrič and others understood the market as a temporary feature of the transition and as a tool for socialism.[14] According to Kidrič, in this transition, centralized planning would be reduced to planning only the proportions of the economy, leaving enterprises to operate based on these proportions and "the law of supply and demand" ([1950] 1979: 89). Thus, as Kardelj envisioned in 1954, enterprises would, "through free competition with other enterprises on the market," become interested in achieving "the best results as regards quality and quantity of goods, lower costs of production and good marketing" (Ward 1958: 569). Thus, the market, another form of decentralization, would replace state intervention in the economy. Already in 1950, the Yugoslav government had converted many fixed prices into market prices (Montias 1959). Over time, new laws made enterprises more autonomous. By the 1960s, the Yugoslavs would abolish central planning, introduce commercial banking to allow for enterprise-driven investment, and open their economy to the world market. As a result, the Yugoslavs created an innovative form of socialism. Hoffman and Neal described the Yugoslav system:

> The Yugoslav economic system is unique and complex. It is socialist: in industry and commerce there is no private ownership except for occasional small service establishments and some retail food stores, yet there is not state ownership . . . The Yugoslav economy is planned; at the same time it is decentralized, and economic enterprises are not administered by the state. The bevy of government ministries and councils for running industries singly or in groups has been abolished. Operating under management of their workers, enterprises are legally independent and function in a competitive and comparatively free market . . . The one general requirement for all of them, as for business under capitalism, is that they operate profitably. (1962: 239)

While, as many scholars have shown, the reality of this system often differed considerably from its plans or its appearance (see, for example, Mencinger 2002; Obradović and Dunn 1978; Zukin 1975), the Yugoslavs did implement the first nationwide experiment in worker self-management and market socialism.

With the apparently permanent expulsion from the Soviet Bloc, Yugoslav leaders sought new international allies and internationalized their socialist experiment. Yugoslav leaders began to work immediately with the relatively new intergovernmental organizations, especially the United Nations, to help them survive in the Cold War world.[15] Most famously, Yugoslavia joined Egypt, India, Indonesia, and other countries to found the nonaligned movement.[16] In the 1950s, many countries found themselves the victims of the Cold War superpowers' whims. These countries sought to avoid aligning with either the United States or the Soviet Union and banded together to escape their dependence on the Cold War superpowers. They also argued for peaceful coexistence among political-economic systems and actively supported anticolonialist movements (Willetts 1978: 18–19). Moving beyond calls for aid, nonaligned countries worked to re-structure world trade and create common financial organizations to benefit the developing world, in which Yugoslavia included itself.[17] More gener-ally, they sought to remove the obstacles in the path to Third World de-velopment and encourage cooperation among the Third World countries.

Tito became a symbol of the nonaligned movement and its potential to create a global alternative to both Soviet socialism and Western capital-ism, as well as an independent foreign policy. "When Tito was in Cairo in 1959, the foreign editor of *Borba* reported that the spectacle of hundreds of thousands of people chanting 'Ti-to, Ti-to' gave him the feeling of be-ing at a mass meeting at home," reported Hoffman and Neal (1962: 473). The first nonaligned conference, in fact, took place in Belgrade in 1961.[18] Within international forums, Yugoslavs stressed the difference between Yugoslav socialism and Soviet socialism (Rubinstein 1970: 41).[19] Yugoslavs saw their own economic system as different and as a potentially helpful model for other developing countries.[20] By 1953, Yugoslavia was sending advisors and consultants around the world. Foreign governments could request these experts to visit their countries or send their own experts and students to Yugoslavia for training. It was reported that between 1954 and the end of 1967:

About 2,500 experts were placed at the disposal of the governments of 32 developing countries; about 2,400 citizens from 75 developing countries completed Yugoslav schools under scholarship grants by this country; some 900 students received spe-cialized training and completed post-graduate courses; and about 2,000 students attended Yugoslav colleges with [sic] they themselves or their government paying for their expenses. (Borgavac 1968: 26)

In addition, Yugoslav enterprises sent several thousand experts abroad (Rubinstein 1970: 214). Around the Third World, one could find fac-tories and mines built with Yugoslav technical and financial assistance, named after Tito or Yugoslavia. The Yugoslav government also provided military assistance to anticolonial movements. For example, the National Committee for the Liberation of Ivory Coast in 1959 asked Yugoslavia for student stipends, stipends for military training, about 200 small arms, scientific help, a design for a movement emblem, and other forms of assis-tance.[21] Yugoslavia sought to play a global role in economic development and anticolonial movements and sought allies for mutual protection from the whims of Cold War superpowers.[22]

Yugoslavia, like many other nonaligned countries, also strategically used the United States and the Soviet Union. Soon after the Soviet expulsion of Yugoslavia from the Warsaw Pact, American government leaders decided to lure Yugoslavia to the U.S. side in the Cold War.[23] In response to Soviet aggression and the possibility of a famine, Yugoslav leaders also had turned for help to the United States and Europe.[24] By 1949, the U.S. government removed the ban on exporting U.S. goods to Yugoslavia and announced its first loan—of $20 million—to Yugoslavia.[25] Between 1949 and 1955, the United States provided $1.2 billion in military and economic aid to Yugoslavia (Campbell 1967: 28). Between 1955 and 1960, U.S. assistance totaled $632.1 million, including surplus agricultural products (under Public Law 480), loans credits, and technical assistance programs (Campbell 1967: 44–46; see also Lampe, Prickett, and Adamović 1990).[26] By 1953, the Soviets also initiated normalized relations with Yugoslavia, which might have freed Yugoslavia from dependence on the United States (Hoffman and Neal 1962: 421–426). Tito began calling Yugoslavia "the bridge between East and West," but Soviet–Yugoslav relations soon broke down again in 1958.[27]

American foreign policy generally encouraged East European countries to remain independent of, and even defy, the Soviet Union. The U.S. government promoted cultural, economic, and military relations with Eastern Europeans as a way to undermine the Soviet Union.[28] Scholarly exchanges of academics were just one way of doing this. The United States did not simply export procapitalist ideas to indoctrinate Yugoslavs according to American interests. Rather, as Berkeley economist Benjamin Ward noted, "In a sense the United States provided the wherewithal for this experiment in socialist economics" (1956a: 340).

Yugoslav Economics

Before the 1948 expulsion of Yugoslavia from the Cominform, Yugoslav economists had practiced Soviet-style economics. Following the Soviet practice, the Yugoslav leadership rejected "bourgeois" neoclassical economics, including mathematical economics, and removed its practitioners from their positions, especially as university professors (Šoškić 1959: 608). To replace them, the Communist Party of Yugoslavia trained new cadres in Marxist-Leninist political economy of socialism and of capitalism, as well as several applied fields. These cadres primarily explored Marxist-Leninist texts to support and develop official government policies (Mencinger 2002). It is likely that some neoclassical economists with mathematical skills worked behind the scenes in Yugoslavia, particularly in high-level planning offices and the military, as they did in the Soviet Union. As throughout the East Bloc, the majority of central planners, however, were trained as engineers and conceived of national planning as an engineering or administrative problem and not as an economic problem.

The official Yugoslav criticism of Soviet state socialism opened many new possibilities to the Yugoslav economics profession. Yugoslavia's form of market socialism suggested to economists that Oskar Lange's work and neoclassical economics more broadly might apply to Yugoslavia. Oskar Lange, a neoclassical economist from Poland who worked for years at the University of Chicago and now worked again in Poland, created the most famous neoclassical model of market socialism. In Lange's model, discussed in Chapter 1, people chose their occupations and consumer items, which had prices or wages determined by competitive markets. There would be no market in production or capital; rather the Central Planning Board would set an initial arbitrary price (or interest rate) and then alter the price (or interest rate) in response to excess supply or demand as, according to Lange, the competitive market corrected itself. Firms would not maximize profit but would follow two rules: Minimize the (average) costs of production, and equate prices with the (marginal) costs of production. This model was socialist because the state owned the means of production, including capital and natural resources, and, in addition to their income, employees would receive a social dividend, part of the income from the capital and natural resources, which would otherwise go to shareholders in capitalism. The Yugoslav experiment added another socialist component, worker self-management, to Lange's competitive model. Lange's model and neoclassical economics more generally appeared to provide tools for "laissez-faire socialism" (Rusinow 1977: 231), in which the state and large monopolistic firms disappeared and worker-controlled, socially owned firms competed on a free market.[29]

Even in 2002, Austrian school economist David L. Prychitko remarked, "Economists tend to consider Yugoslavia the closest practical application of the theoretical model of market socialism devised by Oskar Lange" (37). Many scholars agreed with this view, but they claimed that the Yugoslav leadership was likely unaware of the transnational neoclassical discussion of socialism (Maksimović 1965: 349; Milenkovitch 1971: 101; Rusinow 1977: 62; Ward 1958).[30] According to these accounts, Yugoslav leaders, such as Kardelj, somewhat naïvely had, in the words of Yugoslav economist Aleksander Bajt, "ideas closer to [Austrian School] neoclassical economist Böhm-Bawerk than to Marx" (1988: 185).

Yugoslav leaders may well have read neoclassical economics in the late 1940s. Yet, the similarity between Yugoslav anti-Soviet socialism and neoclassical economics was already overdetermined. As discussed in Chapter 1, neoclassical economics had emerged out of a dialogue about socialism. Neoclassical criticisms of Marxist economic ideas, such as the labor theory of value, and the neoclassical embrace of markets led many Marxist socialists and later Soviet socialists to reject neoclassical economics altogether. With the rejection of the Soviet model, the new Yugoslavia reflected the socialist alternatives available. Soviet political economy textbooks continually referred to bourgeois economics and thus communicated some of its ideas, and some Soviet economists used neoclassical economics for planning behind the scenes. Neoclassical economics had criticized certain aspects of Marxist political economy, offered mathematical methods to manage socialism, and provided market socialist alternatives since the 1920s. Both neoclassical economics and socialism evolved in relation to each other, which helps explain the similarities among neoclassical economics and socialisms critical of the Soviet model.

Communist Party elites, such as Kardelj and Kidrič, allied with neoclassical economists because neoclassical economics worked well with their new vision of Yugoslav socialism. Neoclassical economics fit nicely with anti-statist decentralization, free markets, and worker self-management. These elites provided economists with resources to transform their profession.

Yugoslav economists soon recognized their own colleagues' great and "uncritical" interest in Western bourgeois economics ("Skupština" 1955: 1027; Šoškić 1959: 613; Uvalić 1952: 24). Yet they found neoclassical economics, especially quantitative methods and the theory of prices, to be highly relevant to the creation of Yugoslav socialism (Šoškić 1959). Thus, in the early 1950s, Yugoslav economists, like their Warsaw Pact counterparts, returned to the transnational dialogue among neoclassical economists.

Yugoslav economists learned about neoclassical economics through reading scholarly books, journals, and book reviews and, less often, through scholarly exchanges and international conferences.[31] Their own professional journals published reviews of neoclassical literature. For example, in 1952, the Yugoslav journal *Ekonomist* published a review of French "bourgeois" economist Émile James's *Histoire des théories économiques* (1950), which the Yugoslav reviewer remarked dealt with "questions that concern our country" (Šoškić 1952: 89). Yugoslav professional economics journals also regularly listed foreign works, including neoclassical ones, held in Yugoslav libraries. In 1951, for example, the journal *Ekonomist* reported, among a long list of books, that Yugoslav libraries held E. F. M. Durbin's *Problems of Economic Planning* (1949), which contained articles explaining Friedrich von Hayek's ideas and Durbin's famous application of neoclassical economics to socialism (1936). The Yugoslav libraries also had the work of Lionel Robbins, the neoclassical critic of Durbin and other socialists. Economists sought to acquire new works, especially those from the United States, through book exchanges.[32]

To develop experts for the new system, the Yugoslav government began sending scholars and researchers to Western countries—especially Great Britain, France, Italy, Switzerland, and the United States—for specialized training in 1952. The Yugoslav government also continued to send experts to the Soviet Union and Eastern European countries for training. While not all economists agreed on the supposed benefits of Western training, some number of them, according to one member of this group,

agree[d] with the concept of the need for an intensive studying of contemporary economic thought in the West, especially of that part of it which deals with quantitative methodology as well as with the achievements of objective scientists. They consider that a necessary condition for further development of the young Yugoslav economic thought. (Maksimović 1965: 359; see also Milenkovitch 1971; Šoškić 1959; Sirotković 1959)

These economists thought that they could use certain elements of Western neoclassical economics, especially quantitative methodologies and price theory, for socialist economics. Sending economists abroad became a long-standing Yugoslav policy. Some of the earliest economists who studied abroad were:

Mladen Korač[33]	1953–1954	Cambridge University
Jakov Sirotković	1954–1955	London School of Economics
Ivan Maksimović[34]	1954	Turin
Ivan Maksimović	1955	Paris
Ivan Maksimović	1958	London School of Economics
Branislav Šoškić[35]	1955–1957	Cambridge University
Branko Horvat	1955–1958	Manchester University
Vladimir Stipetić	1957–1958	Oxford University
Vidosav Tričković	unknown	Cambridge University

The Faculty of Economics at the University of Belgrade began to send all its professors on fellowships to foreign institutions abroad, all for at least one month, some for one or two years. They were supposed to take courses, improve their language skills, observe economics education, and visit libraries. The Institute for Economic Sciences in Belgrade sent its researchers and young assistants abroad for "specialization" (*Institut Ekonomskih Nauka* 1969).[36] Rikard Lang, as director of the Institute of Economics in Zagreb, also sent the Institute's most talented students to Western universities, particularly the United States, for graduate study.[37] At the same time, Yugoslavia's lenient border policies allowed students and professors to get in a car and drive to Paris, London, or Vienna when they wished.[38]

Yugoslav economists also traveled to study in the United States.[39] The first Yugoslavs and Americans took part in an exchange in 1955. The Ford Foundation began regular academic exchanges with Yugoslavia in the 1958–1959 academic year (Richmond 1987: 115–116). American and Yugoslav economists already shared a common interest in the neoclassical analysis of market socialism. Yugoslav economists did not arbitrarily choose an American university to visit but rather sought out universities that had specialists in neoclassical economics of socialism with knowledge of Eastern Europe. East European economists often chose to visit Harvard University; Columbia University; MIT; University of California, Berkeley; and Stanford University.[40] Yugoslavs would later add Cornell University, when it became a center for the study of worker self-management in the late 1960s, and Florida State University, which had an entire building devoted to Yugoslav-American studies, as scholarly destinations in the United States.

At international conferences, Yugoslav economists met new colleagues and learned the most recent developments in their field. Journals and newspapers also reported on the proceedings of these conferences. For example, the journal *Ekonomist* reported on the 1956 International Economic Association conference in Rome, which a Yugoslav delegation attended (Stojanović 1956). The author of the report provided an extensive discussion of the presentations by the most famous economists, referring to them only by their last names, suggesting that they might already be known to the readers.[41] Through these conferences, economists could learn about universities to visit and about foreign professors they could invite to speak at Yugoslav universities.[42]

One of the first Yugoslav economists to study abroad was Ivan Maksimović. After finishing his undergraduate degree in 1949, Maksimović immediately began teaching at the University of Belgrade. Maksimović later studied in Turin in 1954, in Paris in 1955, and then at the London School of Economics in 1958.[43] During his visit to Paris, Maksimović met Oskar Lange, the pioneer in neoclassical market socialist models, "discussing with him some theoretical problems of market in a socialist planned economy" (1965: 347). Maksimović returned to Yugoslavia and very quickly published an article on Lange's ideas (in 1955), as well as other works in 1956 and 1958 that explained the entire field of neoclassical economics of socialism. He then brought Lange to lecture in Belgrade in 1957. Maksimović remembered, "When Prof. Lange visited Yugoslavia for the first time at the end of 1957 he was already a well known figure for most Yugoslav experts" (1965: 347).

Maksimović published one of the first Yugoslav books devoted entirely to "bourgeois"—that is, primarily neoclassical—economics. In his dissertation and later book titled *The Theory of Socialism in Bourgeois Economic Science*, Maksimović (1958) demonstrated that he had extensive knowledge of the Western literature on neoclassically based socialism and Western neoclassical economics more broadly. He discussed hundreds of Western economists' works.[44] In opposition to the Austrian School theories that he considered as primarily of historical interest because, at least in his view, the Austrian School lost the socialist calculation debate, Maksimović understood neoclassical economics as a potential normative model for socialism because this "bourgeois" economics was in fact not necessarily about capitalism:

Members of the Austrian and Lausanne schools used the method of deduction of general economic laws from the economic behavior of the detached economic subject, *homo economicus*. Therefore, it was almost natural that they came to the conclusion that in such obtained "laws" there was not anything specifically capitalist. The laws which were formulated in the theory of subjective value and the theory of price and mechanism of exchange ("subjective" and "objective" conditions of equilibrium) had little or no direct connection with the social and institutional framework of the capitalist economy. (ibid.: 17)

According to Maksimović, bourgeois economics provided the tools to determine the optimal production mix and optimal prices to obtain the maximum level of social welfare, which would then provide normative principles for socialist economic policy. While he did voice some reservations about doing this, Maksimović argued for the use of neoclassical economics within extant socialism.[45]

Another one of the first economists to study abroad, Branko Hor-
vat, would become one of the most world-renowned Yugoslav economists.
Around 1955, he and two of his colleagues at the Yugoslav Federal Plan-
ning Bureau went to England for doctoral study.[46] On his return, Horvat
became chief methodologist at the Federal Planning Bureau (Uvalić and
Franičević 2000). He also began writing his *Economic Theory of a Planned
Economy*, published in 1961 in Serbo-Croatian and in 1964 in English.
According to Horvat, the new Yugoslav system required a new theoretical
and analytical apparatus (1961: vii). While continuing to call himself a
Marxist (ibid.: viii), Horvat employed neoclassical economics to build this
new apparatus. He demonstrated an extensive knowledge of the neoclassical economic literature, especially neoclassical discussions of socialism,
as well as current Western economic theories of price, interest, investment, and planning. Horvat stated that Marxist categories like the labor
theory of value applied only to capitalism and had no place in a theory of
socialism:

The whole conceptual apparatus, developed to cope with an essentially different situation, becomes inapplicable. If the socialist economy is to have a theory of value, it
should be a different theory. An attempt to use Marxian categories outside the context of the capitalist political economy would show a complete misunderstanding of
his theory . . . The adequacy of the Marxian theory of value for the capitalist system
is not our concern here and, as we have just seen, it is neither meant for nor applicable
to a socialist economy. (Horvat 1964: 14)

Horvat and his colleagues recognized that Marxism was primarily a critique of capitalism, rather than a blueprint for socialism. Neoclassical economics provided Horvat and others with tools to improve socialism.

The fact that Horvat's book was published in English reflected its
more general significance as a work of neoclassical economics. Horvat's
work had potential relevance inside and outside of Yugoslavia. In his book,
Horvat sought a way of "designing an efficient economic system" that would
maximize production and economic welfare (1961, 1964: 1–2), following
Vilfredo Pareto's definition of the socialist state as the maximizer of social
welfare and the general neoclassical tradition of the social planner. Thus,
he used neoclassical economics as a "normative" tool for building socialism
(1961: 1). Even more importantly, Horvat's experience with Yugoslav socialism allowed him to contribute new ideas to the transnational dialogue
among neoclassical economists. In fact, Yugoslavia provided "almost labo-

ratory conditions" for comparing its system of "'free market' and workers' management" with the Soviet system (Horvat 1964: 118). Continuing the Yugoslav criticism of "etatism" and the Soviet Union, Horvat rejected the Soviet model, which had also fit so well within the neoclassical economic framework. According to Horvat, neither Western nor Soviet economists recognized the importance of institutions and instead took their existing institutions as given (1961: 2). Thus, Horvat criticized the narrow understanding of neoclassical economics, which spoke only about markets or planning, and instead called for a broad understanding of the institutions necessary to realize both central planning and a purely competitive system. Paralleling the new works in economic policy design (Marschak 1959; Tinbergen 1956, 1961), Horvat proposed the optimal choice of institutions themselves. Specifically, Horvat supported workers' councils and the institutions that would allow them to realize their new role as "entrepreneurs" in the sense discussed by Knight and Schumpeter (1961: 150).[47] Horvat and other Yugoslav economists joined the transnational neoclassical discussion and contributed to it new knowledge emerging out of the Yugoslav experiment.

With new possibilities for contributing to the neoclassical discussion, some Yugoslav economists quickly abandoned their former Soviet-style Marxist-Leninist political economy and turned to new areas of economics. Like their Soviet counterparts, small, though increasing, numbers of Yugoslav economists embraced quantitative methods from "bourgeois economics," especially econometrics, input-output modeling, and linear programming. In the new system, planners had to limit their interventions in the free market, merely setting the proportions of the national economy (Kidrič [1950] 1979). Instead of using administrative means, the plan mobilized economic mechanisms to motivate enterprises and individuals to maximize production. The planner thus had to move beyond an engineering perspective to an economic view of the economy as a maximization and minimization problem, such as maximizing production and minimizing costs. With the decentralization of most planning to the enterprise level, the architects of reforms also recognized the need for new training of enterprise managers and members of workers' councils. The economics of enterprise became a growth area. There were new textbooks (Babić 1961; Radičević [1955] 1957) and new courses, which explored profits, entrepreneurship, management, marketing, and foreign markets. As part of the nonaligned movement, Yugoslav economists also turned immediately to the economics of development (Lang 1955). The new Yugoslav system expanded the practice of economics.

Yugoslav policy makers and economists had long complained about the dearth of books on the Yugoslav economic system (Horvat 1968: 14–15; Uvalić 1952: 21). Yugoslav economists began to study their own economic system, coming to "believe" in self-management and to focus on only this system (Gligorov 1998: 333–334). This intense focus on their own country unintentionally brought them into the field of comparative economic systems. This field of economics had established classification systems into which each country would fall—such as developed capitalist, socialist central planning, and undeveloped—describing each economic system and evaluating the advantages and disadvantages of each system. Building on Pareto's welfare economics and its further refinement by Abram Bergson and others, economists sought to design neoclassical measures by which to determine which system was better. Rather than accepting these categories passively, the Yugoslavs asserted that they had developed their own economic classification type, the Yugoslav model (Račić 1955). Yugoslav economists, with the support of the leadership, fleshed out this Yugoslav model as a separate economic system and evaluated the economic, political, and social benefits that might emerge from this system, which fit well into comparative economics worldwide at that time.

Yugoslav neoclassical economists sought an independent center for economic research, where they could control their professional environment and conduct basic research on the Yugoslav system. When Horvat and his colleagues returned from abroad, they immediately proposed a new economics research institute in Belgrade. However, they came up against high-level bureaucratic resistance, which delayed the formation of an independent institute for several years (*Institut* 1969: 1–9). In 1958, they formed a research and methodology section within the planning office, which later became the Institute for Economic Sciences (IEN). Following the expanded areas of economists' practice, the IEN's main areas of work were the Yugoslav system, quantitative planning, and economic development. Horvat organized a research seminar, which invited economists from around the world (*Institut Ekonomskih Nauka* 1969: 87). To develop cadres for the IEN, they chose "the best students" in the country to be research assistants, the best of which would be sent abroad for specialized graduate training. By 1969, of the thirty scientific workers and assistants at IEN, twenty-two had studied abroad. The IEN also developed a graduate program to train students, a computer center, and a library. The IEN became a center for the new economic methods of the new Yugoslav system.

Yugoslav economists also worked to reform economics education for the new system. Economists complained that their science was backwards and did not meet the needs of the new Yugoslav economy (Horvat 1968; Šoškić 1959; Uvalić 1952). They criticized the "mediocre" faculty, the shortage of teachers, the lack of material incentives to lure the best students to university teaching, and the fact that faculty had to teach themselves (Černe [1960] 1966; Karli 1955; Šoškić 1959; Uvalić 1952). Faculty had to use "dogmatic" political economy textbooks or lacked textbooks and other relevant works altogether (Uvalić 1954: 271). These economists also argued that Marxism emerged from worker class engagement with capitalism and thus had other, Western concerns. In their view, the new Yugoslav economic system required a new kind of economics education. By the 1951–1952 academic year, the universities already made some changes in economics education. At the University of Zagreb, courses on econometrics, operations research, and mathematical statistics, as well as on markets, were introduced. By the third year, students had to choose either macroeconomic studies or microeconomic studies (*Ekonomski Fakultet Zagreb* 2005).[48]

By the 1960s, Yugoslav universities had succeeded in making neoclassical microeconomics a standard part of their economics curriculum (Mencinger 2002). American economist and future Nobel Laureate in economics Paul Samuelson's famous *Economics* textbook was also translated and used by the economics faculty of the University of Ljubljana (ibid.). Neoclassically trained economists soon published their own textbooks. For example, France Černe's 1966 *Markets and Prices* was basically a standard Western introductory economics textbook (Milenkovitch 1971: 231).[49] Černe started his textbook by noting, "Here the analysis of market and price as an economic discipline is beginning to more intensively develop" (1966: 5). As with American introductory textbooks, *Markets and Prices* contained graphs and explanations of supply and demand curves, elasticity, indifference curves, and opportunity costs. The text referred to major works by Paul Samuelson, Alvin Hicks, Alfred Marshall, and H. Schultz, as well as Karl Marx.

Černe continued the specific perspective of Yugoslav economics, which criticized state power and sought a kind of laissez-faire socialism. Černe concluded his textbook with a discussion of the Western neoclassical literature on socialism (1966: 235–237). He noted that Western neoclassical economists considered capitalism with its monopolistic structure to be a barrier to market competition and thus unable to supply maximum social welfare. But he also criticized these same economists for assuming that a socialist state could instead realize this full competition. According to Černe, these economists' model of socialism, like capitalism, could only produce incomplete or monopoly competition. Černe then posed an alternative: "Either the theoretical apparatus of these economists is illegitimate for socialism or perhaps we cannot have a socialist economic system, which would be established on such a theoretical basis" (ibid.: 236). Instead of the socialist state, Černe called for prices to be freely formed on a market, like in the "capitalist system of complete competition" and economists' theories of complete competition (ibid.: 236–237), within the conditions of social ownership and workers' management (ibid.: 5).[50] Černe followed the work of Horvat and other Yugoslav economists in arguing for the superiority of independent enterprises interacting on a fully competitive market within a socialist system.

It is clear that not all economists practiced or even knew about neoclassical economics. Some economists continued to practice Marxist political economy in the Soviet manner. Many economists found it difficult to read the major international economics journals and focused primarily on examining their own system empirically, without the methods of neoclassical economics. Some economists and political leaders continued to attack neoclassical economists for their ideas and practices (Horvat 1968). In spite of this, groups of economists in Yugoslavia quickly identified the socialist potential in neoclassical economics. They began to read neoclassical texts, studied abroad and met with their counterparts, and contributed to a transnational neoclassical discussion through their rejection of state socialism and their expansion of Oskar Lange's market socialist model to include not only fully competitive markets but also worker self-management.

In the early 1960s, liberal Yugoslav leaders gained control of the Party-state and began to implement market reforms. These reforms sidelined central planners, pushing them into the opposition (Gligorov 1998: 338).[51] The government implemented further decentralization and market-oriented reforms, while also expanding worker self-management. Between 1963 and 1965, the Yugoslav government began to realize, according to many observers, "market socialism" (Mencinger 2004; Uvalić 1992: 6). Lampe, Prickett, and Adamović noted, "With the economic reform measures enacted in the mid-1960s, they sought to create an unprecedented model of a market socialist economy in which independent enterprises, managed by their workers, would act in response to the forces of the marketplace" (1990: 82). The pure competitive model assumed that enterprises would work autonomously from the state, responding to prices as information. Before 1954, enterprises had had little control over their resources (Dubey 1975: 33). Yugoslav economists supported the autonomy of enterprises, in which workers' councils acted as entrepreneurs. By 1964, the Yugoslav government had abolished state investment funds and increased the role of banks in the allocation of finance (ibid.: 34). Local governments were allowed to create their own banks, which became important sources of capital for enterprises (ibid.: 35). In a related way, central planning itself was abolished, thus further realizing one version of the neoclassical model. The Yugoslav state also reduced the number of prices it fixed, following the neoclassical belief that, in the pure competitive model, markets determine prices and thus equilibrium prices reflect optimal production levels. Neoclassical economists supported a series of reforms informed by their professional training.

Neoclassically trained economists gained influence by working directly on these reforms or providing academic writings that helped shape them.[52] Yugoslav economists helped to explain how this model might best function both to policy makers and to the public. Yugoslav economists used neoclassical economics as a normative theory and promoted reforms to make Yugoslavia function more like the neoclassical model of the competitive firm, influencing policy makers to change the world to fit their theory, as economists often do.[53] As discussed in the following pages, scholars recognized that the reforms made the Yugoslav economy more closely resemble the neoclassical market socialist model, moving in the direction of laissez-faire socialism with worker self-managed firms competing on a market. In the minds of neoclassical economists, Yugoslavia, Lange's market socialist model, and neoclassical economics could not be separated. They were in fact interchangeable elements. The Yugoslav model would soon become a global model.

The Yugoslav Model

While Yugoslavs immediately perceived the relevance of neoclassical economics to their new socialist system and sent scholars and students abroad for specialized training, neoclassical economists outside Yugoslavia took longer to consider the Yugoslav economy relevant to their own professional work. Abram Bergson, as discussed in Chapter 1, had reinterpreted the Soviet Union as central to mainstream neoclassical economics, but this had not been done yet for the Yugoslav economy. Economists around the globe would soon, however, perceive the Yugoslav economy as a core element of mainstream neoclassical economics.

Economists outside Yugoslavia began to consider the Yugoslav economy as relevant to mainstream neoclassical economics, when they learned to view this economy through their own neoclassical framework. In the mid-1950s, an American graduate student in economics at University of California, Berkeley, Benjamin Ward, traveled to Yugoslavia on a Ford Foundation grant and did just this. At Berkeley, Ward studied economics with one of the experts of the Soviet model, Gregory Grossman, and also studied the Russian language. After becoming critical of Soviet socialism, Ward sought what he later called a leftist communitarian solution.[54] He happened to read about Yugoslav worker self-management in a Quaker bulletin on Eastern Europe. He could learn Serbo-Croatian quickly because he already knew Russian, so he chose to go to Yugoslavia. As a result of his pioneering work on the Yugoslav economy, Ward was appointed an assistant professor at Berkeley.

Ward soon noted that Yugoslavia seemed to have realized the neoclassical economic model of market socialism, as envisioned by Italian economist Enrico Barone and Polish economist Oskar Lange, discussed in Chapter 1. In his dissertation, Ward (1956a) evaluated four types of firms—Soviet, Yugoslav, reformed Yugoslav, and capitalist—because, in neoclassical economics, knowledge about the firm provided knowledge about the functioning of the whole economic system, and vice versa. Ward rejected the capitalist firm and economy because the Soviet firm and economy outproduced them, but he also rejected both the Soviet-style economy and firm because "only in Yugoslavia has the Soviet type of enterprise organization been tried, found wanting and abandoned" (ibid.: 47). Ward extensively described the Yugoslav economy, from its Soviet-style beginnings in the late 1940s, to the new Yugoslav worker self-management model starting in 1950, to what he called the "reformed Yugoslav" model created by a 1954 law. The original Yugoslav model created a system and a firm that still had Marxist elements. The new reformed Yugoslav model, however, evoked the greatest excitement from Ward because it incorporated "non-Marxian economic categories such as interest, economic rent and the like, while at the same time preserving the features of socialism as suggested in the market socialist models such as those of Barone, Lange and others" (ibid.: 307). Ward even titled his dissertation "From Marx to Barone" because he understood Yugoslavia as moving from a Marxist-based socialist economic system (from Marx) to a neoclassically based socialist system (to Barone). To Ward, the reformed Yugoslav model was important to neoclassical economics, but he did not perceive the importance of his own work to Yugoslavs. After his comparison of the four types of firms, Ward noted that the comparison was "more relevant for the discussion of the market socialism controversy than it is to Yugoslavia itself" (ibid.: 325).

Most significantly, Ward (1956a) clearly distinguished Keynesianism or state-managed capitalism from market socialism. Market socialism as understood by neoclassical economists was *not* Keynesianism. According to Ward, the 1954 reforms would have implemented a neoclassical form of socialism, the reformed Yugoslav model, but the political leadership almost immediately used "administrative measures" to directly intervene in the economy and counteract the destablizing effects of the reform. As a result, the Yugoslav government did not realize the reformed Yugoslav model and, instead, maintained what Ward considered to be an inferior "market syndicalist" model. To Ward, this unfortunate market syndicalist model was a form of Keynesianism. Just before this state intervention, a Yugoslav policy journal published a review of the famous Keynesian Alvin H. Hansen's *Monetary Theory and Fiscal Policy.* According to Ward:

The reviewer's summary position was that Keynesians such as Hansen are attempting to save capitalism by means of intervention by the state . . . The analogy with the actions taken by the Yugoslav leaders in an attempt to salvage their market syndicalist economy is suggestive. One is tempted by analogy to refer to the period since early 1954 in Yugoslavia as the period of Keynesian socialism. (1956a: 266)

To Ward, the market syndicalist model was a form of Keynesianism. Thus, in the mind of a neoclassical economist, the mixed Keynesianism economy *differed fundamentally* from the neoclassical market socialism that the Yugoslavs had failed to create in 1954. Neoclassical market socialism was not a mixed Keynesian economy to neoclassical economists around the world but rather was a fully competitive market with socialist institutions.

Two years later, in 1958, Ward published an article, "The Firm in Illyria," in the *American Economic Review.* Like many other neoclassical economists studying the Soviet Union, such as Abram Bergson and others,

Ward simultaneously wrote articles both about the concrete Yugoslav system and about mainstream economic concerns, such as "What Is Welfare Economics?" (Ward 1956b). Following the neoclassical tradition, he equated the competitive market model and the market socialist model. Ward compared "the competitive capitalist (or market socialist) model" with the "Illyrian model," Illyria being the historical name of the Balkan region. Ward based the Illyrian model on the unrealized reformed Yugoslav model: "Illyria is in fact an alternative to the existing system in Yugoslavia as well as to those in Western and the rest of Eastern Europe" (1958: 567).[55] In this Illyrian model, the means of production were nationalized, workers' councils managed firms by setting price and output policies "in their own material interest," worker-managers worked to maximize their individual incomes, all enterprise employees shared profits equally, and each firm "operate[d] in a purely competitive market" without state intervention (1958: 566–571). In some sense, for Ward, the neoclassical Illyrian model suggested what Yugoslav socialism might become.

Notwithstanding his own sympathies for the Illyrian model, Ward found a fundamental flaw in it, which set off a long-standing controversy. From his theoretical analysis, Ward found that the Illyrian firm could do as well as or better than capitalist firms (1958: 577). However, he assumed that this firm's worker-managers would maximize their own incomes. As a result, the Illyrian firm had perverse, paradoxical, negative incentives: an increase in demand and prices, for some commodities, would not lead income-maximizing workers to increase the number of employees and thus to increase output. Instead, Ward argued, in response to increases in demand and price, workers would rather maximize their own individual incomes than hire new employees and increase production. Therefore, the Illyrian firm had a negatively sloped supply curve and tended to disequilibrium between supply and demand, thus suggesting its inferiority as both a firm and a system. Over time, economists, including those from Yugoslavia, would criticize Ward's negatively sloped supply curve and his suggestion that worker self-management was inferior to the competitive capitalist model.

Russian-born MIT economics professor Evsey Domar in 1966 recognized the innovation of Ward's *American Economic Review* article but noted that only a few economists had read it, possibly because the article seemed to pertain only to Yugoslavia (Domar 1966: 735). The 1960s brought widespread interest in alternative economic institutions, such as cooperatives and socialist institutions more generally. As a result, Ward's work became popular once again. Domar (1966) himself followed Ward, applying neoclassical economics this time to the case of Soviet cooperatives.[56] As a result, Soviet cooperatives became interchangeable with other forms of socialism within the neoclassical model.

Even more importantly, Cornell University economics professor and Czech émigré Jaroslav Vanek made the Yugoslav case central to mainstream neoclassical economics. Vanek made his name through his neoclassical trade models. His brother Jan, who worked in the International Labor Office, introduced him to Yugoslav worker self-management. According to one, possibly apocryphal, account, Paul Samuelson declared that worker self-management socialism was not part of economics because it did not have a neoclassical context, which led Vanek to create his neoclassical model of the Yugoslav system. In an *American Economic Review* article, Vanek built on the "perfect, competitive and smooth neoclassical world" assumed in Ward and Domar's "pure model" of the Illyrian firm and the Soviet cooperative and evaluated the efficiency of the entire "labor-managed economy of the Yugoslav type," the "type of economy that represents, by and large, the true aspirations of reformers in eastern Europe" (1969: 1006). To Vanek, many economists had incorrectly taken Ward's negatively sloped supply curve as "proof of the absurdity of labor management" (ibid.).

According to Vanek, Abram Bergson had already proven that the Soviet firm was less efficient than the market capitalist model (1969: 1014). In contrast, according to Vanek, the labor-managed economy, with groups able to start new firms and close failing firms (free entry and free exit), produced optimal results and had market structures that were more competitive than those of capitalism.[57] Vanek found the labor-managed economy to be superior to both the Soviet and capitalist models:

Basing myself on ten years of intensive study more than on the present exposition, I cannot forego a set of strongly favorable conclusions; I cannot avoid them, even though I realize that I am contradicting the majority of our profession who have thought about the problem, and even I may risk earning the displeasure of many . . . In brief, the labor-managed system appears to me to be superior by far, judged on strictly economic criteria, to any other economic system in existence. (ibid.: 1013–1014)

In fact, for Vanek, the labor-managed economy provided an ideal toward which both state capitalism and state socialism could converge (ibid.: 1014).

As a result of these models, neoclassical economists found a variety of socialisms to be interesting and relevant to their work. Neoclassical economists could move easily between different types of abstract socialist models and existing socialist forms, as well as moving freely from the various socialisms of firms and economic systems. In 1984, Milenkovitch criticized the situation:

In this state of affairs, from the outside, we can not distinguish between the capitalist, the Langean socialist, or the worker managed enterprise. What appears in the short run as sharp difference between firms' behaviors becomes in general equilibrium a merging of identities. In general equilibrium in competition, all three firms and the economies founded on them are equally efficient. (83)

Yet, this interchangeability of firms and economies increased economists' interest in Yugoslavia and in these new abstract socialist models. These works inspired neoclassical economists at all levels:

A massive body of literature from Ward's seminal model of the "Illyria" firm (1958) and its generalization by Vanek (1970) to date, probably larger than for any other single economic issue, has accumulated on the economic implications of the presumed maximand of self-managed enterprises. (Nuti 1996: 189)

Much of this literature sought to evaluate Ward's assumptions and the negatively sloped supply curve. Yet, neoclassical economists saw many advantages of the Illyrian model. Paul Samuelson (1973) had a short explanation of the Yugoslav model into his famous *Economics* textbook, writing that

the system has been viable, and growth under it has surpassed that of the earlier Stalinist period. Even if the cynicism expressed by insiders concerning the amount of power the workers themselves exercise is justified, this system of syndicalist structure presumably offers some countervailing influence to the power of the bureaucrats. (1973: 875–876)

Neoclassical economists, including the future Nobel Laureate James E. Meade (1972, 1974), turned to modeling the Yugoslav economy and its related forms.

Branko Horvat (1967) made one of the earliest Yugoslav responses to Ward's (and Domar's) work. Following the conventions of neoclassical modeling, Horvat created a model of the behavior of the "Yugoslav firm" and compared it with the behavior of the "capitalist firm." He assumed that both had a freely competitive market with prices formed outside the control of the individual firms, but the capitalist firm maximized profits while the Yugoslav firm maximized income per worker. Horvat argued that Ward based his models and his negatively sloped supply curve, which suggested the inferiority of worker self-management, on the early 1950s Yugoslav economy, when, in fact, the Yugoslav economy had since changed. In fact, economic reforms had made the Yugoslav firm more similar to the pure capitalist firm.[58] Following the views of other neoclassical economists such as Oskar Lange (1936, 1937), Horvat argued that capitalist firms in reality did not act like the model of a purely competitive firm. In the Yugoslav firm, the worker collective took on the role of entrepreneur and, along with other institutions, provided a better environment for competitive markets than capitalism did. To avoid unrealistic assumptions in neoclassical models, Horvat called for more empirical studies of the existing Yugoslav system.[59] Such studies, according to Horvat, would prove that the Yugoslav economy provided the right institutional system for the freely competitive market to function, meaning that the Yugoslav economy optimally reaped the benefits of the competitive market system and that neoclassical economics better describes the Yugoslav economy than the existing capitalist economy.[60] In sum, Horvat established the formal similarity of the capitalist firm and the Yugoslav firm, demonstrating in neoclassical theory that the Yugoslav firm acted rationally and potentially outperformed its capitalist counterpart, and called for empirical research to prove this.

The Yugoslav response to the Ward-Domar-Vanek neoclassical model became part of a transnational discussion among neoclassical economists. Yugoslav economists continued to rethink what the Yugoslav firm maximized—was it income per worker or profits or something else?—and other assumptions of the neoclassical model that seemed to support Ward's finding of the negatively sloped supply curve. They also answered Horvat's call to conduct empirical research to support alternative assumptions (Dubravčić 1970; Horvat 1979; Prašnikar et al. 1994; Šuvaković 1977).[61] The Yugoslav, Illyrian, labor-managed, or participatory model became a core part of neoclassical economics, alongside the pure competitive market, centrally planned socialism, and the empirical example of the Soviet economy. At the same time, the neoclassical economics used to describe the Yugoslav model became, in fact, a resource for remaking the Yugoslav economy.

Yugoslavia as a Global Model

By the 1970s, Yugoslavia had become a global development model for organizations as different as the nonaligned movement and the World Bank. Tito's and Yugoslavia's leadership in the nonaligned movement gave much legitimacy to worker self-management socialism as an alternative. Economists from the former Yugoslavia whom I interviewed adamantly rejected the idea that they had actively advocated worker self-management socialism abroad. Rather, according to these economists, Yugoslav political leaders promoted worker self-management abroad. In contrast, these economists found their counterparts around the world already interested in the Yugoslav case.

The abstract Illyrian and concrete Yugoslav models traveled through networks of intergovernmental institutions, professional associations and conferences, particular universities, and publications, especially professional journals. The Yugoslav government already participated in numerous intergovernmental organizations, such as the United Nations, the International Monetary Fund (IMF), the General Agreement on Trade and Tariffs (GATT), and the many U.N. agencies. Scholars have shown the influence of international financial institutions, such as the World Bank and the IMF, on policy making in many countries (Babb 2001; Broad 1988; Henisz, Zelner, and Guillén 2005; Margold 1967; Woodward 2005). Economists with mainstream neoclassical training have long dominated these institutions. As with all members of such organizations, the Yugoslav government sent representatives, as well as economic and other experts, to join the regular staff.[62] Yugoslav economists had the neoclassical training to work in these institutions. They also had experience in a variety of socialisms that relate directly to neoclassical economics.

Yugoslavia was one of the founding members of the World Bank. As a member, Yugoslavia's socialist government for decades paid dues to, received loans from, and exercised voting power in the World Bank.[63] The government also sent its citizens to work as World Bank governors, alternative executive directors, and regular staff members in the World Bank headquarters in Washington, DC.[64] Most Yugoslav economists had a strong interest in, and commitment to, worker self-management socialism, as well as the neoclassical credentials they needed to be hired in the World Bank. The World Bank also worked from the comparative economics perspective and found Yugoslavia to be a unique economic type, relevant to its work.[65] Yugoslav economists also had special expertise in market transitions and enterprise reorganization from their work at home. They could thus quickly move up the ranks in the World Bank.

For example, Dragoslav Avramović joined the World Bank staff in 1953 and became the chief economist for Latin America and the Caribbean, as well as the director of the development economics department. In 1958, he received his PhD from the University of Belgrade's Faculty of Economics within the emerging system of worker self-management in Yugoslavia. By the 1970s, he began to work for the nonaligned movement, which led to his retirement from the World Bank and his work at the Brandt Commission. After 1989, Avramović returned to Yugoslavia, implemented a stabilization program for the Milošević government, became governor of the Yugoslav Central Bank, was removed from the government, and became a leading political opponent to Milošević (Lewis 2001). Other neoclassically trained Yugoslav economists also later worked at the World Bank.

Not only was the Yugoslav model relevant to academic neoclassical economics, Yugoslavia was also seen as relevant to neoclassically based development practice. After the 1948 break with the Cominform, Yugoslav leaders quickly identified Yugoslavia as a developing country, connecting with other developing countries (Rubinstein 1970: 82). In its nineteenth-century form, development economics focused on the transition from agrarian society to industrial society, while neoclassical economics studied fully industrialized economies in or near equilibrium (Pieterse 2001: 39). As discussed in the first chapter, Soviet economists had worked to reinterpret neoclassical economics for their rapidly changing society. Soviet and other Eastern European economists gave priority to the issues of the transitions from capitalism to socialism and then to communism. Development economists understood that Yugoslavia had begun a "transition." From today's point of view, we might assume that this transition would be a transition to market capitalism. However, this transition, discussed further in the next chapters, was to full market socialism, similar to Ward's reformed Yugoslav model informed by neoclassical assumptions. Because Yugoslavia had already experienced market transition, Yugoslav economists were uniquely qualified to advise other countries making such transitions.

Officially, the World Bank deemed the Yugoslav system a success. In 1972, a World Bank mission visited Yugoslavia; it published its report in 1975 (Dubey 1975). When considering its rapid growth combined with institutional changes, as well as the democratization of the system, the report declared, "The Yugoslav economic system has to be judged a success" (ibid.: 52; see also ibid.: 3, 20). A reviewer of this report concluded that the "theoretical and practical interest in Yugoslavia has shown few signs of decline. . . . the period may well be one of intensified interest in such alternative development futures as that provided by the Yugoslav experience" (Dunn 1978: 633). The reviewer found:

> Few informed observers of workers' management in Yugoslavia would disagree with this general assessment of self-managed enterprises. Still fewer would take issue with the report's observations (p. 48) that economic problems thought to be inherent to the operations of the workers' managed firm—including inadequate levels of reinvestment, excessive personal income payments, a bias toward capital-intensive techniques of production, and allocative inefficiency resulting from capital immobility—are either nonexistent or capable of resolution through appropriate compensatory legislation and policy instruments. (Dunn 1978: 631–632)

The World Bank officials considered the Yugoslav model successful.

The Yugoslav government also worked to create new development institutions. Among other institutions, in 1974, the Yugoslav government created the International Center for Public Enterprises in Developing Countries (ICPE) in Ljubljana, which many countries soon joined.[66] At nonaligned movement meetings, the ICPE was presented as the only institution of the nonaligned movement.[67] According to its Yugoslav founders, the U.N. secretary general was interested in having such a center in Yugoslavia because "such an institution would represent the most natural center for studying the experiences of workers' self-management in Yugoslav enterprises."[68] The ICPE offered services in consulting, training, research, and information and documentation.[69] At its first seminar in 1974, the participants decided that

1. Planning should be treated as imperative for the future development of developing countries,

2. Firms in the public or social sector are considered the motor force of economic development of developing countries, and

3. Self-managing participation of workers in the management of firms in social or public property becomes a necessary and normal practice in the process of strengthening the economies of nonaligned developing countries.[70]

Within the ICPE, Yugoslav economists, such as Janez Prašnikar and Aleš Vahčič, began advising countries based on these assumptions and on Yugoslav experiences. In the context of the nonaligned movement, the ICPE developed and exported the worker self-management socialist model, which had already taken shape within a transnational discussion among neoclassical economists. The ICPE supported management training to improve state-owned firms, global financial cooperation among developing nations, industrial restructuring, the breaking down of large monopolistic enterprises, the formation of small and medium-sized firms, and entrepreneurship.

While most Yugoslav economists claimed that they did not promote worker self-management abroad, two individuals—Branko Horvat and Jaroslav Vanek—did much to spread the Yugoslav model beyond the borders of Yugoslavia. The reviewer of the World Bank report previously mentioned further noticed that the report reflected the conclusions and recommendations made by Horvat, other Yugoslav economists, and Vanek (Dunn 1978: 630–632). Horvat advised governments around the world, published abroad, and brought many economists to Yugoslavia to study the worker self-management system (Uvalić and Franičević 2000). Through a series of institutions and major international conferences, the Yugoslav leadership and economists presented the Yugoslav model to the rest of the world.[71] The large-scale interest in the conferences led to the formation of the International Association for the Economics of Self-Management (IAESM) and the transformation of Horvat's journal *Economic Analysis*, into an international journal, *Economic Analysis and Workers' Management*, published primarily in English.[72] Horvat worked to spread the worker self-management model.

Jaroslav Vanek also did much to promote the Yugoslav model. He published many articles and books on his abstract labor-management models and his understanding of the real Yugoslavia. In 1970 at Cornell University, Vanek created an interdisciplinary social science research and teaching program called the Program on Participation and Labor-Managed Systems (PPLMS), complementing the economics department's graduate specialization in the economics of participation and labor-managed systems. The PPLMS brought students from around the world to study the Yugoslav and other cooperative models, as well as supporting research, organizing conferences and workshops, and maintaining an international system of cooperative documentation and documentation exchange. Tito and other

Yugoslav political leaders promoted worker self-management socialism abroad, especially through the nonaligned movement. Individuals like Vanek and Horvat, as well as institutions like the World Bank and the ICPE, helped to work out the details of this global development model that would take on a life of its own.

Conclusions

Yugoslavia created an innovative experiment in socialism based on worker self-management, decentralization, the market, and the social ownership of the means of production. In response to the difficulties, if not the impossibility, of being a small country independent from Soviet state socialism and Western capitalism, Yugoslavia turned to international allies and organizations. Yugoslav economists in dialogue with other mainstream neoclassical economists around the world developed the Yugoslav model. While neoclassical economics was supposed to be a tool for describing the Yugoslav economy, it also served as a blueprint for introducing and reforming socialism in Yugoslavia and other countries. Through their influence on policy makers, Yugoslav economists, in a sense, changed the world to fit their theory. Through the nonaligned movement and transnational neoclassical economics, the Yugoslav experiment became a global socialist model. However, as is discussed in Chapter 6, this model soon came under attack in Yugoslavia itself.

4

Goulash Communism and Neoclassical Economics in Hungary

AFTER THE SECOND WORLD WAR, the Hungarian Communist Party, like its Yugoslav counterpart, came to monopolize political life, which allowed Party leaders to attempt to replicate the Soviet state socialist model with its central planning, state ownership of the means of production, and hierarchical enterprises.[1] The Party leaders also imposed the Soviet model on the profession of economics. In the Soviet model, economists primarily provided theoretical and ideological support from the works of Marx, Engels, Lenin, and Stalin for political leaders' economic policies. The Party declared that it did not support empirical research and declared neoclassical economics "bourgeois" because it was perceived as providing ideological support for capitalism. The death of the Soviet leader Joseph Stalin in 1953 allowed countries inside the East Bloc to experiment with alternative socialisms, as Yugoslavia already had after its expulsion from the East Bloc. Within this new environment, the Hungarian Party-state implemented a novel form of market socialism, designed by economists, that gained international recognition as "goulash communism."

In Hungary after 1953, groups of economists—known as "reform economists" because of their support of market reforms—gained professional and political resources from their political alliances with Party factions. Scholars have generally understood reform economics as an *ad hoc* economics based on "learning by doing" (Kovács 1990: 224) and "pragmatism," as opposed to ideological or theoretical concerns, isolated from the prewar domestic neoclassical and nonneoclassical traditions (Szamuely and Csaba 1998: 158, 182). These political alliances, however, allowed them to develop a new economics profession and rejoin, unexpectedly, the transnational discussion among neoclassical economists in the 1950s. Reform economists came to use neoclassical economics as an analytical tool and a normative model for market socialism.

Hungary's New Economic Mechanism (NEM) reforms of 1968 realized an innovative form of market socialism. In the eyes of neoclassical economists, market socialism was not a mix of systems, a little bit of socialism mixed with a little bit of capitalism. In a different way than in Yugoslavia, Hungarian reform economists also further developed neoclassical market socialism by calling for socialist institutions competing on a competitive market. Like other neoclassical economists, these reform economists differed most fundamentally not over market versus plan but over whether they advocated hierarchical institutions or decentralizing, democratic institutions as necessary for this competitive market and central planning. At the same time, Hungarian Party-state elites avoided this discussion of institutions and promoted an apparently narrow form of neoclassical economics, which, in fact, maintained existing hierarchical institutions. The Hungarian market socialist experiment of the NEM evoked great excitement around the world, especially among economists, as Hungary became a globally recognized innovator in market socialism. Soon, Hungarian economists would be disappointed by the limits of the NEM, which would lead them further to develop models of market socialism.

Hungarian Reform Economics: New Institutions

However, this turn toward market socialism and neoclassical economics did not happen right away. Immediately after the Second World War, the Hungarian Communist Party led by Mátyás Rákosi worked to implement the Soviet state socialist model.[2] A Soviet-styled planned economy, in the eyes of the Party-state leadership, required new experts and new knowledge. According to Ernő Gerő, the Party's second-in-command and top economic policy maker, the planned economy required economists who were scientifically trained, recognized practical problems, and arose "from the people" (1948: 652). Only socialist economists could help the planned economy because bourgeois economists were "bankrupt" and had protected and praised capitalism (ibid.: 655; Rudas 1948: 658). To create a new generation of socialist economists, Party leaders closed down already existing professional institutions and established new Marxist-Leninist ones that fit within the Soviet model. Between 1947 and 1950, the Party closed the main university faculty training economists (the Közgazdaságtudományi Kar, or Economics Faculty, at the Budapest Technical University), the only independent economics research institute (the Hungarian Institute for Economics Research), economists' main professional journal (*Közgazdasági Szemle*, or *Economics Review*), a wide range of other economics journals, and the Hungarian Economics Association (Bockman 2000: 98–105). They also purged the Hungarian Academy of Sciences of economists (Péteri 1991: 287). Party leaders then established a new Economics University, later called the Karl Marx University of Economics, based on Marxist-Leninist principles, and started the *Hungarian-Soviet Economics Review*.[3] The focus of economics education became theoretical political economy of socialism and capitalism based on the writings of Marx, Engels, Lenin, and Stalin.

Unlike Yugoslavia, Hungary remained part of the Warsaw Pact. Therefore, the Soviet Union continued to have a direct influence on Hungary. Stalin's death in 1953 created a political vacuum, and political factions vied for power throughout the East Bloc. In Hungary, Mátyás Rákosi, Ernő Gerő, and Imre Nagy, a communist marginalized and attacked by the Rákosi regime, vied for power. In 1953, Imre Nagy served as prime minister. While he was in power, groups of economists from the new and the old professional institutions allied with him. These economists began to criticize publicly Stalinist central economic planning and called for market reforms within a socialist system, thus earning the label "reform economists." In exchange for their expertise and support, Imre Nagy provided these economists with professional resources that would allow them to become the mainstream in Hungary.

Being an agricultural economist himself, Nagy was in a particularly good position to make an alliance with economists. He had been an economic researcher at an agricultural research institute in the Soviet Union, which gave him greater professional prestige than most other economists, who had little research experience (Rainer 1996; Szabó, OHA, 1991). In Hungary, he had also personal knowledge of the economics profession because he had been a professor at the Economics University in Hungary since 1948 and a member of the Academy of Sciences' Permanent Economics Committee, in which top economic experts discussed professional and policy issues. From his work in the Agricultural Ministry, he also had experience with the concerns of applied economists. Nagy was a powerful member of the economics community and familiar with economic thinking and practices, as well as with the problems facing economists. Nagy promised a central role for economists in his new system, arguing that economics was so important that it should be placed at the "forefront of the sciences" (Nagy 1954: 24).[4]

Economists who had suffered during the pre-1953 period joined Nagy's army of experts.[5] Indeed, Nagy himself had suffered during the Stalinist period; in 1949, Party leaders had sentenced Nagy to one year of internal exile for his "right-wing views" (Rainer 1996). Other high-ranking Communists, including economists, had suffered similar accusations and punishments.[6] Another economist, Ferenc Donáth, had been jailed on false charges in 1951 and released in 1954, as the result of the changes instigated by Nagy (Péteri 1993: 163).[7] Imre Vajda joined Nagy's group after being in prison on false charges from 1951 to 1954 (Vas 1990: 49). Rákosi had personally forced Tamás Nagy, the Economics University's main political economy lecturer, to divorce his wife because she was politically suspect (T. Nagy, OHA, 1986: 104).[8] Tamás Nagy said it was "natural" for him to join Imre Nagy (ibid.: 118). Governmental agency directors, such as György Péter of the Central Statistical Office, had to continually protect their employees from attacks by the Party. Péter Erdős had been removed from the Communist Party and his job because he was accused of taking part in a "Zionist conspiracy" (Péteri 1996: 367). Nagy mobilized these and other disillusioned elite economists to build his economic and political reform programs. He also included his students and colleagues at the Economics University and the Agricultural University, from his teaching days between 1948 and 1952, into this central core of advisors (Rainer 1996: 449–551).

Nagy advocated changes in the standards of professional economic practice. In 1954, Nagy declared the importance of "scientific criticism, the discussion of a wide range of theoretical questions, and the free battle of opinions" (1954: 22). This marked a significant change in Hungarian economics practice. For example, in 1950, a highly influential economist forbade an economics lecturer from teaching, remarking "He does not understand or feel the essence of socialism."[9] In 1954, in contrast, a participant at an Academy of Sciences' Economics Committee meeting criticized a new statistics textbook as too ideological:

Its entire discussion style was pseudoscientific honey . . . For example, he said "Socialist statistics speaks about the working people and speaks to the working people" . . .

this could have been said in 1945–46 in a propaganda or popularizing article but not in a university textbook in 1953.[10]

The Economics Committee decided to tell the author to remove the "useless examples and quotations," as well as the sections on statistics in classical Marxist works, and to add more discussion of representative statistics and specific Hungarian economic problems. This is just one example of the broad changes in professional standards and practice during the Nagy period.

Nagy also recreated an old role for economists, the independent researcher, to embody this scientific spirit, which also added to his army of experts. This role had ended with the closure of the only independent economic research institute, the Hungarian Institute for Economic Research (HIER), which the Party under Rákosi had condemned as "reactionary."[11] The new Economic Science Institute (ESI), which opened in 1954, provided once again an independent realm for economists to conduct research removed from the problems and concerns of practical agencies.[12] According to its founding document, the most important task of the ESI was "the study of scientific problems arising during the construction of socialism."[13] The ESI was created to eliminate, in Nagy's words, the "backwardness" in economic science through the analysis of "reality," rather than focusing on theoretical or strategic Marxist-Leninist texts (Nagy 1954: 22). By studying existing problems and "concrete events," ESI economists made a sharp break with the traditional work of political economic theorists who formed blueprints for future socialism and communism through textual analysis of classical Marxist works. The ESI economists would study the "objective factors" and "concrete practical questions" and thus provide a "scientific basis" for planning and economic policy (ibid.: 21–22). From the beginning, the economists at the ESI were officially ordered to practice this new empirical research approach.

ESI economists had access to a wide range of materials that had been denied to most economists in the Stalinist period. The ESI library had subscriptions to *Business Week, Economic Notes, Monthly Review of Credit and Business Conditions, Political Affairs, Survey of Current Business, U.S. News and World Report,* and *The Wall Street Journal*.[14] The library also had the works written by those at the HIER. Furthermore, the ESI housed the Economics Document Center, which had originally functioned within the HIER and provided translations of foreign economics literature and data, as well as Hungarian literature and data. Those in the ESI thus had access to a wide range of materials.

The ESI immediately began functioning as a workshop for Nagy's reform programs (Rainer 1996: 452).[15] From its inception, the ESI was the creation of reform economists. Kálmán Szabó, an ally of Nagy, made the plans for the ESI.[16] The first employees of the ESI were also reform economists.[17] Imre Nagy's graduate students also worked in the ESI.[18] János Kornai, the economic columnist at the official party newspaper *Szabad Nép* and part of a group of pro-Nagy journalists, also joined the ESI in 1955 (Kornai 2006: 71).

At the same time, the ESI provided an institutional base from which reform economists exercised control over their own profession. The founders of the ESI envisioned the institute as the organizational center for the economics profession.[19] ESI economists performed many professional functions, which gave them much influence over their discipline. For example, the ESI took on many of the science policy tasks of the Academy of Sciences, including debating theoretical questions brought up by ESI researchers, discussing the scientific plans of the ESI, promoting its connections with practical life, and assessing the theoretical and political level of work from the ESI going to publication.[20] They also evaluated economics dissertations and tested graduate students.[21] Until 1957, ESI members dominated the dissertation committees of graduate students (Péteri 1996: 378).[22] In addition, they could organize committees with experts from outside the ESI to study specific economic questions. The ESI provided reform economists with an institutional center to influence the rest of their profession.

Not only did the Nagy regime support the establishment of an economic research institute and encourage new professional standards, but it also closed the *Hungarian-Soviet Economics Review* and reestablished the prewar *Economics Review*.[23] The *Hungarian-Soviet Economics Review*, as the sole professional journal, had mainly published Soviet articles and articles promoting government policies and thus did not provide a forum for Hungarian reform economists. Reform economists had found extremely limited, if any, opportunities to publish.[24] With the reestablished *Economics Review*, they could communicate their ideas and practices to the rest of the discipline. The journal rarely published Soviet authors and featured articles by reform economists most prominently. Nagy supporters, including members of his government, dominated the editorial board.[25] The journal quickly became extremely popular among Hungarian economists.[26] The

Economics Review provided reform economists with the only professional forum for economic articles and a means to communicate their ideas.[27]

The *Economics Review* promoted Nagy's new vision of economic practice. In the first issue, the editorial board declared that articles should no longer use "scholastic" methods but rather should be based on empirical research ("Közgazdaságtudomány" 1954). In line with Nagy's call for intellectual debate, the editorial board initiated many series of articles discussing common themes. Beyond developing the profession, the editorial board saw the journal as a means to organize economists to solve specific policy problems and provide a "scientific basis" for economic policy (ibid.). The *Economics Review* provided reform economists with a means to promote their practices of empirical research and debate, as well as their policy ideas.

The Nagy regime also implemented a major reform of the universities. Reform economists considered the reorganization of the Economics University essential to end the domination of theoretical political economy and Marxism-Leninism, which, they argued, did not train students appropriately for employment.[28]

Nagy professionalized economic science by creating new institutions, such as the ESI, the new role of independent researcher, and the *Economics Review*, as well as reforming economics education and supporting empirical research and debate. This professionalization changed the power structure within the economics discipline because these institutions provided reform economists with the means to develop and communicate their ideas and practices, and thus break the monopoly other groups had over the discipline. In exchange for this political and professional support, reform economists, and particularly the ESI researchers, developed economic programs for Nagy and promoted Nagy's worldview. Reform economists maintained control of these institutions and infused them with their perspectives, ideas, and practices. As a result, reform economists and their institutions continued to have an impact long after Nagy was removed from power.

Hungarian Reform Economics: New Ideas

Imre Nagy's support allowed economists not only to transform their professional life but also fundamentally to revolutionize the very content of Hungarian economics. "The main methodological mistake of our leadership is overcentralization, bureaucratism," declared György Péter, the head of the Central Statistical Office, in 1954 ([1954] 1986: 74). Péter thus initiated the public criticism of the Stalinist system, though he called it "our leadership," and the public discussion of market reforms. His article provoked great excitement and interest because he called for reforms and mobilized a new economic vocabulary. Péter called for "healthy competition" between "independent" enterprises working for "profits," consumers who can "freely decide" whether and where to buy goods, and prices that take into consideration "demand and supply" (ibid.: 75, 81, 83, 84, 86). While in capitalism market methods function "blindly" and are "destructive," in socialism "they can be turned towards the good of society" (ibid.: 91).[29] In contrast, in the older Stalinist economic vocabulary, the economy and the political sphere were fused, as a space filled with informants, liars, spies, nationalized companies, politicians, planners, and, finally, workers who needed protection and discipline. With this article, Péter introduced a new way of thinking about the economy and launched the lively career of Hungarian reform economics.

Reform economists began immediately to write about what they called the "economic mechanism," which, as I discuss later in this chapter, American economists also developed at this time. Starting sometime in 1954, the term *economic mechanism* became the most important concept in Hungarian economics during the 1950s and 1960s.[30] By envisioning the economy as a mechanism, reform economists presented it as a distinct object that could be altered, tinkered with, or even exchanged for a new one, just as an engine could be. János Kornai ([1957] 1959), former Party newspaper columnist who would soon become one of Hungary's most famous reform economists, wrote extensively about the economic mechanism. According to Kornai, the economic mechanism refers "to the methods in *use* in administering the economy (i.e. to the systems of planning, money, credit, wages, and prices) and to the *forms* of organization of economic activity" (ibid.: 1). The mechanism was generally made up of different smaller "mechanisms," "methods," or "levers." In his model, Kornai specified four "indirect economic" levers and four "direct administrative" levers. The four economic levers controlled investment, the monetary system, the price system, and the wage fund. They were indirect because state authorities did not tell the enterprises exactly what to do but rather manipulated the environment in which individual enterprise sought financial gain to make them do what the state authorities wanted. The four direct administrative levers were the centralized direction of production, the system of material allocation, state regulation of foreign trade, and the system of central allocation of managerial personnel. Through these levers, state authorities told companies directly what to produce, which materials to use, which goods to export, and who could be managers. According to Kornai, state authorities had mainly used direct administrative levers, leaving the indirect economic ones unused or mobilizing them only to buttress central instructions. This meant that the economic mechanism did not work harmoniously or efficiently. Kornai argued that the central authorities should increase the use of economic levers, "real economic forces," and decrease the use of the administrative levers. Through indirect economic means, the central authorities could fulfill plans by using managers' and workers' personal financial interests in increasing profits.

Reform economists argued for an economic mechanism with predominately indirect economic levers, or, as it was later called, a "market mechanism." In contrast to the existing mechanism that primarily used direct levers and vertical connections between planners and enterprises, Kornai argued for a comprehensive reform to create a mechanism with indirect economic levers and horizontal connections. This "market mechanism" would work within the planning system, linking Party leaders and planners with economic actors. At a meeting in early 1957, Tamás Nagy agreed on a plan for economic reform, which "outlined the future model as a socialist economic model, in which administrative measures play a very small role, and planned direction of the economy happens decisively with economic influencing tools built on the market mechanism" (Szamuely 1986: 202–203). For reform economists, the ideal mechanism was a market mechanism, which had as few administrative levers as possible.

The reform economists presented an image of the economy as a sphere separate from politics. Political actors and institutions acted only through indirect means on the world of independent and competitive enterprises. With the correct economic levers, economic actors would act rationally and state authorities would not have to intervene at all. Through profits, prices, and rational economic actors, local company interests would be united with national economic interests. In a committee on reforming the economic mechanism, the economist István Varga spoke about the planned economy as a kind of magic trick:

If a magician gives a deck of cards to someone, telling them to draw a card from anywhere in the deck, but what he draws will certainly be a jack of diamonds, I ask: Is this a planned economy, yes or no? Whatever he draws, he will certainly draw the card that the magician wanted him to. If it is so, then it is a planned economy. (Szamuely 1986: 205)[31]

Another economist questioned whether planners as magicians always had the means to accomplish this trick. Varga responded, "Companies, they should do what they want, but if they see it in their own interests, then they will do what I want; this is a planned economy" (ibid.: 206). Economists promised a self-regulating system, with which politicians and other noneconomic actors would interact only indirectly.[32]

Hungarian economists also began using neoclassical mathematical economics. Small numbers of economists embraced quantitative methods from "bourgeois economics," especially econometrics, input-output modeling, and, later, linear programming. As in Yugoslavia, these economists learned about recent neoclassical economic work through book reviews and lists of foreign works published in the *Economics Review* and the publications of the ESI. As early as 1953, András Bródy created input-output tables within a government ministry (Bekker 1999: 849). Just a few years later, Mária Augusztinovics began organizing input-output models of the entire economy in the National Planning Office (Augusztinovics 1995). While many economists found such "bourgeois" methods politically suspect, these young economists could learn from older economists and mathematicians familiar with these methods.

While the new socialist Hungary represented a break with the past, there were still numerous personal and intellectual ties between economists who had worked before the Second World War and those who worked in the new socialist economy.[33] Many Party-state leaders knew about neoclassical economics. György Péter, the head of the Central Statistical Office, was familiar with neoclassical views of socialism. He was not an economist, but he was well read and had taught himself some economics (Gelegonya 1996: 125–126).[34] During one of his jail sentences for interwar and wartime communist activities, Péter had read the most important prewar Hungarian economics textbook by Farkas Heller (ibid.: 126). Farkas Heller was one of the major proponents of Austrian School marginalism in Hungary and a professor at the Economics Faculty in Budapest (ibid.). Other Communist Party leaders had even more extensive knowledge of neoclassical economics and economics more broadly through their pre-1948 studies at the Economics Faculty. János Szita, a top economic expert beside Ernő Gerő, had received his doctorate from the Economics Faculty in 1946. Kálmán Szabó,

István Hetényi, István Fogaras, Gyula Hevesi, Edit Varga, and Imre Nagy had also studied there at that time. Margit Siklós, who had been a teaching assistant at the Faculty and a skilled planner, and Edit Varga, who had received her doctorate from the Faculty in 1946, both made personnel decisions in the economics profession (Szabó, OHA, 1991: 163). Varga was also one of the leaders of the Communist Party's economic policy department. István Hetényi, a non-Marxist apprentice of Farkas Heller in the Faculty, and István Huszár had both studied at the Faculty and then worked on high-level economic policy in the party state (Hetényi, OHA, 1987: 39; Huszár, OHA, 1990).[35] The Hungarian economic leadership was familiar with neoclassical economics, but, in the post-1953 period, the leadership spoke much more openly about markets, supply and demand, profits and other topics, than about neoclassical economics.

As was the case with Yugoslav economics, the similarities between Hungarian reform economics and neoclassical economics were, in fact, overdetermined. Through the nineteenth century and into the twentieth, neoclassical economists had developed their ideas in dialogue with socialism. Neoclassical criticisms of Marxist economic ideas, such as the labor theory of value, as well as the neoclassical confidence in markets, led many socialists, including those in the Soviet Union and Eastern Europe, to reject neoclassical economics. In spite of this rejection, neoclassical economists continued to develop their ideas in dialogue with socialism, incorporating abstract models of socialist planners and market socialism, as well as concrete Soviet and Yugoslav models, as core analytical and normative elements. Hungarian reform economists rejected the Soviet model, which made other socialist ideas available, including neoclassical economics. Thus, it makes sense that socialists critical of the Soviet model would find themselves interested in neoclassical economics.

In the 1950s, Hungarian economics students also became familiar with neoclassical ideas. By 1954, the newly renamed Karl Marx University of Economics required students to study neoclassical economics, especially in the history of economic thought courses taught for decades by Antal Mátyás. Mátyás had studied at the pre-1948 Economics Faculty, where Farkas Heller worked and wrote his *History of Economic Theory* (Heller 1943). After researching the history of economic theory, including Marxism, Western "bourgeois" economics, and older Hungarian economics, Mátyás began teaching these topics at the Economics University in 1953 (Szentes 1996: 9). In 1954, the university published his lecture notes for his course titled "The History of Modern Bourgeois Economics." By 1955, Hungarian university curriculum presented the major Western contemporary economic schools, though in a very critical way (Csaba 2002: 84).

Indeed, in his 1960 edition titled *Main Trends in Bourgeois Economics after the Establishment of Marxism*, Mátyás explained Western economics literature, in which Hungarian economists had participated until the late 1940s. This book had chapters on the German historical school, the 1870s founders of neoclassical economics, the Austrian School, the further development of equilibrium theory and monopoly theory, and Keynesianism, as well as chapters on specific economists including Austrian School economist Eugen von Böhm-Bawerk, one of the neoclassical founders Léon Walras, and neoclassical pioneer Alfred Marshall. In his discussion of Keynesianism, Mátyás referred to the relatively recent literature, including Samuelson's famous *Economics* textbook (1955), Alvin Hansen's 1953 *A Guide to Keynes*, Lawrence Klein's 1949 *The Keynesian Revolution*, and Keynes's 1936 *General Theory of Employment, Interest and Money*. Mátyás embedded these detailed descriptions within a critical view that bourgeois economics was an apology for capitalism, hid the inherent conflict between capital and workers, and incorrectly presented everyone as interested in productivity (1960: 70). Unlike Yugoslav economists, Mátyás did not suggest that neoclassical economics might be an instrument for socialism. However, he did explain the idea that market equilibrium would realize the maximum social welfare and the optimal use of materials (ibid.: 8), which formed the basis of Western neoclassical economists' understandings of market socialism. Understandably, Tamás Szentes, a development economist, who had worked and studied both modern Western economics and Marxist political economy with Mátyás in the 1950s, wrote that, if university graduates were able to communicate professionally with their Western and developing countries colleagues and if they could understand Western economic theory and methods, "they could thank Antal Mátyás" (1996: 11). Mátyás provided a foundation for a future transnational neoclassical discussion.

Young, mathematically inclined economists could also learn from mathematical economists trained before 1948. For example, from 1950 to 1959, Ede Theiss remained a professor in Eötvös Loránd University's State and Law Sciences Faculty and director of its statistics department. In 1931, Theiss had defended his economics dissertation on mathematical theory of price formation, production, and income distribution using the economic literature of Walras, Pareto, and recent econometrics. With a Rockefeller scholarship, Theiss visited the United States from 1931 to 1933, including the University of Chicago (Köves 1994). He continued to work as a professor until 1959. By 1965, Ede Theiss, along with Central Statistical Office economists, had developed an econometric model of the entire Hungarian economy (Halabuk, Kenessey, and Theiss 1965). Such older scholars remained a resource for younger economists and for socialist experimentation.

Hungarian reform economists did not merely parrot the ideas of neoclassical economists but rather contributed to the neoclassical discussion of market socialism. Some economists sought to combine neoclassical economics and Marxism.[36] Others immediately planned a new kind of market socialism. According to Oskar Lange's famous 1936–1937 model, market socialism would have a market in consumer goods, while a central planner would set initial producer prices and then, in response to excess supply or demand, adjust these prices. Hungarian reform economists moved beyond Lange's model and sought to realize a market in which autonomous enterprises would competitively set prices and around which socialist institutions would function.[37] As a result, centrally planned prices would no longer be necessary, except in special cases, such as in monopolistic industries. In 1954, György Péter called for "healthy competition" between "independent" enterprises working for "profits," consumers who can "freely decide" whether and where to buy goods, and prices that take into consideration "demand and supply" (75, 81, 83, 84, 86). Going beyond Lange's market socialist model, Hungarian reform economists presented a new form of market socialism with a pure competitive market.

The rise to power of Imre Nagy opened up the possibility for a fundamentally new kind of economics profession in Hungary. In the post-1953 period, reform economists gained control of a wide range of professional institutions, which allowed them to spread their ideas. These ideas resembled those of neoclassical economics because they reflected a common understanding of alternative socialisms critical of the Soviet model and official Marxist-Leninist political economy. Hungarian economic leaders were already familiar with neoclassical economics. University students soon also became acquainted with neoclassical economics. Furthermore, small numbers of economists turned quickly to mathematical neoclassical methods as a tool for socialism and began to create new neoclassical theories and models. These developments in the 1950s formed the foundation for Hungarian reform economists' participation in the transnational neoclassical dialogue after 1956.

1956

In early 1956, Soviet leader Nikita Khrushchev condemned Stalin in a secret speech to party leaders, which seemed to allow others to criticize the Stalinist state socialist system. Eastern European intellectuals began to make public criticisms of the Soviet state socialist system and call for reforms. By March, young Hungarian intellectuals gathered as a discussion group under the auspices of the Petőfi Circle, originally organized under the supervision of the Party's youth group (Litván 1996: 39). In May and June, the Petőfi Circle held famous public discussions with thousands in the audience. As Litván found, "The extraordinary nature of these events was a function not only of the subject matter, but also of the quality of the presentations and the hitherto unimaginable open and unrestrained character of the discussions" (ibid.: 40). Economists close to Imre Nagy led two debates on economics in March (Hegedüs and Rainer 1989). During these debates, participants criticized Stalin, arguing that economists should be more involved in policy and planning and that economics itself should be reorganized. The Petőfi Circle showed its great interest in and support for Yugoslav socialist experiments. Many participants called for more information about Yugoslav socialism, especially its self-management system (ibid.: 41, 42, 58). At this time, reform economists argued for workers' councils, which would control managers, replacing central Party-state directives, and allow enterprises to function independently in a market environment (for example, Balázsy [1956] 1986; Kornai [1957] 1986: 143). Reform economists tied together socialism, economic democracy, and markets.

The Hungarian population increasingly took part in protests and oppositional activity in favor of Imre Nagy and against the Party leadership and the Soviet occupation of Hungary. On October 23, 1956, thousands of Hungarians took to the streets, which launched the Hungarian Revolution.[38] Imre Nagy returned to power, declared Hungary's neutrality, and allowed non-Communist political parties to operate. At the beginning of November, however, the Soviets took over the country by force and arrested Nagy. Nagy would eventually be executed.[39]

After arresting Nagy, the Soviet authorities put János Kádár in power in Hungary. Over 200,000 refugees, or 2 percent of the population, escaped across the Austrian border (Cox 2006: xi). The Kádár regime soon carried out retributions against those who had taken part in revolutionary activities. From summer 1957 to fall 1958, Party officials and leading economic experts publicly condemned, among other intellectuals, economists for their part in the revolution.[40] Economists called this period the "terror" (T. Nagy, OHA, 1986: 172). One Hungarian hardliner declared, "Economic science is one of the main retreats of Hungarian revisionism," and, besides writers and newspaper reporters, economists were the most important influence on Imre Nagy.[41] Economists posed a danger because they encouraged the criticism of economic problems and "demonstrated" that the cause of these problems was not specific economic policy but rather the socialist "system."[42] The critic then concluded that the installation of a market mechanism would lead to "capitalist restoration."[43] Another opponent of reform economists wrote, "The new mechanism is not an economic panacea, but rather one of the most pernicious manifestations of revisionism."[44] The *Economics Review* was also criticized for publishing the work of revisionists who had sanctioned the revolution (Bieber, Fábián, and Gulyás 1957).[45] The repression of the revolution brought extensive condemnation of reform economists as "revisionists" and leading instigators of the events of October 1956.

The Party leadership specifically targeted the ESI. At the end of 1957, the Communist Party set up a Revising Committee in the ESI to examine the activities of its members. The Committee asked each economist two questions: (1) Do you agree with Soviet intervention in Hungary? and (2) Do you agree that Imre Nagy and the others were traitors? János Kornai and András Nagy both refused to answer "yes" to these questions and were dismissed from the institute.[46] The ESI director István Friss opposed this committee and its dismissals and also made certain the founding principles of the ESI did not change (T. Nagy, OHA, 1986: 177), which meant that economists there continued to research "economic reality" and did not return to a focus on Marxist-Leninist theoretical texts. In spite of the support of Friss, economists in the ESI experienced direct political intervention in their professional work.

After the revolution, the Party-state decided to depoliticize Hungarian society by reorienting the population toward consumerism. The party leadership sought to restrict politics to the Communist Party, to forbid the discussion of certain topics—such as political reforms, political activity, independent workers councils, a multiparty system, private ownership of the means of production, or any break with the Soviet Union—and to change Party-state policy toward the population, as in Kádár's declaration "those who are not against us are with us." In place of politics, the party leadership offered rising living standards as a basis for legitimacy in hopes that the population would set aside their political demands and work toward individual consumerist goals (Róna-Tas 1997: 84–86; Tőkés 1996: 22; Toma and Völgyes 1977).[47] Reflecting this shift in orientation, in the early 1960s the Hungarian government replaced its Monopoly-style board game "Fulfill the Plan!" with a new one called "Manage Sensibly!" In the new version, players managed their money so they could accumulate an apartment, a car, and household appliances.[48] Economic goals of mass consumption and accumulation of money were supposed to replace political aspirations.

To realize continually increasing living standards, the party called on economists, especially those with quantitative skills, to help reform the economy. In exchange for avoiding "politics," Hungarian economists had the opportunity to join the transnational neoclassical discussion and to exercise some influence over future economic reforms. After 1956, many economists had already chosen to hide away from any activity that could be construed as political. Some of the leading economic policy makers, József Bognár, Imre Vajda, and Jenő Wilcsek, decided to work in the Karl Marx University of Economics because there they would not have political roles (Wilcsek, OHA, 1983: 57).[49] Many economists turned to mathematical economics because its technical language could conceal a wide range of politics.[50] A group of economists gave up political economic themes for mathematical economics as a way to escape (T. Nagy, OHA, 1986: 181). Economists chose to go into mathematical economics rather than political economy because "you had more room" in mathematical economics since censors and politicians did not understand it.[51] Economists could hide their ideas within the formulas and difficult language of mathematics.

The interest in mathematical economics after 1956 turned out to be more than just an escape. It also created what one Hungarian economist called a "new economics" (Wilcsek, OHA, 1983: 61). Hungarian economists considered the end of 1950s and the early 1960s the "golden age" of mathematical economics (Szamuely 1986: 32). The Soviet Union, Yugoslavia, and other East Bloc countries experienced a similar turn toward mathematical economics. Joining the few economists working on input-output analysis and econometrics in the mid-1950s, increasing numbers of Hungarian economists adopted the neoclassical methods of input-output analysis, econometrics, and linear programming as tools for socialism. In his history of Hungarian input-output analysis, economist Róbert Horváth described the new input-output research centers established after 1956:

Nation-wide research was immediately begun, studying the possibility of application of this method as worked out theoretically on the basis of the Walrasian concept of a static equilibrium analysis and as perfected by Leontief and others. His [Leontief's] basic idea of input-output statistics, as derivated from early Soviet economic planning methods at the beginning of the twenties, was quickly understood in Hungary too, as well as the early speculations of Professor Oskar Lange in elaborating input-output statistics and also input-output analysis as a tool of socialist economic planning. (1963: 213)

As mentioned earlier, the Central Statistical Office began developing econometric models of the Hungarian economy. Turning instead to linear programming, Kornai remembered, "In the extremely repressive era, following 1956, I decided to move to a politically less sensitive topic: mathematical planning, more closely the application of linear programming to planning, which brought me very close to neo-classical thinking" (Blanchard 1999: 5). By 1963, Kornai was directing "a little army of 150 to 200 staff members" in the National Planning Office to apply their neoclassical model to national economic planning (Kornai 2006: 151).

Economists further transformed their professional work in several ways. In 1961, the Karl Marx University of Economics was reformed to include more mathematical training and introduced specialized studies in computer science, efficiency, and quantification (Kemenes 1981: 586).[52] Even more importantly, some economists attended international conferences and took part in academic exchanges. Earlier, Hungarian economists had traveled to other Eastern European countries. By the late 1950s, some were receiving invitations to give lectures in Western Europe and the United States. For example, János Kornai was invited to LSE in 1958 to give lectures and conduct a seminar (2006: 159). Although he could not go then, Kornai and his colleague András Nagy successfully attended an International Economic Association conference in 1963 (ibid.: 159–160). During the 1964–1965 academic year, five economists visited the United States, including András Bródy and György Péter, through the Ford Foundation (Bockman and Eyal 2002: 347). Bródy worked closely with Wassily Leontief, the founder of input-output analysis, at Harvard University. Paradoxically, the repression of the 1956 revolution led Hungarian economists to return to the transnational neoclassical economics discussion.

Importantly, these mathematical methods could solve problems without changing the existing power structures (Szamuely and Csaba 1998: 174). Neoclassical economists had long theorized the way that a planner in a highly centralized socialist system could obtain the same optimal results as a purely competitive market system would. In Hungary, economists used neoclassical economics in a very narrow sense because the Kádár regime forbade discussion of politics, institutional change, and, especially, workers' councils. The Soviet Union feared that the Yugoslav system might appear more attractive than the Soviet model and thus forced Eastern European regimes to reject anything that might resemble "Titoism" (Litván 1996: 45). Reform economists focused instead on mastering these highly technical methods, leaving aside the wide range of institutions long considered by neoclassical economists to be necessary to make the market or the plan achieve optimal results. Reform economists thus experienced great excitement experimenting with mathematical methods, but they would eventually become frustrated by the regime's limitations.

Transnational Dialogue among Neoclassical Economists

In the United States, economists worked on "market mechanisms" at the same time as their counterparts in Hungary.[53] In 1949, Paul Samuelson ([1949] 1966) wrote two reports for RAND, which were later collectively titled "Market Mechanisms and Maximization." Basically, the reports explained the new developments in linear programming, which Samuelson knew "from reading unpublished memoranda of Tjalling Koopmans of the Cowles Commission" and George Dantzig (ibid.: 425).[54] After describing how to calculate equilibrium (or what were called "shadow") prices, Samuelson discussed how a central authority might be used to coerce enterprises to use these prices. However, Samuelson also maintained that "a market mechanism can be set up which, more or less automatically and without the use of centralized intelligence or planning, will simultaneously determine both the best price and quantity" (ibid.: 436). Through this automatic system, prices would rise when demand surpassed supply, and prices would fall when supplies surpassed demand, allowing firms to take prices as given and make their own decisions. This decentralized form of planning through a market mechanism understood as a price mechanism is the same as Oskar Lange's market socialism (ibid.: 469). Neoclassical economists in the United States and Hungary shared the idea of an optimizing market mechanism, which allowed them to develop a neoclassical dialogue about socialism.

Hungarian reform economists also acted like the social planner of neoclassical economics. As Pareto originally discussed in the 1890s, a socialist state or a social planner could solve neoclassical equations describing a competitive market economy to obtain equilibrium or shadow prices that would maximize social welfare. Oskar Lange (1936, 1937) suggested that the social planner could use markets and trial-and-error price setting to maximize social welfare. In 1956, Dutch economist Jan Tinbergen took Pareto's ideas a step further, showing that a social planner could not only maximize social welfare equal to that of a competitive market but also could help entire societies jump to a more efficient equilibrium and then rearrange income or even property to get a just result. Therefore, the social planner could realize socialism either by acting like Pareto's socialist state and improving social welfare or by creating a new society that had socialist institutions. Alternatively, the social planner could jump to a new system altogether, such as the capitalist system as discussed in Chapter 6.

The 1960s witnessed an explosion of literature criticizing the narrow form of neoclassical economics, calling for institutions that would allow markets and socialist states to achieve Pareto optimality and provide maximum social welfare. Exemplifying this narrow form, Oskar Lange had not discussed any difficulties with making firm managers follow the rules of market socialism or how the public might let their preferences be known to the Central Planning Board. The highly abstract Arrow-Debreu model also narrowly focused on the core of neoclassical economics, competitive markets and a socialist state. In the late 1940s and early 1950s, as discussed in Chapter 1, economists such as Kenneth Arrow and Gerard Debreu, as well as their Soviet counterparts, had developed their science within the world of the military. This world had encouraged economists to ignore institutions. Economists who did consider decentralizing and possibly democratic institutions did so in a minimal and highly abstract manner (for example, Arrow 1951). After years of not speaking about the institutions necessary for competitive markets or central planning, these economists no longer took for granted the existing, often hierarchical institutions.

To these economists, both competitive markets and the socialist state required institutions to make them successfully maximize social welfare and obtain Pareto optimality (Tinbergen [1956] 1967: 32). In the definitive article on "market failure," Francis Bator (1958) demonstrated the many ways that competitive markets and Langean market socialist states created prices that neglected a range of externalities and information asymmetries and thus failed to produce Pareto optimality. Neoclassical economists in the West and in the East realized that competitive markets required institutions, in particular to deal with the problems of incentives and asymmetric information. The literature on principal–agent relations blossomed during this time. In this literature, principals, such as owners or social planners, seek to delegate tasks to agents, such as managers, which require effective incentives and adequate information. Furthermore, Marschak (1959) and other economists further suggested that economists did not really know whether centralized or decentralized solutions worked more efficiently. Instead, the manager, the economist, or even a social planner should compare economic mechanisms (or institutions) and choose the optimal ones. This optimum would create incentives to maximize social welfare and maintain the efficiencies of the pure competitive system, thus continuing Pareto's view of a socialist state. Thus, in the late 1950s, economists formed the field of mechanism design, remarkably similar to Hungarian reform economics.[55] A social planner would now have to evaluate and implement the necessary institutions. American neoclassical economists continued to develop their discipline through examinations of an abstract model of socialism that had remarkable similarity to Hungarian reform economics.

These economists questioned the very dichotomy between socialism and capitalism, as well as that between centralization and decentralization. They even questioned the distinction between the national economy and the firm because both national economies and firms could have central planning. By the early 1960s, neoclassical economists had begun to ask whether economic systems were in fact converging (Tinbergen 1961). They saw every organization (whether a firm or a national economy, whether socialist or capitalist) as potentially optimally organized and thus as structurally similar (Marschak 1959: 399). Marschak and others no longer focused on the ownership of the means of production or on the ideology of a system but rather on information flows and decision making in organizations. As a result, American neoclassical economics provided tools to both capitalist and socialist economies.

The 1950s and 1960s witnessed a transnational convergence of neoclassical economic methods and concepts across the Cold War borders. Therefore, it is understandable that American and Hungarian economists would be interested in each others' work, though it was not easy to learn about each others' work.[56] Yugoslav economists could study abroad and directly discuss neoclassical economics. In Hungary, there were greater restrictions. However, many of exiles from the 1956 Hungarian Revolution brought knowledge about Hungarian socialist experiments and reform economics with them.

For example, Béla Balassa began studying economics in Budapest in 1946 and finished his doctorate in 1951 (Balassa 1989). He first worked as a planner at a large construction trust and then was internally deported.[57] In the new Nagy government in 1953, Balassa became the organizer of a large construction trust and wrote two economics books. During the revolution, he became a member of a group that took over the Ministry of Construction and planned to teach economics in the Karl Marx University of Economics. After the revolution failed, Balassa escaped to Austria and obtained a Rockefeller Foundation fellowship, arriving at Yale University in April 1957 to study with fellow Hungarian William Fellner (Balassa 1989: 17–18).[58] Balassa's claim that his Hungarian education poorly prepared him for American graduate school seemed unbelievable, given that he completed his course work and published his prize-winning dissertation *The Hungarian Experience in Economic Planning* (1959) within two years (1989: 17–18). He went on to teach economics at Yale University, the University of California at Berkeley, and Columbia University. From 1967, he taught at Johns Hopkins University and worked as a consultant to the World Bank. Balassa identified himself as a lone figure at the World Bank with his "liberal economic philosophy" in contrast to those with a "dirigiste" and protectionist philosophy (ibid.: 19). Yet his approach reflected the Hungarian arguments for competitive markets within socialism. In 1968, Balassa was officially invited back to Hungary to give a public lecture—"announced in the Communist Party newspaper and well-attended"—at the Karl Marx University of Economics (ibid.: 21). From then on, he returned at least once a year to Hungary to lecture and participate in conferences.

The ability for Balassa to communicate with Western neoclassical economists was not common among Hungarian economists, but it also was not unique. Economists János Kornai and Tamás Lipták remained in Hungary after the revolution of 1956 and sent an article manuscript to one of the most prestigious economic journals in the world, *Econometrica*, run by the Econometric Society based at Yale University, which, Kornai recalled, "immediately accepted it without changing a word or a comma"

(Kornai 2006: 139). After publishing that article in 1962, the editor of *Econometrica*, French neoclassical economist Edmond Malinvaud, invited Kornai to the 1963 International Economics Association conference in Cambridge, England (ibid.: 159). At the conference, Kornai met Leonid Hurwicz, Tjalling Koopmans, and other world-renowned neoclassical economists. Kornai remembered that at the conference:

> The plan modeling undertaken in Hungary attracted keen interest from Western colleagues. It was not just a question of the Lange-Malinvaud and Kornai-Lipták models being compared theoretically. Practitioners also compared the structures of the computational models as well as data collection and model application promoted by French, Dutch, and Indian state planning institutions with what was going on in Hungary, with the assistance of the National Planning Office. Our work gained esteem abroad and was seen as a significant intellectual achievement. (ibid.: 154)[59]

Kornai and Lipták's model provided an analysis of a pure centrally planned socialist economy, which was directly relevant to mainstream theoretical debates about Lange and Malinvaud's models of decentralized market socialism and to those interested in evaluating different economic mechanisms like Marschak (1959). *Econometrica* in 1965 published yet another article by Kornai and Lipták "immediately without alteration" (Kornai 2006: 144). Hungarian reform economists had returned to the transnational dialogue among neoclassical economists about socialism.

Moreover, Hungarian economists discussed neoclassical economics with their counterparts in the East Bloc. Polish economist Włodzimierz Brus was one of the most important influences on Hungarian reform economics (Szamuely 1986: 266, 307). In 1961, Brus's *The General Problems of the Functioning of the Socialist Economy* appeared.[60] Hungarian economists quickly learned about his work, which explained Soviet economic ideas from the 1920s, the 1930s neoclassical economics discussion of socialism, the "rich material" on the Yugoslav system "in Polish as well as other languages" (Brus 1972: 138), Hungarian reform economic ideas (ibid.: 70, 73, 82), and the ways to build a "market mechanism" into a planned economy.[61] Brus declared, "More now than ever, it is necessary for us to study Western writings on economic planning, especially since we have become concerned with many problems of the functioning of a socialist economy which we did not deal with hitherto" (ibid.: 41). These Eastern European economists shared a training in neoclassical economics that provided both analytical and normative tools for socialism, as well as a common language for a regional discussion of reform.

Furthermore, some Hungarian economists also worked as consultants abroad, which required neoclassical training. For example, András Bródy, one of the most important mathematical economists and earliest practitioners of input-output analysis in Hungary, headed the economics department at the University of Lusaka in Zambia from 1969 to 1972 and then led the Business and Economics Faculty there from 1974 to 1977. He later went on to teach in India, France, Australia, and Japan (Bekker 1999). Tamás Szentes was trained and taught at the Karl Marx University of Economics in Budapest. From 1967 to 1971, he headed the economics department at the University of Dar es Salaam in Tanzania. Then he went on to work in various U.N. expert groups (Corvinus 2009). As mentioned earlier, Szentes "could thank Antal Mátyás," his professor at the Karl Marx University of Economics, for the ability to communicate with his colleagues in the developing world and understand Western economic theory and methods, as well as Marxist economics (1996: 11). In general, Hungarian reform economists had the neoclassical training to work abroad.

The U.S. government also facilitated this return to a transnational neoclassical socialist discussion. In 1964, the Hungarian economists began receiving Ford Foundation fellowships to conduct research and study in the United States. As discussed in Chapter 2, the U.S. government and the Ford Foundation gave priority to exchanges of economists, and specifically mathematical economists, in Hungary to influence the approaching economic reforms. Scholars have generally assumed that such exchanges exported American economics, which would then support capitalism and American economic power abroad, while undermining socialism. Yet, as we have seen in this and previous chapters, neoclassical economics developed within a discussion of various socialisms. The U.S. government in the name of undermining socialism ironically helped to reconnect the market socialist discussion that had been severed by the early Cold War.

Beyond providing grantees money, resources, and time to conduct research, the Ford Foundation also immersed grantees in the American economics profession, which they documented in their final reports to the Ford Foundation.[62] During their usual ten-month visits, they gained firsthand experience with the American university system through affiliation with one or two top-ranked universities. In addition to studying intensively at their affiliated universities, they also visited numerous prestigious campuses throughout the country. Hungarian economists did not arbitrarily choose an American university. They chose a university or universities that had specialists in neoclassical economics of socialism with knowledge of Eastern European socialism. They could as well be certain that other interesting Eastern European economists would also be there. Hungarian economists specifically chose to visit Harvard University, Yale University, Columbia University, Berkeley, and Stanford.[63]

Hungarian economists took part in many activities at universities abroad. Foreign universities' libraries provided grantees the most excitement.[64] All the economists brought books, periodicals, newspapers, data, and other inaccessible items back to Hungary. One economist, András Bródy, wrote, "Originally I had no intention to make any practical computations, that is, I did not dare to dream that my mathematical growth model—besides theoretical discussion—can be also implemented with good statistical data."[65] They went to seminars, gave lectures, and worked with professors. They also learned new skills, including computer programming and input-output modeling.[66] Through exchanges, Hungarian economists immersed themselves in American economics education.

Hungarian economists were introduced to the American economics profession more generally while in the United States. In their final reports to the Ford Foundation, grantees mentioned that they improved their English language skills during their stay, which increased their professional interactions internationally. Grantees attended professional meetings, such as those of the American Economics Association, American Statistical Association, and the Econometric Society. They made extensive professional contacts. They also received a two-year subscription to any journal of their choice when the program ended.[67] Before attending the program, the participants often did not know about the range of institutions and opportunities for economists in the United States.[68] They left the United States knowing the most important American economics departments, as well as the significant practitioners and professional organizations.

Hungarian economists could use the U.S. government and the Ford Foundation to reconnect with American neoclassical economists and rejoin the neoclassical economic discussion of socialism. Economists both in the East and the West focused on policy and mechanism design, studying institutions important to economies and firms. Their focus on mechanism design had emerged from various socialist discussions. Hungarian economists brought their new ideas about market socialism and neoclassical economics to the United States through émigré economists, their professional writings, and their academic visits. Those with training in neoclassical economics could forge these connections not only with economists in the United States but also with their counterparts in the East Bloc and the developing world.

Neoclassical Economics as a Socialist Blueprint

The Hungarian Party-state introduced the New Economic Mechanism on January 1, 1968. The New Economic Mechanism (NEM) fundamentally altered socialist practice in Hungary. Under the NEM, the state retained public ownership of the means of production but abolished the obligatory output targets for enterprises that had been an essential part of Soviet central planning.[69] The NEM restricted state planning to setting the main national economic objectives and the main proportions of economic development (Swain 1992: 99–100). In place of these obligatory administrative means, planners could use indirect financial or economic means to interest enterprises in realizing the plan. Like Lange's market socialist model and like textbook neoclassical economics, enterprises were to act autonomously, except in major investments directed by the government, and were supposed to maximize profit, which would also act as an incentive for enterprises.[70] Some prices were freed from state control, allowing them to fluctuate on a market, while the state fixed other prices. However, as Chapter 6 shows, the Hungarian state in fact continued to intervene directly in the economy.

Scholars outside of Hungary considered the NEM directly relevant to neoclassical economics because it apparently realized Lange's abstract neoclassical market socialism. George R. Feiwel recognized that most Eastern European reform movements did not follow Lange's model, but "the notable exception is Hungary, where the *basic reform construct* bears rather close resemblance to Lange's prewar model" (1972: 604). In comparative economics textbooks in the United States, Hungary after the NEM became a case study of market socialism, meriting it a separate chapter (for example, Bornstein 1974; Neuberger and Duffy 1976).[71]

Hungarian reform economists' visions of reform did differ from Oskar Lange's abstract market socialist model (Feiwel 1972: 604) in ways that further contributed to neoclassical economics. The Hungarian reform used the market to determine prices more extensively than Lange's model did. The Hungarian model did not assume a closed, isolated national economy but rather removed many barriers between the domestic market and the world market. Béla Balassa (1971) argued that the Hungarian model with its competitive market was even better than Lange's model because reform economists recognized that decision making by enterprises, rather than central planners, would lead to the best results—Pareto optimality—if all enterprises were price takers, thus receiving prices as given. However, as Balassa continued, small socialist countries had many monopolies, which made enterprises price makers and thus produced suboptimal results. By opening the economy to the world market, the Hungarian reform made Hungarian enterprises price takers on the world market. Through such innovations, Hungarian reform economists contributed to the transnational dialogue among neoclassical economists.[72]

Hungarian reform economists used neoclassical economics as a blueprint for market socialist reforms in their country and thus helped to reorganize the Hungarian economy to fit their theory.[73] As already discussed, reform economists had developed the notion of an economic mechanism and the varieties of possible mechanisms. They had turned to neoclassical economics, which complemented their market mechanism ideas, because both reflected a common understanding of alternative socialisms critical of the Soviet model and official Marxist-Leninist political economy. Especially after 1956, they then participated in the transnational neoclassical economics discussion that had evolved, since the nineteenth century, around notions of socialism and the market. Reform economists' work displays a sense of consensus about the general vision of reform, as if there was a linear path that the actual reforms embarked on. This shared consensus emerged from a textbook version of neoclassical economics, which both developed based on a socialist model and provided several models for future socialist states. Thus, neoclassical economic models provided plans for reforms. For example, in Hungary, Kornai argued:

True, the theories of the GE [General Equilibrium] school cannot be accepted as an accurate description or explanation of a *real* economy. But it should be accepted as a plan for designing a *new* world. Should the leaders of a country find themselves in a position in which they are able to develop the functional mechanism of their system themselves—as it happened in the drafting of the Hungarian reform—the system should be formulated according to the models of the GE school. ([1971] 1991: 343)

Neoclassical economics provided several plans for socialist societies. Hungarian reform economists and socialist economists elsewhere shaped reforms with neoclassical economics in mind. Hungarian reform economists brought their visions of true reform either directly or indirectly to the official committees drafting economic reforms.

The NEM also realized a new economy with new kinds of economic actors and new roles for economists within it (Bockman 2000). As Kemenes noticed, "In 1968 when the reform was introduced, the economists' new role became institutionalized. The economic way of thinking, using quantitative terms and observing economic laws and interdependencies, gained ground" (1981: 583). Economists, whom the pre-1953 Rákosi regime had marginalized in favor of engineers and theoretical political economists, now played a central role in the NEM reforms and gained numerous benefits. Most importantly, reform economists became the main experts in the new system.[74]

Though they benefited from the NEM, reform economists soon recognized its narrow nature and called for further reforms that would realize decentralizing institutions. Márton Tardos argued that the NEM was supposed to have also removed obstacles to cooperative and small-scale private activities, ended restrictions in interenterprise trade, freed prices and enterprises from state intervention, and expanded the democratic rights of workers to influence enterprise operations (1982: 297). In the 1970s, neoclassical economics, instead, was used to recentralize the socialist economy and increase the power of the Communist Party, as opposed to workers. Lange's market socialist ideas and the general market socialist interest in spreading economic rationality were also not necessarily in the interest of the workers.[75] In the Hungarian description of the NEM, Friss argued that "one of the main features of our new system [is] the extension and strengthening of our socialist democracy" (1969: 38). Yet the NEM increased the power of the Party and the managers at the helm of monopolistic enterprises. As a result, the NEM realized neoclassically based market socialism but in a way that reinforced hierarchy and did not achieve the socialist political goals of ending worker exploitation and achieving economic democracy.

Conclusions

The criticism of Soviet state socialism and the attempt to create market socialism provided new opportunities for small numbers of Hungarian economists to recreate their profession. These reform economists gained new professional institutions and political resources to spread their ideas throughout the profession. Rather than working in an ad hoc and isolated manner, as is often argued, reform economists developed new concepts that fit well with neoclassical economic trends in the United States and Western Europe, as well as elsewhere in Eastern Europe, and they joined a transnational dialogue among neoclassically trained economists. Building on their own experiences at home, reform economists contributed to this dialogue, especially as principal-agent theory, policy design, and mechanism design became important in American neoclassical economics. By 1968, reform economists helped to shape the New Economic Mechanism reform, which created an internationally recognized form of market socialism. Economists' frustrations with the narrowness of the reform and the political backlash against further reforms would lead economists to participate in a global criticism of neoclassical economics and hierarchical institutions in both socialism and capitalism. This is the topic of Chapter 6. The next chapter, Chapter 5, examines a liminal organization that brought together economists and other social scientists critical of Soviet socialism and Western capitalism, providing a venue for a transnational discussion about socialisms.

5

The International Left, the International Right, and the Study of Socialism in Italy

AFTER THREE CHAPTERS ON ECONOMISTS and their emerging transnational discussion, this chapter focuses on one institutional location where this neoclassical discussion about socialism took place, an Italian think tank funded by transnational and Italian right-wing institutions.[1] Scholars have commonly assumed that transnational networks of right-wing scholars and activists converted the world to neoliberalism. The case of the Center for the Study of Economic and Social Problems (CESES, pronounced *chay-sis*)[2] in Milan, Italy was, to all appearances, just such a right-wing think tank controlled by transnational right-wing activists. However, scholars on the left filled such liminal organizations as CESES, creating new knowledge about a variety of socialisms.

Confindustria, the primary association representing private industry in Italy, created and funded CESES to check not only the influence of the Italian Communist Party but also the influence of a number of Italian capitalists who supported economic planning and experimental forms of socialism, such as the typewriter manufacturer and publisher Adriano Olivetti and the millionaire publisher Giangiacomo Feltrinelli. Functioning from 1964 to 1988, CESES sought to create a new managerial class that supported capitalism and rejected communism by showing members of this class the failures of socialism and the demand for market reforms in Eastern Europe. Members of the Mont Pelerin Society, the transnational network in support of free markets and a limited state, organized and participated in CESES activities. In his memoirs, Milton Friedman

(Friedman and Friedman 1998) presented CESES as part of a broader pro-free-market transnational network centered around himself. Friedman referred to CESES as "the Mont Pelerin Society of the East," which was founded "to promote free-market ideas" (ibid.: 338–339). Milton Friedman, Warren Nutter, and other members of the American New Right that emerged with the Goldwater campaign were active participants in CESES activities. American right-wing foundations also funded CESES.[3] CESES published translations of Hayek, Friedman, and other members of the Mont Pelerin Society in Italian. Warren Nutter wrote in 1968:

> I know of few activities with greater potential payoff for a relatively tiny investment than the conferences and contacts now being arranged through Mieli [the head of CESES]. In many respects, the hope of the West lies in the East. The best prospect for halting the plunge of the West into collectivism is revolt against communism in the East. It would be romantic to expect any single activity to move the course of history, but drops of water can wear away stone if properly concentrated.[4]

The transnational neoliberal network controlled by right-wing activists considered CESES an essential element in the fight to protect and spread capitalism.

The case of CESES, however, reveals that neoliberal ideas did not emerge from Western or American hegemony but from liminal spaces between and beyond American capitalism and Soviet state socialism.[5] In contrast to the usual focus on the actions and plans of the transnational right and/or American activists, this research focuses on the intentions and actions of Italians within their historical and political context. As the previous chapters have shown, Eastern European economists were not passive recipients of American knowledge; groups of them had already begun to study markets and neoclassical economics by the 1950s as tools for building socialism. In fact, Eastern Europeans more broadly had continued a difficult dialogue about socialism with their counterparts in other Eastern European countries, Western Europe, and the United States. At the same time, scholars recognized that transnational right-wing networks and American economists wielded much more power and many more resources than those in Italy and Eastern Europe and thus could fundamentally alter local political contexts. How are we to make sense of these contradictory trends?

With the American backlash against McCarthyism and the Soviet backlash against Stalinism, as well as the emergence of new social movements and new social actors in the early to mid-1950s, groups criticized both Western capitalism and Soviet state socialism and expanded liminal spaces within, between, and beyond these Cold War poles with discussions of alternatives and new institutions like CESES. These spaces were not some homogeneous "Third Way"; they were made up of heterogeneous individuals and groups working along the borders between the Cold War systems, seeking to understand Soviet-style state socialism and divine alternative or dissident socialisms, which they might connect with and build on. As one CESES organizer said, these spaces formed "a galaxy without borders." The left—such as, but not only, Maoists, Trotskyists, market socialists, and libertarian socialists—dominated these liminal spaces because they had the skills, connections, and motivation to do so. Therefore, while most accounts assume the diffusion of preexisting neoliberalism as ideology from the West to the Rest, in fact, neoliberalism developed within liminal spaces, in which the participants created new forms of social scientific, historical, and philosophical knowledge.[6] Knowledge about the Other—Soviet socialism or Western capitalism—could not be obtained directly but rather had to develop within liminal spaces.[7] Working in liminal spaces allowed those on the left in the East and the West to understand actually existing socialism and what socialism could become. The transnational right would later reinterpret this "galaxy without borders" as homogeneous and capitalist, but they could only succeed in this appropriation from a stable hegemonic location, which did not yet exist within the shifting political, economic, social, and cultural context of the 1960s and 1970s. The CESES case shows that the ideas and experiments of the dissident left worldwide, and especially those from Eastern Europe, sit at the heart of neoliberalism.

CESES

Founded in 1964 in Milan, Italy, CESES started with a budget equivalent to $1.2 million in 2006 dollars.[8] A powerful group of Italian industrialists in Confindustria provided the majority of the funding to CESES. They decided to create CESES "to break the monopoly which, in the absence of competitive initiatives, the extreme left has succeeded in establishing . . . among the Italian intellectuals most committed and active in political life."[9] According to the logic of the Confindustria leadership, the most effective way to undermine communism and the left was to teach people about the goals of Soviet socialism and to show how Soviet socialism had failed to reach these goals. CESES was "to introduce to our country's cultural and entrepreneurial milieu—as far as possible—exact knowledge of socialism, understood not as a utopia projected into the future, but rather as a reality already experimented with for a long time in various countries."[10] These conservative industrialists believed that the Italian people, and especially the elites, had to learn about Marxist-Leninist theories and the realities of already existing socialism in the East Bloc to persuade them to support liberal democracy and the market economy at home.[11] To achieve these goals, CESES had three main activities: Sovietology courses and conferences, Sovietology publications, and anticommunist youth leadership training.[12]

Liminal Spaces, Liminal People

Almost immediately, regional members of Confindustria balked at the costs of CESES, and its supporters criticized CESES. Regional Confindustria offices paid the CESES budget through annual subscriptions. They also recommended young students from their regions as participants in CESES activities. When CESES met with Confindustria regional leaders to ask for financial support, these leaders claimed to support the goals of CESES, but they did not want to pay their subscription fees for the organization. Instead, they wanted to use these funds to support certain candidates in local election campaigns and other local political activities. Within the first year and a half, the CESES budget was cut by 40 million lire, about 25 percent.[13]

Confindustria members not only cut the budget but also began to question whether CESES was actually anticommunist. A high-level Confindustria officer attended an international economics conference run by CESES and found that the conference did not "fully adhere to the institutional task of anti-communism, which CESES claims."[14] Confindustria continued to fund CESES, but these criticisms accumulated. A participant in the youth training courses reported that there were "elements oriented to the left" in the courses and the teachers were often left-wing.[15] This criticism forced the CESES leadership to try to sell the idea of CESES once again to the regional offices of Confindustria.[16] A regional leader in Confindustria told the CESES organizers that critics had informed him that the whole ambiance of CESES had taken a turn to the left.[17] Confindustria finally stopped paying for CESES in 1976, though CESES continued to function until 1988. What was going on at CESES?

CESES was created in the liminal space that opened up within, between, and beyond Western capitalism and Soviet socialism after the McCarthy trials and the death of Joseph Stalin in the 1950s. In his famous 1956 criticism of Stalin, Soviet leader Nikita Khrushchev opened the door to reevaluating the Soviet past and suggesting other socialist pathways. Importantly, the new negative label of "Stalinism" for the earlier system allowed the first socialist critiques of the Soviet system as a whole (Strada 1988: 28) and motivated thought about other forms of socialism. Slovenian philosopher Slavoj Žižek has commented on this phenomenon:

Although the Communist regimes, in their positive content, were mostly a dismal failure, generating terror and misery, they simultaneously opened up a certain space, the space of utopian expectations, which, among other things, enabled us to measure the failure of actually existing Socialism itself. (2001: 131)

Žižek argues that, in its "attempt to escape the logic of capitalism," communism itself opened and sustained this space (1999: 9). Similarly, as Falk argues, democratic socialist criticism of existing Communist regimes emerged from a radical and democratic reading of Marxism-Leninism (2003: 25, 61). Yet, the principally negative nature of this criticism, as anti-Stalinist, meant that this liminal space could contain many positive alternatives and traditions. In the United States, the civil rights movement, criticism of capitalist alienation and mass society, and the emerging peace movement similarly opened critical and heterogeneous liminal spaces within liberal democratic capitalism.

The shifting context allowed for liminal individuals and spaces to appear. As one of these spaces, CESES brought together people with politics outside the usual Cold War dichotomies—including former Communists, anti-Soviet socialists, libertarians, anarchists, Eastern European reformers, and Eastern European émigrés—to discuss the nature of socialism, both actually existing and possible future socialisms. In the Cold War, those at CESES had charismatic and dangerous access to Cold War enemies in a world entering into the 1960s and 1970s.

Liminal spaces emerged in Italy precisely because it had a strong Communist party. The revelations of Khrushchev and then the Soviet intervention in Hungary in 1956 caused thousands to leave the Italian Communist Party (PCI).[18] A liminal space emerged as communists rejected the PCI without embracing the party in power, the right-wing Democratic Christian Party (DC), the two main poles in Italian politics. The main founders of CESES were themselves former PCI members: Renato

Mieli, Vittorio De Biasi, and Carlo Ripa di Meana. In the PCI, Mieli had worked directly with Palmiero Togliatti, the party leader, and became the director of the Milanese edition of the party newspaper *L'Unita* (Mieli 1996). Ripa di Meana was the editor of *World Student News*, the major publication of the communist International Union of Students, published in Prague. Mieli and Ripa di Meana left the PCI around 1957, in response to the Soviet repression of the Hungarian uprising (Ripa di Meana 2000). After leaving the PCI, Mieli joined a research center sponsored jointly by the Edison Company and Confindustria, working with Vittorio De Biasi, who had been a close colleague of the famous Marxist Antonio Gramsci and was now a powerful, "visceral anticommunist" leader of the Edison Company (Mieli 1996: 124–125). Ex-PCI members were not trusted by others because their political orientation was not clear.[19] For example, these three figures relentlessly criticized the PCI and the Communist Party of the Soviet Union, while Mieli also declared in 1964 that he was one of the "militants of the Italian workers' movement" and continued to speak at socialist conferences until at least 1988.[20] Mieli repeatedly declared that he was inspired by Khrushchev's revelations about Stalin and was not "anti-communist": "For the same reasons that I became an anti-fascist, I could not feel an anti-communist" (Mieli 1996: 99).[21] Mieli became the director of CESES and its driving force. The founders of CESES did not show a clear anticommunist, antileft identity, although they opposed, like many on the left, the PCI.

This space of former PCI members linked up with an already existing, small anti-Soviet socialist culture in Italy. Italy has had a long history of attempts to create different forms of democratic socialism, which both fascism and the Cold War hindered.[22] For CESES, liberal socialist Andrea Caffi was particularly important.[23] The main biographer of Caffi, Gino Bianco, headed the history section at CESES, while other socialists headed other sections. Giorgio Galli was the head of the sociology section, and Carlo Ripa di Meana ran the cultural section.[24] Reflecting the general atmosphere of CESES, Caffi followed a kind of Proudhonian socialism, an anarchism that rejected the state, corporations, centralization, rationalization, scientific planning, nationalism, and political parties (Bianco 1977). As described positively by a young CESES participant, Caffi supported "direct socialist action to increase the social control of bureaucratic mechanisms and of the oligarchic power of industrial corporations. Only in such a way is it humanly possible to protect the freedom of the individual" (Monti-Bragadin 1971: 62). Caffi argued for the long-term subversive potential of grassroots, underground counterculture, consisting of networks of small groups of individuals, practicing and preaching the Enlightenment virtues of cosmopolitan sociability: friendship, equality, mutuality, tolerance, and open dialogue (Sumner 1996: 150). CESES can thus be seen as an attempt to put Caffi's liberal socialism into practice.[25]

Others within the liminal space did not define themselves as on the left but as "liberals." Reflecting this group, the head of the research section, Renato Pavetto, and the head of the economics section, Giovanni Salvini, came from the newspaper funded by Confindustria, *Il Sole 24 Ore*. Though he never joined another political party after leaving the PCI, Mieli would eventually define himself as a liberal and join the Mont Pelerin Society. Some participants saw the goal of CESES as building "a liberal culture" in Italy.[26] At the same time, a few participants defined themselves as "liberal" only because they would listen to others, as opposed to extremists who would not.[27] In general, however, liberals in Europe primarily supported economic and political liberalism.

While this emerging liminal space was liminal precisely because its members had such differing views, they did share some characteristics. These individuals were strongly anti-PCI, anti-Soviet, antifascist, often anarchist, and often opposed to the political and cultural power of the Catholic Church.[28] Because they often rejected all the existing political parties, many worked in universities, think tanks, journals, and other areas of cultural work in Italy, rather than as politicians.[29] They thus had a great influence on Italian culture (Bobbio [1997] 1999: 83; Teodori 1998: xxvii). They sought to change Italy fundamentally, to move beyond the fascist past, avoid future totalitarianism, and create a new society.[30] In their view, empirical research was an essential part of this new society because, reflecting the influence of Karl Popper's *The Open Society and Its Enemies* ([1945] 1950), dialogue and empirical testing of hypotheses would reveal the lies of ideologies and totalitarianism.[31] They criticized the PCI and "Italian culture" for their commitment to the historicism they found in the work of Karl Marx and Italian intellectual Benedetto Croce, their rejection of modern social science, and, as Italian writer Italo Calvino asserted, having "given us so little with which to understand the world" (Sassoon 1996: 262). Finally, those occupying this liminal space were also interested in European East–West convergence and sought contacts with Eastern Europeans in the Soviet bloc in the hopes that discussions and friendships would make a world war more difficult and would lay the groundwork for reunited Europe.[32] CESES shared these qualities and was one of many such institutions in Italy.

Eastern Europeans, both at home and abroad, brought new knowledge and politics to CESES and other transnationally connected liminal spaces. While some Eastern European dissidents openly condemned Communist Parties, other, more "reform-minded" Eastern Europeans, as Žižek (1999) has observed, did not make these overt condemnations and thus were more useful for East–West dialogues inspired by dreams of détente and convergence, like those at CESES. Former dissident émigrés were deeply divided politically, ranging from "voices truly frightening in their vehement and blind hatred of everything modern, everything progressive, achieved in Russia and throughout the world since the age of Enlightenment" to those who supported democratic socialism in the Soviet Union and elsewhere (Deutscher 1977). More "reform-minded" Eastern European émigrés, rather than vehement anticommunists, played a central role in CESES. These émigrés who participated in CESES activities included Alec Nove, Václav Bělohradský, Andrzej Brzeski, Alfons Clary-Aldringen, Jiří Pelikán, and Eugène Zaleski. Émigrés brought firsthand information about the East Bloc and had a great deal of passion about the events going on in the region.

Americans were also part of these transnationally connected liminal spaces. Many American scholars, often Eastern European émigrés, took part in international conferences to bring together those from the West and East. These scholars included members of the American New Right, who saw those in the Italian liminal space—and in other similar spaces worldwide—as anticommunist, antistate, and pro–free market allies. They did not necessarily understand the heterogeneous nature of this space, communicating in English with the CESES founders who needed funding and who thus had an interest in presenting CESES as a location of stable right-wing identities and allies. Coming from the American political landscape, the American New Right interpreted liminal spaces as allies because it identified the American Left with state-directed programs. The Italian political landscape was much more fragmented and more heterogeneous than that in the United States dominated by just two political parties.[33]

Through the 1960s and 1970s, these liminal spaces expanded. Individuals within these spaces were not centrist or on a slippery slope toward neoconservativism, as in the case of the New York Intellectuals.[34] They formed a heterogeneous network, "a galaxy without borders," that shared some essential characteristics.[35] CESES was one of many institutions that brought heterogeneous groups into dialogue to understand socialism and capitalism, as well as to consider alternative democratic socialisms. The shifting context of the Cold War that allowed this galaxy to emerge would continue to change with the emergence of post-Fordism, new social actors, new social movements, and reforms in Eastern Europe. The nature of this space could be perceived as homogeneous only from some stable political location that would appear to exist only after 1989.

Sovietology and Liminality

The Confindustria leadership funded CESES to counter the PCI, by confronting the world with "what communism is."[36] To do so, CESES imported American Sovietology to Italy. In the United States and Western Europe, Sovietologists, as discussed in the second chapter, studied the Soviet Union and socialist Eastern Europe. Created within the emerging Cold War and the politics of the McCarthy era, American Sovietology, with its theory of totalitarianism, criticized only the Soviet Union, did not criticize the American system, viewed the Soviet Union as fundamentally different—culturally, economically, socially, and politically—from Western countries, claimed moral superiority of the West over the Soviets, and had a knee-jerk anticommunism (Gleason 1995; Meyer 1993). In the minds of the Confindustria and CESES leadership, American Sovietology seemed to provide the perfect antidote to Soviet socialism, the PCI, and the left more generally, but this leadership would soon be disappointed.

The founders of CESES created a Sovietological center that examined the economics, politics, sociology, and history of the East Bloc. CESES began operations with an annual international economics conference to spread knowledge about the Soviet Bloc worldwide. The two- to three-day conferences were held annually in various cities around Italy from 1964 to 1984 and were reported in the mainstream Italian press. At these conferences, internationally recognized experts discussed the Soviet and Eastern European economies. After the first year, Eastern European economists also took part in these conferences. In addition to economics conferences and an economics research section, CESES also held conferences and had research sections covering the sociology, history, and legal systems of the East Bloc. These conferences and the work of the sections were intended to develop and publicize the most up-to-date knowledge about the realities of Soviet socialism and the PCI, as well as to interest a new cohort of recent college students (*laureandi* and *laureati*) and new professors (*assistenti*) in Sovietological research and teaching. To further this research, CESES created an archive of documents about communist movements and a large library, which in its first six months acquired 1,500 volumes, as well as journals from around the world. CESES editors translated and reprinted articles from the top American Sovietological journals *Problems of Communism* and *Soviet Studies*, along with articles by Italians, in their own Sovietological journal, *L'Est*. CESES also published a bulletin of translated articles from the Soviet and Eastern European press, *Documentazione sui Paesi dell'Est*.[37] Within a year of its opening, CESES was a fully functioning center for Sovietological research.[38]

The international economics conferences run by CESES evoked doubts, however, in the minds of its right-wing funders. To the funders, the conferences appeared sympathetic toward communism. For example, as mentioned earlier, one high-level Confindustria officer found that the third international economics conference did not "fully adhere to the institutional task of anti-communism, which CESES claims."[39] There were several reasons why CESES appeared sympathetic toward communism.

In interviews, former CESES participants agreed that CESES used its conferences and publications as "elegant propaganda" or "clever propaganda," but they did not specify for what cause.[40] To these participants, CESES was not overtly anticommunist but rather "pragmatic" and "objective."[41] Mieli sought to show how socialism functioned in Eastern Europe and used Eastern European economists as witnesses to the problems in Eastern European planning to provide intellectually sophisticated proof for the failure of Soviet socialism. However, this scholarly proof did not yet exist in a form simple enough to be packaged as ideology. With the changes in the post-Stalinist period in the Soviet Bloc, it was difficult to know what would happen in the Soviet Union and Eastern Europe. Would Stalinism be reintroduced? Would there be anti-Stalinist revolutions in the region as there were in East Germany in 1953 and Hungary in 1956? Would economic reforms fundamentally change Soviet socialism? As a result, Sovietologists had to study a moving target and could no longer make simple claims about communism. As one newspaper reporter recounted about one of the CESES conferences, "It is difficult to draw conclusions from these conversations . . . the opinions of the experts differ greatly, they say here that it is time to discard simplistic or 'sensational' hypotheses."[42]

By 1960, Sovietologists in the United States and elsewhere had begun a revolution in their own field, condemning the totalitarian framework that had previously dominated Sovietology and calling for comparative politics and comparative economics.[43] As a result of their original totalitarian framework and its structural functionalist assumptions, Sovietologists had presented the Soviet Union as an unchanging system; in their view, the functional subsystems of Stalinism did not have a reason to change. After Khrushchev's attack on Stalin, Sovietologists recognized the shortcomings of the static totalitarian model and sought new tools to understand the changing East Bloc. These new tools were those of mainstream social science, which assumed similar institutions and processes in the East and West. In addition, the East Bloc itself could no longer be described homogeneously. In Hungary, Poland, and Yugoslavia, for example, the Party-state leadership implemented market economic reforms, allowed dissident communities, and witnessed political movements and revolutions. Within Sovietology, those in Eastern European Studies followed these new developments with interest and were considered less conservative than those studying the Soviet Union. The turn away from the totalitarian framework and structural functionalism and toward mainstream social science tools and a focus on Eastern Europe created a new kind of Sovietology in the 1960s.

While CESES covered many areas of Sovietology, it was the only Italian institution that had a research focus on socialist economies.[44] In the 1950s and 1960s, the study of the Soviet Union and Eastern Europe was virtually impossible in Italian universities. Sovietology had a controversial history in Italy. University professors and many others were suspicious of imported American social science and empiricism more generally, which greatly informed the new Sovietology.[45] Comparative politics, which included political Sovietology, entered the universities in the 1960s after much resistance (Morlino 1991). On the economics side of Sovietology, university faculty did not want students to learn Marxist economics, and no one taught Soviet economics.[46] The first comparative economics courses, which covered economic Sovietology, were not taught until 1970.[47] Moreover, Italy had no formal graduate training in any field until the 1980s (Cotta 1996: 340). Italian social scientists began teaching in universities after completing their undergraduate degrees. Because there was no university training in Sovietology, CESES provided previously unavailable training and teaching resources, including its international conferences, published proceedings from these conferences, its translations of the Eastern European press, and its Sovietological journal.

CESES can be seen as one of many institutions—others included Harvard University's Russian Research Center and Columbia University's Russian Institute—simultaneously creating the new Sovietology based on broader changes in the social sciences and in Eastern Europe. Until Stalin's death in 1953, there had been very few interactions between the capitalist and socialist blocs, and thus little information flowed between them. After 1953, scholarly exchanges and other forms of travel were allowed, but it was still difficult to get information about what was happening in Eastern Europe beyond the official sources.[48] Existing books and articles on the region did not provide enough information to assist potential teachers or researchers. As one CESES participant noted, right-wing and left-wing evaluations of Eastern Europe were not helpful because the right-wing ones were polemically negative and the left-wing ones were naïvely apologetic. Reading hundreds of books and articles did not replace talking with Eastern Europeans at CESES conferences or reading the proceedings of these conferences.[49] Informal discussions with Eastern Europeans, where Eastern Europeans seemed to speak more freely, were especially appreciated by the Italian and American scholars. American scholars particularly benefited from CESES conferences because U.S. visa restrictions allowed them even less contact with Eastern European scholars or Eastern European Communist Party members than Italian scholars had.[50] CESES participants provided scarce and invaluable information and translated this information for one side or the other during the Cold War. As one French participant in CESES conferences remembered, "We as go-betweens were happy to translate their contributions into formulations understandable by Western economists" (Lavigne 1997: 481). Scholars practicing the new Sovietology—no matter what their personal political predilections—required heterogeneous networks meeting in liminal spaces like CESES.

Solutions found in the East were seen as applicable in Italy because Italians considered Italy and Eastern Europe as similar. In Italy, as well as elsewhere, there was a great deal of interest in Sovietology. Like the countries of Eastern Europe, Italy had a strong Communist Party. Italy and parts of Eastern Europe had similar levels of industrial development and similar economic problems. Therefore, Eastern European economic reforms could provide lessons for the Italians. A report about a CESES conference stated, "There is no doubt that the Italian reader will find material for reflection and new stimulation to rethink the problems which are also ours."[51] At a CESES conference in 1964, Minister of Finance Pieraccini gave a speech in support of planning. According to the report of a high-level Confindustria official, the minister of finance said:

The Italian government is involved in a grand work, in which the Italian economy will be governed according to an economic plan: he views sympathetically the study of the themes which examine the foreign experiences because our programming should be democratically open to active participation of the people in economic choices.[52]

Italians affiliated with various socialist parties were also great supporters of nationalization and planning (Sassoon 1996: 268), although, as the minister of finance declared, many people were interested in democratic socialism. Thus, Sovietology remained relevant to Italians.

While CESES activities brought together people with a wide range of political orientations, those who identified with the left were the most successful in CESES activities. Those on the left could most easily cross the Cold War divide and speak with a range of individuals with direct knowledge of actually existing socialism. The main organizers and many of the employees of CESES had spent significant amounts of time in the Soviet Union and socialist Eastern Europe, where they had seen actually existing socialism in operation and met Eastern Europeans critical of the Stalinist system. Renato Mieli had frequented the East Bloc while he worked for the PCI. When Carlo Ripa di Meana (2000) worked in Prague, he met many dissidents and visiting Italians interested in meeting dissidents. Dario Staffa, Russian translator and journal editor at CESES, worked at the Casa di Cultura in Moscow and learned then about Russian dissident literature.[53] Those on the left also studied socialist theory and practice, which helped their research. As one participant in CESES activities remembered, those interested in market socialism learned socialist doctrine because

the doctrine was a kind of code; once the code was deciphered it was much easier to understand the books and articles and to read between the lines, an exercise we were all familiar with. Also, for Western economists who wanted and managed to travel to these countries and meet their colleagues, knowledge of the doctrinal code facilitated access to sources and to institutions. (Lavigne 1997: 480–481)

Knowing "the code" and having a left-wing sensibility allowed for contact with Eastern Europeans.[54] In addition to knowing "the code," those on the left who had lived in the East Bloc had language abilities that enabled them to communicate with a variety of Eastern Europeans. These language abilities were also essential to the work of CESES. Employees read the Eastern European press on a daily basis in search of articles for *Documentazione sui Paesi dell'Est*, a journal published every two weeks and containing articles from the Czech, Chinese, Yugoslav, Polish, Hungarian, and Soviet press.[55]

Those on the left also often had the most interest in Eastern Europe. For example, Carlo Ripa di Meana agreed to work with Mieli to set up CESES to conduct Sovietological research, "A task which I found fascinating . . . I had had the occasion to see from the inside the society of my dreams" (Ripa di Meana 2000: 119). Participants in CESES conferences reported that the Italian students there were generally on the left and sympathetic to socialist countries.[56] One economist who was at CESES numerous times said that the Americans were "boring" because they only collected facts from the Eastern Europeans.[57] Those on the left at CESES conferences saw themselves working together with Eastern Europeans on a common project of what we might call market socialism or democratic socialism. One participant in CESES remembered, "for those of us—a minority [in economics]—who believed in a 'feasible socialism', all that revolved around 'market socialism' (including its critics) was significant" (Lavigne 1997: 480). This interest in Eastern Europe and new forms of socialism drove those on the left to a dialogue with their counterparts in Eastern Europe.

For economists, the fascination with market socialism generally covered two broad areas, innovations in planning and innovations in markets, including worker self-management. These represented very different, and often conflicting, understandings of socialism. As discussed in Chapter 2, neoclassical economists since the late nineteenth century had understood that purely competitive market economies and centrally planned socialist economies were mathematically equivalent. Assuming this equivalence, neoclassical economists in the East and the West had developed econometrics, linear programming, and theories of price formation based on neoclassical economics. By the late 1950s, the Soviets and Eastern Europeans began to use econometrics, linear programming, and theories of prices to study their own economies, and they experimented with planning using these methods.[58] Western European and American economists were fascinated in these experiments and the difficulties experienced.

Western European and American economists were also interested in market experimentation in Eastern Europe. As discussed in Chapter 2, because central planning and the Soviet Union were perceived as central to neoclassical economics, neoclassical economists in the East and the West also incorporated various socialisms, including decentralized market socialist models and the new Eastern European market socialist experiments, into the center of neoclassical economics. CESES started just as Eastern Europe was implementing major economic reforms. For example, in 1968, Hungary created a market mechanism within its planning system. At CESES conferences, Eastern European economists were invited to make presentations about these reforms and the difficulties involved. These experiments into how markets functioned within various planning and managerial structures had never been done before, and they provided new knowledge about the institutional requirements for markets. Even more exciting for the participants were discussions of worker self-management experiments in Yugoslavia and East Germany. Milton Friedman himself visited Yugoslav factories in 1967 and 1973 to pursue his interest in systems of worker ownership and self-management (Friedman and Friedman 1998: 423–424).[59] There was a common interest in nonstate institutions to escape the oppression of the state in both the East and the West. The market socialist experiments in Eastern Europe interested Western economists because these experiments offered new knowledge about planning, markets, and worker self-management, as well as about neoclassical economics.

To its funders, CESES seemed sympathetic to communism also because the new Sovietology produced a new kind of scholarly interaction. Confindustria members and the CESES organizers wanted to include Eastern European participants as "witnesses" to the failures of communism whose calls for reforms, often market reforms, provided "validation of the capitalist and market economy."[60] Eastern Europeans were assumed to be naïve witnesses who did not understand Western economics but merely reported the facts from the communist world (Bockman and Eyal 2002). Yet, to the Confindustria leadership, the Eastern Europeans and other participants did not seem procapitalist. According to one report, the conference presenters from Austria, Belgium, Bulgaria, Czechoslovakia, West Germany, Britain, Yugoslavia, Poland, and Romania sought only to convince others of the existence of a "third way" between liberal and Marxist economics.[61] The Westerners response to these ideas disturbed this high-level Confindustria official: "The scholars of the West present at the meeting seemed all pervaded by a strong dose of good faith credulity, which is upsetting." To him, it would have been logical to "refuse hospitality" to the Eastern European "Marxists."[62] In fact, "no one at this meeting had thought to propose the verification of the postulates of this so-called Marxist theory."[63] Yet, the CESES leadership sought a new kind of East–West interaction. In response to demands that CESES participants automatically condemn any Marxist ideas, Vittorio De Biasi responded:

We would betray our duty, would lose our task, if we limited ourselves to the "instrumentalist" teaching, without having first confronted and resolved the problem of knowledge, deeply studying that which has been the basis of the most tragic tyranny of all times.[64]

Reporting on a CESES event, one newspaper reporter wrote that Sovietology "becomes a proposal of civility through approaching communism and its realizations with a new, modern attitude and interests, . . . humanistically, relegating to the past the place of ideological brawls, political dilettantism, pathological mistrust."[65] Sovietology provided an arena for knowledge production based on a new form of East–West scholarly interaction.

This Sovietological discussion, however, was not by any means easy. The participants had to work to obtain knowledge they could use within the changing terrain of the Cold War world: They had to "read between the lines," seek ways to talk informally, build some kind of common language, try not to offend each other, deal with "voices truly frightening" coming from certain right-wing émigrés, endure speakers participating for political rather than professional reasons, recognize that visa restrictions would keep some speakers away, and make sense of the knowledge and often depressing news emerging out of Eastern Europe. This discussion would develop a new Sovietology, which depended on skills, experiences, knowledge, and specific interests of those identified with the left working within a liminal space. The necessity of social ties and trust across the Cold War border for Sovietological knowledge production meant that CESES participants were politically ambiguous and potentially dangerous.[66] The right-wing hegemonic project to use ideologically secure Sovietology to proselytize against communism was undermined by the changing nature of the Cold War, the revolution in Sovietology, and heterogeneous nature of transnationally connected liminal spaces.[67] The potentially liberatory nature of Sovietological knowledge would become apparent in CESES's youth training programs.

Youth Training Seminars

Mieli and the other founders of CESES gave priority to Sovietological research because they needed more knowledge about the Soviet Bloc to make strong, scholarly anticommunist arguments and because they personally wanted to know more.[68] At the same time, the Confindustria leaders wanted a new managerial elite indoctrinated into anticommunism and liberal democracy. They criticized Mieli for focusing on Sovietological research rather than on training this new managerial elite (Pistolese 1996: 6). They successfully—though temporarily—forced CESES to make the youth training seminars its primary activity.[69] However, with the changing nature of Sovietology and the shifting political, economic, social, and cultural context, this indoctrination depended on left-wing participation and had consequences unintended by Confindustria.

There were two main youth training programs: one for only Italians and another for both Italians and Americans. The Italian youth training program began in 1966 and continued until 1976. The program worked on a two-year cycle. In the first year, fifty or so youths (preferably undergraduate students [*laureandi*] or graduates working in university departments [*laureati*]) would take the first introductory course that would last two weeks. After that first course, twenty-five to forty-five participants would be selected to continue with the training, taking four two-week courses culminating in a group research project. From this course, some would be chosen to conduct individual research projects funded by scholarships. Each year, a new group of students would start in this program.[70] The other youth training program brought Italians and American students together to learn specifically about Sovietology for two weeks each year. These Italian–American meetings were organized by Warren Nutter, a Sovietologist at the University of Virginia and a leader in the American New Right, and were funded in part by right-wing foundations. These meetings took place annually from 1967 to 1977 (Mieli 1996). Both of the youth training programs invited speakers to lecture on specific topics and chose students from all parts of Italy in hopes of spreading the impact of the programs throughout the country.

Like the international economic conferences, the youth training seminars did not function as Confindustria had intended. Confindustria members participating in these courses found themselves confused and angered. One "bitterly disappointed" participant in the courses reported that (1) the courses were too short to deal with any topic sufficiently, (2) the students were not all well prepared for the courses, (3) there were "elements oriented to the left" in the courses, and (4) the teachers were sometimes insufficiently prepared and also often left-wing.[71] Within Confindustria, there were "insistent voices" that saw CESES "as promoting the training of the left."[72] Another member warned that Vittorio De Biasi, as one of the leaders of CESES, might not be aware of the real workings of the courses because the courses had a completely different character when he visited.[73]

The instructors for the Italian–American meetings were primarily from CESES's international economics conferences, while the Italian-only program was mainly taught by Italians. In response to criticisms of the Italian instructors, Vittorio De Biasi stated that it had always been difficult to get teachers with any deep knowledge of Sovietology or Marxism-Leninism. De Biasi recognized, "There is no doubt that among the invited teachers there are those of the 'left,'" but at the same time all were unsympathetic to communism.[74] The instructors included Giorgio Galli; Lucio Colletti, an ex-communist and director of the journal *La Sinistra*, a journal funded by the extraparliamentary left and noted for publishing instructions for making Molotov cocktails (Galli 2000: 108); Leo Valiani, who had left the PCI with the Hitler-Stalin Pact in 1939 and remained on the left;[75] Gustav Wetter, a Jesuit Sovietologist, one of the foremost scholars of Soviet philosophy and a participant in the Korcula Summer School in Yugoslavia (Comey 1967; Ramet 1985: 306; van der Zweerde 2003); Ugo Finetti, who wrote on dissent within the PCI, criticized the Italian party system and became a high-level PSI official in the Lombardy region;[76] Giulio Seniga, a former high-level PCI official who remained on the left;[77] and Paolo Spriano, an official in the PCI and historian of the PCI (Galli 2000: 164).[78] There were also instructors from more conservative liminal spaces including Bruno Leoni, Augusto Del Noce, and Italy's prominent political scientists, Giovanni Sartori and Nicola Matteucci. CESES chose instructors who had the skills, experiences, and knowledge of the anticommunist left, as well as those from other liminal spaces, necessary to create not only the new Sovietology but also knowledge about left-wing politics in Italy.

The main topics in the courses for the Italian students were Sovietology, political science, and the philosophy of science. CESES, perhaps paradoxically, chose to indoctrinate the youths into capitalism through the introductory course "Marxism: Theory and Practice":

1st Monday: (1) Genesis of historical materialism in the thinking of the young Marx up until Engels, (2) the evolution of Marxist philosophy in the USSR: The contribution of Lenin and Stalin.

1st Tuesday: (1) systematic analyses of current Soviet philosophy: materialism, (2) Marxist dialectics.

1st Wednesday: (1) Materialist conception of history, (2) Relations among political power and religious tradition in the USSR.

1st Thursday: (1) Soviet society yesterday and today, (2) National minorities in the USSR.

1st Friday: (1) Principles of civil law in the USSR, (2) Soviet economic planning.

1st Saturday: The political thinking of Mao Zedong.

2nd Monday: (1) Cuba, (2) The Soviet press.

2nd Tuesday: (1) Yugoslavia, (2) The Third International.

2nd Wednesday: (1) The Arab Middle East, (2) History of PCI (1921–45)

2nd Thursday: (1) The ideology of PCI, (2) PCI in the face of Italian socio-economic evolution (1946–1967).

2nd Friday: The crisis in the relations among communist states.

2nd Saturday: Union policy of the PCI.[79]

CESES intended the students to gain enough knowledge about Marxism and actually existing socialism to be able to argue successfully with Italian communists. At the same time, the students were exposed to a wide range of Marxist and socialist ideas, original Marxist works, and criticisms of Leninism and Stalinism from within the anti-PCI left.

In addition to Marxism, the students also took two-week courses on Italian politics and conducted research on Italian political parties.[80] This research emerged out of the current research projects of Giorgio Galli, who, in the view of a high-level Confindustria official, did not take a "decisive anti-Marxist position."[81] Galli had written for Italian socialist journals and had extensive contacts with the Italian left that gave him remarkable access to trends within the PCI and the socialist parties in Italy.[82] As with many others on the anti-PCI left, he worked with groups importing American social science, such as Il Mulino and the Cattaneo

Institute. American political science can be seen as reformist rather than revolutionary because it focused on the political system, political parties, and elections (Morlino 1991). At the same time, the youths in CESES programs conducted research on "the most significant texts of Croce, Einaudi, Mosca, Coppola, Corradini, Corridoni, Rocco, Gentile, Salvemini, Gobetti, Toniolo, Sturzo, Turati, Gramsci, etc."[83] In 1969, the students' individual research projects included "The theory of political obligation in Lenin and Gramsci," "Research on the hypotheses of societal transformation by the PCI," "Research on the hypotheses of societal transformation by Italian socialism," "Research on the hypotheses of societal transformation by Italian liberals," "Research on the Marxist-Leninist left in Italy," "Catholic dissent groups in Italy," "Marxism-Leninism and new power," "Marxism and Cuba," and "Political science research on the Italian model."[84] These readings and research topics within the shifting Italian political context, in which social movements and extra-parliamentary groups emerged as strong new actors, challenged the intended reformism of a political science education. In addition, Italian public and elite opinion had long been critical of political parties and saw the political system as corrupt (Lupo 2004). The instructors at CESES often gave the students an anti-PCI left-wing interpretation of political parties and the political system itself.

Philosophy of science became a popular topic at CESES because it seemed to offer a way to establish a cosmopolitan public sphere free of ideology commensurate with the liminal spaces of CESES. Many important texts in philosophy of science had been recently published: Thomas Kuhn's *The Structure of Scientific Revolutions* in 1962, Carl G. Hempel's *Philosophy of Natural Science* in 1966, and Karl Popper's *The Logic of Scientific Discovery* in English in 1959. A group of students started their own journal, *Controcorrente [Countercurrent]*, which CESES funded. In this journal, which ran from 1969 to 1976, the students discussed anarchism, socialism, liberalism, and other topics of related interest, including philosophy of science. To the students at *Controcorrente*, the issues of "burning timeliness" were operationalization, models, definitional schemes, analytic and classificatory concepts, and typologies (Zucchini 1970). These seemingly strange objects of fascination were exciting because social science methodology was cutting edge in Italy at the time and, I argue, discussing politics through empirical methods was another way of discussing politics. Mieli and others had created CESES as a place for dialogue, empirical testing of hypotheses, and persuasion, rather than the conversion supposedly practiced by both the PCI and the Catholic Church. The *Controcorrente* students sought to persuade other university students to use social science methodology, Popperian discussion, and critical rationality that they learned at CESES, rather than accept ideology. However, the *Controcorrente* students found that "while the ardour and zeal was huge, the result did not satisfy. We are still a long way from our proposed model. Maybe we were too optimistic" (Scano and Zucchini 1969). The Popperian project of CESES seemed very difficult to realize, and the *Controcorrente* students' attempts to deal with these difficulties ultimately failed when the journal ceased publication in 1976.

While persuasion and conversion could fail, a person's attempts to persuade others might result instead in that person being persuaded by others. The industrialists agreed with CESES that knowing their enemy— the Soviet Union and Marxism-Leninism—was important, but they also felt that this knowledge might be dangerous and might lead to communist sympathies. As one industrialist told Vittorio De Biasi, "The communist idea for decades has succeeded in influencing and seizing the good faith of millions of youth—and non-youth—around the world . . . I am convinced that actually in this lies the danger of the CESES courses."[85] This comment suggests the many ways that students and instructors could use the Sovietological and broader social scientific knowledge developed at CESES. In addition, the historical context of these courses altered their intended propagandistic nature. The CESES courses began during the first student occupation of the University of Turin in 1967. The student movements of 1968 and the turmoil of the 1970s flooded into the classroom. Through the workshops and conferences, students learned about Marxist economic theory, economic alternatives to capitalism attempted in Yugoslavia, Eastern European dissident movements, the ideas of Mao and many others, criticisms of the state, calls for autonomous forms of organizing, the ideals that the Eastern European socialist regimes were not living up to, old Italian anarchist traditions, and so on. At CESES, researchers and students were supposed to study the East Bloc to condemn Italian communism, but Eastern European dissent also provided them a model for Italian dissent.

As a result of their belief in an independent, cosmopolitan public sphere, in which dialogue and empirical testing of hypotheses would reveal the lies around ideologies and totalitarianism, Mieli and others planned to invite youths from all political persuasions in hopes of having an open debate that would be naturally critical of Soviet socialism and the PCI once the realities were revealed. When the Confindustria regional leaders heard the criticisms of "left elements" in the CESES courses, the regional leaders decided that only those with a solid anticommunist orientation should be allowed to take part, and those left elements that "infiltrate" the courses should be "eliminated."[86] Vittorio De Biasi responded that Confindustria members were to blame for the "left elements" because they chose the students.[87] De Biasi argued that the youths only "appear" left wing to those who did not understand Marxism-Leninism. In fact, to De Biasi, many of the participants in the courses were not particularly bright and incorrectly saw those who sought to understand Marxism-Leninism as left wing.[88] The CESES leadership would continue to argue with the Confindustria members about the choice of students for the youth training seminars. Students in the seminars did change their political alliances, but in a variety of directions. For example, one student in the CESES seminars, Silvano Alessio, turned to the left and joined the PSI; another student, Vittorio Moccagatta, later became the right-hand man of Berlusconi; another student, Maurizio Vaudagna, became a leader in the student occupation of the University of Turin and then a professor of American History; Federico Avanzini, who was briefly at CESES, became a central participant in the university occupations.[89]

The CESES youth training seminars were intended to create a new managerial elite indoctrinated into anticommunist and pro–liberal-democratic views. However, the many liminal actors participating in CESES activities sought to realize many different projects at CESES. As Giorgio Galli remembered, referring particularly to the youth training courses, CESES "seemed to me an example of those heterogeneous ends which Hegel placed among the principle makers of history" (2000: 104). As a result, these seminars had unintended consequences. The often left-wing instructors taught students about the Soviet Union, Eastern Europe, Marxism-Leninism, and a range of new ideas from Sovietology, political science, and the philosophy of science. Further complicating the indoctrination process, the students were immersed in the university protests and the political upheavals of 1968 and the 1970s. Moreover, Italian politics, economics, and society, as well as its counterparts in Eastern Europe, changed so fundamentally during this time that the study of these topics could not be packaged as ideology or propaganda; rather the instructors, researchers, and students at CESES participated in the very changes they were studying. CESES provided a heterogeneous education that led the students to different political and professional pathways.

Conclusions

The right-wing hegemonic project to use an ideologically secure Sovietology to destroy the left and recruit adherents to the right was undermined by the shifting terrain of the Cold War, changes in actually existing socialism, the revolution in Sovietology, and the heterogeneous nature of transnationally connected liminal spaces. In fact, in the 1970s, Confindustria and American right-wing foundations stopped funding "the Mont Pelerin Society of the East," which meant the end of the youth programs, *Controcorrente, L'Est, Documentazione sui Paesi dell'Est, Notizie Est*, and the Cultural Libera book series.[90] Mieli could then reorient CESES to his favorite areas of study—Sovietology and the PCI—but he had to search continually for funding, which he found through small grants from the Bank of Italy and other organizations.[91] The international economics conferences continued until 1984, bringing together famous Sovietologists and Eastern European economists from around the world. CESES continued to publish books and articles on the PCI until it was closed in 1988. Mieli died in 1991. While CESES exposed students and scholars to Sovietology, we can see that these programs did not last long and had unpredictable consequences. Thus, CESES can be seen as a failed hegemonic project.

At the same time, the actual activities of CESES produced new knowledge needed by right-wing activists to reorient and realize their hegemonic projects. When Milton Friedman (1998) called CESES "the Mont Pelerin Society of the East," this was just one of many times that right-wing activists would appropriate and shape liminal spaces for their battles back home. Their success was not in their prognostication or their propaganda but in their ability to appropriate the liminal discussions of alternative democratic socialisms. By the end of the 1980s, right-wing activists could argue that they had been correct all along, and they declared the success of the global neoliberal hegemonic project organized around Milton Friedman, the Mont Pelerin Society, right-wing think tanks, right-wing foundations, and certain economics departments (Friedman and Friedman 1998; Hartwell 1995; Yergin and Stanislaw 1998). In addition, after CESES had substantially decreased its activities and later shut its doors, right-wing activists could present CESES in any way they pleased. In the more stable ideological period of the early 1990s, the right could co-opt liminal spaces like CESES by enframing them or by forcing them into a dichotomy between Western neoliberal capitalism or a defunct Soviet socialism.[92] As a result, knowledge from the liminal spaces changed the core of Western capitalism, while maintaining the hegemony of the core. Only through its failure did CESES, in fact, realize the—now altered—right-wing neoliberal hegemonic project.[93]

However, the actual activities of CESES produced new knowledge needed also by left-wing activists to reorient and realize their own democratic socialist projects.[94] We should not misunderstand the antistate, promarket language of socialist economists and elites as moving on a slippery slope toward neoconservativism or a "Third Way" compromise.[95] There had been a long tradition of antistate, promarket ideas among socialists. Changes in the nature of industrial production and the state, as well as the resulting new social actors and new social movements, demanded changes in socialist practice and knowledge. In parallel with worldwide criticisms of the state and calls for worker power, Eastern Europe and other parts of the world made significant innovations, especially Yugoslavia's worker self-management socialism and Hungary's reform economics. Innovations in socialist practice and socialist knowledge moved through liminal spaces like that of CESES, where scholars from East and West criticized Soviet state socialism, studied these innovations, and discussed the future of socialisms. The Cold War hindered direct interaction with the Other—Western capitalism or Soviet state socialism or reform socialist Eastern Europe—which meant that detailed knowledge about the Other could not be obtained directly but rather had to emerge from liminal spaces. Left-wing interest in Eastern Europe continued through the "postsocialist transition" in new institutions based on the CESES model.[96] For many socialists, including economists, 1989 seemed like the year to finally realize decentralized market socialism and a broad form of neoclassical economics, which we turn to in the next chapter.

6

Market Socialism or Capitalism?
The Transnational Critique of Neoclassical Economics and the Transitions of 1989

IN 1989, THE WORLD APPEARED TO EMBRACE wholeheartedly capitalism and free markets. The seemingly Reaganite or Thatcherite devotion to free markets surprised many observers at the time. Through research that took me around the world, I found that most neoclassical economists entered the year 1989 with a belief that market socialism might finally be possible. Naomi Klein similarly recognized that Eastern Europeans understood this year as a time of possibility: "In 1989, history was taking an exhilarating turn, entering a period of genuine openness and possibility" (2007: 184). Ralf Dahrendorf at the time also noted, "The countries which have shed really existing socialism have not embraced another system such as capitalism instead, they have chosen the open society in which there are a hundred different ways forward to freedom, and a handful on offer at any one time" ([1990] 2005: 116–117). Eastern European economists spoke continually of the need for real markets. They had embraced markets; there is no question. Our bewilderment comes from the current acceptance of a necessary connection between markets and capitalism and a necessary disjunction between markets and socialism. In the minds of many neoclassical economists around the world in the 1980s, markets were essential for constructing a socialism more socialist than anything seen in the East.

In this chapter, we examine the period from the 1970s to 1989. At the beginning of this period, neoclassical economists around the world perceived a great crisis in their field and began to criticize themselves. This was surprising given that neoclassical economists had just gained

new forms of political and social influence worldwide. Scholars have focused on the battle between Keynesians and monetarists, often understood as a battle between those who supported the state and those who
supported the market. However, neoclassical economists assumed that
pure competitive markets would produce optimal results.[1] They also assumed that a central planner would produce the same optimal results as
these markets.[2] Neoclassical economists differ over the institutions they
consider necessary to make these ideal models reality. Many called for
decentralizing, democratic socialist institutions, while others called for
hierarchical, authoritarian institutions, either capitalist or state socialist.
Conservative political elites in the capitalist West and the socialist East
co-opted a very narrow idea of neoclassical economics, accepting existing hierarchical institutions as given, which served to bolster their own
elite power. Economists who did not support this co-optation began to
question their own neoclassical practices, often successfully advocating
decentralizing reforms. As a neoclassical economic institution, the World
Bank also took in these perspectives, battles, and best practices.

For many neoclassical economists, 1989 marked the end of Soviet
state socialism, which they had criticized for so long. Finally, market socialism seemed possible. For example, Branko Milanović, an economist in
the World Bank and former student and colleague of Branko Horvat in
Belgrade, remembered that around 1990 he happened on Jeffrey Sachs
in a bookstore. Jeffrey Sachs had Milanović's new book, which he asked
Milanović to sign. Milanović recalled:

> I thought for a second and wrote: "To Jeff Sachs, who is trying to save socialism."
> Jeff was kind of shocked, and he said, "I do not want to save socialism; I want to
> bury it." I was surprised then but realized later: I was still behind the curve regarding
> what was happening. I saw the early reforms in Poland as a way to introduce market
> elements into socialism, the same way that Keynesian economics introduced some
> state control into capitalism. Pushing the parallel further, I saw the socialist crisis
> of the 1980's as a way toward the creation of a reformed and sustainable socialism.
> But Jeff (rightly) saw it as the end of socialism and the beginning of the transition
> to capitalism.[3]

Milanović was by no means the only neoclassically trained economist who
envisioned the realization of market socialism, not capitalism, in and around
1989.

Transnational Neoclassical Critique
of Neoclassical Economics

Neoclassical economists had reason to feel quite successful in the policy realm. Yugoslav and Hungarian economists had helped implement major reforms in the 1960s, which began to create two forms of neoclassical market socialism of great international interest. These reforms had expanded positions for economists within the government and the economy and allowed neoclassical economists to reform economics education in line with their own research. Increasing numbers of these Yugoslav and Hungarian economists took part in the emerging transnational neoclassical dialogue. In the United States, neoclassical economists also sensed their own professional success. In his 1964 presidential address to the American Economic Association, George Stigler declared, "I am convinced that economics is finally at the threshold of its Golden Age—nay we already have one foot through the door" (1965: 17). In the United States, economists experienced growing demand and growing salaries in business and government (Heller 1975: 8).[4] Worldwide, neoclassical economists had gained broad areas of influence in government and society (Babb 2001; Coats 1981, 1986; Dezalay and Garth 2002; Fourcade 2009; Markoff and Montecinos 1993). Yet, by 1970, neoclassical economists around the world began to question their own practices and assumptions.

For decades both Austrian School and Marxist economists had criticized neoclassical economics.[5] Neoclassical economists had ignored many of these criticisms.[6] Now, neoclassical economists themselves perceived their discipline as in crisis and began what was later called "an epidemic of self-flagellation" (Coats 1977). In the 1970s, in the context of worldwide movements against authoritarianism and technocracy, as well as the abandonment of market reforms in Eastern Europe, many neoclassical economists criticized the cooptation by conservative political elites in the East and the West of a seemingly narrow neoclassical economics that would maintain the hierarchical status quo. In the socialist East, in light of new developments in computer technology, some political leaders and economists believed that neoclassical central planning might finally be feasible and imagined replacing the markets of market socialism with computers and central planners (Gerovitch 2002). Neoclassical central planning would allow elites to maintain their hierarchical control over the economy and hierarchical control in large monopolistic (or nearly monopolistic) firms. In his "The Computers and the Market," Oskar Lange himself agreed:

> Were I to rewrite my essay today my task would be much simpler. My answer to Hayek and Robbins would be: so what's the trouble? Let us put the simultaneous equations on an electronic computer and we shall obtain the solutions in less than a second. The market process with its cumbersome *tâtonnements* [groping, or trial and error] appears old-fashioned. Indeed, it may be considered as a computing device of the pre-electronic age. (1967: 158)

This notion of centrally planned socialism based on neoclassical economics is as old as neoclassical economics itself, but this particular vision left intact the hierarchical institutions of Eastern European state socialism.

In the United States, in addition to similar uses of neoclassical economics in the military, the New Right presented another narrow view, in which markets would spring up as the state retreated from the economy. In fact, the New Right advocated particular institutions, especially private property and hierarchical corporations, as necessary for efficient markets and efficient economies more broadly. Both American and Eastern European conservative leaders supported large monopolistic companies, argued against broader democratic and socialist institutional reform, reinforced centralized political authority, and encouraged individual consumerism to support their system. Criticisms of neoclassical economics thus occurred in the context of this professional and political battle within neoclassical economics itself, as well as in the context of the worldwide battle over authoritarianism, democracy, and power. We now examine these criticisms in Hungary, Yugoslavia, and the United States.

Hungarian Critiques of Neoclassical Economics

As discussed in Chapter 4, in 1968, the Hungarian government implemented a major economic reform that fascinated economists worldwide. This New Economic Mechanism (NEM) reform realized a type of market socialism inspired by Oskar Lange's neoclassical market socialism, but reformers also hoped to move beyond this model to have truly competitive markets within a more democratic socialism. Economists with neoclassical training benefited from the NEM in a great variety of ways (Bockman 2000, ch. 5). For example, the Party-state leadership supported mathematically based neoclassical planning methods and created long-term planning offices within ministries to implement these methods. At the same time, the NEM remained a very narrow neoclassical reform that maintained the institutions of Party-state power. The NEM supposedly ended direct state intervention in the realm of enterprises, allowing the state to intervene indirectly through financial means. Yet the NEM did not incorporate the institutional changes that economists felt necessary for indirect state intervention. Economists recognized that Hungary had "neither market nor plan" (Bauer 1983) and called for further reforms, which the Party-state rejected for several years. During this time, the NEM remained a narrow neoclassical reform that maintained hierarchical Party-state power, which now included very powerful managers of state industrial and agricultural enterprises (Eyal, Szelényi, and Townsley 2000; Lampland 1995).

Frustrations with the NEM led Hungarian reform economists to criticize their own tools and assumptions. Most famously, even as he continued working on neoclassical planning models, Hungarian economist János Kornai ([1971] 1991) launched his attack on neoclassical economics in his book *Anti-Equilibrium*. While writing this book and discussing it with his colleagues at the ESI in Budapest, Kornai also visited and discussed his critique with some of the most famous neoclassical economists in the United States, including Kenneth Arrow and Tjalling Koopmans (ibid.: xvi–xvii). These 1968 and 1970 visits landed him in the United States during the "epidemic of self-flagellation," which was really a battle within neoclassical economics itself.

By his own account, Kornai had worked on the NEM and found neoclassical economics inadequate for reform work.[7] He specifically criticized general equilibrium theory, most typified by Arrow and Debreu's highly abstract model. Kornai found that such models did not reflect reality but rather were valid only for a very restricted, artificial world and dealt with an "extremely narrow" range of questions (ibid.: 28–30). In his view, earlier "naïve" Hungarian reformers, who focused only on market reforms; "Western neoliberals," who argued against any state intervention; and those for "pure" central planning all used "essentially *the same* unrealistic assumptions" to prove their views (ibid.: 334).[8] The abstract Arrow-Debreu model, as well as the proposals of Western neoliberals and East European naïve economists, did not describe how economies really functioned or the institutions required for their functioning. This abstract model also did not predict or help resolve the immense difficulties economists experienced trying to implement market reforms. Therefore, Kornai declared, "To ask,

'Planning or market'—is to ask the wrong question" (ibid.: 334). Kornai sought to create a new language and conceptual apparatus to describe existing economic systems.

Kornai was not the only economist frustrated by unrealized reforms. Economists across the East Bloc experienced the cyclical history of crisis, reform, and political backlash against the reform (Bockman and Eyal 2002: 238–239; Campbell 1991: 213; Seleny 1993: 101). Hungarian economists had envisioned the NEM transforming the centrally planned state socialist system into decentralized market socialism. According to Erzsébet Szalai, many Hungarian intellectuals thought of the market mechanism as a means to "loosen the rigid hierarchy of the power structure and therefore not only to expand the opportunities for individual freedom, but also to make societal control over the power conglomerate possible in the long run" (2005: 17; see also Antal 1999: 90). However, the NEM was followed by the usual backlash, which maintained the hierarchical political and economic system. Reform economists understood that neoclassically based markets and neoclassically based planning could not by themselves change the system but rather required new institutions that would alter the power structure.[9] Partial reforms were not enough. The neoclassical economists' frustrations led them to see political elites as the primary obstacles to comprehensive economic reforms.[10]

During the 1970s, reform economists remained committed to markets, socialism, and enterprise autonomy. They turned to several specific institutions to make markets function effectively. First, they sought to move beyond monopolies and create a competitive market. Antal (1982), Bauer (1984), and Máriás et al. (1981) called for a larger number of economic units to encourage competition and for a radical reorganization to end the dependence of companies on the state and thus to create a real self-regulating market. Révész argued that the NEM and its turn toward intensive development required small enterprises (1979: 47, 60). Varga claimed further that the new epoch in the world economy required small enterprises that could adapt quickly to changes happening globally (1978: 229).

Second, reform economists sought to encourage entrepreneurship. Entrepreneurship as a socialist concept took Hungary by storm, thanks to the charismatic and controversial economist—also known as "a prophet and a daredevil" and a "miraculous healer"—Tibor Liska (Bársony 1982: 422). In contrast to the Yugoslav view of workers' councils as entrepreneurs, Hungarian officials and economists saw managers as entrepreneurs (Tardos 1982). Liska, however, argued that socialism should have individual entrepreneurs who would not own the means of production. According to Liska, socialism allowed the realization of the entrepreneurial spirit because the end of private property and the further development of commodity relations liberated everyone for entrepreneurship (Bársony 1982: 426–427). In Liska's socialist entrepreneurial system, each citizen would receive a social inheritance, which could be used to bid on a market for leasing a business or for starting a new business. Businesses and social inheritance would be returned to society, not passed on to heirs, on the death of their possessors. There would be a competitive market in leasing—rather than owning— the means of production, individual accumulation of wealth (without inheritance), openness to the world market, and free market prices (Bársony 1982; Swain 1992: 110–111).[11] In 1978, Liska headed the Research Group on Entrepreneurship at Karl Marx University (Szabó 1989), where he collected around him those working in the emerging second economy. He developed ideas with such practitioners and held very popular public debates each week. Starting in 1981, he tested his ideas in a series of enterprise experiments.[12] Entrepreneurship in a variety of possible forms became an essential institution for a competitive market within a socialist system.

Third, reform economists revisited the notion of socialist property, considering control and ownership separately. In Hungary, as opposed to Yugoslavia, socialism had always been premised on state ownership of the means of production and, simultaneously, state planning. To encourage enterprise autonomy, Hungarian economists argued for a variety of ownership arrangements that would retain social ownership but sever its connection with the state, for example by giving enterprise ownership to worker collectives or handing the ownership of worker self-managed enterprises to nonstate holding companies, which would issue their own shares (Swain 1992: 135).[13] These economists sought to make enterprises independent of the state, thus eliminating the state administrative aspect of property and giving administrative control, but not ownership, to other entities (Voszka 1991: 58). Economists placed these ownership alternatives on the table in the 1970s and 1980s.

In 1982, the Hungarian government gave workers the right to create work partnerships, semiautonomous subcontracting units of workers from enterprises that produce goods or services during the off hours using factory equipment (Stark 1989).[14] Most importantly, in 1985, the Hungarian government set up enterprise councils in three-fourths of all state enterprises (Voszka 1992).[15] The enterprise council law gave councils the right to appoint a director and decide on the fate of the firm, such as mergers, the splitting up of the firm, joint ventures, and stock companies with state assets. According to Révész ([1988] 1989), with this reform, "the practice of ownership moved toward self-government and the majority of property rights (with the exception of founding or closing state enterprises) were formally removed from the hands of state organs" (69). This reform was an attempt to decentralize property rights from the state to the firm, giving the means of production to the workers as a group, specifically not as a form of privatization. Economists thought that factory democracy would bolster enterprise independence and collective material interests. Groups of reform economists had long supported workers' councils and other forms of worker democracy within firms.

Hungarian reform economists participated in the transnational self-criticism of neoclassical economics as part of their own frustration with, and criticism of, the Hungarian Party-state's narrow approach to reforms, which reinforced centralized power. These critical reform economists turned to decentralizing, democratic institutions to make markets run effectively and without political interference, not to introduce capitalism. The Hungarian Party-state, in fact, began to realize these institutions—new enterprises of various sizes, autonomous enterprises, workers' councils, entrepreneurship, and new forms of social property—that economists deemed necessary for competitive markets. Yugoslav neoclassical economists sought, in the end unsuccessfully, to do the same.

Yugoslav Critiques of Neoclassical Economics

In 1965, Yugoslavia implemented major market reforms, which, according to one of the most famous economists there, Branko Horvat (1967), made the socialist Yugoslav economy and its firms more closely correspond to neoclassical models and to rational behavior than capitalist economies or firms did. These reforms had led to much excitement abroad.

However, neoclassical economists soon found themselves in a rapidly changing political environment. The New Left in the universities and the Zagreb-based *Praxis* group attacked the economic reforms, markets, and trends they regarded as capitalist (Lampe 1996: 295).[16] In 1968, student strikes spread through Yugoslav universities, calling for the realization of worker self-management and Yugoslav socialist goals, in contrast to consumerism and markets. This coincided with increasing anti-Yugoslav nationalism, especially visible in Croatian Spring from 1968. The Yugoslav leadership decided to turn against liberalism, nationalism, and technoc-ratism (Ramet 2006: 260).[17] By the end of 1972, Tito and the leadership had dismissed liberal and nationalist leaders from the communist parties of the individual republics (Lampe 1996: 304).[18] The Yugoslav government turned away from market reforms to a new kind of socialism. Yugoslav neoclassical economists who supported market socialism found them-selves in the opposition, alongside nationalists and central planners who had been pushed into the opposition during the 1960s market reforms.[19]

The Yugoslav government sought to end technocracy and markets and further develop worker self-management socialism by creating a "con-tractual economy" and "contractual socialism." Yugoslav socialism, as discussed in Chapter 3, was based on decentralization, worker self-man-agement, social ownership of the means of production, and use of the market. Economists had understood decentralization as the transfer of economic and political authority to enterprises, thus allowing for enter-prise autonomy (Milenkovitch 1977: 56). However, the Yugoslav leader-ship transformed this idea. On the one hand, decentralization became the devolution of federal power to the republics, thus retaining the state in a republican form (Ramet 2006: 327). On the other hand, the 1974 con-stitution introduced a new, more participatory and contractual form of planning. In 1976, enterprises were broken up into even smaller basic or-ganizations of associated labor (BOALs) within the firm.[20] These BOALs were relatively small and were supposed to be independent of each other and the firm they were part of. BOALs created their own plans, which were then integrated into a larger nationwide social plan, thus making planning more participatory. The system was contractual because BOALs related to each other and to the Party-state through contracts.[21] In the 1970s, the Yugoslav government developed new kinds of decentralization in fact at odds with economists' models and views.

The overwhelming majority of Yugoslav neoclassical economists supported worker self-management, but, at the same time, they very much opposed these reforms (Gligorov 1998: 349–350). They understood these re-forms as abandoning the market and the 1965 reforms, replacing them with contracts formed through the intervention of political authorities (Drutter 1990; Vojnić 1989).[22] In a 1972 outspoken interview that brought official criticism, Branko Horvat argued, "The terminology is self-management, but the reality is that the state dictates what has to happen," meaning the liquidation of the market economy, which, for Horvat, indicated "a

return to Stalinism" ("Razgovor" 1972: 1752–1753). As a result, economists could no longer assume that the Yugoslav model had or would soon
have a freely competitive market.[23] Horvat, the lifelong socialist, called for
the return of markets and radical expansion of self-management, including expansion into the political realm itself. Also, as a result, Horvat and
his colleagues were punished for their ideas. Horvat later recalled, "From
1972 repression was again introduced. I then warned the public that the
country was being pushed into disaster. The public prosecutor reacted and
I, among others, lost the possibility of teaching at the university" (1989: 5).
Horvat remembered being publicly called "an enemy of Yugoslavia," even
as he continued to promote the Yugoslav model around the world (ibid.:
31). One of his students in Ljubljana told me that, during this "terrible
time," students could no longer study abroad, and talking about markets
made one a "dissident." In contrast to Hungarian reform economists, Yugoslav neoclassical economists would have to wait much longer, until the
mid-1980s, to begin to realize the institutions they deemed necessary for
socialist competitive markets.

Yugoslav neoclassical economists also began to criticize neoclassical economics, participating in the worldwide self-criticism. In contrast
to Hungarian reform economists, however, Yugoslavs focused their criticisms specifically on the neoclassical "Illyrian" worker self-management
model developed by American-based neoclassical economists Benjamin Ward and Jaroslav Vanek in *The American Economic Review*. Yugoslav economists had criticized the assumptions of the abstract "Illyrian"
model, especially Ward's negatively sloping supply curve, which assumed
that, in response to increases in demand and price, workers would rather
maximize their own individual incomes than hire new employees and
increase production. The negatively sloping supply curve seemed to make
the case that worker self-management socialism worked in perverse and
irrational ways. Branko Horvat recognized that Benjamin Ward had been
"progressive" and well educated in neoclassical economics, but according to Horvat, Ward had assumed that workers maximized their wages
without examining whether this was actually the case in Yugoslavia (1979:
168). In Horvat's view, Ward's article had been revived by those who opposed workers' self-management:

As socialist movements and trade unions began to press towards workers' management, it became necessary to show that this was an inferior system. The article was
rediscovered, the term "Illyrian" discarded and replaced by "workers' managed" and

a ready-made proof was obtained for the inferior allocational efficiency of the labour-managed economy. The proof was then included into the standard courses on comparative economic systems. (ibid.)[24]

Transnational right-wing networks had begun to use criticisms of the Yugoslav system to argue for the necessity of markets, private property, and hierarchical management.

Ljubo Sirc, Eirik Furubotn, and other economists mobilized the Yugoslav case and neoclassical economics to prove that self-management would never work.[25] After fleeing Yugoslavia in the 1950s, Ljubo Sirc wrote works critical of both central planning and self-management. In contrast to economists who supported self-management, Sirc argued that the economic problems building up in the late 1970s resulted from the lack of a "clear link between the enterprise and the workers who are expected collectively to take decisions concerning that enterprise" (1979: 242). Sirc continued:

It is, therefore, destructive to wage a class struggle against those persons most successful in managing capital and organising production, because they have contributed to the prosperity more than anybody else; they have made possible the present level of productivity, without which there is no prosperity. (ibid., 244)

In making his case, he mobilized the critical writings of Yugoslavs themselves:

Because of such persistent accusations of prejudice, I have developed the habit of supporting my views by continuously referring to what the communists themselves write. As a rule, their detailed criticisms are valid although they cannot do much about them since they are a consequence of the system which they are bound to praise as a great success and achievement. (ibid.: xv)

He removed the criticisms and their debates from the context within which economists were calling not for private property but for real socialism with actual worker self-management and social ownership. He saw that Yugoslavia provided real lessons for those in the West:

As for the West, Yugoslavia seems to show what happens if enterprises are managed by people who are not dependant [sic] on those legally linked to their capital. In this respect, it also shows where the West is heading if many ideas tried out in Yugoslavia and found wanting nevertheless gain currency here. (ibid.: xvii)

Economists in right-wing networks used the case of Yugoslavia as proof of the need for hierarchies and private property.

Yugoslav economists created an entire industry rethinking the assumptions of the neoclassical model, showing that Yugoslav worker self-management socialism worked rationally and in fact better than capitalism (Dubravčić 1970; Horvat 1979). Their colleagues abroad also took part in this work (Drèze 1989; Marschak 1968; Meade 1989; Wachtel 1973).[26] Yugoslav economists also turned to the task of empirically studying the reality of worker self-managed firms and relating their findings to neoclassical economics (Petrović 1988; Prašnikar 1980; Prašnikar et al. 1994; see also Wachtel 1973). Economists searched through a variety of heterodox economic schools to add to the toolbox of neoclassical economics. For example, young Yugoslav economists around Branko Horvat looked for a way to extend neoclassical economics to analyze and overcome obstacles to realizing true worker self-management market socialism. Neo-Ricardian economics, specifically the work of Piero Sraffa, was of particular interest to this group.[27] They also integrated the radical political economy of the American New Left (Franičević 1983) and, to a lesser extent, the Austrian School.[28] After years criticizing the neoclassical Illyrian model, Aleksander Bajt finally stated, "The model of the Illyrian firm is completely irrelevant, in reality it leads one astray, in search of problems where there are none" (1988: 53).

As in Hungary, many Yugoslav economists also understood that competitive markets—in the words of Aleksander Bajt, "the only acceptable model of the socialist economy is the model of free competition"—required certain socialist institutions.[29] One of these institutions was entrepreneurship. Bajt wrote, "The main problem of workers' firms is not found where Ward looked for it at all. It is entrepreneurship" (ibid.: 53). Tea Petrin recognized that entrepreneurship had emerged as a fundamental institution not only in Yugoslavia: "The eighties will be remembered as an era of entrepreneurship. We are witnessing the emergence of an entrepreneurial movement in the West as well as the East" (1991: 7). In Yugoslavia, officials and economists had long accepted worker collectives as entrepreneurs, practicing socialist entrepreneurship (Dubravčić 1970; Horvat 1961, 1967). However, Yugoslav economists, as well as other social scientists, criticized the lack of real worker participation in Yugoslavia (for example, "Razgovor" 1972; Županov 1969). Since the 1970s, Yugoslav leaders, such as Edvard Kardelj, as well as various economists, criticized social property as leading to managerial, rather than worker, control and sought various forms of nonprivate, nonstate ownership (Uvalić 1989:

114). By the 1970s, the Yugoslav government allowed individuals to pool their own capital and labor with those of other individuals in a new organization called COALs (contractual organizations of associated labor) based on self-management, thus starting their own businesses (Uvalić 1989). During the 1980s, economists closely connected with Branko Horvat worked on various workers' shareholding plans and entrepreneurial training programs, which they regarded as essential for competitive markets and autonomous enterprises in socialism.

For example, around 1986 with Slovenian government support, economists Tea Petrin, Janez Prašnikar, and Aleš Vahčič formed a consulting firm originally called AGEA and then renamed YUGEA (Yugoslav General Entrepreneurial Agency), to restructure Yugoslav enterprises.[30] They argued that market competition within socialism required the restructuring of these monopolistic firms, the creation of small- and medium-sized firms, and "entrepreneurship" (Petrin and Vahčič 1988). These economists had criticized state ownership for decades and sought to develop other nonstate social forms. Neoclassical economic theory assumed that, in a competitive market, firms could freely enter and exit the market and that firms were price takers because a large number of firms would compete without monopolies—price makers—forming. To create these firms, these economists traveled around Yugoslavia helping workers to create spin-off companies financed by workers' funds, much like Employee Stock Ownership Programs. According to David Ellerman, who visited them in mid-1989, YUGEA not only laid the groundwork for worker buyouts but also started business incubators and entrepreneurship clubs to create a culture of "socialist entrepreneurship," "namely, entrepreneurship oriented towards forms of democratic worker ownership" (1990b: 215). Now, workers would own and democratically control the means of production. Workers in the self-management system could hire capital, in contrast to capital hiring workers as it occurs in the capitalist system (Wachtel 1973: 59). In a sense, these economists seemed to understand these new ownership forms as allowing, in Tito's words in 1950, "Factories belonging to the workers—something that has never yet been achieved!"[31] In the context of Yugoslavia at this time, Yugoslav economists understood worker self-management, worker ownership, market competition, and entrepreneurship as mutually necessary for socialism.

Yugoslav neoclassical economists joined the transnational criticism of authoritarianism and technocracy embodied both within their profession and by ruling political elites. Political elites around the globe mobilized a very narrow version of neoclassical economics to support their own elite power against the threat of the democratic socialist institutions that many neoclassical economists found necessary for truly competitive markets.

American Criticisms of Neoclassical Economics

Scholars have cast the 1970s debates among U.S. economists as a battle pitting monetarists against Keynesians, market advocates against state interventionists. Indeed, conservative monetarist economists themselves presented the debates in this manner, as reflected in Milton Friedman's 1970 *The Counter-Revolution in Monetary Theory* and Harry G. Johnson's 1971 "The Keynesian Revolution and the Monetarist Counter-Revolution." Yet, as this book has shown, monetarists and Keynesians may have disagreed over policy, but they all practiced neoclassical economics. In spite of public conflicts, American Economic Association President Walter Heller emphasized (possibly too optimistically) a consensus within mainstream economics:

Even where disagreement flourishes—most visibly, perhaps, between Keynesians and monetarists—the public may not discern that the analytical and empirical ties that bind us are far stronger than the forces that divide us. Our controversies take place within the context of basic consensus on the nature of methods of economic theory and inquiry. (1975: 4) [32]

As mentioned earlier, Paul Samuelson emphasized that economists "do agree on much in any situation," which meant that "I could disagree 180° with his [Milton Friedman's] policy conclusion and yet concur in diagnosis of the empirical observations and inferred probabilities" (1983: 5–6). Milton Friedman did not practice a capitalist economics, while Paul Samuelson used a socialist or Keynesian economics. In fact, the monetarists and the Keynesians shared neoclassical economic methods that had, as we have seen, both a competitive market and central planning at the center, so the cause of the criticisms and debates lay elsewhere. [33]

The 1964 campaign of Barry Goldwater and the 1969 election of Richard Nixon confused the public about the nature of economics because conservative leaders mobilized both the Austrian School that criticized neoclassical economics and the Chicago School that embraced it. Austrian School economists like Friedrich von Hayek and Chicago School economists like Milton Friedman were, in the words of economist Richard B. McKenzie, "defenders of individual freedom, critics of government, developers of market economics, and believers in rational discourse," but "members of both schools frequently dismiss (in private) one another as muddle-headed or even perverse in their theoretical attachments" (1980: 1).[34] The Austrian and Chicago schools disagreed fundamentally about methods and, thus, about a wide range of theories, concepts, models, and findings.

American criticisms of neoclassical economics resembled those in Eastern Europe in part because groups of American neoclassical economists confronted a similar narrowing of neoclassical economics and cooptation of neoclassical economics by conservative political elites.[35] Therefore, these criticisms did not reflect so much a self-criticism as a continuing split within the profession. Milton Friedman and other conservative supporters publicly advocated neoclassical economics as a reflection of reality that required hierarchical institutions. During the 1960s, the Chicago School of neoclassical economics maintained and further developed a narrow version of neoclassical economics that had long suited conservative forces. Other neoclassical economists disagreed with this approach.

Milton Friedman's *Price Theory* textbook (1962b) represented this narrow form, which in fact assumed concentrated political and economic power centers. The textbook mobilized the same neoclassical tools as other textbooks, but it had a particular perspective described well by Mirowski:

To risk caricature of this position, its first commandment is that the market always "works," in the sense that its unimpeded operation maximizes welfare. Its second commandment is that the government is always part of the problem, rather than part of the solution. (2002: 203–204)

Friedman and others used neoclassical economics as a convenient fiction, in which one assumed that individuals were completely rational and markets were completely competitive even when one knew otherwise (McKenzie 1980: 7). For example, in his textbook, Friedman wrote:

This description implicitly supposes the existence of effective competition in translating consumer wishes into productive activity. It is assumed that people can affect their incomes only through use of their resources and not through interference with the price system . . . What the market does is primarily to determine the return per unit of resource, and there is no reason to believe that the market aggravates the inequality in the ownership of resources. Moreover, any given degree of inequality is a much more serious one in an economy which is governed largely by status or tradition than in a market economy where there is much chance for shifts in the ownership of resources. Historically, the fundamental inequality of economic status has been and is almost certainly greater in economies that do not rely on the free market than in those that do. (1962b: 11)

Yet this seemingly narrow view of markets working on their own, in fact, assumes a strong state to enforce private property rights and disregards, in contrast to the earlier Chicago School tradition (Simons 1934), centralized economic power within and among corporations that undermine competition. As a result, like neoclassical advocates of central planning in Eastern Europe, the Chicago School came to advocate a version of neoclassical economics that assumed existing hierarchical institutions as given.

Neoclassical economists who did not support conservative elites rejected these assumptions. The president of the Econometric Society, Frank Hahn, devoted his 1968 presidential address to criticizing his field: "Equilibrium economics . . . is easily convertible into an apologia for existing economic arrangements and it is frequently so converted" (1970: 1). To Benjamin Ward, neoclassical economics had narrowed its scope and "is based on an ideology, which in practice restricts the range of problems considered" (1972: 239–240). Ward continued, "The accepted procedures are at best only applicable to the consideration of marginal changes in the status quo," rather than fundamental changes (ibid.: 240). Like their Eastern European counterparts, these neoclassical economists argued that these unrealistic models could not help economists to solve real economic problems and thus made economics irrelevant to policy discussions (Leontief 1971; Morgenstern 1972; Phelps Brown 1972; Worswick 1972). To Frank Hahn, "The gap between theory and fact is far too large, and in some sense becoming larger" (1972: 206). Neoclassical economists called for empirical research, especially to test the underlying assumptions of their field, and for recognition of the need for institutions and interdisciplinarity (Leontief 1971; Phelps Brown 1972). They criticized their profession's focus on abstract models with unrealistic assumptions and an uncritical enthusiasm for mathematics (Leontief 1971: 1; Morgenstern 1972). Economists came to question such assumptions as the very existence of equilibrium (Rothschild and Stiglitz 1976), complete information (Akerlof 1970; Arrow 1963; Rothschild and Stiglitz 1976; Spence 1973), and rational actors especially in times of risk and uncertainty (Sandmo 1971), arguing that institutions and incentives matter (Mirrlees 1971). These economists rejected their highly abstract, narrow models and sought to expand these models to deal with the urgent questions of the day.

American economists also explored institutions similar to the ones their counterparts did in Eastern Europe. They opened the black box of the firm. They returned to the topic of entrepreneurship in response to the late 1960s economic slowdown and 1970s economic crises.[36] Scholars in management and business schools had long been interested in entrepreneurship, but economists began to show an interest in this area. Economists also argued that worker participation and worker ownership of the means of production were fundamental to competitive markets. Economists in both East and West had criticized state ownership with its related intervention in supposedly independent enterprises and debated various social property rights alternatives. In the United States, Alan Blinder recognized "the current surge of interest in profit sharing, employee stock ownership, worker participation, and the like" (1990: 3). New laws in the 1970s allowed Employee Stock Ownership Programs (ESOPs)—that pay benefits in company stock rather than in cash—which led to thousands of employee-owned companies (Ellerman 1990). Property could take on different forms, often more social forms.

Neoclassical economists around the world shared methods and a language, as well as common criticisms of how their knowledge had been used. Conservative political elites supported a narrow view of neoclassical economics that maintained hierarchical institutions of the status quo and allowed elites to maintain power. In contrast, by the 1970s, most economists from East and West agreed that market economies—whether socialist or capitalist—required a variety of institutions: autonomous companies, competition, worker participation, economic democracy, political democracy, and entrepreneurship. They also argued against government overspending, political and economic monopolies, inflation, and state socialism. These institutions were perceived as best practices for socialism and had emerged from experiments in the socialist and developing world.[37] Economists, however, did not agree on the other "lessons" of socialism. Significant areas of dispute remained around forms of ownership, privatization, the proper role of the state, and the nature of neoclassical economics itself.

The Social Planner and Reform

In spite of this battle over neoclassical economics and the supposed decline of Keynesianism, all mainstream neoclassical economists—from the University of Chicago to Harvard and MIT to Eastern Europe—used socialisms for macroeconomic modeling. For example, Friedman compared the impact of an income tax versus an excise tax by stating:

Let us suppose that we are dealing with a community of many identical individuals—identical in tastes and preferences and also in kind and quantity of resources owned by each individual. In this community every individual will have the same income and consume the same bundle of goods, so we can represent the position of the community by the position of any one individual. (1962b: 61)

In the minds of economists, all members of a community can be considered identical and thus replaceable with one individual, whom economists called the "representative agent" or the "social planner," which they use as the baseline for all macroeconomic modeling. In 1977, the term *social planner* appeared overtly in the professional economics literature (Carlton 1978; Grossman 1977; Khalatbari 1977; Mayshar 1977; Mussa 1977). These models entered the macroeconomic textbooks in the late 1980s (Bryant and Portes 1987) and continue to be taught today. The Chicago School (for example, Becker, Murphy, and Grossman 2006)[38] and rational expectations school (Hansen and Sargent [1994] 1996; Kydland and Prescott 1982; Lucas 1972; Lucas and Prescott 1971), as well as the more left-leaning market failure school (Dasgupta and Stiglitz 1980a,b), base their models on a hypothesized social planner.[39]

Interestingly, the method of the social planner emerged publicly as neoclassically trained economists from Eastern Europe continued to criticize the central planning model of the Soviet Union and implemented a competitive market socialist model that might lead toward stateless communism. Many neoclassical economists also followed these market socialist models with great interest, while central planning remained at the center of their models. This use of the term *social planner* also came at a time when more conservative economists began to attack macroeconomic state policies. Robert E. Lucas famously argued that macroeconomic policies are ineffective and that markets were effective. In a different direction, Joseph Stiglitz and others argued that market failures are pervasive, and thus markets require state intervention. Both groups used the same socialist model as their fundamental method.[40]

Neoclassical economists continued to consider their methods relevant to both capitalist and socialist economies. The neoclassical economist as the social planner could seek to improve economic systems, so as to reach a Pareto-optimal equilibrium and maximize social welfare. As one of the most famous comparative economics textbook authors, Morris Born-stein, explained, "One may argue that the ultimate purpose of comparing economic systems is to find ways of improving the performance of a given system (in light of its social preference function)" (1989: 11). Economists had long criticized the Soviet socialist system (Grossman 1963) and sug-gested ways that this system could be improved. They found interest and excitement in various market socialist experiments, particularly in Yugo-slavia and Hungary, which led them to think about ways to improve these economic systems, as socialist systems.

These economists made a distinction between mere policy change and reform, which meant moving to a Pareto-optimal equilibrium.[41] Since Pareto, neoclassical economists had considered both the competitive market and the socialist state, in the abstract, as equally efficient, given necessary institutions, and thus thought of each as having a stable, Pareto-optimal equilibrium. In 1956, economist Jan Tinbergen took Pareto's ideas a step further, showing that a social planner could not only maximize so-cial welfare equal to that of a competitive market but could also help entire societies jump to a more efficient equilibrium and then rearrange property rights to get a just result. Economists also argued for other possible Pareto-optimal equilibria, such as the worker self-management market socialist system or an "infinity" of possible reforms or systems. As economist Ste-phen Rosefielde remarked:

Thus, from an efficiency point of view there exists not one model of socialism but an infinity of models each characterized by a unique social welfare function, and each demonstrating unique behavioral characteristics dependent on the institutional ar-rangements required for the realization of a particular set of ends. The proper task of the student of socialist economics is the explicit sorting of alternative socialist ends into different general equilibrium frameworks so that the relative merits of al-ternative social economic systems can be objectively determined both in theory and practice. (1973: 242)

In 1932, Lionel Robbins, a famous British follower of the Austrian School, similarly argued, "Without economic analysis it is not possible rationally to choose between alternative *systems* of society" ([1932] 1945: 155). The social planner could evaluate these many possible systems to see whether they were Pareto optimal and what kinds of benefits they might provide. Reform could improve the system or lead to a new system, though not necessarily to a capitalist one.

Neoclassical economists came to regard the Soviet system in practice, as opposed to the abstract central planning model, as stable yet inefficient and thus in need of some sort of reform. Such a system was stable because it had a coherent set of institutions that work together well, though these institutions produced inefficient outcomes. Neoclassical economists mathematically recognized that there might be more than one stable equilibrium in a system (Bryant 1983; Diamond 1982). In 1989, former president of the Econometric Society Michael Bruno explained, "The concept of economic reform is described as a planned shift from one, Pareto inefficient, but quasi-stable, equilibrium (or 'trap') to a new Pareto superior equilibrium which is, or is designed to become, stable too" (275). The Soviet centrally planned model could be understood as one of these traps. At this time, economists then revived an earlier notion of the "big push" to argue for a jump to a better equilibrium with a coherent, comprehensive set of institutional changes (Murphy, Shleifer, and Vishny 1989).[42] Worldwide, economists ran into political obstacles to the implementation of a range of macroeconomic policies, including structural adjustment in Latin America and worker self-management reforms in Eastern Europe. These economists were well aware of the political difficulties involved and began studying reform strategy itself to understand the political conditions for a successful push, jump, shock, or transition to a new equilibrium (Marschak 1973; Milanović 1989; Portes 1972).

At the same time, it should be remembered that market reform or transition did not necessarily mean a transition to capitalism. In fact, neoclassical comparative economists questioned the very characteristics of economic systems. According to Bornstein,

The trend in the study of economic systems is to downgrade the significance of ownership as a critical element in the nature and operation of economic systems, on the ground that it is less important than the pattern of resource allocation and income distribution. Thus, it is now commonly held that "capitalism" and "socialism" are not useful classifications of economic systems, and that such distinctions are more of ideological or political significance. (1989: 9)[43]

In the same textbook, Neuberger declared, "Ownership rights, in themselves, may signify very little. They may mean anything from complete control over the owned object to virtually no control at all" (1989: 19). Neoclassical economists had long believed that their tools could improve any economic system.[44] Moreover, socialists understood socialism as much more than state ownership of the means of production and central planning. For example, Rosefielde called for a more socialist model than Oskar Lange's market socialism, which, in his words, "To put the matter bluntly, the Lange model of market socialism is capitalism without capitalists" (1973: 239). To define socialism as merely state property and central planning meant that socialism might include wage labor and labor exploitation more generally, which seemed to contradict its very values and goals. In the 1980s, economists sought to improve economic systems, compare economic systems, evaluate which are Pareto optimal, and realize the preferences determined by society.

Neoclassical Economics within the World Bank

The World Bank could not avoid the new developments in neoclassical economics and in market socialism. World Bank economic expertise has long been based on neoclassical economics and, more specifically, on comparative economic systems.[45] We know that comparative economists criticized the Soviet socialist system. Following comparative economics, World Bank economists sought to improve various economic systems and knew market socialist experiments because they figured prominently in comparative economics publications and were based on neoclassical economics. Socialism formed the basis of various, significant neoclassical models. Therefore, no matter their politics, neoclassical economists found socialism in all its theoretical and abstract forms professional relevant and interesting.

Those with a variety of politics and neoclassical training could work in the World Bank. An American economist who would soon enter and quickly rise up the ranks of the World Bank wrote, "I am seeking to integrate the neoclassical theory of the self-managed economy with the libertarian and Marxist theories of the transition to socialism" (Knight 1975: 10–11). These ideas and commitments did not contradict the neoclassical economics used in the World Bank. As World Bank economists had told me, the World Bank hired "lots of leftists," as well as those on the right. Those on the left were sent to countries that might interest them, such as Nicaragua or Ethiopia, while those on the right were sent to other countries. We must remember that neoclassical economists understood their professional methods as helpful to a wide range of systems. Mainstream comparative economics textbooks argued that ownership was no longer relevant to the field. The more important distinction within neoclassical economics was between those who advocated decentralizing, democratic institutions and those who supported hierarchical, authoritarian institutions. World Bank economists would not have necessarily accepted that competitive markets required private property and capitalism.

In 1987, the World Bank published a report titled "The Bank's Analytical Approach to Socialist Countries and Economic Reform" (Schrenk 1987). The author, Martin Schrenk, who had written the 1979 World Bank report on Yugoslavia (Schrenk, Ardalan, and El Tatawy 1979), started by framing the World Bank's analytical perspective as that of comparative economic systems, specifically referring to the work of Morris Bornstein (ibid.: 1–2).[46] According to Schrenk, the "obvious meeting ground for a productive dialogue [between the Bank and socialist member countries] is the realm of policies . . . System changes . . . are subject to a productive dialogue only if the principal choices have been made by the country" (4). By system changes, Schrenk seemed to mean moving between stages of socialism, not moving from socialism to capitalism. Referring to the work of Hungarian economist János Kornai, Schrenk presented socialist economies on a continuum from the first phase of a "heroic-enthusiastic" system, to the second phase of "bureaucratic-hierarchical command economy," and to the third phase of "market socialism" (ibid.: 5–6). According to Schrenk, the World Bank should focus on the "transition from Phase 2 to Phase 3," which

poses both formidable analytical challenges and unique opportunities to the Bank. The range of opportunities are those which the Bank always saw its major contribution: the design of effective sub-systems under decentralization, institution-building, and the development of policies. (ibid.: 10)

According to Schrenk, the turn toward market reforms in Eastern Europe meant that a bureaucratic-hierarchical command economy, Phase 2, was no longer an option, and the World Bank should help countries move to Phase 3, market socialism.

Therefore, at this time, the World Bank planned to help build and improve market socialism. According to the economic literature, Phase 2 was quite stable, and any market reforms might cause a reversion to this phase. Therefore, economists felt that a comprehensive set of reforms was needed to move completely to Phase 3, which seemed to be a stable location that would function much as did other market economies: "In Phase 3 presumably similar institutions and policies would be appropriate in many instances as in pure non-socialist market economies" (ibid.: 10). According to the report, important areas of reform would include: (1) expanding the range of ownership forms to include state or social ownership and other ownership forms "compatible with socialism: from private ownership of small firms, a variety of cooperative and collective ownership of small firms, to mixed ownership and control"; (2) abolishing annual planning; and (3) making state-owned firms market oriented (ibid.: 16).

In the report, neoclassical economics played a problematic role. Schrenk argued that the neoclassical paradigm offered models of capitalist market economies and "the centrally planned economy of the textbook" but not of socialist economies (ibid.: 4). He declared that nothing was truly known about socialist economies—there was no "universal model" of socialism—and comparing them with perfect competition was not helpful (ibid.: 4). Socialist economies in transition from Phase 2 to Phase 3 thus had special characteristics and problems that neoclassical models could not capture. In these rhetorical moves, he severed socialism from its role as original model for neoclassical economics and the role that neoclassical economics had played in actually existing socialism. However, because market socialism of Phase 3 was similar to pure nonsocialist market economies, those countries that successfully created market socialism could then use neoclassical economics to evaluate and improve their economy.

Schrenk relied on the work of Eastern European economists, especially the work of Kornai, demonstrating the continuing relevance of Eastern European socialism to neoclassical economics and to the World Bank in particular.[47] Schrenk's report reflected Kornai's 1970s criticism of neoclassical economics that the "uncritically modified model of neo-classical origin" did not recognize how institutions and the system more generally create different results and behaviors (ibid.: 4). His report also called for socialist best practices coming out of Eastern Europe—to discontinue annual planning with targets and quotas, create market-oriented efficient enterprises, and establish a variety of ownership types (ibid.: 16)—and envisioned Eastern Europeans as having helpful experiences: "The positive and negative experiences of other socialist economies who went through a similar process at an earlier stage, can be more helpful in designing the appropriate approach" (ibid.: 15).

Eastern European economists, in fact, had neoclassical training and were part of the transnational dialogue about neoclassical economics.

Yugoslavia had been a member of the World Bank since its beginnings. Romania then joined in 1972, Hungary in 1982, and Poland in 1986, with other Eastern European countries joining after 1989 (Hardt and Kaufman 1995: 192–193). The World Bank had long considered Yugoslav worker self-management socialism a "success" in regards to economic development (Dubey 1975: 52). Eastern European economists had actually experienced market transitions—within socialism—and were well aware of the political difficulties involved. Thus, they would increasingly be involved as economists and consultants within the World Bank.

Schrenk's report remained within the comparative economic mission of the World Bank to improve economic systems. World Bank economists continued the neoclassical economic interest in markets and a variety of socialisms that lay at the core of their practice. They did not associate markets necessarily with capitalism but rather saw markets as necessary for both socialism and capitalism. This focus on improving systems helps to explain the book inscription made by World Bank economist, Branko Milanović, in 1990, which was cited earlier in this chapter: "To Jeff Sachs, who is trying to save socialism." Milanović was certainly not the only one who thought that economists were saving socialism.

Realizing Market Socialism

In 1985, Mikhail Gorbachev became the general secretary of the Communist Party of the Soviet Union. By 1987, he had implemented reforms devised to realize *perestroika* (restructuring) and *glasnost* (openness) as a way to renew socialism. According to Gorbachev (1996), *perestroika* meant ending totalitarian systems and introducing democratic reforms and freedoms, a pluralistic economy (with many types of ownership, including privatization, free enterprise, and shareholding), and a free market economy. This might sound like capitalism to observers looking back in hindsight, but at the time it represented the most advanced understanding of socialism among economists in both East and West. In other words, these were seen as best practices in socialist economics transnationally. In the minds of many Eastern European socialists, the Soviet Union was finally catching up. The Soviet Union's own reforms also removed obstacles to reforms throughout the East Bloc. Many economists around the world thought that market socialism might finally be possible.

János Kornai (1990b) remarked, "We witness a very strange revival of market socialist ideas in Eastern Europe" (Kornai 1990b: 141).[48] In the late 1980s, Eastern European economists continued to think in terms of reforms, rather than considering a transition to capitalism (Voszka 1991: 80).[49] Market socialism was the model for the late 1980s reforms. According to Kornai, "In Hungary, and also in a number of other socialist countries, the principle of 'market socialism' has become a guiding idea of the reform process" (1990b: 50). Eastern European economists had long envisioned reform as a process that could move forward or backward, as "stages" or "waves" of reform (Szamuely 1982, 1984), but essentially as a linear process, a single path. In the 1970s, Party-state factions had halted market reforms. For economists, the 1980s brought a return to the market reform path. These economists often presented reform proposals in 1988 and 1989 as the continuation of previous reforms, such as those from the 1950s and 1968.[50] The experience of recurring political obstacles to reform had made economists interested in *radical* economic reform, which, in the context of the late 1980s, meant "genuine" competitive markets and socialist institutions, especially socially owned, nonstate enterprises and worker self-management.[51] The pure form of market socialism that brought together competitive markets and socialist institutions had a long tradition in neoclassical economics, since the 1930s at least, and evoked a great deal of excitement in late 1980s Eastern Europe and elsewhere.[52] The transition offered the possibility of radical economic reform and the final realization of market socialism.

East European economists carried on their decades-long criticism of centrally planned socialism.[53] For example, Hungarian economist Tamás Nagy (1989) argued that the current Hungarian system was neo-Stalinist and in crisis. During the late 1980s, Eastern European economists continued to discuss the centrally planned model because, in their view, their economies still acted like this model and it represented a Pareto equilibrium point. Czechoslovak economist Vaclav Klaus ([1989] 1990) observed that the highly centralized Czechoslovak economy had "reached a very stable equilibrium . . . it is actually a point of a kind of Pareto optimum" (45).[54] Kornai also judged this "classical system" stable and internally coherent (1992: 377–379). However, the classical socialist system lagged behind capitalism in productivity and growth and would do so increasingly, which impelled policy makers to implement market reforms (ibid.).

Economists talked extensively about the impending economic crisis of the centrally planned economy. Hungarian Mihály Laki (1989) warned that, if the economy was only minimally reformed, "the traditional Soviet-type socialism will continue to exist, and the market will not be, even later on, an integrating power in the economy. If the system is completely transformed, market economy will develop" (251). Therefore, radical, comprehensive reform was needed as a "big push" to move away permanently from Soviet state socialism, a seemingly Pareto-inefficient trap, and to a new Pareto-optimal location.

Around the world in the late 1980s, politicians, even those on the left, embraced markets, as noted by Mudge:

> In the 1990s the rise of market-friendly politics across the political spectrum became an unmistakable phenomenon. . . . the most effective advocates of policies understood as neo-liberal in Western Europe (and beyond) have often been political and intellectual elites who are sympathetic to, or are representatives of, the left and centre-left. (2008: 723)

Yet this was not a new phenomenon among Eastern European economists. By 1989, they called for a "genuine market economy" and socialism. Polish economist Leszek Balcerowicz (1989) insisted on a market economy, which true market socialism would have. He (1992) later explained, "The term 'market socialism' should be used, in my view, only with respect to those models that envisage a genuine market, which includes free price-setting" (11n13). Hungarian economist Béla Csikós-Nagy used the term *socialist market* but also called for a market economy: "The socialist market economy cannot be basically different from that of the modern market economy" (1989: 218). To economists throughout Eastern Europe, markets were essential to all economic systems, capitalist or socialist (Hegedűs 1989: 225). This new socialism should realize the reform ideal and include markets, especially the provocative capital and labor markets.[55] According to this view, only through the market would Eastern European countries stave off economic crisis and collapse. At the end of 1988, the top Hungarian Party-state economic policy maker Miklós Németh declared, "The market economy is the only way to avoid a social catastrophe or a long, slow death" (McDonald 1993: 219). Vaclav Klaus's infamous demand for "a market without adjectives" thus fit within neoclassical traditions of socialism. These economists did not necessarily equate markets and capitalism.

From their linear, reform perspective, Eastern European economists understood that severe economic crisis had pushed Communist regimes to move forward again, after the backward movement of the 1970s, on the reform path. During socialism, Eastern European reform economists, as well as the previously mentioned World Bank document from 1987, understood "market transition" as a movement toward market socialism:

1. centrally planned state socialism →• market socialism

By the late 1980s, only radical reform would create the "big push" to the new equilibrium of market socialism. The goal of radical reform was not capitalism, but it was a system fundamentally different from the centrally planned socialist system. This market transition had several complex components.

After decades of halfhearted reforms followed by backtracking, these economists believed that they needed to implement comprehensive reforms quickly. They feared that because the Party-state bureaucracy always fought against market reform partial market reforms might cause a return to the classical state socialist model (Kornai 1992; see also Nuti 1988). Vaclav Klaus (1990) argued, "In the real world one can never stop halfway, because the marginal point, which is stronger, less strict, less demanding, etc. will always prevail . . . That is why we cannot, under any circumstances, consider the question of replacing one system with another to be simple or to have ready-made answers" (47). If one believed that the centrally planned model was a Pareto equilibrium point and an economy did not make it to another Pareto equilibrium point, then the economy would naturally tend back toward the centrally planned model. Therefore, a market transition might follow one of two tracks:

1. centrally planned state socialism →• market socialism

2. centrally planned state socialism →• market socialism →• centrally planned state socialism

To these economists, a genuine market economy would not merely simulate capitalism. Oskar Lange's abstract model of market socialism came to be seen as simulated capitalism.[56] The model was based on a narrow form of neoclassical economics that did not include the necessary institutions to avoid monopolies and hierarchies and did not allow real competition and the necessary institutions to enable workers' power and create real socialism. Some scholars had wondered what exactly made Lange's model socialist. To Balcerowicz (1992), many market socialist reform packages would merely create "simulated capitalism," an economic system with capitalist institutions, like joint-stock companies and stock exchanges, but without capitalists (13–14). Balcerowicz argued that these simulated forms would eventually evolve into capitalism. Therefore, market socialism in this form was not a stable Pareto-optimal equilibrium point but rather an unstable transit point. We now see three possible transition scenarios:

1. centrally planned state socialism → market socialism

2. centrally planned state socialism → market socialism → centrally planned state socialism

3. centrally planned state socialism → (simulated) market socialism → market capitalism

For some, market socialism was the goal of the transition, while for others it provided a rest stop on the road to capitalism.[57] American economist Steven Rosefielde (1992) even understood David Lipton and Jeffrey Sachs as advising the Soviet government to create "some acceptable form of market socialism that suits its purposes and those of the developed West" (8). Simulated capitalism could lead in several directions.

Beyond Lange's "capitalism without capitalists" and other forms of simulated capitalism, economists assumed that another Pareto-optimal socialist form existed. Balcerowicz (1992) noted very briefly that the inevitable slide from market socialism to capitalism could be avoided through "the model of the labour self-management economy" (14n20). The Illyrian firm based on the Yugoslav worker self-management model remained a potential and desirable endpoint of market transition. During the 1960s and 1970s, economists around the world had shown great excitement about the Yugoslav socialist model, especially because Yugoslavia had some of the highest growth rates in the world.[58] In the 1980s, however, the world witnessed Yugoslavia descend into debt crisis, inflation, nationalist violence, the slow collapse of the state, and general economic crisis (Lampe 1996; Lydall 1989; Woodward 1995). By 1984, Alec Nove said in an interview, "I think any serious Yugoslav economist would instantly admit that what is happening now is, to put it mildly, rather unfortunate, not to say a mess" (Stephanson 1984: 105). Yet, in spite of the crisis in Yugoslavia, worker self-management remained a model for many in the East Bloc, a model that might finally be realized with the right economic reforms.[59] Kornai recognized the strong popular support for this system (1992: 473). Hungarian economist K. A. Soós ([1989] 1990) wrote, "In the present period, full of political and economic uncertainties and radical changes, the practice of self-management, which, after all, has become accepted in our society, could be preserved as a valuable element of the status quo" (471). Worker self-management socialism remained a transition option.[60]

The Illyrian model, abstracted from the Yugoslav case, existed as a viable option to which the social planner could help an economy jump. According to Balcerowicz (1989), the market economy in socialism would not have private ownership of means of production but rather some form of socialist ownership: Illyrian socialism, workers' property, leasing of the social capital as discussed by Tibor Liska and Boris Brutzkus, or capitalist institutions without private capitalists as discussed by Márton Tardos (185–186). To Balcerowicz, these were "pure models," not hybrid models mixing planning and markets (ibid.: 186).[61] Economists argued that partial reforms or hybrid mixed models, like Keynesianism, would not lead to these pure Pareto-optimal models, like the laissez-faire Illyrian model. Thus, it is possible that, when Vaclav Klaus supposedly stated that the Third Way was the surest road to the Third World, he was rejecting mixed systems, not the variety of pure models. Because the Illyrian model would not collapse into capitalism, at least in Balcerowicz's mind, it continued as an option. Therefore, we have another market transition model:

1. centrally planned state socialism → market socialism
2. centrally planned state socialism → market socialism → centrally planned state socialism
3. centrally planned state socialism → (simulated) market socialism → market capitalism
4. centrally planned state socialism → (simulated) market socialism → Illyrian model[62]

The market transition had several possible destinations, including the Illyrian model based on Yugoslav worker self-management.

Throughout the 1980s, Eastern Europeans seemed to implement the "lessons" of socialism. They handed state-owned enterprises over to workers, in hopes of realizing enterprise autonomy, workers' control, entrepreneurship, and the withering of the state. By the end of the 1980s, workers' self-management existed throughout Hungary, Poland, and Yugoslavia (Milanović 1992). According to Orenstein, in Poland "employee councils, moreover, were reinvigorated in 1988 and 1989 . . . Roundtable negotiations between Solidarity and the communist regimes in 1989 reaffirmed the rights of worker self-management" (2001: 27). Paczyńska argued that the reaffirmed rights "solidified the opinion among workers that the enterprises belonged to the employees. Hence, workers assumed that privatization meant that formal ownership rights would be transferred directly to them or that at the very least they should have a decisive say in the design and implementation of restructuring" (2009: 135). In 1987–1988, Soviet reforms gave more rights to work collectives, encouraged cooperatives, and leased assets to work collectives (Logue, Plekhanov, and Simmons 1995). By August 1991, more than 111,000 cooperatives were in operation in the Soviet Union (Nelson and Kuzes 1994: 29). The 1991 privatization law, according to Logue and his coauthors, gave employee ownership the key role in privatization (1995: 5). Throughout Eastern Europe, economists also called for the leasing of state enterprises and the ownership of these enterprises by nonstate entities. These reforms, in the eyes of economists, would create the essential condition for market competition, enterprise autonomy, and socialism.

For some, the Illyrian model became an amorphous, positive goal. Yugoslav economist Milica Uvalić (1992) reinterpreted "socialism" as the Soviet state socialist model in opposition to Yugoslav worker self-management model. She declared:

The socialist features of the Yugoslav economy inherited from the traditional centrally planned economy have seriously undermined the ultimate goal of all economic reforms in Yugoslavia of introducing a self-managed market economy, thus reproducing problems, typical of the socialist economy, of economic inefficiency, inadequate incentives and lack of entrepreneurship. (ibid.: 65)

For Uvalić and others, real Yugoslav worker self-management required the eradication of state socialism. To many economists, the problems of the 1990s did not prove that worker self-management was unworkable.[63] Some Yugoslav economists also understood the East and the West as converging toward a new system based on entrepreneurship, economic and political democracy, and liberation from state domination (Kalogjera 1990: 42; Milanović 1989). Balcerowicz (1989) asked: "Is it possible to pass from socialist systems to these models? Would they last or transform into another system?" Worker self-management socialism remained an option, but it was unclear where it might be heading.

After the recurrent political backlashes against previous reforms, economists argued that only radical democratization would open the door to genuine market reform and socialism. The necessary "big push" toward this model would require the expansion of economic and political democracy, thus creating new social actors personally interested in the system. Tamás Nagy, former top economic advisor in the Hungarian Communist Party, wrote, "It is the economic restructuring itself that necessitates the elimination of the party and state apparatus' rule over the economy. The way to arrive at this end is to make the political power pluralistic (to create a multi-party system) and thus subject to social control" (1989: 264). According to Branko Horvat (1989), socialism envisions an equitable society, which does not have concentrations of economic or political power (233). Polish economist Jan Mujżel called for the deepening of self-management and democratization "as fast as possible" to create a "critical mass" as a "'guarantor' against withdrawing from the comprehensive and far-reaching systemic changes and even from slowing down the pace of these modifications" (1988: 86). A comprehensive reform would be necessary to stop resistance by the state and create new supporters of a worker self-management system. If such a reform failed, according to Mujżel, a technocratic market reform, privileging managers and experts over workers, would result.

In 1988 for the Branko Mikulić government and even more so for the 1989 Ante Marković government, Yugoslav economists joined government commissions to finally realize the reforms they had hoped for since the 1960s. Yugoslav economists continued to condemn the state socialist model, as they had done for decades, and to criticize the 1974 reforms that sought to eradicate markets (Popov 1989). Dragomir Vojnić (1989), for example, called for a "new socialism" based on market pluralism, ownership pluralism, and political pluralism. Hungarian reform economists' proposal "Turnabout and Reform" similarly called for markets, a pluralism of ownership, and democratization (Márkus 1996). By November 1988, the Hungarian Central Committee had decided it was necessary to build a "market economy" with mixed property forms, but, judging from the minimal discussion of economic reform, the Central Committee seemed much more concerned about political reform (*Magyar Szocialista* 1994: 489). Political democracy and new international actors would fundamentally change the political context, removing market socialism as a possibility and paving the way for a transition to capitalism that had not previously been part of any major reform plans.

Conclusions

Since the Soviet New Economic Policy of 1921, the Soviet Union and then Eastern Europe had experienced "transitions," market reforms, and various market experiments. The changes of 1989 were no more rejections of socialism than these earlier reforms had been. After decades of political resistance to reforms, Eastern European economists sought genuine markets and democracy within the socialist economy and the polity. With the turn toward enterprise autonomy, new rights for workers' councils, new entrepreneurship laws, and the end of the Communist Party's political monopoly, the transitions in Eastern Europe could be seen as a continuation and realization of the market socialist tradition within neoclassical economics. Even by 1994, two economists deeply involved in the transition noted the continued prevalence of market socialist discussions within economics:

> One of the most enduring proposals in modern economics is market socialism . . . A reasonable person might expect that recent events in eastern Europe would put this proposal to permanent and well-deserved rest, Instead, these events seem to have given hope to the market socialists. (Shleifer and Vishny 1994: 165)

Neoclassically trained economists rejected Soviet central planning and envisioned a range of possible market transition destinations.

The year 1989 was the time to realize a market economy, economic democracy, and political democracy within a socialist system. Yet, by November of that year the situation had changed dramatically. We now turn to how the goal of transition transformed from realizing market socialism to destroying socialism and creating capitalism. The political renarration of 1989 and the troubled connection between socialism and neoclassical economics since 1989 are the topics of the next chapter.

7

Post-1989
How Transnational Socialism Became Neoliberalism without Ceasing to Exist

THE YEAR 1989 OPENED THE POSSIBILITY of finally realizing the democratic, decentralized socialism that many Eastern Europeans had sought for so long. The post-1989 period, however, fundamentally changed the political terrain and political options worldwide. As Michael Burawoy and Katherine Verdery (1999) argue, the collapse of the Party-states broke down the "macrostructures" and opened up space for "micro-worlds" and local improvisation within new rules and limits. While some celebrated the victory of dissident culture and civil society (Garton Ash 1990), others made apocalyptic predictions of, as Ken Jowitt's 1992 book title put it, a *New World Disorder*. Scholars soon noticed that elites no longer considered socialism an option (Devine 1993: 243; Estrin 1991: 194; Keren 1993; Nuti 1992; Porket 1993; Swain 1992). As Pekka Sutela noted, "More widely than ever before, the non-viability of socialism is taken as evident, all the more so after the popular revolutions of the autumn of 1989" (1992: 67). Neoliberalism replaced market socialism as a goal. Neoliberalism advocates a set of four general ideas:

1. competitive markets
2. smaller, authoritarian states
3. hierarchical firms, management, and owners
4. capitalism

This chapter explores the ways that neoliberals used neoclassical economics to support this fourfold political and economic agenda.

This book has sought to demonstrate that neoliberalism is not synonymous with neoclassical economics. Scholars have incorrectly used these two concepts interchangeably. Those economists labeled "neoliberal"—such as Leszek Balcerowicz, Milton Friedman, Vaclav Klaus, and Jeffrey Sachs—and Eastern European socialists—like Włodzimierz Brus, Branko Horvat, Oskar Lange, and Ota Šik—practiced neoclassical economics. They would not have agreed on economic policies, but they did share professional economic methods and models. Since the nineteenth century, neoclassical economists had considered their discipline universally applicable to any economic system. They also developed their theories and methods through thinking about socialism, capitalism, and markets. From the 1950s, economists in socialist Eastern Europe used neoclassical economics as an analytical and normative tool to build market socialism. Western economists had worked with them as colleagues since the late 1950s, thus developing their ideas and methods transnationally. In the socialist East and the capitalist West, neoclassical economists could easily speak a neoliberal language because a pure competitive market system existed at the core of their discipline. They talked the language of markets, supply and demand, prices, entrepreneurship, competition, and profits, although this did not necessarily mean that they wanted to create capitalism. The victory of neoliberalism was in spite of, not because of, the majority of neoclassical economists.

This chapter starts with a comparison of the ideas of Jeffrey Sachs and Joseph Stiglitz, two world-famous neoclassical economists. This comparison helps to illuminate the debates among such economists worldwide, not only in the early 1990s but throughout the history of neoclassical economics. They did not battle over unfettered markets or state intervention in the economy, nor about disembedding or embedding the market, but rather they differed over whether the market required authoritarian or democratic institutions. In 1989, as discussed in the previous chapter, this debate seemed settled in the name of the democratic institutions of market socialism, but the opening of the Eastern European political fields to new actors brought this resolution back into question. The chapter then turns to the ways in which neoclassical economics could be used to support neoliberalism, in contrast to its earlier support of socialisms, and explores the actors interested in mobilizing neoclassical economics in this neoliberal way. The transition was, in the words of anthropologist Katherine Verdery, "a project of cultural engineering in which fundamentally social ideas are resignified" (1999: 54). The transition also brought a deep economic crisis, tremendous decline in living standards, vast corruption, and politicians' endless opportunism. Hungarian economist Iván Major related, "What started as a realization of long-awaited dreams by the peoples in Eastern Europe has been turning into a nightmare" (1993: 1). In this chapter, I seek to explain how this revolution in thought and practice happened after 1989 while at the same time recognizing that socialisms embedded within neoclassical economics remain latent within neoliberalism.

Jeffrey Sachs versus Joseph Stiglitz

On January 1, 1990, Poland became the first government in the former East Bloc to implement shock therapy, followed by Czechoslovakia and Bulgaria in 1991; Russia, Albania, and Estonia in 1992; and Latvia in 1993 (Marangos 2007: 42–43). American economists David Lipton and Jeffrey Sachs had advised the new Solidarity-led government in Poland and laid out a reform program for all Eastern European governments. According to Lipton and Sachs (1990a), the following policies should be implemented quickly and simultaneously:

1. Stabilization. This meant austerity through balancing the budget, ending subsidies, increasing interest rates, devaluing the exchange rate, making the currency convertible, and limiting wage growth through taxes.

2. Liberalization. This entailed deregulating prices, opening the country to free international trade, and removing restrictions on the private sector.

3. Privatization. In contrast to the two other policies, privatization would be a longer process of selling off or giving away state-owned firms to create a private sector.

Lipton and Sachs advised the rapid implementation of these policies to avoid inevitable "populist" or other political resistance to them (ibid.: 87). They also discussed other essential steps, such as the restructuring of enterprises and a social security net, but these were given much less emphasis than the first three items.[1]

Economists like Jeffrey Sachs, David Lipton, Olivier Blanchard, Richard Layard, Milton Friedman, Anders Åslund, and Andrei Shleifer publicly espoused a narrow view of neoclassical economics, arguing that markets would emerge from the retraction of the state and create the institutions necessary for their own functioning. Sachs later wrote, "Markets spring up as soon as central planning bureaucrats vacate the field" (1993: xiii). Similarly, Åslund and his coauthors wrote, "The evidence suggests that institutional development is stimulated by early and radical reform" (1996: 249). Yet this language of disembedding the market from the state obscures the very clear argument these economists made for particular state and corporate institutions necessary for markets to thrive.

Lipton and Sachs (1990a) wrote one of the most famous articles by this group, "Creating a Market Economy in Eastern Europe: The Case of Poland." This article represented an important reinterpretation of Eastern Europe and its lessons. Lipton and Sachs understood Eastern Europe as in "crisis" and suffering from "unnecessary decay" caused by its "Stalinist legacy" (ibid.: 76, 80–86). Although they acknowledged several times that economies in the region differed, in the end, Lipton and Sachs presented socialist economies as basically the same: defined by Stalinism, central planning, state ownership, distorted relative prices, heavy industry, large firms, "a virtual absence" of small and medium-sized firms, chronic excess demand, and autarchic production (ibid.: 80–86). For example, Lipton and Sachs mentioned that Hungary and Poland had private sectors, but "even in these last cases," they insisted, "the private firms have been heavily restricted by administrative barriers, punitive tax laws, shortages of inputs, and unavailability of foreign exchange and credit, the allocation of which has been almost entirely directed to the state sector" (ibid.: 82). Time and again, throughout the article, the authors recognized and then disregarded the significant variation in Eastern European economies, reinforcing the view that socialist economies were essentially Stalinist and defined by central planning. After decades of experimentation in markets, property, prices, and entrepreneurship, as well as extensive foreign trade and marketing, Lipton and Sachs wrote off the entire Eastern European socialist experience: "There are tens, if not hundreds, of thousands of officials whose professional experience lies in a lifetime of bureaucratic planning of economic life, with close links to party-appointed managers in the state enterprises" (ibid.: 88). Their vision of Eastern European economies as essentially Stalinist suggested that the only solution was to destroy this immoral legacy and create a wholly new system.[2]

"The strategy of transition" presented by Lipton and Sachs was a one-size-fits-all program to move from a "Stalinist" centrally planned state socialist economy to a market economy, jumping from a once Pareto-efficient equilibrium to a new Pareto-efficient equilibrium. Lipton and Sachs, in fact, channeled many of the criticisms of Eastern European economists, but they did so for a particular neoliberal agenda that, in fact, bolstered the central state that Eastern Europeans had criticized. Inspired by Hungarian economist János Kornai's work, Lipton and Sachs presented Eastern Europe as lacking "normal" market relations or efficient enterprises (ibid.: 80). Repeating the arguments of many Eastern European economists, they asserted that the lessons of socialism had shown that a rapid and "comprehensive" reform, rather than piecemeal changes, was needed (ibid.: 99). Most importantly, Lipton and Sachs did not see anything worth retaining in the Eastern European countries. The authors were encouraged by the fact that the Polish government had introduced "a host of legislative and executive initiatives aimed at wiping away the remnants of the previous economic system and building a legal and institutional foundation for a market economy" (ibid.: 111). To Lipton and Sachs, such so-called shock therapy was the best plan.

The strategy of transition, contrary to its own liberal rhetoric, relied on and empowered a strong authoritarian state, ironically similar to the Stalinist state.[3] Lipton and Sachs did warn that one must guard "against the inadvertent creation of new concentrations of enormous political and economic power in society" (ibid.: 130). Yet, in opposition to Eastern European economists' criticisms of Soviet state socialism and calls for decentralization, Lipton and Sachs declared that only a strong government could ignore populist dissent and implement shock therapy.[4] Workers were their primary obstacle. By this time, Eastern European governments had in effect given most factories to the workers.[5] Lipton and Sachs recognized that "workers wonder what the fuss is about, because of course *they* own the firms" and ominously declared, "Privatization should begin by establishing that the central government owns the enterprises and has the exclusive power to engage in privatization" (1990a: 128).[6] In Poland, Hungary, and Yugoslavia, the state recentralized ownership rights that had been de facto workers' property.[7] Thus, in the name of private corporate property, Lipton and Sachs called for the state reappropriation and nationalization of what was de facto workers' property.

Their strategies resembled Stalinist ones in other ways. Lipton and Sachs, as well as their counterparts in Eastern Europe, shared a Stalinist rejection of the past and call for drastic change (Raman and West 2009).

Even more importantly, as Reddaway (2001) noted, they used "authoritarian methods to impose quasi-market institutions on Russia." Markets were the law of the land, except when workers wanted to sell their labor power on the market. Lipton and Sachs rejected the full wage liberalization "supported by some Polish economists" (1990a: 115) because it would lead to inflation. So, the state would have to keep wages below market value, which had also been the case under Stalinist socialism. Lipton and Sachs also recognized the fundamental reorientation of the economy: "The transformation of the economy will require a massive resource reallocation, with delays between the freeing up of resources and their reabsorption elsewhere" (ibid.: 124). Lipton and Sachs called for rapid privatization, not by employees or managers but rather by state authorities, foreign corporations, and other investors.[8] Friends and family of the new (and old) political elite and its economic experts acquired these businesses (Wedel 2001), which resulted in corporate ownership, oligarchy, close ties between government and business, and high levels of corruption. As with their Eastern European counterparts, American economic elites and economists professed a narrow neoclassical economics, which declared that markets would create efficient institutions, while, in fact, accepting the status quo, the hierarchical institutions of the past in a new form.

Former World Bank chief economist and Nobel Laureate in economics Joseph Stiglitz has been one of the most important critics of shock therapy and the Washington Consensus. Those on the left have embraced his criticisms of "market fundamentalism" and globalization.[9] Many readers of Stiglitz's work, however, have misunderstood his message because they view economists as standing along a continuum from free market advocate to state advocate. Readers of Stiglitz have understood him as on the side of state intervention, in opposition to the market or capitalist side. However, Stiglitz, like those who supported privatization, practiced neoclassical economics with a commitment to competitive markets.[10]

Like Lipton and Sachs, Stiglitz also appropriated the views of Eastern European economists, but in a different way. Stiglitz himself had participated in East–West dialogues about neoclassical economics and socialism and viewed the market transition as a process that began during socialism. In the preface to a set of lectures given in 1990 titled *Whither Socialism?* Stiglitz remembered that during his graduate school days he had "made an expedition to the Central School of Statistics in Warsaw to talk with Lange and Kalecki and their disciples" (1994: xi). Oskar Lange and the other Polish economists and planners shared a common neoclassical economic language with Stiglitz and most mainstream economists in the United States. In contrast to Lipton and Sachs's interpretation of Eastern Europe defined by an immoral and failed Stalinist legacy, Stiglitz understood the Eastern European experience as relevant to neoclassical economics:

We have learned a lot from these [socialist] experiments, but because they were hardly controlled experiments, what we learned remains a subject of some dispute. While government ownership is clearly no panacea, there remains scope for further experimentation. (ibid.: 277)

Also in contrast to Lipton and Sachs, Stiglitz perceived the changes in 1990 as connected with past changes within socialist systems and socialist debates. Stiglitz found himself interested in "transition" starting not in 1989 but already in the early 1980s:

My interest in the problems of transition was first piqued in 1981, at a meeting sponsored by the National Academy of Sciences and the Chinese Academy of Social Sciences in Wingspreads, Wisconsin, . . . and a return visit in Beijing the following summer. Since then, I have had the good fortune to make several visits to Hungary, Czechoslovakia, Romania, Russia, and China, but I cannot claim, on the basis of these quick glimpses, to be an expert on the host of problems that these countries face. I hope, and believe, that the theoretical insights may be of some value. (ibid.: xi)

Stiglitz knew that the socialist world had long discussed the transition to markets within socialism, which, for Stiglitz, continued into the 1990s.

Stiglitz agreed with Lipton and Sachs that the socialist experiment in Eastern Europe had failed (ibid.: 2). However, Stiglitz also made a surprising claim: "The failure of market socialism serves as much as a refutation of the standard neoclassical model as it does of the market socialist ideal" (ibid.). The failure of socialism meant the failure of mainstream neoclassical economics? Readers unacquainted with history narrated here would be surprised, but it is clear that his conclusion is logical. According to Stiglitz, the failure of market socialism disproved a certain kind of neoclassical economics.[11]

Stiglitz first disparaged Eastern European governments for using the "standard neoclassical model," defined as the famous and highly abstract Arrow-Debreu model from the 1950s, to attempt to create market socialism. Both the Arrow-Debreu model and Oskar Lange's neoclassical model of market socialism assumed perfectly competitive markets with economic units acting on perfect information provided by prices. For decades, Stiglitz and other economists had carried out pioneering work that sought to move beyond such abstract models, creating a "new paradigm" with a more realistic understanding of markets (ibid.: 5). After declaring the end of socialism and the end of the standard neoclassical model, Stiglitz wrote, "The socialist economies never really took seriously the market socialist ideal" (ibid.: 197). In fact, he remarked, "Had the neoclassical model provided a good description of the market economy, market socialism would have had a much better running chance of success" (ibid.: 137). Neoclassical economists with a better understanding of the real, imperfect functioning of markets could have helped create a better form of socialism.

Stiglitz also criticized neoclassical economists such as Milton Friedman and Jeffrey Sachs for what he later called their "market fundamentalism" (Stiglitz [2002] 2003: 36). Like Eastern European governments creating market socialism, market fundamentalists relied on an abstract, unrealistic model of markets, not as a model for socialism but as a model for capitalism. As a result, such neoclassical economists presented the transition to capitalism as relatively straightforward; state enterprises merely needed to be privatized and markets freed. Stiglitz argued instead that markets did not necessarily need private property.

While Lipton and Sachs advocated privatization, Stiglitz argued for establishing institutions that would allow for competition, "not pure price competition but simply old-fashioned competition, the rivalry among firms to supply the needs of consumers and producers at the lowest price with the highest qualities" (1994: 255). Stiglitz did not believe that privatization, especially in Eastern Europe, would create this competition and thought that it would likely maintain monopolies (ibid.). Competition required active state policy to break up monopolies, restructure enterprises and industries, encourage small enterprises, and promote new enterprises. Stiglitz considered privatization much less important than encouraging market competition (ibid.: 260–261). In addition, reforms to improve competitiveness would allow the new business forms that had developed during socialism to continue, rather than be eradicated as part of the old defunct system in Lipton and Sachs's shock therapy.

According to Stiglitz, "The seeming failure of market socialism has led many to conclude that there is no third way between the two extremes of markets and state enterprises" (ibid.: 253). Instead of viewing the options as either market or state, according to Stiglitz, Eastern European leaders should have created a system with intermediary institutions, such as cooperatives and local community organizations, that help markets (ibid.: 253). He further called for worker involvement in enterprise management to combat "alienation" (ibid.: 271):

While government ownership is clearly no panacea, there remains scope for further experimentation. For instance, we need to study forms of economic organization involving more worker participation and ownership. (ibid.: 277)[12]

Stiglitz thus worked within the tradition of neoclassical economists in East and West, who, by the late 1980s, understood that markets required economic democracy, enterprises functioning independently from the state, entrepreneurship, laws encouraging small and medium-sized firms, deregulation of most prices, a variety of property forms (including nonstate social, local community, cooperative, and private ownership), and political democracy. He concluded his book:

As the former socialist economies set off on this journey, let us hope that they keep in mind not only the narrower set of economic questions that I have raised in this book but the broader set of social ideals that motivated many of the founders of the socialist tradition. Perhaps some of them will take the road less traveled by, and perhaps that will make all the difference, not only for them, but for the rest of us as well. (ibid.: 279)

Stiglitz thus continued to find the Eastern European legacy important for neoclassical economics specifically and for the world more generally.

By early 1991, Jeffrey Sachs had begun advising the Slovene government, which brought him into conflict with Yugoslav neoclassical economists.[13] Economists from Slovenia and elsewhere in the former Yugoslavia did not passively accept Sachs's calls to erase the socialist past in its entirety. For example, Slovene economist Jože Mencinger, who had received his PhD at the University of Pennsylvania, remarked:

Unlike other socialist countries, SFR Yugoslavia had been an open country; many economists had studied abroad, acquiring a solid understanding of mainstream Western economics, and were therefore not easily awed by foreign advisers. Most had participated in rather free debates on economic reform in the 1980s; thus they were not surprised by the breakup of socialism. (2004: 76)

Many Yugoslav economists shared a neoclassical profession with American advisors and had actual work experience in market transitions. Yugoslav neoclassical economists, including Aleksander Bajt, Dragomir Vojnić, and Kiro Gligorov, had already worked on the 1960s market reforms and created the new reform plan for the federal Yugoslav government led by Ante Marković in the late 1980s. According to Mencinger, most economists did not consider the Yugoslav socialist legacy as Stalinist or as a waste but rather as the basis for a market economy:

> Owing to a decades-long series of reforms during SFR Yugoslavia's existence, many of the essentials for a successful transition were at least partly met before 1989: enterprises were autonomous, basic market institutions existed, and the system of macroeconomic governance enabled the use of many standard economic policy tools. (ibid., 72–73)[14]

According to this view, the market transition had taken place over several decades, which meant that the old system could be built on, rather than destroyed. In opposition to Sachs's policies, Aleksander Bajt resigned in November 1989 (Meier 1999: 109). The next year Jože Mencinger and others resigned. Yugoslav economists found the one-size-fits-all program unacceptable.

Yugoslav and other Eastern European economists who had long rejected state socialism understood Western experts like Lipton and Sachs as advocating, in the name of markets, a model similar to the Soviet one that Yugoslavs and Hungarians, in particular, had rejected since the 1950s. The Hungarian and Polish governments renationalized and centralized social property, much as the Soviets had decades earlier: "Hungary and Poland were pushed in the apparently contradictory position of seeking to recentralize assets only a few years after some assets had become quasi-owned by workers, and after management rights had been transferred to workers' councils" (Milanović 1992: 53). Yugoslavs, in particular, found such calls for the renationalization of the means of production particularly infuriating because they had worked for decades against the centralized Soviet model and for decentralized workers' power.[15] As Bateman has recognized, the "market fundamentalist" approach of Sachs and others meant that the "potential for building upon existing institutions and assisting incipient reform trajectories, particularly at the local level, was simply not taken seriously" (2000: 196). As in Poland, Sachs along with old and new Slovene elites sought to destroy the past and create a new form of (state) capitalism.

In Slovenia, Sachs advocated mass privatization through free distribution of shares, which seemed to realize the Second Fundamental Welfare Theorem derived from Pareto. According to Pareto's ideas, mass privatization was exceedingly fair because it redistributed property throughout society. Theoretically, by redistributing wealth at the outset, the competitive market could then produce optimal and fair results. While criticizing this view, World Bank economist from the now former Yugoslavia Željko Bogetić explained, "Only in the case of free distribution of shares (or vouchers) to citizens, will Pareto improvement in privatization be achieved. When shares are traded in the market, no one will be worse off than they were before, and those whose shares command positive prices will be better off" (1992: 90). However, this view did not take into account other forms of power, such as political and cultural capital, "*ex post* inequities" possibly "more substantial than the alternatives" (ibid.), information asymmetries, and the continuation of state socialist institutions.

Some Eastern European economists did support mass privatization, though in ways consciously designed to avoid the state control that Sachs supported. Some Hungarian neoclassical economists advocated "spontaneous privatization" by employees and often managers because it avoided direct state intervention and state control of social property once again (Milanović 1992: 66; see also Róna-Tas 1997: 175). For example, Hungarian reform economist Iván Major criticized the transition ideas of Western experts for seeking to impose the same transition policies on all of the East Bloc as the Soviet Union had tried (1993: 153). Major asked, why should the state and central planners control the privatization process? To him, privatization should at least be controlled by democratic organs, such as a democratically accountable Parliament rather than a governmental agency (ibid.: 135). Like Stiglitz, Major argued that privatization, in fact, avoided necessary restructuring of enterprises that would have made them competitive (ibid.: 127).

Through the 1980s, economist and future Slovene Minister of Economy Tea Petrin and Slovene economist Aleš Vahčič advocated markets, entrepreneurship, and policies to encourage small and medium-sized enterprises within a socialist system. After 1989, together with David Ellerman, a colleague of Joseph Stiglitz who later worked with Stiglitz at the World Bank, Petrin and Vahčič actively worked against mass privatization. In their 1992 article, they criticized giving away shares to everyone because it overly dispersed ownership and did not create effective owners

(Ellerman, Vahčič, and Petrin 1992). Instead, they called for a decentralized model of spontaneous privatizations and employee ownership that would quickly create effective owners. Sachs's mass privatization appeared as a program biased against workers: "In the absence of plausible arguments, opposition to western-style employee ownership may turn out to be little more than a thinly disguised class bias against workers as the 'wrong sort of people' to have private ownership" (ibid.: 139). Hungarian and Yugoslav economists criticized the mass privatization plans of Sachs and others.

Neoclassical Economics and Neoliberalism

The disagreements between Sachs and Stiglitz were not specific to them as individuals or as American economists. Gil Eyal (2003) found similar lines of contention among Czechoslovak economists. Béla Greskovits (2002) discovered that these lines of contention repeated those of the eighteenth and nineteenth centuries between those who viewed legacies of the past as obstacles to reform and those who understood these legacies as positives assets for reform.[16] I, however, suggest that Sachs and Stiglitz represented a more fundamental, historical division within neoclassical economics itself: the division between those who argue that effective markets (or central planning) require authoritarian institutions and those who argue that effective markets (or central planning) require radical forms of democracy.

International and domestic elites could exploit this historical division and mobilize the more authoritarian neoclassical economists to support neoliberalism because of the nature of neoclassical economics itself. To begin with, neoclassical economists had always believed that their methods and theories were universally applicable to any economic system.[17] For these theoretical reasons and due to their actual experiences with market transitions within socialism, neoclassical economists felt that they could improve all systems and assist those moving through market transitions to various systems.

Neoclassical economists of all political persuasions use the social planner model to evaluate policy options and recommend policy or even system changes. Sachs and hundreds of other economic advisors themselves acted like central planners creating a market economy. At least in part, the social planner model conditioned them to think about their role in this way. The social planner as a kind of benevolent dictator seeks to maximize social welfare and reach Pareto optimality, in which one could not increase the welfare of one individual without worsening the condition of another. As discussed in Chapter 1, Vilfredo Pareto (1896, 1897a) developed this model as a "socialist state" model. One can use these tools to describe the economy, evaluate various tax policies, or even compare different social systems to "rationally" choose an alternative system (Robbins [1932] 1945: 155). Since the 1950s, neoclassical economists had shown that one could jump to new Pareto optima based on the planner's or society's preferences (Tinbergen 1956). Following Pareto, a competitive market could produce a Pareto optimum if those who benefit from a change could potentially compensate those who did not, through lump-sum transfers (taxes or subsidies) or even the equal distribution of income or company shares across individuals. Neoclassical economists of all political commitments used this model and improved it, seeking to correct its unreal assumptions.[18] The transition offered a perfect opportunity for economists to realize their role as social planners.

After 1989, however, the role of social planner seemed strange and incongruous with the transition away from central planning, as economist Arye L. Hillman noted:

The terminology of the mainstream economic models is also somewhat inappropriate for application to the transition. The models, which purport to describe private-property based democratic market economies, are nonetheless replete with references to benevolent dictators, social planners, exogenously specific social weights as the basis for distribution, and "representative" consumers who can be interpreted to portray the "needs" of a diverse population. The lump-sum taxes and transfers of these models appear also to assume the feasibility of the communist ideal of production according to ability and consumption according to need. (1994: 194)

As Eastern Europeans had rejected centrally planned state socialism, neoclassical economists in the name of competitive markets continued to use terms like *the social planner* and *lump-sum transfers* developed from a nineteenth-century model of socialism. Criticisms of the idea of a social planner are practically nonexistent.[19] In 2000, University of Chicago economist Gary Becker noted that "an all-powerful social planner lies behind many discussions by economists of political choices" and argued that "the social planner approach is a fairy tale and is not relevant to understanding which regulations, taxes, and subsidies get implemented" (1149, 1150). In spite of his criticism, in 2003 Becker argued, "Given these weaknesses of the planner model, it is important to have an analysis that includes the planner model as a special case but also incorporates differences in the political power of various interest groups" (Becker and Mulligan 2003: 296). Thus, Becker did not reject the planner model and, in fact, continues to use the model.[20] Even free market advocates strangely and tellingly continued to envision themselves as social planners.

Eastern European economists with a hierarchical understanding of neoclassical economics—such as central planners—could make the transition most effortlessly from planning to neoliberal reform. According to Gligorov, those who supported nonmarket central planning "could more easily adapt to the process of liberalization" because "all they needed to do was to substitute the normative, i.e. administrative, determination of wages and profits by appropriate market mechanisms" (1998: 341). Those with a commitment to expanded worker self-management and other institutions, by contrast, "had to give up everything they stood for" (ibid.). Similarly, Mencinger called Sachs's policy "a typical central planer's [sic] approach to the economy" (1992: 12). In fact, the neoclassical social planner approach, without any attempts at economic democracy or more participatory forms of political democracy, made it seem that the transition would be easy.

Neoclassical economists also employed concepts that in the transition took on multiple interpretations simultaneously.[21] The transition resignified social ideas, which fundamentally changed the situation after 1989, while at the same time retaining the decades-old Eastern European reform rhetoric. Therefore, economic concepts had a variety of interpretations, both socialist and neoliberal, which made it difficult to discern what was being discussed. During this time, the idea of "the transition" itself took on new meanings. Socialists advocated "transition" for decades, whether from capitalism to socialism, from state socialism to worker self-management socialism, or from state socialism to a market economy within socialism, as the World Bank also understood it in the late 1980s.[22] Socialists had long used the term *transition*. Political leaders now reinterpreted "the transition" as moving away from socialism of all sorts and toward a market economy understood either overtly or covertly as capitalist. In the period immediately after 1989, many Eastern European officials did not use the term *capitalism*, considering a transition to capitalism as too radical (Brus

1992: 7; Sutela 1992, 85).[23] Even David Lipton and Jeffrey Sachs in their famous 1990 article on Polish reforms did not use the term *capitalism* to explain the necessary reforms in Poland.[24] They declared that the Polish government sought to create "market economies with large private sectors" (ibid.: 75). In a World Bank publication, Hillman and Milanović wrote, "It is also often not clear what is meant by 'market economy'" (1992: 1). We can understand that in the new political space the "market economy" retained old interpretations and also became connected with capitalism.

The multiple, simultaneous understandings of economic concepts made the transition also appear to some as the natural continuation of previous market reforms. Observers have noted that the shift from economic reforms to the transformation of economic systems was surprisingly smooth (Szamuely and Csaba 1998: 196), though few were prepared for the economic and financial crises that ensued. During socialism, Eastern European economists, especially those in Hungary and Yugoslavia, had worked for decades on market reforms and attempted transitions to market socialism. During the 1970s and 1980s, economists also gained skills in market research, management, and accounting (Bockman 2000: ch. 5).[25] They were familiar with international policy advice and the neoclassical economics on which it was based. Greskovits recognized this: "By the time of the collapse of communism, Hungarian and Polish experts knew and, more to the point, had already tried most of what they could have learned from international advisers" (1998: 61; see also Bockman and Eyal 2002). Hungarian and Yugoslav economists, in fact, used their own experiences with market transition during socialism to advise other countries in their market transitions. As anthropologist Alexei Yurchak (2006) found in the former Soviet Union, people had realized that "although the system's collapse had been unimaginable before it began, it appeared unsurprising when it happened"; in fact, they "found themselves prepared for it" (1). During socialism, many people had creatively reinterpreted socialist ideology to deal with new situations, which allowed the Soviet system to appear immutable, while changing its very nature, preparing them for a new society. "Everything was forever, until it was no more," states the title of Yurchak's book. Similarly, Eastern European neoclassical economists found themselves prepared for the transition because they had organized repeatedly for market transitions, though within socialism, and participated either directly or indirectly in transnational neoclassical discussions since the 1950s.[26] In the transition, economic concepts had multiple interpretations, thus making it unclear whether there was revolution, evolution, or no change at all.

Since the nineteenth century, neoclassical economists had considered the competitive market and a centrally planned socialist state as mathematically identical, which created a narrow neoclassical core, when in fact they always discussed or assumed institutions required for both. This core endows all neoclassical economists with the language of markets and the language of central planning. Economists or political elites at times did not discuss institutions for political reasons, as happened in the Stalinist and McCarthyist 1950s, and focused instead on these core elements. This narrow or disembedded neoclassical economics lent itself well to arguments for neoliberalism, which appears as disembedded liberalism.

In addition, because they shared this core neoclassical economists could appear to have formed a consensus, for example, in support of neoliberalism, when in fact individual economists might reject its essential components. Economists themselves could not always recognize significant differences within the discipline. Lipton and Sachs (1990a), as well as other neoclassical economists, presented a consensus around the world for private property and corporate capitalism. John Williamson (1990) presented his now famous Washington Consensus. According to Murrell, while economists like Lawrence Summers perceived a "striking degree of unanimity" among economists about advice for the transition, economists who supposedly agreed actually could not perceive their fundamental differences and contractions (1995: 164, 173). In part, economists seemed to agree because they all could speak about markets and planning.

Dynamics within academia worldwide further reinforced these trends. As discussed in Bockman and Eyal (2002), American economists unaware of the transnational nature of the dialogues in which they participated found consensus around markets and assumed that their colleagues had diffused American ideas to passive recipients around the world. In the eyes of Western advisors and their Eastern European interlocutors, Eastern Europe had become a wasteland (Gille 2007).[27] The Yugoslav wars had further proven, to many observers, that Eastern Europe was a wasteland. These Yugoslav wars also fragmented the former global leader of the nonaligned world into several small, relatively provincial countries. Socialist Eastern Europe came to be seen as isolated from the West. The West was also seen as isolated and pure from any interaction with socialism. Lipton and Sachs therefore suggested that it was necessary to remove the broken vestiges of the old system to expose the tabula rasa on which to create a Western European capitalist system. Eastern Europeans thus appeared as the passive recipients of knowledge that they themselves, ironically, had created (Bockman and Eyal 2002).

Outside observers also often could not distinguish neoliberal policies from the new socialist forms. Critics and advocates of neoliberalism have assumed that markets are capitalist, while neoclassical economists have understood markets as both capitalist and socialist and that socialism, in fact, might provide the best conditions for competitive markets. These critics and advocates have also often assumed that Soviet state socialism was the only form of socialism. East European economists' apparent mass conversion to free markets after 1989 supported the neoliberal triumphalist view. In Table I.1 on page 11 in the introduction, we can see how Yugoslav socialism differed from Soviet socialism, but also how Yugoslav socialism resembled neoliberalism in some aspects, such as in its distrust of the state and acceptance of the market. However, besides sharing a promarket, antistate stance, Yugoslav socialism and neoliberalism had very different institutions. If one viewed Eastern European economic debates as market versus planning, then one would easily conflate neoliberalism with the new forms of socialism. In their narrow forms, neoliberalism and alternative socialisms appeared the same, but they were fundamentally different.

As we have seen throughout this book, neoclassical economists found a range of socialisms relevant to their professional work, which became problematic after 1989. Neoclassical economists over time incorporated various socialisms—abstract central planning, abstract decentralized planning, actually existing socialism in the Soviet Union, decentralized market socialist models, the Illyrian model, actual experiments in neoclassical socialism in Hungary and Yugoslavia, the "social planner" model—into the center of neoclassical economics. These socialisms were mutually reinforcing, often contradictory, and frequently perceived as interchangeable. As discussed in Chapter 3, Milenkovitch had criticized the confusion in economics:

In this state of affairs, from the outside, we can not distinguish between the capitalist, the Langean socialist, or the worker managed enterprise. What appears in the short run as sharp difference between firms' behaviors becomes in general equilibrium a merging of identities. In general equilibrium in competition, all three firms and the economies founded on them are equally efficient. (1984: 83)

All these economic systems were Pareto optimal, and thus the social planner could help a society jump to any of these.

In general, as discussed in the previous chapter, neoclassical economists perceived several possible market transitions:

1. centrally planned state socialism → market socialism

2. centrally planned state socialism → market socialism → centrally planned state socialism

3. centrally planned state socialism → (simulated) market socialism → market capitalism

4. centrally planned state socialism → (simulated) market socialism → Illyrian model[28]

Neoclassical economists did not consider these to be mixed economies, like Keynesianism, but rather as pure models. Mixed or "Third Way" options would lead to systems that were not Pareto optimal. Around 1989, neoclassical economists saw several possible Pareto optimal systems.

However, the post-1989 Eastern European economic crises brought these Pareto-optimal destinations into question. The debt crisis and then wars in Yugoslavia delegitimated the Illyrian model. Economists questioned whether market socialist destinations were Pareto optimal and stable. In 1989, Balcerowicz asked, "If it were possible to introduce the envisaged systems, could they last? To put the question another way, do they not have some in-built tendency to transform themselves into some other system?" ([1989] 1995: 32). Market socialism in its worker self-management form remained essentially untried, and thus it was unclear whether it would work or might lead to another Pareto equilibrium of unknown character. As Mario Nuti explained, the economic crisis made a known destination desirable:

Obtuse procrastination on the part of past and present socialist leaders (including also—indeed especially—Mikhail Gorbachev) has made it impossible for anything but a version of capitalism to be the target model for Central Eastern European countries: when a boat is sinking, it is no time to experiment with the floating properties of alternative rafts. (1992: 20)

With the transition, market socialism became understood as an unstable system that could never have worked (Kornai 1990a; Sachs 1993: 33–34).

How Did the Shift to Neoliberalism Happen?

What I have shown is that neoclassical economics did not cause neoliberalism. Individuals used a particular understanding of neoclassical economics, a narrow version that hid its authoritarian requirements, to support neoliberalism. According to my definition mentioned earlier, which reflects my understanding of the 1990s debate in and around Eastern Europe, neoliberalism is a set of ideas and related polices that support competitive markets; smaller, authoritarian states; hierarchical firms, management, and owners; and capitalism. In the world of neoclassical economics, markets could help both socialisms and capitalisms. In addition, markets were not identified with private property but rather could have a variety of property ownership structures. According to Harvey, the neoliberal *utopian* project, which called for the end of the state in the name of the free market, masked the reality of the neoliberal *political* project, which transformed and mobilized the state to "re-establish the conditions for capital accumulation and to restore the power of economic elites" after the early 1970s economic crisis and possibility that socialist candidates and programs might be politically successful (2005: 15, 19). Thus, neoliberalism advocated a strong, though smaller, state. The definitive characteristic of neoliberalism, however, is its reaffirmation of the hierarchical control managers and owners, while simultaneously attacking workers. The turn to neoliberalism coincided with the renationalization of workers' property, the freezing of wages, the mass firing of workers, the eradication of self-management, and the narrowing of democracy.[29] The class struggles on a global scale during the transition shaped the nature of neoliberalism.

However, as Eyal, Szelenyi, and Townsley (1998) and Szalai (2005) have argued, Eastern European countries did not have capitalists to make capitalism. Eastern European Communist Party technocrats—economists and enterprise managers—were the surprising revolutionaries against the old regime of ideological bureaucrats, gaining power not as owners but as experts and managers (Eyal et al. 1998). During socialism, economists and enterprise managers had long wished to implement market reforms, which would allow them to move beyond direct control of the economy to neoliberal guidance. However, for decades, party leaders and bureaucrats had frustrated the technocrats' attempts. Technocrats then allied with the democratic opposition in roundtable negotiations in 1989 and 1990 and successfully ended the political monopolies of the communist parties.

These old technocratic elites and new domestic political elites led the revolutions of 1989 and played the decisive role in shaping the postsocialist world as neoliberal (Appel 2004; Soltan 2000).[30] At least during the Hungarian roundtable talks, the opposition unified against the political monopoly of the Communist Party and for multiparty elections, but the opposition and the Party could not find consensus on economic issues (Bozóki 2002: xxiii; Pető 2002: 121; Ripp 2002: 4). With the successful end of the Communist Party's political monopoly, the introduction of a multiparty system, and the fall of the Berlin Wall, the political opportunity structure changed fundamentally, while the goal of economic policy remained unclear.[31] New and old political elites could take advantage of the transformed political terrain to find new allies and constituents, as well as to declare their rejection of socialism and their embrace of markets and democracy in vaguely defined form.

International financial institutions acted as allies for some in these battles. With the worldwide debt crisis of the 1980s, international financial institutions gained new forms of influence and could impose devastating structural adjustment conditionalities (Greskovits 1998; Stiglitz [2002] 2003; Woodward 1995).[32] In Eastern Europe and Latin America, political elites marginalized from the mainstream could adopt neoliberal ideas to please these international capitalist constituencies, as opposed to international socialist constituencies, and to fuel their own rise to power worldwide (Babb 2001; Dezalay and Garth 2002; Markoff and Montecinos 1993). These political leaders joined forces with like-minded economists in international capitalist networks, isolating themselves from other domestic stakeholders and mobilizing neoclassical economics in a narrow, disembedded way, to support neoliberal policies (Blyth 2002; Harvey 2005).[33] Political elites and economists thus allied themselves with and depended on these international capitalist actors (Szalai 2005: 50).

With their reoriented alliances, political and economic elites then reneged on agreements made with workers earlier in the transition. For example, at the Polish and Hungarian roundtables, the state had given workers more control over enterprises. According to political scientist Agnieszka Paczyńska, in Poland, "The control that the councils and trade unions held over enterprises solidified the opinion among workers that the enterprises belonged to the employees" (2009: 135). Privatization would thus mean ownership, either privately or collectively, by the workers. In the new political environment, however, workers soon appeared as part of the problem, as obstacles to efficiency. A former Polish deputy minister of privatization told Paczyńska, "Privatization did not so much entail getting the state out of enterprises, but rather getting worker self-management out of them" (2009: 6). Also, as already discussed, in Yugoslavia workers were seen as "the 'wrong sort of people' to have private ownership" (Ellerman, Vahčič, and Petrin 1992: 139). Political elites instead sought foreign investors, domestic banks, and other organizations as owners.

Because Eastern Europe did not have capitalists to create capitalism, and workers were deemed inadequate owners of the means of production, technocrats and political elites sought to create new actors interested in a new neoliberal system (Greskovits 1998: 50). Instead of advocating competition, they promoted privatization through recentralization, which allowed them to handpick managers and boards of directors, use political discretion in awarding state property, and thus create new allies, who would not let the system return to any form of socialism (Róna-Tas 1997: 192). Róna-Tas has noted that, in the Hungarian case, "recentralization thus provided the governing coalition with the opportunity to build a political clientele. Given the short history of the coalition parties, the temptation to use privatization to fabricate a solid social base for themselves proved irresistible" (ibid.: 192). In contrast to the calls for radical democracy and market socialism in the late 1980s, political elites used hierarchical institutions to reinforce and expand their own power.

The role of the transnational right in the spread of neoliberalism has been well documented. Many observers have demonstrated that the New Right propagated a neoliberal message through an effective network building. According to these accounts, certain economists worked with other activists to develop transnational networks and spread neoliberal ideas. Most importantly, economists Milton Friedman and Friedrich von Hayek helped to construct right-wing networks by creating the Mont Pelerin Society and connecting it with right-wing think tanks, foundations like that of the Scaife family, and economics departments at the University of Chicago and elsewhere (Bourdieu and Wacquant 1999; Cockett 1995; Diamond 1995; Hartwell 1995; Harvey 2005; Kelly 1997; Klein 2007; Mirowski and Plehwe 2009; Smith 1993; Valdés 1995; Yergin and Stanislaw 1998). These economists also offered their academic credibility, their reinterpretations of economic ideas, and their organizational skills to the expanding network.

They published a wide range of books, pamphlets, and articles, which passed through the ever-increasing number of institutions in this network. Think tanks, networks, and intellectuals worked together to create a hegemonic constellation that supported certain transnational capitalist interests and blocked attempts at considering alternatives to neoliberal capitalism (Gill 1990; Plehwe, Walpen, and Neunhoffer 2005).

The transnational right has long promoted ideologies that cobble together a contradictory plurality of discourses (Hall 1988, Mirowski 2009).[34] The right-wing network included economists from very different, often contradictory traditions. The neoclassical economist Milton Friedman and the critic of neoclassical economics Friedrich von Hayek could thus appear in right-wing ideology as in agreement, when they worked in entirely different traditions. Austrian economists inspired by Hayek's evolutionary thought became the strongest supporters of shock therapy (Aligica and Evans 2009: 78; Prychitko 2002), thus allying with Jeffrey Sachs and his neoclassical colleagues who also supported shock therapy. In the name of spontaneous order and evolution, the Austrian School organized a dense network of institutions working very unspontaneously for major social change. Later, the right wing criticized Sachs and the IMF for shock therapy and Sachs's "top-down planning approach" (Easterly 2008), when, in fact, Austrian School economists had also supported these policies. By bringing together economists with contradictory views, the right accumulated resources both to present neoclassical economics as an argument for free market capitalism and to criticize the neoclassical economics of others as inherently socialist. As a result, the opportunistic use of diverse economists allowed the right wing to make almost any argument for neoliberalism. Think tanks and foundations within this network repackaged these ideas from a wide range of traditions as a course of action and had the resources to promote this package worldwide (Campbell 1998).

Right-wing neoclassical and Austrian School economists presented Eastern Europe as a blank slate naïvely embracing capitalism without any serious economic training, even though, as this book has shown, Eastern Europeans had participated in transnational neoclassical discussions at least since the 1950s. According to Aligica and Evans, Marxism had already collapsed in Eastern Europe before 1989 and left no alternative, leaving a tabula rasa even in economics: "The contact with Western science and academic community was truly reactivated only in the 1990s" (2009: 50). Neoclassical economics as neoliberalism filled this vacuum: "It was mainly the intellectual rottenness and vacuity of Marxism that explains the extraordinary efficient way in which the Western epistemic communities promoted neoclassical and neoliberal ideas through the very networks of the Marxists after 1989" (ibid., 96–97). Those on the right reinforced an image of the old socialist East defined by Stalinist central planning and Marxist-Leninist political economy, in contrast to the capitalist West defined by markets, private property, and neoclassical economics.

Elites reinforced dichotomies and sought to eradicate the liminal spaces in which economists and others developed alternatives to both Soviet state socialism and American neoliberal capitalism. For example, according to Hungarian economist Péter Márkus (1996), the Hungarian policy debates were limited to either state property or private property, ignoring a range of social property forms. Neoclassical economists with a commitment to authoritarianism in the name of markets also suggested a new choice between dictatorship and disorder. In line with this thinking, Shleifer and his coauthors (2003) argued that sometimes dictatorship and corruption were necessary and efficient, especially when, for example, fighting left-wing insurgents in Peru:

> From the perspective of Peruvian institutions, these deals reflect a move to eliminate disorder and increase dictatorship, which was probably efficient. Although this move is not attractive, neither were the tradeoffs that Peru faced. Eventually, as Fujimori tried to consolidate his dictatorship, the democratic process worked and he was driven out of the country. Not surprisingly, disorder increased as well. (614)

Dictatorships allowed not only for order and efficiency but also for freedom. According to Mirowski, Friedrich von Hayek stated in an interview that "a dictatorship may limit itself, . . . and if self-limited it may be more liberal in its policies than a democratic assembly that knows of no limitations" (2009: 446). Later in the same interview he continued, "I would prefer to temporarily sacrifice, I repeat temporarily, democracy, before having to do without freedom, even if temporarily" (ibid.). In *The Myth of the Rational Voter*, Bryan Caplan (2007) argued against democracy on the grounds that individuals do not understand that their rational interests lie in free trade and free markets. While he claimed that market actors best know their interests and would support economically correct policies, a neoclassical social planner or at least a transfer of power to some faction of professional economists would be required to create this outcome. Dividing the world's choices into dictatorship or disorder erases the movements worldwide for participation and radical forms of democracy going far beyond the national elections that 1989 represented.[35] Through such dichotomies, elites suppressed a range of alternatives (Kumar 1992; Yurchak 2006).

The strategic work of the transnational New Right has helped to spread neoliberalism not because the New Right created the ideas but rather because they successfully exploited and distorted others' ideas (Bockman and Eyal 2002). Right-wing activists co-opted social movements and discussions taking place outside the Cold War dichotomy of capitalism versus socialism to obtain and develop new forms of knowledge. CESES, the topic of Chapter 5, was not the only institution of its kind but part of "a galaxy without borders." Many institutions brought together individuals interested in convergence between East and West, South and North, to talk about socialism, human rights, social justice, and many other topics.[36] In these discussions, participants criticized Soviet state socialism and discussed what socialism might be if it was not necessarily Soviet. Right-wing activists could mobilize these people and their criticisms for their battles at home. They reinterpreted liminal discussions and pushed these galaxies into clear binaries: centrally planning socialism or free market capitalism, state property or private property.[37] They decisively argued that socialism had failed, that Milton Friedman and Friedrich von Hayek were always right, and that there is no alternative to capitalism, markets, and private property. We can see right-wing activists as a reactive force that exploited the creative struggles occupying Cold War liminal spaces.[38]

The victory of neoliberalism was not only the work of right-wing activists and politicians. David Harvey (2005) argued that neoliberalism is primarily a political project to restore capitalist state power, which did not have to be the project only of the New Right. Stephanie Mudge noted:

There is a problematic tendency to conflate neo-liberalism with the political right . . . Though they featured important variations, in the 1990s the rise of market-friendly politics across the political spectrum became an unmistakable phenomenon. (2008: 723)

Yet, both socialists and neoliberals could have just as easily practiced market-friendly politics. More importantly, neoliberals supported hierarchical institutions, managers, and owners in opposition to the employees or the workers defended at least in principle by socialism. Thus, when considering the role of the left in the spread of neoliberalism, a distinction should be made between the neoliberal left—possibly the Democratic

Leadership Council—and those on the left looking for alternatives out-side the dichotomies of power.

Greskovits (1998), Szalai (2005), and others have noted that, in the 1990s, the neoliberal transition and its economic crisis did not provoke populist uprisings or mass protest, in spite of the many warnings by schol-ars like Jeffrey Sachs, Andrei Shleifer, and others. Why did the popula-tions not revolt against the change in system? It is clear that the citizens were frustrated with the problems of the previous system, but opinion polls did not find that they necessarily preferred capitalism.[39]

In contrast to Poland, where workers had organized earlier and gained some leverage in negotiations with the state (Paczyńska 2009), workers in Eastern Europe generally did not have the institutional re-sources to protect their 1980s gains. Many scholars had recognized that Yugoslav socialism never fully realized worker self-management (Comisso 1981; Obradović and Dunn 1978; Zukin 1975), and socialist regimes had often discouraged democratic participation and encouraged the atomiza-tion of its citizens (Stark 1992; Szalai 2005). In 1988 and 1989, however, workers had gained new control over their places of employment. The new best practices of socialism at that time had been worker self-management and possibly worker ownership of the means of production, thus poten-tially moving from socialism (where the state owns the means of pro-duction) to communism (where the state withers away). Yet, there was not time to develop and strengthen the institutional resources—such as democratic worker self-management, nonstate social property laws, coop-erative banks—to protect workers' interests. Also, without the "big push" to advance self-management and democratization "as fast as possible" advocated by Mujżel (1988), workers instead allowed another "big push" predicted by Mujżel, technocratic shock therapy in the interests of new political elites, managers, and a certain group of neoclassical economists. The second economy and then the new political parties acted as safety valves (Greskovits 1998; Szalai 2005). Workers lacking social movements and protective institutions had few attachments to social property and thus let it go relatively easily (Szalai 2005). Political and economic elites sought to create new allies to support a shift away from worker control and own-ership. These elites took away workers' property because workers did not have the adequate institutions to protect themselves and develop radical economic and political democracy (Klein 2007; Nelson and Kuzes 1994). Without such institutions, new and old Eastern European elites with the help of transnational corporations and international financial institutions could then fully exploit this situation and implement neoliberalism.

Conclusions

During and after 1989, the shifting political terrain offered Eastern European elites new alliances to create neoliberalism. Political and economic elites allied with and dependent on international capitalist actors used a narrow view of neoclassical economics, which, in fact, assumed hierarchical institutions, to support neoliberalism. With a view of impending economic and political chaos, the new elites presented their options as technocratic change or decline into this chaos. They then rejected market socialist options, presenting a seemingly narrow but actually authoritarian understanding of neoclassical economics to support neoliberalism, and reneged on the socialist commitment to workers in the name of other social actors, including managers, potential owners, and technocratic experts. In this manner, these elites transformed the transition to democratic market socialism into the transition to capitalism.

Conclusions

NEOLIBERALISM HAS SPREAD AROUND THE WORLD but still remains misunderstood. Economists seem to support and even to proselytize for neoliberalism, an ideology that seeks to expand the reach of markets and supports strong states, enterprise owners and managers, and capitalism. I argue, however, that the majority of mainstream neoclassical economists have not advocated neoliberalism. Many observers assume incorrectly that economists support either the market or the state. This dichotomy blends into others: markets versus central planning, monetarism versus Keynesianism, neoliberalism versus socialism, and neoclassical economics versus Marxism. As a result, neoliberalism is incorrectly conflated with neoclassical economics, and a "galaxy" of alternatives is forgotten. I have sought to rediscover the history of the liminal spaces within which this galaxy formed.

As a means to retrieve this history, I first relocated Keynesianism and the socialist calculation debate from their usual place at the center of the history of economics, which brought into view the variety of ways that neoclassical economists, no matter their political commitments, have used socialisms as both analytic and normative models. In the nineteenth century, neoclassical economists decided that a pure competitive market, based on certain assumptions, produced optimal results and built a set of equations to describe how this market worked so optimally. They also soon decided that a hypothetical socialist state could use these equations to plan the economy and obtain the same optimal results. This socialist state model, which simplified the world even more than the model of the market itself, allowed economists to compare economic policies and the benefits they provided. As a result, a model of a pure competitive market and a model of a socialist state sit at the core of neoclassical economics. This core led neoclassical economists to find a range of socialisms—an abstract socialist state, real Soviet central planning, abstract decentralized planning, the Hungarian decentralized market socialist experiment, the abstract Illyrian model based on the Yugoslav worker self-management socialist system, the real Yugoslav system, and so on—directly relevant to their professional work. Some economists realized that they could use their analytical models as guides for a new socialist society.

Those who have not studied the socialist world that emerged from the Bolshevik Revolution in 1917 have often assumed that East Bloc economies had only Soviet-styled state socialism and that economists there practiced only Marxist political economy. Small but very influential groups of economists there, however, argued that because Marxist political economy primarily described a capitalist economy neoclassical economics in fact provided the best tools to create and improve socialist economies. Economists in the East and the West initially worked separately and in parallel on neoclassical models, while experiencing similar political pressures in the early Cold War. Working within the closed worlds of the military-industrial complexes of their countries, neoclassical economists both in East and West suffered a narrowing of their discipline, in which they could not discuss the institutions that might improve the functioning of either the pure competitive market or the socialist state but rather had to assume the continuation of the existing hierarchical institutions. After the death of Joseph Stalin and the end of McCarthyism, these economists began to communicate and work together, forming a transnational dialogue about socialisms, capitalisms, and markets.

Starting in the 1920s and 1930s, socialist economists rejected authoritarian models and turned to a variety of democratic market socialisms based on neoclassical economics. They brought together radical forms of economic democracy and markets, which they argued worked even better under socialism than under naturally monopolistic capitalism. In the early 1950s, Yugoslav economists fascinated their colleagues abroad with their use of neoclassical economics to build a new kind of socialism. In their never fully realized model, worker self-managed companies would compete with each other on competitive markets, thus creating a kind of laissez-faire socialism. Hungarian economists developed another model of decentralized market socialism and contributed both their neoclassical models of socialisms and their knowledge of their own economic experiment to the transnational discussion among neoclassical economists. New knowledge about neoclassical economics and socialism emerged out of transnational liminal spaces, institutions that brought together heterogeneous networks of individuals critical of both Soviet state socialism and Western capitalism. These individuals from around the world encountered similar economic problems and envisioned a convergence of systems that would solve these problems, moving beyond the confining and unhelpful binaries of socialism versus capitalism or market versus plan.

In the 1970s, in the socialist East and the capitalist West, conservative political leaders once again supported a narrow version of neoclassical economics, a disembedded economics, which did not speak about the institutions required for competitive markets or effective central planning and thus in practice maintained the hierarchical institutions of the status quo and the power of these leaders. The 1980s brought renewed calls for democratic market socialisms. Eastern European workers gained new rights to control their firms and seemed on the road to owning, either socially or privately, the means of production. Eastern European economists also realized a variety of reforms that might eventually build market socialism and might bring about the withering away of the state, some form of communism, and true workers' power. By 1989, it looked as if market socialism might finally be realized.

However, the political terrain changed dramatically in 1989 and 1990, which allowed old and new elites to capture and expand their political and economic power by forging alliances with international capitalist institutions and by leaving behind alliances with international socialist institutions. These postcommunist elites then reneged on their promises to workers and to society more generally, while expanding their support to managers, future owners, and technocratic experts. Thus, around 1989, these elites began to implement neoliberalism, defined in Chapter 7 as a set of ideas and related policies advocating competitive markets; smaller, authoritarian states; hierarchical firms, management, and owners; and capitalism. Terms that had in fact once been part of socialist discussions, including "market transition," retained their old meanings and took on new capitalist ones. The market transition to create "genuine markets" and radical economic and political democracy within socialism transformed into a transition to capitalism and representative democracy.

Neoliberalism thus had socialist origins. Not only economists, but also dissidents, members of social movements, and participants in reform circles within Communist Parties developed new ideas about socialism, which elites then co-opted and distorted into neoliberalism. In my view, we must not overlook economists' long-standing and ongoing transnational socialist dialogues and their real battles in the field of economics, which did not pit those for markets against those for planning but rather those for authoritarian technocracy against those for radical democracy. In 1989, the new political environment allowed certain neoclassical economists with a commitment to authoritarianism and opposition to radical democracy to gain influence and implement neoliberalism. The victory of neoliberalism was in spite of, not because of, those economists who developed models of democratic market socialism that they had hoped to implement after 1989.

The Lives of Socialisms

The early 1990s were a time of exhaustion and confusion among many socialists. As British political scientist Christopher Pierson wrote of his own socialist politics:

There is my use of the "S" word. For some, it will seem at best archaic and at worst sheer willfulness to write about the prospects for socialism. Either socialism belongs amongst that set of ideas which are fit only for deconstruction or else it is shorthand for a history of political hubris, bloodily misconceived and now entirely exhausted. Even "on the left," . . . it is something which is best kept at arm's length. I have some sympathy with the latter view at least. (1995: ix)

Earlier, Krishan Kumar also noted that East Europeans considered communism and socialism "dirty words" (1992: 334-335). David Stark and László Bruszt (1998), as well as other scholars, found that Eastern Europeans sought a transition from socialism but that the goal of this transition was very unclear, leading them instead to use the term *transformation*. Socialism, however, continued in a wide variety of ways, though obscured by the increasingly hegemonic dichotomy of capitalism versus defunct socialism, as well as by the capitalist triumphalist narrative of transition.

Socialism remains concealed within neoliberalism itself.[1] In contrast to Jeffrey Sachs's dismissal of the Eastern European socialist legacy as a wasteland, David Stark perceived the socialist past as a necessary resource for the future:

instead of an institutional vacuum we find routines and practices, organizational forms and social ties, that can become assets, resources, and the basis for credible commitments and coordinated actions. . . . In short, in place of the disorientation that the political scientists find so alarming or the tabula rasa that the economists find so attractive, we find the metamorphosis of subrosa organizational forms and the activation of preexisting networks of affiliation. (1992: 300)

Enterprises from the socialist period continued throughout the region, retaining interfirm network ties, informal connections, and strategies for working within the market transitions that had developed long before 1989. Agnieszka Paczyńska (2009) demonstrated that Polish union movements gained resources, institutions, and historical experiences during socialism, which enabled some workers in Poland to organize and protect their ownership rights during the transition. Socialist-era institutions, networks, strategies, and experiences provided a range of resources for the transition and thus remain within neoliberalism.

Right-wing groups—with left-wing assistance—have labeled previously socialist ideas "capitalist" or "neoliberal." The knowledge about socialism and capitalism that developed out of liminality now appears as nothing more than a precursor to neoliberal ideology, but only because what Timothy Mitchell has called the "narrow window of the neoliberal imagination" makes invisible the discussions and the alternatives, leaving only hegemony in view (1999: 32). In fact, following the Italian Autonomist tradition, we can see the liminal spaces that criticized Soviet socialism and Western capitalism as laying the groundwork for the "communism of capital":

If we can say that Fordism incorporated, and rewrote in its own way, some aspects of the socialist experience, then post-Fordism has fundamentally dismissed both Keynesianism *and* socialism. Post-Fordism . . . puts forth, *in its own way*, typical demands of communism (abolition of work, dissolution of the State, etc.). Post-Fordism is the communism of capital. (Virno 2004: 111)

Knowledge from the liminal spaces changed the core of Western capitalism, while maintaining its hegemony. Liminal spaces in a co-opted form helped the—now altered—right-wing neoliberal hegemonic project. At the same time, socialist ideas remain latent within this neoliberal project.

No matter the political beliefs of neoclassical economists, socialism remains central to their methods and knowledge. The neoclassical pioneers had based their ideas on considering how a socialist economy might work neoclassically. Socialist models formed the origins of the Austrian School of Mises and Hayek, which they later rejected, leading them to transform the Austrian School away from the neoclassical mainstream. During the 1930s, neoclassical economists made fundamental innovations simultaneously in general equilibrium theory, such as measuring marginal utility, marginal cost, and demand elasticity, and in the study of socialism. Yugoslav and Hungarian economists later used neoclassical economics to envision economic reforms and to create two different kinds of market socialism. American economists modeled Eastern European economies and socialist firms to build new knowledge about some of the most popular topics of the 1950s and 1960s: decentralization, centralization, mechanism theory, optimal choice of systems, and policy analysis, including cost-benefit analysis.[2] Eastern European economists found their work relevant transnationally. After 1989, these economic methods and concepts did not disappear, but their socialist origins were concealed.

Even after the devastating critiques of Soviet centrally planned socialism, the "social planner" remains at the core of macroeconomic neoclassical modeling and appears often now in mainstream textbooks (Ljungqvist and Sargent 2004; Mankiw 2008; Mankiw and Taylor 2006) and professional articles (Arnott and Stiglitz 1991; Åslund et al. 1996; Sachs 1989: 288; Summers, Gruber, and Vergara 1993).[3] At the very core of neoclassical economics, there is a perspective of the world from the view of a planner. Jeffrey Sachs and hundreds of other economic advisors in Eastern Europe and elsewhere themselves have acted as central planners. This planner perspective, much more than any particular interest in capitalism, pushed economists to take part in the transitions of the 1990s.

While using a social planner model, many neoclassical economists continued to reject authoritarianism, both within their own disciplinary models and within the reality of Soviet state socialism and Western capitalism. The socialist alternatives they envisioned also remain latent within neoliberalism. Since the 1920s, socialists criticized Soviet state socialism with its central planning and, in response, developed market and democratic socialist alternatives. In his early 1950s social choice models, neoclassical pioneer Kenneth Arrow refused to consider a dictator determining social preferences and asked how a democracy might ascertain and realize these social preferences. Even after 1989, economist Michael Keren wrote, "I nevertheless believe that the dream of a better society under market socialism is not dead" (1993: 333). The market transition models to nonstate socialism, discussed in Chapter 6, remain today ready for use: market socialism, the Illyrian model (a perfected model abstracted from real Yugoslav worker self-management), entrepreneurial socialism, cooperatives, and so on. Democratic, decentralizing forms of socialism remain in co-opted and distorted form within neoliberalism.

Hungarian economic sociologist Erzsébet Szalai remarked, "Although the greatest socialist experiment so far has failed, the challenge that had created it has not lost its validity, even for those paths that ultimately branch off from it" (2004: 63). After 1989, the conditions ripe for socialist revival, such as class conflict, exploitation, and alienation, remained. Creed agreed, "The utility of socialism as a vehicle for protest in a supposedly postsocialist context gave it a new purpose and a new lease on political life" (1999: 240). Former Communist Parties returned to power in new forms in the 1990s.[4] American economist James Millar suggested that these new socialist governments "put up a monument to the advocates of shock therapy, whose single-minded devotion to an undeviated policy that has immiserated the general population has made the political revival of socialism thinkable and possible" (1996: 5). Kumar (1992) revisited Bauman's view of socialism as "the counter-culture of capitalism," calling for socialist movements to remind capitalism of the universalism of its promise through relentless critique of its practices, whether as loyal opposition or revolutionary challenge.[5] Socialism continues to play an important role in the supposedly postsocialist world.

These are just some of the ways socialist ideas have remained latent within neoliberalism. We can see right-wing activists as a reactive force that exploited the creative struggles occupying Cold War liminal spaces, naming artificial constellations according to their political whims in what is, in fact, a "galaxy without borders." I have sought to reconnect the liminal spaces that have since been divided into dichotomies, a dualistic world of power, to reconnect the history of neoliberalism with that which has been excluded from its history: socialism, Eastern Europe, and the transnational left.[6] Those in transnational liminal spaces still seek to understand the post-1989 convergence, what postcommunism is, what neoliberal capitalism is, and what socialism might be. This book is for them.

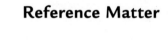

Reference Matter

Notes

Introduction

1. With the economic crises in 1998 and in 2007, scholars have suggested that neo-liberalism as a set of policies is no longer hegemonic (Darden 2009; Fourcade 2006; Harvey 2005). Others have argued that neoliberalism was never hegemonic on a global scale but rather has always competed with other ideologies and experienced continuous criticism and protest against it (Munck 2003). Some have asked whether neoliberalism is merely the continuation of state capitalism, state socialism, or oligarchic-corporate states (Nonini 2008).

2. Sociologists have shown that economists do not merely observe or predict but sometimes produce the phenomena they supposedly observe (Callon 1998; MacKenzie 2006; MacKenzie and Millo 2001; MacKenzie, Muniesa, and Siu 2007).

3. Mirowski and Plehwe (2009) have argued, I think correctly, that this package of neoliberal ideas has taken time to develop.

4. Aligica and Evans most strongly argue that neoclassical economics was a Western creation that undermined Eastern European Marxism: "The spread of economic ideas in Eastern Europe—the 'neoliberal revolution'—was solidly grounded in the core, main-stream economics" (2009: 23).

5. Blyth (2002), Duggan (2003), Sklair (2001), and many others also understand neo-liberalism and globalization as a class project.

6. Similarly, social scientists have shown how economists form "epistemic communities" or networks of like-minded experts, who influence policy worldwide through agenda setting, framing alternatives, diffusing policies, and implementing policies (Haas 1992; Hall 1989). Dobbin, Simmons, and Garrett (2007) critically review the wide litera-ture on policy diffusion.

7. This approach is influenced by the work of Kipnis (2008) and Nonini (2008).

8. As Mirowski (2009) and Plehwe (2009) correctly argue, since neoliberalism as a package of ideas evolved over time, one cannot give a definitive, universal definition. My

understanding of neoliberalism likely resembles those of earlier historical periods and other locations, though it is by no means universally applicable.

9. The core of neoliberalism is generally described as "an ideological system that holds the 'market' sacred" (Mudge 2008: 706) in an almost religious way (Fourcade and Healy 2007) and seeks to "intensify and expand the market, by increasing the number, frequency, repeatability, and formalization of transactions" (Treanor [n.d.]: 6).

10. As discussed later, in the early 1990s, Jeffrey Sachs and other economists had warned of the rise of "populism" and called for a strong state and especially a strong executive to push through shock therapy. Karl Polanyi recognized economic liberals' mobilization of the state for laissez faire: "The road to the free market was opened and kept open by an enormous increase in continuous, centrally organized and controlled interventionism. . . . Thus even those who wished most ardently to free the state from all unnecessary duties, and whose whole philosophy demanded the restriction of state activities, could not but entrust the self-same state with the new powers, organs, and instruments required for the establishment of laissez-faire" ([1944] 1957: 140–141).

11. Similarly, Paul Krugman (2007) hailed the professional research of Milton Friedman, while criticizing his work as an ideologue.

12. Weintraub (1985) and Arnsperger and Varoufakis (2006) provide particularly helpful descriptions of neoclassical economics.

13. Historians of economic thought have long questioned whether there was a real revolution in thought or merely a long evolution (Blaug 1972; Howey 1989; Niehans 1994: 162). I treat marginalism and neoclassical economics as essentially the same for simplicity, but they do, in fact, differ.

14. Economists, like the members of other occupations in the nineteenth century, sought to professionalize and legitimate their jurisdictions through such new scientific techniques and educational programs to gain the benefits of an exclusive labor market (Abbott 1988; Furner 1975).

15. Economists have shown that the traditional assumptions about market equilibrium have been misleading when applied to policy.

16. Hartley points out that Hansen and Sargent reinterpreted the social planner model as a decentralized competitive model, but Hartley finds that, in the end, their model acts just like the centralized model (1997: 68–70).

17. In contrast, heterodox economists, such as those of the Austrian and Marxist schools, generally do not use these neoclassical models.

18. The social planner does not necessarily have perfect knowledge. Some economists choose models of complete information and thus assume perfect knowledge, while other economists use models of incomplete information and thus do not make such assumptions.

19. Callon (1998), Latour (1988, 1999), Mitchell (2002), and Ross (2002) have similarly studied the heterogeneous networks that create knowledge.

20. Similarly, Nancy Fraser (2009) demonstrated how elites used second-wave feminism's critique of the family wage and welfare state paternalism to, for example, "end welfare as we know it." Kristin Ross (2002), as well as Luc Boltanski and Eve Chiapello

(2005), have found that management theorists co-opted New Left critiques of corporate capitalism to develop and legitimate a new flexible capitalism that was supposed to liberate individual creativity.

21. Hardt and Negri argue that "the multitude is the real productive force of our social world, whereas Empire is a mere apparatus of capture that lives only off the vitality of the multitude" (2001: 62).

22. This approach is again similar to that of Callon (1998), Latour (1988), Mitchell (2002), and Ross (2002) who seek to discover the heterogeneous networks that create knowledge. However, Hardt and Negri have recognized that the current paradigm of power has moved beyond binaries and essentialisms also to support hybridity, fluidity, and difference and thus thrives on criticisms of dichotomies (2001: 138).

23. Following Turner (1967), this heterogeneous, liminal space can be seen a "realm of pure possibility" and might become a source for innovations and future structure. As Moncada and Blau argue, the "billions of poor, traditionally living on what they grow, find, or catch, possess rare knowledge of how societies function and self-govern—as cooperatives, participatory democracies, collectives . . . From them westerners will, we venture, learn more than we can now imagine" (2006: 121).

Chapter 1

1. Scholars have continued to debate the nature of Mises's argument and whether Hayek actually altered it (Lavoie 1985; Murrell 1983; Steele 1992).

2. As mentioned in the Introduction, elites often "enframe" the world into dichotomies to bolster their own power (Mitchell 1990).

3. Coats also agrees that histories of economics have overemphasized the role of Keynes and suggests that we look at the broader context (1982: 18).

4. However, as Niehans has discussed in his history of economics textbook, "According to the conventional historiography, the two phases of the marginalist era were separated by the 'Marginalist Revolution.' This was supposed to have taken place in the 1870s through the path-breaking achievements of William Stanley Jevons, Carl Menger, and Léon Walras, the three 'founders' . . . The historical research of the last two decades has shown convincingly that this interpretation, largely fostered by the Viennese, cannot be maintained" (1994: 162).

5. Lerner noted that even by the 1930s many socialists still remained "suspicious in the extreme of such new-found allies coming from the 'idealogical' centre of the enemy's camp" (1934b: 52).

6. Some economists believed that their criticisms had helped socialism: "It was, however, only after economics had taken a scientific character that socialism, by antagonizing the newly established science, was first clearly formulated" (Gide 1904). In contrast, Heimann wrote, "The economic theory of a socialist system has been developed independently of any influence of socialist theory, entirely on the basis of modern so-called orthodox theory and by academic theorists" (1939: 88).

7. While Sidgwick did not recognize any positive influence made by socialism on economics, he did recognize that the socialist criticism had caused economists to stop

justifying the status quo and laissez faire and to turn to studies of the distribution of wealth and income (1895: 340).

8. For example, Pareto (1897b) remarked on the severe criticism of his work.

9. Howey discusses Wicksteed's neoclassical criticism of *Capital* in 1884 for a socialist magazine. The socialist George Bernard Shaw restrained his public criticism of Wick-steed because "Shaw even felt that Marx might have a good deal of the Jevonian theory of utility tucked away in the yet unpublished volumes of *Das Kapital*, a circumstance that would make any defense of Marx against Wicksteed useless" (1989: 121).

10. This translation comes from Cirillo (1980: 300).

11. Walras's ideas about the nationalization of land parallel those of Henry George's immensely popular *Progress and Poverty*, first published in 1879. Discussing England, Pease stated that *Progress and Poverty* "had an enormous circulation in the early eighties, and beyond all question had more to do with the socialist revival of that period in England than any other book" (1916: 240). Henry George's ideas had worldwide popularity.

12. The quotation is Walras ([1896] 1969: 144–145), taken from Cirillo (1980: 300). Cirillo (1976) also discusses Walras's socialist ideas.

13. The connection between Walrasian neoclassical economics and socialism is well known (Mirowski 2002; Young 2005).

14. As economist Carl Landauer noted, these critics developed economic models of socialism: "It is true that in the last years before the First World War that groundwork was laid for the great advance of socialist theory in the interwar period, but this preparatory work was done in the main by some of the critics of socialism and not by the socialists themselves" (1959: 1611).

15. Hayek criticized both classical economics and the historical school, as well as Marxism, for "successfully smothering all attempts to study the problems any constructive socialist policy would have to solve" ([1935] 1938a: 14; see also 9–14).

16. Therefore, socialism has been a laboratory for economic knowledge in a theoretical form even before the 1920s, as Bockman and Eyal (2002) found, since the 1890s at least.

17. While Pareto and Walras differed over many issues, Pareto made several significant contributions to the Walrasian general equilibrium model ("Vilfredo Pareto, 1848–1923").

18. Pareto used the term *ophelimity*, rather than *utility*.

19. Pareto wrote, "We will say that the members of a collectivity enjoy *maximum ophelimity* in a certain position when it is impossible to find a way of moving from that position very slightly in such a manner that the ophelimity enjoyed by each of the individuals of that collectivity increases or decreases. That is to say, any small displacement in departing from that position necessarily has the effect of increasing the ophelimity which certain individuals enjoy, and decreasing that which others enjoy, of being agreeable to some and disagreeable to others" ([1927] 1971: 261). A Pareto-efficient position is not necessarily fair and may be "perfectly disgusting" because, for example, a slave society could obtain maximum social welfare while maintaining slavery and severe inequalities (Sen 1970: 22).

20. As with other neoclassical economists, Pareto criticized Marxist socialists, but he also criticized "socialists of the chair," economists and sociologists of the German histori-

cal school around the *Verein für Sozialpolitik* who supported conservative state socialism (1897a: 54). In opposition to state socialism or a socialism that would merely help the bourgeoisie, Pareto became an admiring observer of socialism as a political movement and envisioned socialism based on free competition and Walrasian neoclassical economics as a way for "popular" socialism to defend liberty against "bourgeois" statist socialism (Pareto 1897a; Mornati 2001: 23-24). He sought to develop an economically viable socialist alternative to state socialism. However, when popular socialism became, in his eyes, authoritarian and classist, Pareto stopped supporting it.

21. Bergson noted that "as far as we know, Barone is the only writer in the field of socialist or welfare economics who has counted up and matched equations and unknowns" (1948: 420). Heimann, however, argued that Weiser developed a system of equations that anticipated Barone's work (1939: 90).

22. Heimann recognized that earlier "political aspects of the problem had not been seriously considered by these authors [critics of socialism] because socialism appeared to lie beyond any limit of practical possibility" (1939: 92).

23. While Neurath criticized Austrian neoclassical economics, he also continued to practice it (Uebel 2004: 56).

24. Block (2003) and Krippner and Alvarez (2007: 228) find Polanyi's rejection of laissez faire policy and embrace of markets contradictory, but it in fact reflected a popular neoclassical view.

25. Market socialist economists included Eduard Heimann, Carl Landauer, Emil Lederer, Franz Oppenheimer, Klara Tisch, and Herbert Zassenhaus. Heimann (1934) wrote, "A planned system would retain the institution of a free market" (1934: 503).

26. Cassel emphasized that he left unexplored whether socialism was practically possible or desirable.

27. Mises himself had later reiterated: "Thus the alternative is still either Socialism or a market economy" (1936: 142).

28. Mises's *Die Gemeinwirtschaft* from 1922 makes no reference to socialists' new ideas. The English translation, called *Socialism: An Economic and Sociological Analysis*, has an appendix and several pages (1936: 136–142) responding to these new ideas. Mises (1923) wrote quite positively of Eduard Heimann's market socialist writings, while repeating that rational calculation required private property.

29. Craver brings up Hans Mayer, an economics professor at the University of Vienna, who practiced neoclassical economics and did not consider Mises's political conclusions as inherent in it (1986: 10). Becchio discusses Polanyi and Neurath, who criticized the political approach of Mises but used the same analytical tools (2005: 16).

30. Brus (1972), too, perceived Mises and Hayek shifting to purely political criticism concerning the relationship between planning and individual freedom (1972: 34).

31. Today, the LSE is famous for the battles between the welfare state supporter William Beveridge and the Austrian School welfare state critic Hayek.

32. This quotation is used by Kurz (1995: 24). A. C. Pigou, who took over Marshall's Chair of Political Economy at Cambridge University, developed the neoclassical social welfare function and followed a socialism similar to that of the Fabians (Spiegel 1991:

to Spiegel, in contrast to those in Continental Europe, British socialists
to Marx's labor theory of value and "became early converts to Jevon's
ew theory of value. In the absence of a divisive struggle over the theory of
al members of a later generation of British academic economists such as
Pigou a... s. Robinson could start their march into socialism without having to accept
the ponderous legacy of the labor theory of value and without relinquishing the standard
toolbox of academic economics" (1991: 514).

33. "The London School of Economics 1895–1945" (1946) discusses this time period.

34. Before 1929, as LSE graduate student Ronald Coase remembered, "The analytical
apparatus used by students was quite crude by modern standards . . . The 1930s brought
about a great improvement in the analytical tools available to economists" (1982: 31).

35. Smith remarked: "Some twenty-five years ago I suspect that nearly every young
economist had a pricing system for factors and products in a socialist state tucked away
in his desk" (1955: 418).

36. Hayek used the term *collective ownership* on this page, but from the rest of the
text he meant state ownership (ibid.). Michelini also argues that Hayek put together a
"cacophony" of different voices (2001: cxxvi).

37. Bockman and Eyal (2002) discuss the general use of supposedly "naïve" witnesses
from Eastern Europe for battles in capitalist countries.

38. Lange asserted: "The capitalist system is far removed from the model of a competitive economy as elaborated by economic theory. And even if it would conform to it, it
would be, as we have seen, far from maximising social welfare. Only a socialist economy
can fully satisfy the claim made by many economists with regard to the achievements of
free competition" (1937: 127).

39. Lange also allowed for other forms of ownership outside of the means of
production.

40. One of the many included "especially the professor here at Columbia to whom I
owe so much, both intellectually and personally, Harold Hotelling" (Arrow 1978: 476).
Technically, Arrow won the Sverige Riksbank Prize in Economic Sciences in Memory of
Alfred Nobel. They are still called Nobel Laureates.

41. In his *Russian Economic Development*, Dobb (1928) agreed with these views, but
then later rejected them (Lerner 1934b: 54).

42. According to Caldwell, as Hayek became more involved in debates over socialism,
he "decided that a more integrative approach to the study of complex social phenomena
was necessary, that standard economic analysis taken alone might itself be inadequate, if
not misleading, for understanding the problems of socialism" (1997: 1857).

43. In the nineteenth and early twentieth centuries, Russian economists contributed
to neoclassical economics and took part in a transnational neoclassical discussion (Barnett 2005). According to Howard and King (1995), Russian Marxists in particular promoted neoclassical economics in Russia.

44. As mentioned earlier, Coase envisioned the firm in this way as well.

45. Katsenelinboigen wrote, "Thus, the Western economic-mathematical trends,
which did have practical application, were partially developed even in the USSR of the
1920s" (1980: 13). Several scholars argue that Soviet rejection of mathematical economics

was not mainly ideological, but rather Soviet rulers refused to wait for the further development of economic tools; there was an unresolved contradiction between equilibrium and stable growth, on the one hand, and revolution and forced growth, on the other; and many officials had a personal interest in low mathematical literacy (Katsenelinboigen 1980: 12; Smolinski 1971: 149–152).

46. Immediately after the Revolution, Stanislav Strumilin, a Russian Marxist who would become an academician in 1931, proposed an early Russian neoclassical approach to the economics of socialism, by which planning is "solving a mathematical problem on how to allocate the productive resources of the country so as to bring about the maximum satisfaction of social needs at a minimum of labor costs" (Sutela 1991: 9–10).

47. This quotation comes from a *Pravda* article from October 31, 1930, cited in Smolinski (1971: 148).

48. Káldor (1949) is a Hungarian source that reflects the general Stalinist model implemented in the Eastern Bloc at that time. This discussion primarily relies on Bockman (2000).

49. According to Katsenelinboigen, Stalin was the top economic expert, followed by Nikolai Voznesenskii (whom Stalin later killed) and then Konstantin Ostrovitianov (1980: 18).

50. This information comes from both the 1952 plans for the Marxism-Leninism Evening University in Budapest, Hungary (Budapesti Bizottság 1952) and the first political economy textbook in Hungary, *Politikai Gazdaságtan: Tankönyv* ([1954] 1956). This discussion primarily relies on Bockman (2000).

51. This discussion primarily relies on Bockman (2000).

52. For an example of attacks on empirical work, see the personal reflections of Russian mathematical economist Katsenelinboigen (1980).

53. Pollock found that, at these discussions, "all agreed that fear of making a mistake hindered scholarly exchanges and dissuaded people from publishing their work" (2006: 193). Stalin and the Party leadership had encouraged this fear by such activities as arresting fifty people from the Institute of Economics in 1949 (ibid.: 178).

54. In the 1940s, Stalin attacked an economist for his neoclassical ideas, which caused Sutela much later to remark, "The fact that such a campaign was deemed necessary shows that the neoclassical efficiency approach to the economics of socialism had survived the Stalinist decades" (1991: 17).

55. This isolation was not complete. For example, throughout the 1920s and 1930s, Western intellectual "fellow-travellers" visited the Soviet Union (David-Fox 2003; Hollander 1981).

56. Kantorovich was one of the founders of the theory of semiordered spaces—later called K-spaces in his honor. He had met foreign mathematicians, who had also turned to economic questions, such as John von Neumann and A. W. Tucker, at the Moscow Topological Congress in 1935. Unless otherwise stated, the information on Kantorovich comes from Bockman and Bernstein (2008).

57. In 1975, Kantorovich would win the Nobel Prize in economics with Tjalling Koopmans for these 1939 discoveries. Technically, this award is the Sveriges Riksbank Prize in Economic Sciences in Memory of Alfred Nobel.

58. He presented his work in 1939 at Leningrad State University, in 1940 at the Leningrad Polytechnical Institute, and in 1943 at the Institute of Economics, and his work was reproduced in 1,000 copies (Johansen 1976: 72; Kantorovich 1960: 366–367; Sutela 1991: 29). In 1940, he taught a seminar with Novozhilov at the Leningrad Polytechnical Institute (Josephson 1997: 207–208).

59. The articles appeared on April 2, 1944, and July 2 and 3, 1944.

60. Schumpeter ([1954] 1966) later thought that Landauer overestimated the change occurring.

61. Lange (1936–1937) hardly mentioned the Soviet Union at all.

62. Most of this information comes from Bergson's short memoir (1992) and the author's discussion with Bergson in 2000.

63. As a student in the Soviet Union, Leontief had written a report on the Soviet national account system. Before moving to the United States, he studied in Berlin, where he likely came into contact with the Central European debates about neoclassical socialism. In 1973, Leontief would win the Nobel Prize in economics.

64. Bergson remembered, "From the beginning, I have been able, I think with some success, to organize my research in the light of contemporary neo-classical analysis. Should that not have been possible, I doubt that I would have persisted in working on the Soviet economy in any substantial way" (1992: 62).

65. The Soviet Union had declared itself socialist only in 1936. Bergson's research covered the years 1928 and 1934, thus before the Soviet declaration of socialism.

Chapter 2

1. There were rare opportunities to meet, such as the Moscow Economic Conference in 1952. According to one of the participants, this conference brought together about 470 participants from forty-nine countries, "afforded an unusual opportunity for western economists to visit the Soviet Union and meet Soviet economists," and allowed discussions in private, which "continued, with short breaks for sleep, through the entire fortnight" (Cairncross 1952: 113–114). This rare occurrence deserves further research but lies outside the concerns of this chapter.

2. Sovietology in some sense continues in the field of Slavic studies, the Association for Slavic, East European, and Eurasian Studies (ASEEES), and the association's publications.

3. I discuss these ideas more fully in the introduction.

4. Breslau (2003) and Mitchell (2002) have argued that between the 1930s and the 1950s social scientists and governments helped to shape "the economy" as a distinct sphere, an object of social science, statistical enumeration, and government policy. However, in the early 1950s, American and Russian economists did not agree that the Soviet economy and the American economy were similar.

5. Bernstein notes that "the eminent British economist Joan Robinson could argue in 1975 that neoclassical economics had more applicability in a planned or wartime economy than in a decentralized market setting" (2001: 89n44).

6. Technically, Kenneth Arrow and Tjalling Koopmans won the Sveriges Riksbank Prize in Economic Sciences in Memory of Alfred Nobel. They are still called Nobel

Laureates. See the Nobel Prize website: http://nobelprize.org/nobel_prizes/economics/shortfacts.html.

7. Scholars and journalists have revealed the historical connections between intelligence agencies and academia. During World War II, the OSS was filled with academics, and some went on to work at the newly established CIA (Katz 1989; Winks 1987). Former OSS staff also joined the new area studies centers at prominent American universities, continuing many of the same activities they began during the war with military and other government funding (Cumings 1998; Diamond 1992; O'Connell 1990). Many revelations about intelligence connections emerged in the 1960s (Johnson 1989). For example, the CIA covertly funded intellectual activities, such as those organized by the Congress for Cultural Freedom (Saunders 2000) and by other CIA-front organizations (Johnson 1989). The intertwining of the CIA and academia goes much deeper than this, however. Johnson has documented the multitude of ways that academics work for intelligence agencies, including by running covert operations, recruiting foreign students, providing professional opinions either informally or on a paid contractual basis, reporting on trips abroad, and so on. This literature has sought to evaluate the costs of the close connection between intelligence agencies and academics.

8. All five members of the Russian Institute faculty had lived in the Soviet Union in the 1920s and 1930s (Byrnes 1976: 23). One of these five, U.S.-born law expert John Hazard, even had a law degree from the Moscow Juridical Institute (Engerman 2009: 30). Interestingly, between 1943 and 1946, many Soviet students had taken a special eight-month intensive program in English and American history and government at Columbia University (Barghoorn 1960: 57).

9. Harvard University Archive. Wassily Leontief papers. Russian Research Center correspondence and other papers, c. 1940s. HUG 4517.16, Letter from Fred Warner Neal, State Department, to Leontief, June 3, 1947.

10. The main anthropologists of this method were Clyde Kluckhohn, the first director of the Russian Research Center, and Ruth Benedict.

11. Alfred G. Meyer wrote to the director of the Russian Research Center, "Through informal channels (Embassy purchasing officer) we are getting a slow but steady supply of price lists, they said; and we should not make the Soviet officials wise to the importance we attach to a knowledge of prices." Harvard University Archive. Merle Fainsod papers. Correspondence relating chiefly to the Russian Research Center, Box 4, Ru-Z. Memorandum from Meyer to Clyde Kluckhohn, October 9, 1951. Confidential.

12. Harvard faculty member Alfred G. Meyer complained to the director of the Russian Research Center about the poor quality of the visiting speakers and that some of these people, known Nazis, had "such a dirty political record that a decent citizen would not ordinarily shake hands with them." Harvard University Archive. Merle Fainsod papers. Correspondence relating chiefly to the Russian Research Center, Box 2, G-M. Memorandum from Meyer to Kluckhohn, May 5, 1952.

13. Koopmans (1960) recounted this history (p. 363). In response to this account, Flood later wrote to Koopmans, "There seems no need to me to include the phrase 'a mathematician whose duties included the reading of Russian technical literature,' after

naming Max Shiffman, because I am confident that Max simply cam [sic] across the Kantorovich abstract in the course of his normal work as a good research mathematician." Yale University Archive, Koopmans Papers, Box No. 14, Folder No. 251 "Kantorovich, Translations, 1960," Letter from Flood to Koopmans, June 13, 1960: 2.

14. Yale University Archive, Koopmans Papers, Box No. 13, Folder No. 237, "Kantorovich, Leonid V., 1956–59," Letter from W. W. Cooper at Carnegie Institute of Tech to Dr. C. J. Hitch at RAND Economics Division, Jan. 13, 1958.

15. Kestner discusses one OSS group studying the Soviet economy through open sources at the Library of Congress, but the OSS classified their reports (1999: 24).

16. As Mirowski has remarked, "Linear programming and game theory grew up in compartmentalized spheres in each country, with only a very few figures with security clearance having substantial access to cutting-edge research in both" (2004: 205). Mirowski states further: "There was also the phenomenon of some scientists having special access to Soviet developments through their military ties, but not fully acknowledging the nature and extent of their influence" (ibid.: 215).

17. The question was 29a: "Has any group or person accused anyone on this faculty here of being a subversive or of engaging in any un-American activities in the past few years?" The results were Yes, 1,122 or 45.8 percent of respondents; No, 1,185 or 48.3 percent of respondents; Don't Know, 133; and Not Applicable (ibid.: 11).

18. According to Lazarsfeld and Thielens, communism acquired a new overall meaning in postwar period, as a more widespread and threatening danger, covering all things from espionage for a foreign power to distasteful unconventionality, and "there appears to have been a considerable enlargement in scope of the kinds of thoughts and acts which were supposed to reveal an individual's hidden Communism" (ibid.: 57).

19. Americans could buy Soviet books from, for example, the Four Continent Book Corporation in New York, which also bought American scientific publications for the Soviet government (Barghoorn 1960: 55).

20. These quotations come from O'Connell (1990: 137, 136), who used FBI reports from 1948 and 1949.

21. Solberg and Tomilson (1997) document the firing of Howard Bowen at the University of Illinois in 1950.

22. A student asked one political scientist, "Do you want to live in Russia? . . . If not, why do you talk so much about it?" (Meyer 1993: 168).

23. In contrast to much of the Cold War literature (for example, Chomsky et al., 1997; O'Connell 1990; Robin 2001; Simpson 1998), Engerman found, "Neither the field nor its founders were dominated by the fervent anti-Communists who appear in familiar depictions of postwar reaction; it was instead a wide-ranging group determined to build expertise and to make itself useful in intellectual life, public debate, and foreign policy" (2009: 4).

24. Mirowski (2002) and Amadae (2003) have also shown the ways that the military and government environment made economics narrow, leaving behind concerns that only later would become central to economics. Goodwin (1998) confirms that the McCarthyist atmosphere and the state encouraged a more technical, mathematical economics.

25. This theory assumed that totalitarian states had "an official ideology, consisting of an official body of doctrine covering all vital aspects of man's existence, to which everyone living in that society is supposed to adhere to at least passively" (Gleason 1995: 125).

26. The U.S. government demanded data and analysis on the Soviet Union, specifically related to policy, which meant simple histories and predictions (Cohen 1985; Motyl 1993: 81). Many political scientists and other scholars criticized Sovietologists for this nontheoretical stand. See Armstrong (1973) on fact collecting.

27. Originally, eight Russian Institute graduate students had applied for visas, but the Soviet Embassy accepted only four of them (Randall 1955: 2). The four students were Ted Curran, Gay Humphrey, Jeri Lidsky, and Frank Randall, two women and two men.

28. The police or soldiers would arrest them for taking particular pictures (Randall 1955: 5).

29. As Oushakine (2001) has shown, dissidents' oppositional discourse was not separate from the official discourse but rather mimicked this discourse. Similarly, Burawoy writes, "Rather than endorsing alternative values, the working class embraced the regime's values as its own, which became a basis for opposition to the regime's actual practice" (1992: 777).

30. Barghoorn's 1960 book is titled *The Soviet Cultural Offensive*.

31. In the early 1920s, there had been many ties with the Soviet Union, as described by Sivachev and Yakovlev (1979). During the 1930s, 1,500 U.S. specialists worked in the Soviet Union (ibid.: 102).

32. According to Raymond, two–thirds of these foreign students studied in regular Russian universities and specialty schools, while the rest studied at Patrice Lumumba People's Friendship University in Moscow (1972: 137).

33. Reflecting this policy, an internal report of the Ford Foundation from 1961 stated that of the 269 Polish scholars brought to the United States only forty were from the physical sciences, engineering, architecture, and city planning. The 229 remaining were from the humanities and social sciences "with an emphasis on economists." Those coming from Yugoslavia were also drawn similarly from these fields. FF R2346 64-432, Nov. 10, 1961. Internal report by Ford Foundation's International Affairs Department "Educational Relations with Eastern Europe."

34. Such agreements seemed strange at the time. One of the organizers of the first study abroad program with the Soviet Union, Robert F. Byrnes, wrote, "Formal exchange agreements undermine free trade in ideas, increase the role of our government over intellectual activity, and grant legitimacy to governments that deny the freedoms essential to civilized life" (1976: 7).

35. FF R2346 64-432, Nov. 10, 1961: 2. Internal report by Ford Foundation's International Affairs Department, "Educational Relations with Eastern Europe."

36. FF R2346, 64-432, December 1963.

37. FF R2346, 64-432, May 6, 1965. Letter from Shepard Stone of the Ford Foundation to Earl O. Heady at Iowa State University.

38. FF R2346, 64-432, Feb. 14, 1967. Interview of György Varga.

39. FF R2346, 64-432, Feb. 7, 1964. Letter from S. T. Gordon to Shepard Stone of the Ford Foundation.

40. Others connected to the Ford Foundation sought to make changes beyond economic reform: "I hope, also, the Foundation can arrange to bring to the United States several individuals who have official positions in higher education in Hungary, for a massive overhaul of their entire university system is in order." FF R2346, 64-432, March 8, 1965. Letter from Hubert Heffner at Stanford University to Shepard Stone at the Ford Foundation's International Affairs Program.

41. FF R2346, 64-432, Feb. 26, 1968.

42. FF R2346, 64-432, Nov. 18, 1961: 1. Letter from John Michael Montias to Shepard Stone at the Ford Foundation's International Affairs Program.

43. FF R2346, 64-432, Nov. 30, 1962. Letter from Earl O. Heady at Iowa State University to Dr. Charles Hardin at the Rockefeller Foundation.

44. FF R2346, 64-432, April 20, 1965: 2. Letter from Earl O. Heady at Iowa State University to Shepard Stone at the Ford Foundation.

45. The Library of Congress was the main organizer of these exchanges. After the Second World War, in 1946, the library exchange resumed.

46. This quotation comes from Richmond 2003: 148.

47. In Bockman and Bernstein (2008), the East–West connection between Koopmans and Kantorovich is discussed in detail.

48. Harvard University Archive. Wassily Leontief papers. Correspondence, General, 1961–65. Handwritten letter from Leontief to Karin [most likely his assistant in Boston], May 30, 1962.

49. According to the council's brochure, "this book distribution program is financed from a private, non-governmental source which prefers to remain anonymous." International Advisory Council (IAC) brochure. Harvard University Archive. Wassily Leontief papers. Correspondence, General, 1961–65. HUG 4517.5. Memo from Patricia Graham, Executive Assistant, IUCTG. Written: From Pattullo to Various people who may be interested in item II. 6-7-63.

50. Harvard University Archive. Wassily Leontief papers. Correspondence, General, 1961–65. HUG 4517.5. Box Harvard Economic Research Project to International Statistical Institute, File "I." Letter from Leontief to International Advisory Council, Inc., May 9, 1963. Leontief also received books and translations from a "Mr. Gilbert": "Dear Mr. Gilbert: Enclosed is the translation of the Russian article which you secured for me. Thanks for the most useful 'Survey of Soviet Economists and Economic Research Organizations' (I assume it was sent by you)." Harvard University Archive. Wassily Leontief papers. Correspondence, General, 1961–65. HUG 4517.5 Box F to G (general), File "G." Letter to Mr. George Gilbert, Room 304, 545 Technology Square, Cambridge, from Leontief, May 20, 1963.

51. To build a grassroots-based public sphere outside conventional politics and the Cold War blocs, intellectuals sought to create numerous organizations, including the Congress for Cultural Freedom, *Recontres internationales de Geneve*, and *Societa europea di cultura*. Many writers have demonstrated the role of the CIA in the Congress for Cul-

tural Freedom in particular (Saunders 2000). Yet people participated in these conferences for a variety of reasons. For example, Norberto Bobbio (1999) worked in the 1950s with these organizations to reunite Europe and considered those who sought out East–West connections in the West as naturally on the left. Berghahn (2001) finds similar characteristics among a smaller group of intellectuals around the Congress for Cultural Freedom.

52. At Harvard, Leontief established his Harvard Economic Research Project (HERP), which lasted from 1948 to 1977. HERP brought together some of the most famous names in economics, such as Hollis Chenery, Robert Solow, and James Duesenberry, to work on input-output modeling. Economists from around the world sought to be visiting fellows at HERP. From 1956 to 1962, ninety-nine economists (as well as other visiting delegations) from twenty-eight countries, including Soviets and Eastern Europeans, spent anywhere from a day or two to an entire academic year at HERP. Harvard University Archive. Wassily Leontief papers. Correspondence, General, 1961–65. HUG 4517.5. Box Harvard Economic Research Project (cont'd) to International Statistical Institute, File "HERP 1961," List of Visiting Scholars, July 1956–June 1962. The international conferences included many former HERP visiting scholars.

53. Leontief understood his work as neoclassical. According to his autobiography, in 1931, he sought to "formulate a general equilibrium theory capable of empirical implementation" ("Wassily Leontief—Autobiography," 1973).

54. According to Ellman, "Much of the 'new' Western economics of the post World War II period, such as the discussion of the economic problems of the developing countries, growth models and input-output, was simply the rediscovery and development of the fruitful Soviet work of the 1920s" (1973: 1).

55. In 1965, Zoltán Kenessey, a high-level expert in the Hungarian Central Statistical Office, wrote to Leontief: "For me the whole history of I-O seems to be a fascinating subject. During the development of it some geographical and other frontiers were, for everybody's advantage, so successfully crossed." Harvard University Archive. Wassily Leontief papers. Correspondence, General, 1961–65. HUG 4517.5. Letter from Kennesey to Leontief, May 11, 1965.

56. This information comes from a personal conversation with John T. Dunlop in 2000. The Econometric Society and other groups also arranged international conferences with Eastern Europeans and Russians (Bockman and Eyal 2002: 325–326).

57. They received 179 returned completed questionnaires. They were studying Sovietological experts who had traveled to the Soviet Union in 1966–1967.

58. Bockman and Bernstein (2008) discuss the interaction between Kantorovich and Koopmans more extensively.

59. Yale University Archive. Tjalling Charles Koopmans papers. Correspondence, Group No. 1439, Series No. I, Box No. 13, Folder No. 237, "Kantorovich, Leonid V., 1956–59," Letter from Tjalling C. Koopmans to Professor L. Kantorovich, Nov. 12, 1956.

60. Ibid.

61. Yale University Archive. Tjalling Charles Koopmans papers. Correspondence, Group No. 1439, Series No. I, Box No. 13, Folder No. 237, "Kantorovich, Leonid V., 1956–59," Letter from Koopmans to Robert W. Campbell, March 27, 1958.

62. Yale University Archive. Tjalling Charles Koopmans papers. Correspondence, Group No. 1439, Series No. I, Box No. 14, Folder No. 239, "Kantorovich, Leonid V., Cooper-Charnes discussion, 1960, 1961," Letter from Koopmans to Herb [Scarf, most likely], Dec. 7, 1960.

63. Dantzig's simplex method was unquestionably a pathbreaking discovery, but the Nobel committee did not consider him an economist. Therefore, Dantzig was not eligible to win the Nobel Prize in economics.

64. Yale University Archive. Tjalling Charles Koopmans papers. Correspondence, Group No. 1439, Series No. I, Box No. 14, Folder No. 239, "Kantorovich, Leonid V., Cooper-Charnes discussion, 1960, 1961," Letter from Harold Kuhn to R. M. Thrall, July 14, 1961.

65. Yale University Archive. Tjalling Charles Koopmans papers. Correspondence, Group No. 1439, Series No. I, Box No. 14, Folder No. 239. "Esteemed Prof Thrall," handwritten letter from Kantorovich, translated by Richard Judy, Dec. 31, 1960: 7 (typed translation).

66. As Collins and Restivo have recognized, "Significant historical shifts in the social organization of science" through new patrons or new institutions provide resources for scientific competition and alternative norms for scientific practice (1983: 200).

67. Koopmans Papers, Box No. 14, File No. 250, "Kantorovich, Translations, 1958–60," Letter from C. West Churchman to Koopmans, March 13, 1959.

68. Yale University Archive. Tjalling Charles Koopmans papers. Correspondence, Group No. 1439, Series No. I, Box No. 14, Folder No. 246, "Kantorovich, Papers and Bibliographic Materials, 1957–60," Inquiry. From Marlow, Serial 6648/58, March 18, 1958. Marlow said he had been told "a colorful story" about how the text was obtained. Yale University Archive. Tjalling Charles Koopmans papers. Correspondence, Group No. 1439, Series No. I, Box No. 13, Folder No. 237, "Kantorovich, Leonid V., 1956–59," Letter from Marlow to Campbell, April 7, 1958.

69. Yale University Archive, Koopmans Papers, Box No. 14, Folder No. 251. "Kantorovich, Translations, 1960," Letter from Tucker to Koopmans, June 13, 1960.

70. Cramer (1965) states that between 1917 and 1950 one billion copies of books protected by foreign copyright were published in the Soviet Union. Through the 1950s and into the 1960s, the Soviet Union did not adhere to any international copyright treaties. Tsarist Russia also did not respect international copyrights. At the same time, the United States did not sign the Berne Convention for the Protection of Literary and Artistic Works until 1988 (World Intellectual Property Organization, available at: www.wipo.int).

71. The boundary between spying and scholarship relies on presumptions of trust within the scientists' social worlds and the social knowledge required to determine whether someone is trustworthy (Shapin 1994). To evaluate knowledge claims, one must also be able to evaluate the knowledge creator. When social worlds collide, trust and knowledge about members of the social world come into question.

72. Project Camelot was a U.S. military–sponsored study to predict and control development and revolution in the Third World. Publicly, this project was condemned as espionage masquerading as science (Herman 1998: 101–104).

73. Discussion with a participant on an exchange to the Soviet Union.

74. "Expert on Soviet Society: Frederick Charles Barghoorn" and "Arrest in Soviet Union Shocks Scholars," *New York Times*, Nov. 13, 1963.

75. Harvard University Archive. Wassily Leontief papers. Correspondence, General, 1961–65. HUG 4517.5. Letter from Houthakker to L. Klein, Leontief, Malinvaud, Ruggles, Wold, June 6, 1964.

76. Harvard University Archive. Wassily Leontief papers. Correspondence, General, 1961–65. HUG 4517.5. Letter from Koopmans to Leontief, Oct. 29, 1964.

77. Harvard University Archive. Wassily Leontief papers. Correspondence, General, 1961–65. HUG 4517.5. Letter from Leontief to Federenko, Dec. 22, 1964.

78. Harvard University Archive. Wassily Leontief papers. Correspondence, General, 1961–65. HUG 4517.5. Letter from Houthakker to Leontief, March 16, 1965.

79. Harvard University Archive. Wassily Leontief papers. Correspondence, General, 1961–65. HUG 4517.5. Letter from Leontief to Houthakker, May 13, 1965.

80. Harvard University Archive. Wassily Leontief papers. Correspondence, General, 1961–65. HUG 4517.5. Letter from Houthakker to Leontief, May 18, 1965.

Chapter 3

1. In 1918, Slovenes, Croats, and Serbians united in a single kingdom, which collapsed after the Axis powers invaded in 1941. Yugoslavia as a socialist federation came into existence on November 29, 1945 (Curtis 1990).

2. Milenkovitch agreed, "Soviet influence was so complete that the Yugoslavs hastened, well before their comrades elsewhere in Eastern Europe, to nationalize the means of production and to commence central planning. Yugoslav leaders regarded the Communist Party of the Soviet Union as the sole authority on the interpretation of Marxism" and the practice of socialism (1971: 55).

3. The Cominform was the Communist Information Bureau, which included the Communist Parties of the USSR, Bulgaria, Hungary, Czechoslovakia, Rumania, Poland, Yugoslavia (expelled in June 1948), France, and Italy (Morris 1953: 368).

4. As Callon, MacKenzie, and others have argued, economics does not merely describe the economy but also "performs the economy" (Callon 1998; Callon et al., 2007; MacKenzie 2006; MacKenzie and Millo 2003).

5. In 1948, before the expulsion, about half of Yugoslavia's foreign trade was with the Soviet bloc (Campbell 1967: 23). Yugoslav trade with the East Bloc dropped by seven-eighths in 1949 and came to a near standstill in following years (Montias 1959: 294).

6. Within the United Nations, as early as fall 1949, Yugoslav representatives denounced Soviet aggression (Campbell 1967: 17) and supported other countries' criticisms of aggressive Cold War powers. The Yugoslav government also began imprisoning "Cominformists," those who supported the Soviet Union and its form of socialism. By 1952, 14,000 "Cominformists" had been imprisoned (Rusinow 1977: 30).

7. Boris Kidrič ([1950] 1979) made a similar argument about the new stage.

8. Kidrič remarked in a 1951 speech, "We actually are carrying out the withering away of the state" (Ramet 2006: 190–191).

9. This term reflected the intentions of some in the regime rather than the reality of the new system.

10. This quotation comes from Milenkovitch (1971: 66–67).

11. Juhász (2001) states that these workers' councils began spontaneously and were later made legal through the Basic Law in the Management of Enterprises by the Working Collectives passed on June 27, 1950.

12. According to Prout, "By the time of the new Constitution in 1953, the workers' collective had replaced the state *in law* as the manager and trustee of industrial resources in Yugoslavia" (1985: 15).

13. Trotsky's 1932 words are quoted in Nove (1987: 37). According to Woodward (1987), Yugoslav leaders—especially Kardelj and Kidrič—had been Trotskyist since at least 1946.

14. According to Kidrič in 1949, the law of value "becomes a mighty weapon of planning, a means of carrying out the tasks of socialist construction which were thought out in advance and established by the plan" (Milenkovitch 1971: 58).

15. Yugoslavia soon joined the U.N. Security Council, where its representatives worked regularly with India and Egypt, building the foundation for their later work in the nonaligned movement (Willetts 1978).

16. According to Willetts (1978), the 1956 Suez-Hungary crisis brought the leaders of the future nonaligned movement together in a new way. In 1956, Israel, Britain, and France invaded Egypt to stop the Egyptian nationalization of the Suez Canal. In the very same month, the Soviet Union had invaded Hungary to quell a national revolution there. India and Yugoslavia, as well as other countries, came to support Egypt in opposition to the Great Powers and mobilized the United Nations to remove British and French troops from Egypt (Willetts 1978: 3–4).

17. For example, at the first nonaligned conference, Tito called for a "universal economic organization" to remove barriers to world trade caused by closed regional economic groupings, which led to the formation of the U.N. Conference on Trade and Development (UNCTAD) in 1964 (Rubinstein 1970: 170–172).

18. Willetts (1978) argues that the nonaligned movement began in the late 1950s and not at the Bandung Conference in 1955 (3).

19. Furthermore, Yugoslav leaders began presenting socialism as a "world process," taking place simultaneously in the socialist camp, the West, and the Third World (Rubinstein 1970: 74).

20. Yugoslav leaders soon changed their view of Yugoslavia from needing aid to exporting assistance to the world. In 1952, the Yugoslav government formed the Federal Institute for International Technical Cooperation to organize U.N. assistance to Yugoslavia. By 1953, however, this agency had changed its orientation to providing Yugoslav aid to developing countries (Rubinstein 1970: 213).

21. Archives of Serbia and Montenegro, Fond 142 (Socijalistički savez radnog naroda Jugoslavije), 41 (Materijali komisije za medjunarodne veze), 1951, 1955–57, 1959. 142-41-137, Ivory Coast.

22. By 1983, the Yugoslav government had numerous institutions that coordinated economic cooperation and technical assistance with developing countries: the Yugoslav Bank for International Economic Co-operation; the Solidarity Fund for the Non-Aligned and Other Developing Countries; the Federal Administration for International Scientific, Educational, Cultural and Technical Co-operation; as well as Yugoslav ministries involved in foreign affairs, banks, and enterprises (*Yugoslavia* 1983).

23. Willetts states that at first Yugoslavia adopted "a pro-Western alignment in the Cold War" in the early 1950s, which later changed to nonalignment (1978: 4).

24. According to Ramet, the Soviets planned to invade Yugoslavia and remove Tito from power: "Throughout 1950 and early 1951, there were repeated war games and military maneuvers designed to practice for invasion. By then, armed strength levels in Hungary, Romania, and Bulgaria were two to three and a half times the levels permitted by the Paris Peace Treaty" (2006: 177–181).

25. The United States permitted the Yugoslav purchase of a $3 million steel finishing mill from the United States with this loan from the Export-Import Bank (Hoffman and Neal 1962: 148).

26. The United States terminated military aid in 1957 (Campbell 1967: 39).

27. According to Hoffman and Neal, Tito made this remark in 1955 (1962: 428).

28. Campbell recognized that "on the American side there was at least some expectation that the mere fact of growing economic, cultural, and military relations would inevitably tend to draw Yugoslavia toward the West and to encourage changes at home, almost in spite of the regime's wishes" (1967: 22).

29. While exploring the ideas of Yugoslav economists, American economist Benjamin Ward noted their free market views, "The result was not that the economy was left to the tender care of some invisible hand (though one may easily get that impression from the writings of Yugoslav economists of the period)" (1956a: 87).

30. Maksimović argued, "Prof. Lange's model of market socialism, which was formulated by him in 1936/7, was the closest, in our opinion, to the Yugoslav model of economic system, and at a time when one knew little about him" (1965: 349).

31. Some economists had studied economics abroad in the 1930s (Uvalić 1954: 262), and neoclassical economics literature likely remained in libraries, though not necessarily accessible to most readers. For example, Radivoj Uvalić had graduated from the Institut de Statistique and the Institut des Hautes Études Internationales at the Sorbonne in the 1930s, after which he published an article on price movements on world markets and then became a professor of political economy. From 1948 to 1951, Uvalić was dean of the Faculty of Economics in Belgrade and soon after that president of the Serbian Association of Economists (UNESCO 1960).

32. In their 1954–1955 report, the University of Zagreb's Faculty of Economics remarked that in the last year they had sought to get rid of "weaknesses" in their collections and found it especially important to purchase American literature. They also found that they lacked economic literature from the war period and immediately afterward. Also they lacked documentation of economic-financial and social research. For teaching and

research, they needed materials published by the OECD, the U.S. Congress, the IMF, and different organizations that dealt with the collective economy, urbanism, housing, and so on ("Skupština" 1955: 1014).

33. Korač was likely one of the earliest to study abroad after the Second World War. He studied at Cambridge University in 1953–1954 in an economics seminar led by Piero Sraffa, a critic of neoclassical economics (*Ekonomski Fakultet* 2007: 46).

34. See University of Belgrade, Faculty of Law (n.d.).

35. See Montenegrin Academy of Sciences and Arts (n.d.).

36. Interviews with faculty at the Faculty of Economics, University of Belgrade.

37. See University of Zagreb, Faculty of Law (n.d.).

38. Interviews with faculty at the Faculty of Economics, University of Belgrade.

39. For example, Branislav Šoškić studied in 1962–1963 at Harvard and the University of California, Berkeley (Montenegrin Academy of Sciences and Arts, n.d.).

40. Benjamin Ward and Gregory Grossman worked at the University of California, Berkeley. Abram Bergson, Anne Carter, and Wassily Leontief worked at Harvard. MIT employed Evsey Domar.

41. The main speakers were Dennis Robertson, Jacob Viner, Francois Perroux, Gottfried Haberler, and Erik Lundberg (Stojanović 1956: 595).

42. Uvalić reported, "Any faculty may invite a foreign professor to give a series of lectures on some aspect of his special subject. The economics faculties have not so far made the use of this right that other faculties have done" (1954; 274).

43. See University of Belgrade, Faculty of Law (n.d.).

44. Maksimović also explained the Austrian School "neoliberal" criticism of neoclassical economics and socialism, including the arguments made by Friedrich von Hayek.

45. In his conclusion, Maksimović argued against allowing consumer prices to drive the entire socialist economy because the neoclassical equilibrium model assumes a static situation in which prices adjust gradually, which in a developing country would not be the case. In a developing country, neoclassical prices and "economic automatism" would be mixed with direct investments.

46. Branko Horvat studied at Manchester from 1955 to 1958, getting a second PhD.

47. Horvat noted that "entrepreneurship, and the corresponding category of profit, represent the weakest link in formal economic theory" (1964: 114).

48. At the University of Belgrade in 1958, the Economics Faculty created two divisions: General Economics (dealing with the national economy) and Economics of the Enterprise. Within General Economics, students took courses in economic development theory, the theory and policy of prices, and a seminar on *Capital*. The students also took an Economic Doctrines course, which included discussions of the socialist calculation debate. These courses were taught by economists, who had studied abroad and were trained in neoclassical economics (*Ekonomski Fakultet* 2007).

49. This book was originally published in 1960 in Slovenian, then published in Serbo-Croatian in 1966.

50. Černe also stated that the prices of productive means would be formed somewhat differently (1966: 237).

51. Gligorov noted, "The opposition to the mainstream consisted largely of those who believed in central planning" (1998: 329).

52. For example, in the early 1950s, economists worked in discussion groups to form the new system ("Izveštaj" 1953: 61). Later, according to Černe (1966), the Federal office for economic planning, the Federal statistical office, the Economic Institute SRS, and other agencies worked on the second economic plan of 1957–1961. Economists trained abroad in neoclassical economics influenced these discussions. They based their work on the writings of economists, including V. Tričković, B. Šefer, E. Berković, V. Franković, E. Vajs, and I. Turk (ibid. 58–59).

53. I am referring here to the performativity literature (for example, Callon 1998; Callon, Millo, and Muniesa 2007; MacKenzie and Millo 2003).

54. Personal communication with Benjamin N. Ward in 2007.

55. Later in the article, Ward wrote, "The model's relevance to Yugoslavia may be somewhat increased if it is assumed that the legal framework is descriptive of an ultimate purpose on the part of the Yugoslav leadership" (1958; 585).

56. Domar wrote, "Imagine that most of the obstacles facing Soviet kolkhozes (collective farms) today . . . suddenly vanish, and the *kolkhozes* find themselves in a Lange-Lerner type of a competitive world where everything can be bought and sold at a market price, and where peasants are free to run their own affairs *provided the essential structure of the kolkhoz is retained.* How would Soviet agriculture, or for that matter any economic sector so organized, fare in such a wonderland?" (1966: 734). As with all neoclassical modeling, he posited both this cooperative model and its "capitalist twin," which is formally equivalent to the cooperative model and provides a comparative case (ibid.: 737). With this article, Domar brought the cooperative into the neoclassical mainstream.

57. The firms also had to have the same technology. The labor-managed economy was more competitive because it encouraged decentralization and smaller firms.

58. In particular, Yugoslavia had opened its economy to the world economy and thus had more competition and prices were even more exogenous.

59. Horvat argued against "postulating what should be rational" and for observing the actual practices of Yugoslav enterprises (1971: 105).

60. According to Horvat, the freely competitive market can function automatically if it has the right institutional system and thus can avoid all "administrative intervention" (1967: 7).

61. Marschak (1968) and Wachtel (1973) also used empirical data.

62. The Archives of Serbia and Montenegro have numerous lists of experts sent to intergovernmental organizations.

63. At least through 1971, Yugoslavs were never executive directors but rather just alternates (Mason and Asher 1973: 869).

64. From interviews with World Bank economists from the former Yugoslavia, I learned that some of them independently obtained their jobs.

65. Hollis Chenery wrote about Béla Balassa, a highly influential, long-term consultant in the World Bank: "The Bank's orientation is comparative, as is Bela's in most of his work" (1991: xiv).

66. The Yugoslav government also had a hand in the creation of UNCTAD (Rubinstein 1970).

67. According to archival documents, the ICPE remained the only center of nonaligned countries (*"ostane samo centar nesvrstanih zemalja"*). Archives of Serbia and Montenegro, fond 465, popis br. 57, fasc. br. 46, UN Upravljanje preduz., U javnon vlasništvu uzu, 1971–1977. From the start, the Yugoslav founders assumed that the ICPE would become part of the U.N. system and the nonaligned movement.

68. According to the future ICPE director, Anton Vratuša, the ICPE would be the most natural organization for teaching the experiences of worker self-management in Yugoslav enterprises. Archives of Serbia and Montenegro, fond 465, popis br. 57, fasc. br. 46, UN Upravljanje preduz., U javnon vlasništvu uzu, 1971–1977. Letter from Dr. A. Vratuša (deputy state secretary) to Ing. Marko Bulć, member of the SIV, March 23, 1971.

69. The organizers also planned to create a Graduate School of Management in Public Enterprises and a Graduate School of International Transfer of Science and Technology.

70. Archives of Serbia and Montenegro, fond 465, popis br. 57, fasc. br. 46, UN Upravljanje preduz., U javnon vlasništvu uzu, 1971–1977. File: Interregionalni projekat: "Medjunarodni centar za upravljanje preduzecima u javnon vlasništvu," Information about the International Center.

71. According to Deutsch,

The Yugoslavs played a pivotal role, beginning with an international conference on worker self-management in 1972 that began a critical networking of international researchers and practitioners. The Inter-University Center of Post-Graduate Studies in Dubrovnik hosted a series of international seminars on worker participation during the 1970s that helped to both generate interest and publicize activities worldwide. Yugoslav economist Branko Horvat, who published the journal *Economic Analysis and Worker Self-Management*, played a leading role in forming the international economists' organization on self-management. Meanwhile, Yugoslavian sociologists such as Rudi Supek played a parallel role in starting the International Sociological Association Research Committee on Worker Participation and Self-Management in 1978. Yugoslavian researchers published a great deal and played a vital role in stimulating an international community interest in self-management. (2005, 647)

72. This journal joined other new journals, such as *Autogestions: Revue Trimestrielle*, which had this advertisement in *Economic Analysis and Workers' Management* in 1980: "'Autogestion' is everywhere: in books and pamphlets, in people's heads and written on walls." *Economic and Industrial Democracy: An International Journal* also began in this year, while the Peruvian *Socialismo y Participación* began in 1977.

Chapter 4

1. For simplicity, I use the more generic term "Hungarian Communist Party" for the Moscow-connected communist party in Hungary, which changed its name several times during its decades-long existence.

2. There is much debate about when the Party actually decided to implement the Soviet system. Zhelitski assumes that the Hungarian Communist Party had a plan to

establish a "totalitarian regime" as early as 1945 (1997: 79). Swain and Swain (1993) argue that Stalin had no blueprint for the sovietization of Eastern Europe before 1947 (33, 54). Roman agrees with Swain and Swain: "There is no shred of evidence that the soviets had such a program" (1996: 167). According to Roman, the Soviet Union was the most influential foreign power in Hungary, but the Soviet Party leaders did not call for the Sovietization of Hungary after the Second World War. In fact, Stalin insisted on multiparty coalition and the presence of non-Communist politicians in the government. This situation changed in 1948 when the Soviet Union broke with Tito (ibid.: 222). At this point, the Hungarian Communist Party gained a monopoly over the political sphere and began Sovietizing Hungary, which included the imposition of Soviet economics.

3. The Hungarian economics profession was left only with this one journal, which even Party leaders recognized as publishing "low-level" Russian material. PIA 690/5/1948: 46. Notes about the economic press to Andor Berei, April 1, 1948.

4. Reinforcing Nagy's point, the Third Conference Party Conference in May 1954 had ordered the development of economic science (Szabó 1954). One economist remembered that, while he worked in the Party administration from October 1953 to December 1954, the majority of those promoted were neither workers nor peasants but rather economists and intellectuals (Szabó, OHA, 1991: 147). Economists called 1954 the year of the "revival of economic science" (ibid. 1991: 135).

5. Not everyone had formal economic degrees. Some of the older generation worked in economic positions without degrees but identified themselves as economists.

6. For example, Zoltán Vas (1990) had been removed from his post as president of the National Planning Office and sent to the countryside to be a company director due in part to his refusal to allow the Party to dictate his employment policies. In 1953, Vas expected to be put on trial during anti-Semitic purges connected to Stalin's retaliation against the supposed Doctors' Plot. However, Stalin's death ended this process (ibid.: 113). Vas helped prepare Nagy's economic programs and speeches.

7. Donáth and Nagy represented factions of the agriculture bureaucracy that did not support forced collectivization.

8. Imre Nagy and Tamás Nagy were not related. When discussing Tamás Nagy, I use his full name or T. Nagy.

9. HAS 182/3/1950. Notes on the Business and Trade College lecturer Tibor Andersen by Margit Siklós to the Academy of Sciences, May 16, 1950.

10. HAS 183/3/a/1954. Minutes of Permanent Economics Committee, July 19, 1954.

11. PIA 276/115/17/1948: 1–2. Report to Zoltán Vas from László Timár and Dr. Siklós at the National Planning Office's Economic Division, Dec. 13, 1948. The Party-state leadership had originally replaced the Hungarian Institute for Economic Research with a new Economics Institute, but it too was soon shut down. Applied economists conducted research in the Party-state apparatus but were constrained by the immediate concerns of their agencies (Bockman 2000).

12. In Hungarian, the ESI is called the Közgazdaságtudományi Intézet (KTI).

13. HAS 183/1/1954: 2. Suggestion to establish the Economic Science Institute, Nov. 5, 1954 (also dated Dec. 6, 1954).

14. HAS 183/4/a/1955. Letter from István Rusznyak to Nándor Gyöngyösi, Economics Documentation Center, Feb. 23, 1955.

15. In fall 1954, the ESI worked out the details of his economic program. ESI economists also wrote confidential reports and published articles developing economic ideas and promoting Nagy's worldview. The ESI, however, did hire economists who did not support Nagy or his programs, such as István Friss, Rákosi's top economic expert and head of the ESI. While Friss had been a Stalinist economic expert, he was a close friend of reform economists, such as György Péter (Szabó, OHA, 1991), and a great asset to ESI economists (Péteri 1996: 378). While not all ESI economists agreed with Nagy, he could rely on the majority of them to determine economic policy tasks, to evaluate the performance of economic measures, and, above all, to discredit Rákosi's policies.

16. HAS 183/4/a/1954. Letter from Klara Fejér to István Rusznyak, both at the Hungarian Academy of Sciences, Nov. 4, 1954. In the April 1954 issue of Economics Review, Szabó called for an economic research institute (62, 73). The secretary for economics within the Academy of Sciences tried to present a separate proposal, but Szabó said that only he would determine the plan for the ESI. Academy of Sciences officials were not allowed even to give a opinion on Szabó's ideas; rather his proposal went straight to the Politburo.

17. Tamás Nagy, an important supporter of Imre Nagy, was one of the founding members of the institute (Péteri 1993: 166). The ESI incorporated the Agricultural Organizational Institute headed by Ferenc Donáth, an ally of Nagy and one of his deputy ministers. Donáth became the deputy director of the institute (Péteri 1993: 163).

18. The graduate students included Ferenc Fekete, Ernő Csizmadia, and Béla Csendes (Rainer 1996: 457).

19. HAS 183/1/1954: 2. Suggestion to establish the Economic Science Institute, Nov. 5, 1954 (also dated Dec. 6, 1954).

20. HAS 183/1/1954. Suggestion to establish the Economic Science Institute, Nov. 5, 1954 (also dated Dec. 6, 1954).

21. In Hungarian, these graduate students are called aspiráns. HAS 183/7/1956. Report originally written by Friss on work and problems at the Economic Science Institute, Feb. 1956.

22. Péteri notes that the ESI "ranked first with an unusually high share (47 percent) of peer positions in the assessment of dissertations from institutes of applied economics and, just as notably, even in terms of their share over dissertation from departments of political economy" (1996: 378).

23. In Hungarian, this reestablished journal was called the Közgazdasági Szemle.

24. In the April 1954 issue of Economics Review, Szabó called for "an independent economic theory journal because the publishing opportunities are limited" (73). Other publications also lacked Hungarian authors. A report from 1953 on the publishing of economics books found the following:

1. Financial book publishing—no Hungarian authors, the readers were mainly Soviet financial and accounting experts.

2. Statistics book publishing—the readers were mostly from the Soviet Union.

3. Planning economics book publishing—the only authors were National Planning Office employees in the Soviet Union.

4. Nepszava publishers—no Hungarian authors.
HAS 182/8/1953. Report about the situation in economics book publishing.

25. Nagy's graduate student, Ferenc Fekete, was also the chief editor of the journal (Rainer 1996). Tamás Nagy was a member of the *Economics Review* editorial board. According to his account, the board was very "progressive." Those who were proreform were István Antos (director of Party's Planning, Finance, and Trade Division), István Benke, József Bognár, Ferenc Erdei (Nagy's minister of justice), Ferenc Fekete, Tamás Nagy, and Kálmán Szabó. Those who were antireform were László Hay, György Lázár, and G. Szabó (T. Nagy, OHA, 1986: 147–148).

26. Most economists who worked in the early 1950s remembered the impact of the journal's articles.

27. Furthermore, pro-Nagy economists were also put on other editorial boards, such as on the board of the *Social Review* (*Társadalmi Szemle*). The editorial board of the *Social Review* included Kálmán Szabó, Ferenc Fekete, and Andor Berei (Szabó, OHA, 1991: 125). Imre Nagy also made Antal Gyenes the economic editor of this journal (Rainer 1996: 452).

28. HAS 183/2/1954. Meeting minutes of the Permanent Economics Committee, May 3, 1954.

29. Péter also cited Stalin as supporting the use of these tools for the good of society (1954: 91). Pollock (2006) discusses Stalin's complicated views on economic reform.

30. While the term was not new, Szamuely states that its first use in postwar Hungary was during discussions of a comprehensive economic policy program ordered by the Central Directorate at the beginning of October 1954 (1986: 15). According to Kornai, by 1955 the economic mechanism was the topic of discussion in Hungary ([1957] 1959: 186). This term was forbidden or ignored for some time in other Eastern European countries, but by the late 1970s it had become fashionable in many Eastern European countries and used in official documents (Szamuely 1986: 9–10). In Hungary, by the 1980s, it had become "one of the most often used technical expressions" (ibid.: 9).

31. I use words "jack of diamonds" for clarity in English, but Varga uses the term "green jack." A green jack is a weak card in a Hungarian card deck. Varga's choice of color suggests that the person who draws the card is in a weakened position. In the context of his next sentence, his choice of color reveals that he presents the companies in a weakened position in relation to the planners.

32. The self-regulating economic mechanism, of course, did require human agents (Bockman 2000). Politicians, companies, and consumers required economists to mediate between them and the mechanism. Therefore, arguments about the economic mechanism also embodied arguments about the role of economists. In contrast to these models, the Communist Party also continued to intervene directly in the economy.

33. My research has disproven the claim made by Szamuely and Csaba that "there was a total lack of personal and/or intellectual ties between the pre- and post-1945 community of scholars in economics" (1998: 158).

34. Gelegonya also mentions that Péter's father also was an autodidact and a great follower of Henry George (1996: 126), who was discussed in Chapter 1.

35. Tamás Nagy, one of the main organizers of the new Marxist-Leninist economics university, discussed the structure of the future university with students from the Economics Faculty, such as István Hetényi and Kálmán Szabó, who had studied at the Faculty from 1946 (Hetényi, OHA, 1987: 39). The second Party-state economic expert István Friss had also studied economics at the London School of Economics (LSE) for a short period of time.

36. In his memoirs, Kornai recognized, "András Bródy gave a masterly demonstration of how, using Leontief models, one might describe the famous 'reproduction schemes' in the second volume of Marx's *Capital*" (2006: 142).

37. Kornai made a similar point about György Péter's ideas (1994: 78).

38. In Hungary and elsewhere, there has been a politically and emotionally heated debate about the name of the events that took place in October 1956. The official Communist Party term was *counterrevolution* until 1988, when Imre Pozsgay, a member of the Parliament, called it a "popular uprising." Pozsgay's declaration was considered "tantamount to an open challenge of János Kádár's entire regime" (Litván 1996: xii). One of the earliest declarations of the first freely elected parliament in 1990 was "to preserve the memory of the Revolution" (ibid.: x). I use the term *revolution* because it is now the commonly used term.

39. After the Soviet intervention, Nagy had escaped to the Yugoslav embassy. After being promised safe passage, Soviet troops arrested him. He was executed in 1958 (Cox 2006).

40. In late 1956 and early 1957, the new Kádár regime organized committees with many reform economists to work out a new government program and then turned against economists.

41. PIA 288/23/1957/25, "Revisionism and Economic Science": 1.

42. Ibid.: 2.

43. Ibid.: 6.

44. Ibid., "Ideological Fight against Revisionist Economic Views": 22. Most likely Andor Berei wrote this around May 24, 1957.

45. In a Central Committee meeting on May 17, 1957, the minister of the interior specifically criticized the *Economics Review* for publishing revisionist views (Balogh 1993: 331).

46. Personal communication with András Nagy in 1995. András Nagy was no relation to Imre Nagy.

47. Party leaders saw economic success as an achievable goal, as exemplified in a 1957 Party ruling to "use results in the economic area and correct measures to strengthen Communist Party authority." Ruling about Party organizational tasks in economic organizing work, July 30, 1957: 89 (*Magyar Szocialista* 1964: 88–93). Lampland (1995) describes the encouragement of individualism and other proto-capitalist values in Hungarian agriculture.

48. The *HVG* magazine described this game in a 1997 article "Egy játék színeváltozásai: Kapitalizz okosan!" Róna-Tas discusses "Manage Sensibly!" in detail, placing it within the context of the emerging division between private life and the public realm of work (1997: 85–86).

49. Berend also discusses how the intelligentsia in general after 1956 "shied away from politics and involvement in government" (1990: 72). In his 1960 address to the Academy of Sciences' annual congress, Jenő Fock, the secretary of the Party's Central Committee, recognized that the majority of economists avoid work on reforms because "at one time they were closely connected with them . . . [and this being so] strayed unwittingly on to revisionist ground . . . There are also economists who dare not venture on this rocky ground having been 'put wise' by the example of the others" (Berend 1990: 86–87). B.-J. (1960) reviewed this speech in the *Economics Review*.

50. Lewin (1974) found economists making similar retreats into mathematical economics in the Soviet Union.

51. Personal communication with András Bródy in 1995.

52. Kovács noted, "Our colleague Dr. Béla Kreko proposed and started another new faculty at the University of Economics: 'Planning and Economics,' where the students began to study economics, mathematics and computer science for the first time in the history of Hungarian universities (1960)" (2008: 4).

53. As Mirowski (1989) has discovered, in the nineteenth century, neoclassical economists developed their new ideas by applying knowledge from physics to economics. Economists across Europe saw the economy as a mechanism, a machine that could be re-engineered. Thus, the idea of a "market mechanism" was not new. Also see Nelson (1997).

54. By 1955, Samuelson knew about similar linear programming work by Russian economists ([1955] 1966).

55. One of the most famous pioneers in this area was future Nobel Laureate in economics Leonid Hurwicz, who had studied with both Ludwig von Mises and Friedrich von Hayek and had worked as a research assistant for both Paul Samuelson and Oskar Lange.

56. There was an enormous amount of interest in Hungarian economic reforms. By 1983, Rezler noted, "A bibliography on the Hungarian economic reform, compiled by G. F. Horchler of the Library of Congress, contains 1,620 entries" (143).

57. After finishing his doctorate in sampling theory and working as a planner, Balassa was internally deported, meaning that, due to his high-status family background, he could no longer live in Budapest and could no longer do intellectual work (Balassa 1989: 16). During his deportation, István Varga provided him with books on economics, and Balassa continued to write (ibid.: 17).

58. Further information comes from a *New York Times* obituary: "Bela A. Balassa, 63, Economics Professor Who Fled Hungary," *New York Times*, May 11, 1991. Retrieved on August 25, 2010, from www.nytimes.com/1991/05/11/obituaries/bela-a-balassa-63-economics-professor-who-fled-hungary.html.

59. Kornai used Hungary as a case study and "never worried that readers may suspect provincialism in that" (2006: 311).

60. Brus's book appeared in England and the United States as *The Market in a Socialist Economy* (1972).

61. In January 1964, Hungarian economist Tamás Nagy made a public presentation and discussed Brus's work (T. Nagy [1964] 1986: 307–311).

62. One has to be careful with accepting the stories presented by grantees in final reports, but these reports do provide some interesting and useful information.

63. Wassily Leontief (input-output analysis founder), Abram Bergson, and Anne Carter worked at Harvard. Yale University employed John Michael Montias and William Fellner. Gregory Grossman was at the University of California, Berkeley. Kenneth Arrow worked at Stanford University. A Hungarian economist noted that "This mathematical-economic school which was recently developed around Arrow, Hurwicz, Uzawa, etc., is very noteworthy and deserves more attention with us." FF R2346, 64-432, Aug. 12, 1968: 1. Final report of György Kondor.

64. One economist wrote about the "tremendous quantity of literature in the Harvard libraries." FF R2346, 64-432, Nov. 1966: 4. Final Report of Lajos Ács.

65. FF R2347, 64-432, July 28, 1965: 1. Final report of András Bródy.

66. Among others, Lajos Ács said that he learned about computers (FF R2346, 64-432, Nov. 1966: 1). Bródy learned programming and other computing knowledge from professors at Harvard (FF R2347, 64-432, July 28, 1965: 1).

67. FF R2346, 64-432, List of 1966–67 participants.

68. An American economist mentioned this problem (FF R2346, 64-432, April 20, 1965: 1–2, Letter from Earl Heady to Shepard Stone at the Ford Foundation). András Raba said, "Before departure from my country I cannot say to have had sufficient information about where and in which universities in the United States I could possibly find the best opportunities for professional work in my specific field" (FF R2346, 64-432, Sept. 18, 1968).

69. Information about the NEM comes from Brus (1990), Friss (1969), Kowalik (1990), and Swain (1992).

70. As Brus noted, "The real behaviour of actors in capitalist markets is by no means determined by the propositions of general equilibrium theory, whereas socialist managers are to be *instructed* to follow the textbook rules" (1990: 165).

71. Hare, Radice, and Swain similarly wrote, "The Hungarian economic mechanism has proved itself to be a viable alternative to the traditional centralised Soviet model of a planned economy" (1981: 3).

72. Of course, the deregulation of trade is quite controversial because it places often smaller industries in direct competition with multinational corporations.

73. The Hungarian case also shows that economists are not often successful in realizing their blueprints.

74. Economists around the world had become quite influential in government and international agencies (Coats 1986).

75. According to Feiwel (1972: 616), Lange later called for the participation of workers in management.

Chapter 5

1. An earlier version of this chapter was published as "The Origins of Neoliberalism between Soviet Socialism and Western Capitalism: 'A Galaxy without Borders.'" *Theory and Society* 36(4, 2007): 343–371.

2. CESES was known as either *Centro studi economici e sociali* or as *Centro studi e ricerche su problemi economico-sociali.*

3. CESES programs were funded by the William Volker Fund, the Scaife Foundation, the Earhart Foundation, and the Relm Foundation (Moore 2003: 23).

4. Library of Congress, William J. Baroody Sr. Papers, confidential memorandum to W. J. Baroody and others from G. W. [Warren] Nutter, Subject: CESES Seminar, Florence, September 14–16, 1966. September 29, 1966: 5–6. Reprinted from Bockman and Eyal (2002): 336.

5. To understand how CESES functioned, I conducted research in the archives of Confindustria, interviewed twenty-two CESES organizers and participants, and read CESES publications and secondary sources. I interviewed fourteen Italian participants in the summers of 2004 and 2005, six American participants from 2000 to 2002, and two Hungarian participants, one in 2000 and the other in 2002. The archival research was conducted in summer 2005 at the Confindustria Historical Archives, located in Rome. The Confindustria Historical Archives are referred to as "Confindustria" in the notes.

6. Eyal (2000) and Chabot and Duyvendak (2002) have shown the shallowness of most understandings of transnational diffusion, which see knowledge as fully formed, flowing from the United States or the West to the Rest, and used unproblematically in the new environment. Globalization theorists who criticize the theses of cultural imperialism and related global homogenization support these arguments (Hannerz 1997; Tomlinson 1999; Tsing 2001).

7. Knowledge production is in fact most intense along borders because "the boundary is that from which *something begins its presencing.*" Martin Heidegger, "Building, Dwelling, Thinking," quoted in Bhabha (1994: 1). Many excellent studies of the cultural cold war have started from a study of the intentions of the Cold War superpowers (for example, Scott-Smith 2002; Saunders 2000). Rather than assume the Cold War divisions between East and West, this chapter examines knowledge production that can only take place on borders and in liminal spaces.

8. Confindustria 15.1/1, File A. Centro Studi e Ricerche su problemi economico-sociali, CESES, 1964–67, File 1964, inner file "Seminario CESES," Letter from Vittorio De Biasi to Dr. Furio Cicogna, Nov. 6, 1964. According to this letter, the costs of the first year, 1964, would be 125 million lire.

9. Confindustria 15.1/1. File A. Centro Studi e Ricerche su problemi economico-sociali, CESES, 1964–67. File 1964, inner file "Seminario CESES," "Relazione sull'Attività del CESES," Oct. 7, 1964. Attachment 3: "Schema operativo di un centro di studi sui problemi del socialismo": 1.

10. Ibid.

11. One CESES participant noted that if CESES founders had wanted to convert Eastern Europeans to capitalism they would have discussed Western capitalism directly (Author's interview, May 28, 2004).

12. As a reflection of the importance of Sovietology to Confindustria, according to one observer, there was a central committee of top-level Confindustria industrialists— called by some "the twelve apostles of Christ"—in which one of the "apostles" was tasked to develop the study of Communism (Pistolese 1996: 5–6).

13. Confindustria 15.1/1. File A: Centro Studi e Ricerche su problemi economico-sociali, CESES, 1964–67. File 1966. File: Corrispondenza, "Relazione sulle finalità e attività del CESES," July 18, 1966: 13.

14. These unsigned notes were most likely written by Gennaro Pistolese. Confindustria 15.1/1, File A. Centro Studi e Ricerche su problemi economico-sociali, CESES, 1964–67, File: 1966, File: Seminario Internationazionale di Firenze: 14/16-9-66, "Appunto per il Segretario Generale," n. 131, Sept. 19, 1966: 5.

15. Giuliano Cittanti, a participant in the CESES courses, reported his criticisms to Confindustria. His report is described in Confindustria 15.1/1, CESES B., File: 1968, File: Programma, "CESES—Corso propedeutico Ottobre 1967, Relazione Dicembre 1967 del dott. Cittanti (Ferrara)," Jan. 16, 1968.

16. Confindustria 15.1/1. CESES B, File 1968, File: Programma. Letter from Vittorio De Biasi to Dr. Angelo Costa, President of Confindustria, Jan. 16, 1968.

17. Confindustria 15.1/12. Letter from Luigi Valenti of the Centro Studi Attivita Economiche to Vittorio De Biasi, Oct. 31, 1969.

18. In the literature, there seems to be some agreement that about 200,000 people left the PCI between 1956 and 1958 (Bracke and Jorgensen 2002: Appendix; Galli 2000: 51; Groppo and Riccamboni 1987: 112). However, people also left the PCI before 1956 (Blackmer 1975: 54).

19. Mieli (1996) remembered that it was difficult for him and many other former "communists by profession" to find work after leaving the PCI because many did not trust ex-communists, and the "anticommunists" felt satisfied by the PCI crisis without doing anything to help the ex-communists (122–124).

20. In 1964, Mieli had written a book with many others on the Italian Communists who had died during the Stalinist purges. After quoting Rosa Luxemburg calling for freedom of thought, the authors identified themselves as "militants of the Italian workers movement" (Zaccaria 1964, 7).

21. In 1964, Mieli published his revelations about Togliatti's official role in the killing of Polish Communist Party members, after, Mieli claims, being inspired by Khrushchev's revelations ([1964] 1988: 17).

22. Urbinati and Canto-Sperber ([2003] 2004) and the translations edited by Urbinati (1994, 2000) reveal the Italian tradition of bringing together liberalism and socialism. In this chapter, I am speaking about a broader and more heterogeneous group than just liberal socialists.

23. Caffi lived from 1887 to 1955. Caffi was exiled from Russia, after his participation in the 1905 revolution, and saw himself on the left. Caffi returned to the Soviet Union

and worked there in the early 1920s only to leave again after being arrested. In Italy, Caffi worked against the Mussolini government and was tortured by the Nazis in prison (Bianco 1977).

24. Before working at CESES, Gino Bianco was the editor of *Critica Sociale*, the main journal of the autonomous socialist movement. Galli had also written for this journal (Galli 2000: 21). The autonomous socialist movement sought to be independent from the Soviet socialist movement and was formed long before Antonio Negri's Autonomia Operaia emerged in 1973 (Wright 2002). One of the editors at CESES, Alfredo Azzaroni, later became the editor of *Metropoli*, a journal of this later Autonomia movement.

25. Caffi and his close colleague Nicola Chiaromonte had much earlier talked about establishing a small publishing house, a journal, and a commune (Bianco 1977: 90). Chiaromonte popularized Caffi's ideas in the United States while working at the *politics* journal, which included Dwight McDonald, Mary McCarthy, and Gaetano Salvemini (Sumner 1996).

26. Author's interviews: May 19, 2004; May 20, 2004; July 22, 2005.

27. Author's interview, May 28, 2004. Another person in the CESES youth programs said that CESES hoped to create a "pragmatic" political elite like those in the American political system, where elites, according to this view, could have debate (Author's interview, May 17b, 2004).

28. This group often defined itself as *laico*. While *laico* means secular, some Italian intellectuals have denied that it is antireligious and have expanded its meaning to include European liberalism (for example, Giorello 2005).

29. They worked at such journals as *Il Politecnico* (*The Politechnic*), *Mondo operaio* (*Worker's World*), *Il Ponte* (*The Bridge*), *Comunità* (*Community*, later called *Critica sociologica* [*Sociological Criticism*]), *Nord e Sud* (*North and South*), *Il Mondo* (*The World*), *Tempo Presente*, *Problemi del socialismo* (*Problems of Socialism*), *Rivista storia del socialismo* (*Historical Review of Socialism*), and *Tempi Moderni* (*Modern Times*) (Tranfaglia 2005: 279–289).

30. Gramsci's "war of position" reflected a widespread Italian belief in the need to wage a cultural war to control civil society. The CESES founders had all worked in journals of either the PCI or the international communist movement as leaders of the cultural wing of the PCI, and thus were well acquainted with the PCI's strategies.

31. Mieli himself had long been committed to a Popperian process of reevaluation of his political beliefs and called for the use of the "experimental method" in politics to verify one's political beliefs in a laboratory (1984: 146).

32. For example, Norberto Bobbio ([1997] 1999) worked in the 1950s with the Congress for Cultural Freedom, *Recontres internationales de Geneve*, and *Societa europea di cultura* to reunite Europe.

33. The Kennedy and the Johnson administrations had also supported liminal spaces because they were seen as a way to combat communism. The CIA and other American government agencies used those from the anticommunist left, through such organizations as the Congress for Cultural Freedom, to fight the cultural Cold War (Saunders 2000; Scott-Smith 2002). However, by 1964, American funding priorities had changed, and CESES could find support only from the American New Right.

34. According to Wald (1987), the "New York intellectuals" abandoned their Trotsky-ist origins to embrace Cold War liberalism and then neoconservativism. Critics of Wald have pointed out the more complex nature of the American anti-Stalinist left and found that the path from Trotskyism to neoconservativism describes only a part of this group (for example, Lipsitz 1988; Wolfe 1988).

35. The attempts to bring together these groups into umbrella parties continued to fail throughout the Cold War (Bobbio [1997] 1999; De Grand 1989).

36. Confindustria 15.1/1. File A. Centro Studi e Ricerche su problemi economico-sociali, CESES, 1964–67. File 1966. File: Corrispondenza. Letter from Vittorio De Biasi to Dr. Angelo Costa, July 19, 1966.

37. From 1967 to 1971, CESES also published *Notizie Est*, a news service for news-papers and magazines, and a book series, Cultura Libera. In the Cultura Libera series, CESES published seventeen books, including those by Friedrich von Hayek, Milton Friedman, François Fejtő, and Hannah Arendt; Neil J. Smelser's *Theory of Collective Behavior*; and Adam Ulam's work on the Russian Revolution. While one might have expected CESES to highlight Hayek's and Friedman's works, the CESES report of its activities in 1969 noted the "most significant works" in the series: Wittfogel's *Oriental Despotism* and J. Thayer's *Italy and the Great War*. Confindustria 1969–70. File: CESES: Relazioni. "Relazione sull'attività svolta nel 1969": 10. One CESES participant remem-bered that only seventy copies were made of some of the Cultura Libera books (Author's interview, June 4, 2004).

38. CESES was consciously modeled on the Cattaneo Institute in Bologna, which opened in 1956 and became a center for empirical social science research focused on the Italian educational system and electoral politics (Catanzaro 2000; Galli 2000: 101). Cat-taneo imported American social science, after establishing a relationship with the Ken-nedy administration and American foundations. Giorgio Galli had worked at Cattaneo before joining CESES. Similar to CESES, Cattaneo and its related publishing house Il Mulino published social science journals and books, trained students and young profes-sors in social science methods, and conducted social science research. More generally, American foundations sought to export American social science to Europe "in hopes of discouraging the expansion of Marxism in social and political studies" and strengthening "Western democracies using the social sciences to stimulate social and economic reform" (Gemelli and Row 2003: 183).

39. Confindustria 15.1/1, "Notes for the Secretary General," n. 131, Sept. 19, 1966: 5.

40. Author's interviews: May 19, 2004; June 3, 2004.

41. Author's interviews: May 17b, 2004; May 19, 2004; August 13, 2004.

42. Confindustria 15.1/12. Newspaper clippings sent Aug. 5, 1970. Pino Querenghi, "Dove passano i confini della mappa del potere," *La Voce Repubblicana*, July 24/25, 1970.

43. Gleason considers Robert Tucker the person who initiated this revolution: "Tucker was the first to express a feeling that was almost certainly more broadly shared: that study of the Soviet Union was taking place in too isolated an arena. He contended that a more comparative approach was necessary, since the comparison entailed in totalitarianism, pri-marily that between Nazi Germany and Communist Russia, was too narrow" (1995: 128).

The American Council of Learned Societies invested large sums of money in the development of comparative Communist studies through new publications, associations, and retooling in the 1960s, while the American Political Science Association and other associations had broad debates about the future of Sovietology (Fleron 1969: 28). In comparative economics, Gregory Grossman was one of the pioneers and a long-time participant in CESES international economic seminars.

44. The Gramsci Institute worked on historical and political topics. The Feltrinelli Institute studied historical topics. The Trieste Institute for the Study and Documentation on Eastern Europe (ISDEE) focused primarily on trade.

45. Sovietology and earlier Slavic studies had long existed in Italy. Slavic studies was associated with Mazzini Europeanism and then was used by the Italian fascist state in its attempts to take over Eastern Europe (Santoro 2003).

46. Author's interviews: May 19, 2004, and May 31c, 2004.

47. Author's interview, May 31a, 2004. Many Italian students went abroad to do graduate work. While some went to the United States or England, others went to Poland and Hungary, where the most exciting innovations in economics were happening in the 1960s.

48. Even in 1993, Motyl remarked, "Except for the Smolensk materials and a smattering of other documents, until recently scholars had no direct and unimpeded access to Soviet archives. Soviet evidence filtered, screened, selected, misrepresented" (85).

49. Author's interview, May 31a, 2004. It was even better to travel to Eastern Europe. CESES participants used their contacts with Eastern Europeans to organize research trips to Eastern Europe and meet a wide range of specialists there.

50. Author's interviews: May 17a, 2004, and May 20, 2004.

51. In interviews, CESES participants insisted that knowledge about the East Bloc was necessary for understanding Italy. For example, one had to understand the Communist Party of the Soviet Union to understand the PCI. The reforms in Eastern Europe were seen as equally applicable in Italy. Author's interviews: June 4, 2004; July 19, 2005; July 22, 2005. The quotation comes from a CESES report on the proceedings of its international economics on economic planning in 1968. Confindustria 15.1/1, File B. Centro Studi e Ricerche su problemi economico-sociali, CESES, 1968–70. File 1969–1970. File: CESES: Relazioni—Programmi Giovani—Bilancio, "Relazione sull'attività svolta nel 1969": 9.

52. Confindustria 15.1/1, File A. Centro Studi e Ricerche su problemi economico-sociali, CESES, 1964_67. File 1964, inner file Seminario CESES. Notes for the General Secretary, Nov. 12, 1964, n. 240: 2.

53. Author's interview (May 20, 2004) and Staffa 1975.

54. One CESES participant told me that he had "credibility" with those on the left because his scientific works revealed "socialist values." Author's interview, May 28, 2004.

55. The CESES press office also sought to "reveal problems that do not have a solution" (inside cover of *Documentazione sui Paesi dell'Est* 1965), which drove them to trawl the less censored provincial papers looking for these problems. The CESES leadership determined, "We have reason to think that only CESES, in Italy, is able to supply news and information that only systematic scrutiny of the minor presses of the USSR

and the satellites allows." Confindustria 15.1/1. File A. Centro Studi e Ricerche su problemi economico-sociali, CESES, 1964–67. File 1964, File Seminario CESES. "Relazione
sull'attività del CESES," Oct. 7, 1964: 5.

56. Author's interviews: May 17a, 2004, and May 31a, 2004.

57. Author's interview: May 17a, 2004.

58. Eastern European economists had actually used economic models to fix prices,
which was of great interest to those outside Eastern Europe. Participants in the first
CESES international economics conference agreed that there were great developments in
linear programming—a field within mathematical economics—taking place in the Soviet
Union. Confindustria 15.1/1, File A: Centro Studi e Ricerche su problemi economico-
sociali, CESES, 1964–67, File: 1964, inner file Seminario CESES, "Notes for the General
Secretary," N. 243, Nov. 13, 1964: 1.

59. He also visited Yugoslavia in 1962 where he conducted research at a Yugoslavian
bank and gave talks. Friedman wrote, "One of our major interests during successive visits
was how worker ownership functioned. That led to visits to a number of enterprises and
extensive discussion with their managements" (Friedman and Friedman 1998: 293). During his 1967 visit to Yugoslavia, Friedman traveled with Warren Nutter before a CESES
meeting (ibid.: 423).

60. Confindustria 15.1/1, File B. Centro Studi e Ricerche su problemi economico-
sociali, CESES, 1968–70, File 1968, File: Programma attività CESES 1968; Corso
formazione giovani, "Appunto per il segretario generale," N. 3, Jan. 12, 1968: 6. "The
'proof' could be offered above all by those who were witnesses of various experiences collected personally." Confindustria 15.1/1, "CESES—Corso propedeutico Ottobre 1967,
Relazione Dicembre 1967 del dott. Cittanti (Ferrara)": 6.

61. Confindustria, "Notes for the General Secretary," N. 131: 3.

62. Ibid.: 2.

63. Ibid.

64. Confindustria 15.1/1. "CESES—Corso propedeutico Ottobre 1967, Relazione
Dicembre 1967 del dott.Cittanti (Ferrara)," Jan. 16, 1968: 7.

65. Confindustria 15.1/12. "Un 'Bisturi Analitico': Storia del Ceses," *Il Gazzettino*,
July 21, 1970.

66. As Shapin points out, social theory assumes that objectivity comes from the soli-
tary intellectual or the stranger free from social ties, which "allowed truth to be looked
directly in the face and told to others" (1994: 40). However, as Shapin argues, free action
required for objectivity is based on extensive social ties and trust. Similarly, Jasanoff
writes, "Scientific knowledge, in particular, is not a transcendent mirror of reality. It both
embeds and is embedded in social practices, identities, norms, conventions, discourses,
instruments and institutions—in short, in all the building blocks of what we term the
social" (2004: 3).

67. Similar to CESES, the conservative Italian funders of the Cattaneo Institute and
its related publishing house Il Mulino sought to create an anticommunism of the right
but instead found the participants to be "a-communists of the left" and, in response,
stopped the funding in the mid-1960s (Catanzaro 2000: 6). By the time CESES sought

American funding, American mainstream foundations had already turned their focus from independent social science research institutes and toward funding Italian university reform and European integration studies (Gemelli and Row 2003).

68. Mieli wrote, "I wanted to liberate myself from false truth. I wanted to know how things really happened in the Communist world. What was the real history?" (1996: 127).

69. Carlo Ripa di Meana left CESES in 1966 because he did not like the shift from Sovietology to influencing Italian politics (2000: 119).

70. CESES continually (and unsuccessfully) proposed to expand this program to train 100 youths, who would then establish regional CESES branches and spread CESES training throughout all the regions of Italy. Confindustria 15.1/12. "Progetto: Nuovo programma per la formazione dei giovani," n.d.

71. Confindustria, "CESES—Corso propedeutico Ottobre 1967, Relazione Dicembre 1967 del dott. Cittanti (Ferrara)": 1.

72. Confindustria 15.1/12. Letter to Luigi Valenti from Vittorio De Biasi, Nov. 13, 1969: 2.

73. Confindustria 15.1/12. Letter from Luigi Valenti to Vittorio De Biasi, Oct. 31, 1969: 1.

74. Confindustria 15.1/1, File B. Centro Studi e Ricerche su problemi economico-sociali, CESES, 1968–70. File 1969–1970, CESES: Relazioni—Programmi Giovani—Bilancio, Untitled. By 1966, De Biasi had already planned to invite "socialist and communist" speakers to participate in the courses "because they could be subjected to criticism." Confindustria Archives, 15.1/1. File: Corso Propedeutico: November 1966, "Appunto per il Segretario Generale," Nov. 21, 1966, No. 178. One former student remembered four to six teachers "from the left" at the 1968 courses (Author's interview, May 17b, 2004).

75. A short biography can be found at the website of Archivio storico del Senato della Repubblica. 2006. Catalogo delle pubblicazioni dell'Archivio storico, 2002–2006: 14. Available at www.senato.it/documenti/repository/relazioni/archiviostorico/catalogo_archiviostorico.pdf.

76. His works *Il dissenso nel PCI* (1978) and *La partitocrazia invisibile* (1985) reflect his critical stance. He was arrested during the Clean Hands investigation. "Tangenti, condannato Ugo Finetti. L'ex segretario psi accusato da Chiesa," *Corriere della Sera*, May 15, 1997.

77. A former student remembered Seniga as a teacher at CESES (Author's interview, May 17b, 2004).

78. Spriano is famous for numerous works on the PCI, including *Storia del Partito comunista italiano* (1967) [*History of the Italian Communist Party*].

79. Confindustria 15.1/1. File B. Centro Studi e Ricerche su problemi economico-sociali, CESES, 1968–70. File 1968. File: Programma attività CESES 1968; Corso formazione giovani. "Il Marxismo: Teori e Prassi, Secondo Corso Propedeutico, Milano, 6–18 novembre 1967."

80. CESES also offered at least one course on economics in 1970. Confindustria 15.1/1. File B. File: Corrispondenza. Letter from Renato Mieli to Mario Morelli (secretary general of Confindustria), Feb. 3, 1970.

81. Confindustria, "Notes for the General Secretary," N. 131: 4.

82. This information about Galli comes from his autobiography: Galli 2000.

83. Confindustria, "Relazione sull'attività svolta nel 1969": 3.

84. Confindustria, "Relazione sull'attività svolta nel 1969," Attachment: "Elenco delle ricerche effettuate nel 1969 nell'ambito del Programma Giovani."

85. Confindustria 15.1/12. Letter from Luigi Valenti to Vittorio De Biasi, Dec. 29, 1969: 2.

86. Confindustria 15.1/12. Letter from Luigi Valenti to Vittorio De Biasi, Oct. 31, 1969: 1; and Letter from Luigi Valenti to Vittorio De Biasi, Dec. 29, 1969: 2.

87. In addition, Confindustria regional offices could not find adequate students, so CESES often invited students suggested by former CESES participants.

88. Confindustria 15.1/12. Letter from Vittorio De Biasi to Luigi Valenti, Nov. 13, 1969: 2.

89. This information about the CESES students comes from Galli (2000: 105–108). Maurizio Vaudagna's professional appointment as an American history professor can be found at www.lett.unipmn.it/docenti/vaudagna/default_en.htm.

90. However, an American foundation did continue to pay for American scholars to travel to CESES international economic conferences until at least 1982. University of California, Berkeley, economics professor Gregory Grossman showed me his letter, dated September 18, 1982, to Dr. John H. Moore of the Hoover Institution thanking him for covering his airfare to a CESES conference. Many reasons have been given for the end of Confindustria's funding: Soviet pressure on Italian industrialists who wanted Soviet business (Finetti 2004), general economic crisis (Paolo Savona, personal correspondence), disagreement over Mieli's focus on research (Pistolese 1996: 6), and the historic compromise between the PCI and the DC (Author's interview, July 22, 2005).

91. One interviewee mentioned funding from the Bank of Italy, the Italian Ministry of Foreign Affairs, and the city of Milan (Author's interview, May 21, 2004).

92. Mitchell uses the concept of "enframing" (1990: 547). Similarly, to Douglas (1966), symbolic boundary maintenance seeks to turn the liminal and ambiguous into the category of the sacred, removing its ambiguity.

93. Ferguson (1994) and Zimmerman (2005) discuss how colonial ideologies failed but, in their failure, succeeded in creating a desired outcome for the colonial powers.

94. As Mitchell writes, "The violent, the actual, and the exceptional—all of which the law denounces and excludes, ruptures itself from and supersedes—are never gone. They make possible the rupture, the denunciation, and the order" (2002: 79).

95. Only very small numbers of left-wing activists became neoconservatives (Klatch 1998; Lipsitz 1988; Wolfe 1988).

96. In 1984, with the end of the CESES international conferences, CESES participants formed the Italian Association for the Study of Comparative Economic Systems (AISSEC). One year after CESES closed, former CESES participants created the European Association for Comparative Economic Studies (EACES), with 40 percent of its members from Eastern Europe and the Soviet Union. The first leaders in EACES were overwhelmingly CESES participants: Vittorio Valli, Bruno Dallago, Alberto Chilosi, Silvana Malle, and D. Mario Nuti. Vittorio Valli was the first president, and many other

CESES participants became future presidents (see http://eaces.gelso.unitn.it/eaces/brief-his.htm). Participants in CESES activities also have played a central role in the formation of the International Association for the Economics of Participation (IAFEP), an international association of scholars engaged in research and teaching on worker ownership and participation, and its journal *Economic Analysis: A Journal of Enterprise and Participation*, continuing their interest in worker self-management.

Chapter 6

1. This model is based on several highly unrealistic assumptions.

2. This model, like the pure competitive one, is based on highly unrealistic assumptions.

3. E-mail communication with Branko Milanović, January 4, 2008.

4. In the United States, the 1973–1974 and 1974–1975 academic years also witnessed a surge in enrollments in economics courses, especially in introductory economics courses (Heller 1975: 8).

5. Austrian School economists, such as Friedrich von Hayek, had been pioneers in neoclassical economics, but the debates of the 1930s caused them to reject neoclassical economics and turn to more political and philosophical discussions. In 1974, Hayek continued his criticisms of neoclassical economics: "The responsibility for current world-wide inflation, I am sorry to say rests wholly and squarely with the economists, or at least with that great majority of my fellow economists who have embraced the teachings of Lord Keynes" (1978: 192). Marxist political economists in East and West had also protractedly attacked neoclassical economics for focusing on equilibrium, leaving aside broader class relations and historical developments, and thus supporting bourgeois capitalism.

6. Mirowski and Hands have argued that neoclassical economics changed to some extent in response to criticisms and innovations: "Rather than saying it [neoclassicism] simply chased out the competition—which it did, if by 'competition' one means the institutionalists, Marxists, and Austrians—and replaced diversity with a single monolithic homogeneous neoclassical strain, we can say it transformed itself into a more robust ensemble . . . Each subprogram had the capacity to absorb certain forms of criticism and thus deflect those criticisms away from the vulnerable areas in other subprograms" (1998: 288–289). Yugoslav and Hungarian economists often could not ignore critics who had control over employment and other resources.

7. Kornai wrote, "It was my exasperation with its inadequate and unworkable character that inspired this book. This exasperation finds expression also in the sharp tone of the work. In some places, criticism turns into outright attack . . . However, a sharp tone may prove useful, as certain maladies can be better remedied by shock treatment than by sedatives" ([1971] 1991: xvi).

8. Kornai used the term *neoliberal* as understood in the 1970s, which differs from my definition.

9. Stark and Nee recognized Hungarian economists' focus on institutions: "It was in Hungary, above all, that social scientists attempted to identify the distinctive institutional processes by which state socialism was stably (if inefficiently) reproduced" (1989: 9).

10. This focus on politics was also inspired by Eastern European antipolitics (Eyal 2000).

11. Tibor Liska revived an older tradition of market socialism (Brutzkus [1922] 1935), which Leszek Balcerowicz recognized as well (1992: 13).

12. He tried out his theories in several towns in 1981.

13. Márton Tardos and Sándor Kopátsy proposed separating the ownership function, organized by banks interested in profits, from the manager function and state planning. Kopátsy further suggested the issuing of shares. Tamás Bauer and László Lengyel argued for "workers' autonomy" and social ownership. See Voszka (1991).

14. Stark and Nee noted, "Far from convergence as a likely outcome of market reform in state socialist economies, the societies of China and Eastern Europe are giving rise to a new diversity in social life that stems from dynamics peculiar to state socialism" (1989: 30).

15. According to Adam, "In 1985, approximately 60 percent of enterprises became self-managed" (1992: 55n7).

16. Branko Horvat and other economists were also closely connected to the Praxis group (Soltan 1984: 334).

17. Ramet noted that conservatives condemned "anarcho-liberals" for right-wing deviation (2006: 210). For examples of the attacks on liberalism, see Marković and Kržavac (1978). See also Woodward (1977) for a discussion of this period.

18. In Croatia, in particular, but also in Slovenia, liberals allied with nationalists in opposition to conservatives, who sought centralization. Tito and the Yugoslav Communist Party leadership decided to crackdown on nationalist activities in Croatia in 1971 and Serbia in 1972, removing nationalists and their liberal allies from power.

19. Gligorov argued that "the opposition to the mainstream consisted largely of those who believed in central planning" (1998: 329).

20. In Serbo-Croatian, BOALs were known as *osnova organizacija udruženog rada*, or *OOUR*.

21. There were two kinds of contracts, "social compacts" and "self-management agreements," which Estrin and Uvalić discuss (2008: 668n2).

22. Konrád and Szelényi (1979) discuss similar bureaucratic moves against experts in Hungary.

23. Milenkovitch writes: "The active involvement of political organizations in the economic affairs of the BOALs was legitimized" (1977: 56), and "The new interpretation of the role of the market asserted that it was a transitional mechanism to be transcended. It was to be superseded by the system of social agreements" (ibid.: 58).

24. In 1979, Horvat wrote, "Thus, the case for comparative superiority of the two systems boils down to what neoclassical economics can teach us" (168).

25. Tyson also recognized that economic critics of labor-managed firms, such as Sirc (1979) and Furubotn (1976), internationally used the distortions and inefficiencies of Yugoslav economic performance to condemn self-management and "bolster their belief that economic efficiency is attainable only in a hierarchical system in which managers make the economic decisions and control an otherwise undisciplined and wage-hungry labor force" (1980: 107).

26. Nobel Laureate economist James Meade dedicated his 1989 text as "A Tract for the Times Addressed to All Capitalists and Socialists Who Seek to Make the Best of Both Worlds."

27. In the 1970s, Branko Horvat created the JUNASET group, where young economists could present their dissertation research. The group decided that they needed more than neoclassical tools. Some of the students had studied Sraffa's ideas while in England. This information comes from interviews with economists in Belgrade, Ljubljana, and Zagreb.

28. The integration of these other traditions reflects the way that neoclassical economics, according to Mirowski and Hands, "transformed itself into a more robust ensemble" (1998: 288–289).

29. Bajt's 1971 quotation is from Tajnikar (1977: 87).

30. According to Bateman (2000), in late 1970s and 1980s Slovene and Croatian officials and economists strongly supported the development of small enterprises. Prašnikar left the consulting firm around the time it became YUGEA.

31. Chapter 3 contains a discussion of Tito's statement.

32. There are separate schools within neoclassical economics. Mirowski (2002) discusses three main ones, the MIT, Harvard, and Chicago schools of neoclassical economics.

33. In Friedman's *Price Theory* textbook, the appendix has a list of recommended texts, which represent the mainstream in neoclassical economics. While he long criticized the use of Walrasian tools to study concrete problems and called for the use of Marshallian ones instead, Friedman did find, for example, the Walrasian demand function "an extremely useful abstract conception" (Friedman 1949; Friedman 1962b: 27, 56).

34. For instance, in 1975, Friedman wrote to Hayek about a conference held in Hayek's honor, "There was sharp disagreement between the enthusiastic Austrians, who follow Mises on the praxeological method, and myself as a believer with Popper in the testing of scientific hypotheses by attempting disproof or inconsistency of observations with implications." Friedrich A. von Hayek papers, Hoover Institute Archives, Box 20, File 19, Friedman, Milton. Letter from Friedman to Hayek, Sept. 11, 1975. See also Mirowski 2009: 442–443; Skousen 2005.

35. According to Feiwel, the "new conservative trend is a subject of considerable disquietude" for Paul Samuelson, an American pioneer in neoclassical economics. He even referred to this trend in his 1970 Nobel Prize lecture: "An American economist of two generations ago, H. J. Davenport, who was the best friend Thorstein Veblen ever had . . . once said: 'There is no reason why theoretical economics should be the monopoly of reactionaries.' All my life I have tried to take this warning to heart, and I dare to call it to your attention" (1982: 76).

36. Baumol noted this trend: "The great productivity crisis of the past fifteen years has brought with it renewed concern over entrepreneurship" (1983: ix).

37. This argument extends that put forth by Bockman and Eyal (2002).

38. Becker, Murphy, and Grossman state, "We do not model the sources of these preferences, but assume a 'social planner'" (2006: 11).

39. In contrast, heterodox economics, as exemplified by the Austrian and Marxist schools, does not use these neoclassical models.

40. Hansen and Sargent state, "We use a standard method of computing a competitive equilibrium by solving a Pareto or fictitious social planning problem, a method that was used for this type of model by Lucas and Prescott [1971]" (1990: 7).

41. Tinbergen (1956) makes a distinction between quantitative policy change, qualitative policy change, and economic reforms, which change the foundations of an economy.

42. Rosenstein-Rodan (1943) first developed this idea.

43. Bornstein does go on to say, "Nevertheless, although ownership is not decisive in determining the character of the economic system, it is significant both as a factor in income distribution (an important feature of any system) and as a source of power in the formulation of the community's preference function" (1989: 9).

44. These ideas were reflected in other areas of economics, such as mechanism design, to cope with externalities and incentive problems discussed in Chapter 4.

45. In his economics of transition textbook, Gérard Roland asserts that the Washington Consensus, of which the World Bank is a part, is rooted in (1) standard neoclassical price theory; (2) standard macroeconomics and the experience of stabilization policy; and (3) a broad body of knowledge in comparative economic systems (2000: 328). As mentioned earlier, Hollis Chenery wrote in a book honoring economist and World Bank consultant Béla Balassa: "The Bank's orientation is comparative, as is Bela's in most of his work" (1991: xiv).

46. Schrenk started the report, "This is a first attempt at advancing some generalizations about the Bank's analytical work on socialist economies. It is based on a very selective review of Bank work on socialist member countries, and of the literature in the field of comparative economic systems" (1987: 1).

47. Schrenk also turned periodically to Chinese reforms, which seemed to contradict Kornai's ideas.

48. Anders Åslund's 1992 book title *Market Socialism or the Restoration of Capitalism?* reflected the fact that market socialism was an option and that there was a real question at the 1990 conference he had organized.

49. As I discuss in the following pages, even when speaking about transition or "system" change, it was unclear whether the new "system" might be another kind of socialism, capitalism, or something else altogether.

50. Rajko Tomaš wrote, "The newest economic reforms announce a radical change and seek to be the first successful economic reform in socialism" (1989: 2880). Vladimir Gligorov referred to the 1989 reforms in Yugoslavia as "the fifth and truly systemic reform" (1998: 338).

51. In 1989, British specialist of the Soviet economy Alec Nove was disturbed by the popularity of these ideas in Eastern Europe: "It may be tempting to adopt a 'socialist-market-laissez-faire philosophy', and there were some who believed (believe?) that laissez faire would work better under socialism than it can under monopoly capitalism" (105).

52. Neoclassically trained economists also wrote a surprising number of works about market socialism (for example, Bardhan and Roemer 1993; Brus and Laski [1989] 1992; Le Grand and Estrin 1989; Meade 1989, 1993; Nuti 1988; Pierson 1995; Šik 1991).

53. As O'Neil noted, by late 1988 there was a new mass opposition within the Hungarian Communist Party "committed to saving socialism by opposing the Soviet 'bolshevik' system that had clearly gone awry" (1998: xiii).

54. Similarly, Russian reformer Yegor Gaidar (1999) remembered that in the 1960s he realized Soviet system was "an exceedingly stable system that no mere pinpricks would ever budge" (16).

55. Polish economists Brus and Laski ([1989] 1991) argued, "We shall call *market socialism proper* (MS) a consistently reformed system, which although still based on state ownership in one form or another includes a capital market along with product and labour markets" (105).

56. In addition to Rosefielde mentioned earlier (1973: 239), Italian economist and expert on the Polish economy D. Mario Nuti criticized Lange's model for creating "capitalism without capitalists" (1988: 383). Kornai harshly criticized simulation:

> I daresay that I am not the only one around who is fed up with this practice of simulation. We have already tried out hand at simulating quite a number of things. The state-owned firm simulates the behavior of the profit-maximizing firm. Bureaucratic industrial policy, regulating the expansion or contraction of various branches of production, simulates the role of competition. The Price Control Office simulates the market in price determination. The most recent additions to this list are the simulated joint stock companies, the simulated capital market, and the simulated stock exchange. Together, these developments add up to Hungary's Wall Street—made of plastic!" (2006: 350)

57. Marangos (2004) discusses two forms of market socialism as transition models.

58. According to Estrin (1982), for each year from 1952 to 1973, "One can observe Yugoslavia's impressive development record, with the growth of industrial output exceeding 10% per annum on average, based on 9% average annual increases in the capital stock, 5% in employment and productivity, and modestly rising capital-labour ratios" (73).

59. Nuti wrote, "The only genuinely new model – i.e. different from the various versions of the basic Soviet-type model – already in existence, is the Yugoslav model," though he found that the Yugoslav experiment had not performed well and "may well prove to be a diversion" (1988: 357, 383).

60. In Poland, worker self-management played a central role in Solidarity: "While understanding socialism differently—as democratic, decentralised and participatory—Solidarity's left wing also viewed the future economy as socialised although under the self-management of the working class" (Zubek 1994: 802).

61. French economist and Eastern Europe expert Marie Lavigne similarly remarked, "A market socialism is not tantamount to a 'mixed economy' of the type one may have in countries where there is a strong state sector along with a private sector" (1989: 251). Market socialism was not a hybrid but a pure model, models in general that neoclassical economists preferred.

62. Economists later considered the Chinese model in a similar way. Lau, Qian, and Roland (2000) model the Chinese dual-track approach to market liberalization, which they argue implements "efficient Pareto-improving economic reform, that is, reform achieving efficiency without creating losers" (120; see also Naughton 1995).

63. Sociologist Josip Županov (1990) argued that the failure of Yugoslav socialism did not mean that one should give up on worker self-management. To Županov, worker self-management remained possible. See also Estrin and Uvalić (2008).

Chapter 7

1. At the same time, another American economist John Williamson (1990) published his first article on what he termed the "Washington Consensus." Williamson compiled the reforms that he thought "Washington"—meaning "both the political Washington of Congress and senior members of the administration and the technocratic Washington of the international financial institutions, the economic agencies of the U.S. government, the Federal Reserve Board, and the think tanks"—could agree were required in Latin America by 1989 (ibid.). Marangos has called the Washington Consensus a kind of "lowest common denominator" (2007: 37). While not completely identical to shock therapy, the Washington Consensus and shock therapy are very similar.

2. Lipton and Sachs argued, "It is one thing to be poor, but it is quite another to have become impoverished needlessly as a result of the failure of the communist system. It is the sense of unnecessary decay, as much as the deprivation itself, that motivates the impulse toward change" (1990a: 76).

3. Many scholars, including neoclassical economists, have, in fact, argued that these Western economic experts and their counterparts in Russia were "market Bolsheviks" (Cohen 2000; Klein and Pomer 2001; Reddaway and Glinski 2001; Stiglitz 1999), though the term *market Stalinist* seems more appropriate. Hungarian economist László Szamuely commented on the speed of shock therapy, "Does it not resemble Stalin's famous slogan: Let's fulfill the five year plan in four years?" Szamuely's 1993 quotation comes from Hedlund (2005: 266).

4. Lipton and Sachs declared, "Only decisive actions by a reformist government can keep these populist pressures in check" (1990a: 87). The call for strong government also makes sense coming from those associated with the IMF, which sought repayment of loans, regardless of popular pressures.

5. For more information, see Chapter 6. In addition, early forms of privatization were employee buyouts. In the case of Poland, the International Labor Organization reported, "In some 1,100 cases since 1990, state enterprises were directly privatized, i.e. *sold, contributed in kind to a new company or leased to their employees.* Employee lease buy-outs were used in 70 per cent (some 800 cases) of these 'direct' privatizations" (Schliwa 1997: ix).

6. Lipton and Sachs wrote, "On grounds of social equity, the government should reject the workers' claims to full ownership of the enterprises, since the industrial work force represents only 30 percent of the labor force and 15 percent of the population" (1990a: 128).

7. In 1990, the Hungarian state recentralized ownership rights under the State Property Agency (Róna-Tas 1997: 191).

8. In another 1990 article, Lipton and Sachs argued that (1) state enterprises be converted into "Treasury-owned joint-stock companies"; (2) a portion of the shares be given or sold at a low price to employees; (3) a portion of the shares be given to financial inter-

mediaries such as mutual funds and banks; (4) households then receive shares in these intermediaries; and (5) the government keep a portion of the shares of each enterprise to sell to "core investors" who would take a key management role in the enterprise (1990b: 299).

9. Stiglitz has specifically condemned the "market fundamentalist" policies of the IMF that in his mind caused economic disaster in Asia and Russia in the late 1990s ([2002] 2003: 58, 221).

10. For example, Stiglitz wrote: "I believe that globalization—the removal of barriers to free trade and the closer integration of national economies—can be a force for good and that it has the potential to enrich everyone in the world, particularly the poor" ([2002] 2003: ix). I discuss his support of competition in the following pages.

11. In spite of his claims, he continued to practice neoclassical economics. Hodgson (1999) explains how Stiglitz could perceive himself as nonneoclassical: "Stiglitz (1994) defined 'neoclassical' more narrowly, as the general equilibrium approach characterised by Arrow and Debreu. He was thus able to characterise his own approach as nonneoclassical" (35).

12. Stiglitz questioned the relevance of Yugoslavia: "Not too much should be read into the failures of the worker-managed firms in the former Yugoslavia, for these involved peculiar (and obviously unsatisfactory) arrangements with respect to the transfer of property rights, as well as other institutional details which, both ex ante and in hindsight, were not conducive to success" (1994: 277).

13. In Yugoslavia, Janez Drnovšek, the new Slovene chair of state presidium, invited Jeffrey Sachs to advise the government (Meier 1999: 109).

14. According to Mencinger, "The majority of domestic economists considered the legacy of the past an exploitable advantage; to many foreign and a minority of domestic economists, however, it would impede rather than assist the transition" (2004: 76).

15. Economists from the former Yugoslavia told me this during my interviews with them. Franičević (1999) has discussed fear felt by Croatian economists and the general Croatian public that there would be a "reétatization" of the Croatian economy, which did in fact happen.

16. Greskovits demonstrated that Albert O. Hirschman had earlier outlined similar lines of contention.

17. In the 1920s and 1930s, Ludwig von Mises rejected this universalism, which led him to question and then abandon neoclassical methods.

18. As discussed in the introduction, according to Hartley, Hansen and Sargent reinterpreted the social planner model as a decentralized competitive model, but their model still acts like the centralized model (1997: 68–70). Even in the same journal issue as Lipton and Sachs's 1990 criticism of socialism, Lawrence Summers and his coauthors published a study based on a model of a "social planner" and a "government planner" (Cutler, Poterba, Sheiner, and Summers 1990: 20, 50).

19. James Buchanan (1959) has criticized the omniscience of the planner in economic models but continues to use a less omniscient planner in his work.

20. In 2006, Becker and his coauthors wrote, "We do not model the source of these preferences but assume a 'social planner'" (Becker et al. 2006: 46).

21. In Hungary, economist Éva Voszka wrote, "We are bewildered not only by the multitude of words but also by a confusion of terms intensified by societal uncertainty that is rooted in rapid political changes and produces conceptual chaos" (1991: 58).

22. The previous chapter contains a discussion of the World Bank's interpretation of transition.

23. According to Szamuely and Csaba, in 1989, János Kornai's *The Road to a Free Economy* "was the first open platform advocating fully-fledged private capitalism at a time when most democratic parties were still a long way from stating this point clearly" (1998: 198).

24. In one footnote, Lipton and Sachs (1990a) referred to an article with *capitalism* in the title. They used the term *capitalist* once in the text and once in a footnote, but these references were not to any goal of the transition.

25. Laki similarly argued, "In Hungary, it was possible to acquire such skills [market research, sales, and organizational skills] not only in the private domain but also (and equally well) in the flexible sub-units of the reformed state sector, in the traditional industrial and agricultural co-operatives, and in the various hybrids of state ownership plus private initiative" (1996: 230).

26. Another explanation of the smoothness of the shift to system change is that Eastern European countries were never truly socialist and the transition was rather a move sideways, shifting from one variant of capitalism (bureaucratic state capitalism) to another (multinational capitalism) (Callinicos 1991).

27. The language of waste is part of the larger moral project of neoliberalism, its praise of markets, and the call for purification after 1989 (Eyal 2000; Fourcade and Healy 2007). János Mátyás Kovács similarly presents a world of waste, "The components of the official legacy, i.e., the systemic features of communist economies and polities such as large-scale nationalization, obsolete industrial structures, environmental pollution, huge state bureaucracies and lack of entrepreneurial spirit, were regarded as factors which— due to their inertia— would in the beginning slow down the transition to capitalism . . . Essentially, they were seen as the *inactive* (deactivated) trash of the old system, ready for removal" (1994: xiii).

28. As discussed in Chapter 6, Chinese socialism could also fit in this model.

29. Burawoy argues that neoliberalism is "a borrowed ideology that is opportunistically deployed to justify new forms of exploitation and dispossession" (2001: 1112).

30. While neoliberalism has core characteristics, national conditions, including political systems and class alliances, shape the actual realization of neoliberalism (Babb 2001; Dezalay and Garth 2002; Fourcade 2006; Fourcade-Gourinchas and Babb 2002; Prasad 2006). Political entrepreneurs, especially in more adversarial political systems such as the United States and Britain (as opposed to France and Germany), could exploit discontent of the growing numbers of upwardly mobile "victims" of welfare state policies (Prasad 2006). In Eastern Europe, political entrepreneurs could also exploit the discontent of a wide variety of groups. Also, those working in the second economy became interested in transforming the system (Lampland 1995; Róna-Tas 1997; Seleny 1993).

31. This lack of clarity on economic policy continued during the government dominated by the Hungarian Democratic Forum, from 1990 to 1994, which adopted the slo-

gan of a social market economy without specifying what this might mean (Szamuely and Csaba 1998: 199).

32. According to Susan Woodward, "Yugoslavia's dissolution began with fundamental changes in the international environment," which included past IMF conditionalities—that intensified decentralization, empowered republics, and dismantled the federal state—and the end of the Cold War and Yugoslavia's liminal role within it (1995: 47–68).

33. Greskovits has called this the "syndrome" of the "loneliness of the economic reformer" (1998: 35). O'Donnell (1973) and Markoff and Montecinos (1993) also find similar forms of isolation from domestic stakeholders in Latin America. Csaba correctly notes that Hungarian reformers much earlier mobilized the opinions of international financial institutions to convince political elites (1995: 216).

34. In England, for example, these think tanks and foundations, as Stuart Hall recognized, "stitched together" a plurality of discourses to create Thatcherism as a unified "discursive formation" or "regime of truth" (1988: 53). All the while, this unity retained its contradictory nature. Hall rejected the idea that these individuals suffered from false consciousness but rather argued that ideology shaped one's very subjectivity and spoke to a real crisis in 1970s Britain.

35. Centeno (1994, 1998), Markoff and Montecinos (1993), and many others have demonstrated the technocratic nature and distrust of democracy among economists. Centeno (1998) specifically focuses on Hayek's profound distrust of democracy.

36. There were many other institutions, such as the Korcula Summer School, the Inter-University Center in Dubrovnik, the International Economic Association, and many more.

37. Shleifer and Vishny (1994), for example, state: "Under all forms of market socialism, from Lange (1936) to the present, the state ultimately controls the firms" (165). Austrian School–trained economist David Prychitko noted that the Austrian School "seemed to equate socialism with central planning" and focused exclusively and incorrectly on central planning (2002: 2).

38. As mentioned in the introduction, Hardt and Negri argue that "the multitude is the real productive force of our social world, whereas Empire is a mere apparatus of capture that lives only off the vitality of the multitude" (2000: 62). Similarly, Lotringer writes, "Capital affords us to project ahead, work it from within, knowing all too well that it will be quick to instrumentalize any creative move, turning it into binary oppositions, however radical they claim to be, proven recipes that failed repeatedly *because they have become inadequate to think the complexity of the contemporary reality*" (2004: 17–18).

39. In 1989, for example, a Czechoslovak poll showed only 3 percent opting for a "capitalist way," 41 percent for a "socialist way," and 52 percent wanting a "merger of capitalism and socialism" (Kaser 1990: 597–598).

Conclusions

1. Raman and West recently also noticed that "the traces of socialism are still to be found in the spaces now claimed by neoliberalism" (2009: 14).

2. After the 1980s privatizations in Europe and the United States, as well as the Eastern European debate about privatization, neoclassical economists turned to studying auction design, which also emerged from socialist models. In a foundational article in the

early 1950s, Leo Herzel advocated the auctioning of FCC television licenses. Herzel later remembered his own "adolescent attraction to socialism" and interest in Abba Lerner's work (1944) as "a blueprint for an efficient socialist economy" (1998: 524). In his FCC auction article, Herzel applied Lerner's market socialist model to TV licenses and other "situations where the ownership of private property did not provide a satisfactory solution" (ibid.: 524). The licensing of use, rather than ownership, had been advocated by many socialists, including the charismatic Hungarian advocate of entrepreneurial socialism Tibor Liska.

3. Since 1990, Jstor reports that over 1,500 articles in economics journals discussed a "planner" without references to "Soviet," "socialist," or "urban planner." Some other authors use the term *representative agent*.

4. According to Grzymala-Busse (2002), all East Central European Communist Parties survived the transition and remained politically active. Communist political practice had provided these leaders with important resources, such as skills at recruitment, negotiation, and policy reform. Their experience with policy reform and their claim to some kind of socialist agenda remained. Socialism still mattered to Eastern Europeans. For example, as discussed by Creed (1999), Bulgarians voted in the Communist successor party in 1990 and again in 1994, and "still, significant allegiance to the Socialist Party remains." In local settings, Bulgarian villagers interpreted socialism in various ways, but socialism was still relevant (ibid.).

5. While severely criticizing the Soviet Union, Bauman argued that socialism remained "the counter-culture of capitalism": "The power of socialism, as we saw before, consisted in its status as the counter-culture of capitalism, and in its role as a thoroughly critical utopia, exposing the historical relativity of capitalist values, laying bare their historical limitations, and thereby preventing them from freezing into an horizon-less commonsense" (1976: 99)

6. However, as mentioned in the introduction, Hardt and Negri contend that the current paradigm of power now supports hybridity, fluidity, and difference, thus thriving on criticisms of dichotomies (2000: 138).

Bibliography

Archives

Archives of Serbia and Montenegro, Belgrade, Serbia.

Confindustria Archives, Rome, Italy.

Ford Foundation Archives (FF), New York, NY

Harvard University Archives, Cambridge, MA

Hoover Institution Archives, Stanford, CA.

Hungarian Academy of Sciences Archive (HAS, MTA), Budapest, Hungary

Hungarian Communist Party Institute Archive (PIA), Budapest, Hungary

Library of Congress, William J. Baroody Sr. Papers, Washington, DC

Oral History Archives (OHA), Budapest, Hungary, interviews of István Hetényi (1987), István Huszár (1990), Tamás Nagy (1986). Kálmán Szabó (1991), and Jenő Wilcsek (1983).

Yale University Archives, New Haven, CT

Published Sources and Scholarly Papers

Abbott, Andrew. 1988. *The System of Professions: An Essay on the Division of Expert Labor.* Chicago: University of Chicago Press.

Adam, Jan. 1992. "The Possible New Role of Market and Planning in Poland and Hungary." In *Market Socialism or the Restoration of Capitalism?* edited by Anders Åslund, 47–66. Cambridge, UK: Cambridge University Press.

Akerlof, George A. 1970. "The Market for 'Lemons': Quality Uncertainty and the Market Mechanism." *The Quarterly Journal of Economics* 84: 488–500.

Aligica, Paul Dragoş, and Anthony John Evans. 2009. *The Neoliberal Revolution in Eastern Europe: Economic Ideas in the Transition from Communism.* Cheltenham, UK: Edward Elgar.

Amadae, S. M. 2003. *Rationalizing Capitalist Democracy: The Cold War Origins of Rational Choice Liberalism.* Chicago: University of Chicago Press.

Antal, L. 1982. "Thoughts on the Further Development of the Hungarian Mechanism." *Acta Oeconomica* 29: 199–224.

———. 1999. "What is left of 'reform economics?'" *Acta Oeconomica* 50(1–2): 89–102.

Appadurai, Arjun, ed. 2001. *Globalization*. Durham, NC: Duke University Press.

Appel, Hilary. 2004. *A New Capitalist Order: Privatization and Ideology in Russia and Eastern Europe*. Pittsburgh: University of Pittsburgh Press.

Armstrong, John A. 1973. "Comments on Professor Dallin's 'Bias and Blunders in American Studies on the USSR.'" *Slavic Review* 32: 577–587.

Arnott, Richard, and Joseph E. Stiglitz. 1991. "Moral Hazard and Nonmarket Institutions: Dysfunctional Crowding Out of Peer Monitoring?" *The American Economic Review* 81: 179–190.

Arnsperger, Christian, and Yanis Varoufakis. 2006. "What Is Neoclassical Economics?" *Post-Autistic Economics Review* 38(1). Retrieved on June 29, 2010, from www.paecon .net/PAEReview/issue38/ArnspergerVaroufakis38.htm.

Arrow, Kenneth J. 1951. *Social Choice and Individual Values*. New York: John Wiley & Sons.

———. 1963. "Uncertainty and the Welfare Economics of Medical Care." *The American Economic Review* 53: 941–973.

———. 1978. "A Cautious Case for Socialism." *Dissent* 25 (Fall): 472–480.

Arrow, Kenneth J., and Gerard Debreu. 1954. "Existence of an Equilibrium for a Competitive Economy." *Econometrica* 22(3): 265–290.

Åslund, Anders, ed. 1992. *Market Socialism or the Restoration of Capitalism?* Cambridge, UK: Cambridge University Press.

Åslund, Anders, Peter Boone, Simon Johnson, Stanley Fischer, and Barry W. Ickes. 1996. "How to Stabilize: Lessons from Post-Communist Countries." *Brookings Papers on Economic Activity* 1996(1): 217–313.

Augusztinovics, Mária. 1995. "What Input-Output Is About." *Structural Change and Economic Dynamics* 6(3): 271–277.

B.-J. 1960. "Közgazdaságtudományi előadások a Magyar Tudományos Akadémia 1960. évi nagygyűlésén." *Közgazdasági Szemle* 7: 751–767.

Babb, Sarah L. 2001. *Managing Mexico: Economists from Nationalism to Neo-Liberalism*. Princeton, NJ: Princeton University Press.

Babić, Šimun. 1961. *Uvod u ekonomiku poduzeča*. Zagreb: Školska knj.

Bajt, Aleksander. 1988. *Samoupravni oblik društvene svojine*. Zagreb: Globus.

Balassa, Béla A. 1959. *The Hungarian Experience in Economic Planning: A Theoretical and Empirical Study*. New Haven, CT: Yale University Press.

———. 1971. "Discussion (with Edward Ames)." *The American Economic Review* 61: 436–439.

———. 1989. "My Life Philosophy." *American Economist* 33: 16–23.

Balázsy, Sándor. [1956] 1986. "Üzemi munkástanács, vállalati önállóság, iparvezetés . . . ." In *A Magyar Közgazdasági Gondolat Fejlődése, 1954–1978*, edited by László Szamuely, 156–166. Budapest: Közgazdasági és Jogi Könyvkiadó.

Balcerowicz, Leszek. 1989. "On the 'Socialist Market Economy.'" *Acta Oeconomica* 40(3–4): 184–189.

———. [1989] 1995. "On the Socialist Market Economy." In *Socialism, Capitalism, Transformation*, 28–34. Budapest: Central European University Press.

———. 1992. "The 'Socialist Calculation Debate' and Reform Discussions in Socialist Countries." In *Reform and Transformation in Eastern Europe: Soviet-Type Economics on the Threshold of Change*, edited by János Mátyás Kovács and Márton Tardos, 5–18. London and New York: Routledge.

Balogh, Sándor, ed. 1993. *A Magyar Szocialista Munkáspárt ideiglenes vezető testületeinek jegyzőkönyvei*. Vol. 3. Budapest: Intera Rt.

Bandera, V. N. 1963. "New Economic Policy (NEP) as an Economic Policy." *The Journal of Political Economy* 71: 265–279.

Baran, Paul A. 1944. "New Trends in Russian Economic Thinking?" *The American Economic Review* 34: 862–871.

Baranzini, Roberto. 2001. "Léon Walras: il singolare socialismo di un marginalista atipico." In *Marginalismo e Socialismo nell'Italia Liberale, 1870–1925*, edited by Marco E. L. Guidi and Luca Michelini, 35–65. Milan: Fondazione Giangiacomo Feltrinelli.

Bardhan, Pranab K., and John E. Roemer, eds. 1993. *Market Socialism: The Current Debate*. New York: Oxford University Press.

Barghoorn, Frederick C. 1960. *The Soviet Cultural Offensive: The Role of Cultural Diplomacy in Soviet Foreign Policy*. Princeton, NJ: Princeton University Press.

———. 1964. *Soviet Foreign Propaganda*. Princeton, NJ: Princeton University Press.

Barghoorn, Frederick C., and Ellen Mickiewicz. 1972. "American Views of Soviet–American Exchanges of Persons." In *Communications in International Politics*, edited by Richard L. Merritt, 146–167. Urbana: University of Illinois Press.

Barna, Tibor, ed. 1963. *Structural Interdependence and Economic Development*. Proceedings of an International Conference on Input-Output Techniques, Geneva, September 1961. New York: St. Martin's Press.

Barnett, Vincent. 2005. *A History of Russian Economic Thought*. New York: Routledge.

Barone, Enrico. [1908] 1938. "The Ministry of Production in the Collectivist State." In *Collectivist Economic Planning: Critical Studies on the Possibilities of Socialism*, edited by F. A. von Hayek, 245–290. London: George Routledge & Sons.

Bársony, J. 1982. "Tibor Liska's Concept of Socialist Entrepreneurship." *Acta Oeconomica* 28 (3–4): 422–455.

Bateman, Milford. 2000. "Small Enterprise Development in the Yugoslav Successor States: Institutions and Institutional Development in a Post-War Environment." *Most* 10: 171–206.

Bator, Francis M. 1958. "The Anatomy of Market Failure." *The Quarterly Journal of Economics* 72: 351–379.

Bauer, Tamás. 1983. "The Hungarian Alternative to Soviet-Type Planning." *Journal of Comparative Economics* 7: 304–316.

———. 1984. "The Second Economic Reform and Ownership Relations: Some Considerations for the Further Development of the New Economic Mechanism." *Eastern European Economics* 22: 33–87.

Bauman, Zigmunt. 1976. *Socialism: The Active Utopia*. New York: Holmes & Meier Publishers.

Baumol, William J. 1983. "Preface." In *Entrepreneurship*, edited by Joshua Ronen, ix–x. Lexington, MA: Lexington Books.

Becchio, Giandomenica. 2005. "Two Heterodox Economists: Otto Neurath and Karl Polanyi." Working paper No. 11/2005. University of Torino. Retrieved on January 15, 2010, from: www.cesmep.unito.it/WP/2005/11_WP_Cesmep.pdf.

Becker, Gary S. 2000. "A Comment on the Conference on Cost-Benefit Analysis." *Journal of Legal Studies* 29: 1149–1152.

Becker, Gary S., and Casey B. Mulligan. 2003. "Deadweight Costs and the Size of Government." *Journal of Law and Economics* 46(2): 293–340.

Becker, Gary S., Kevin M. Murphy, and Michael Grossman. 2006. "The Market for Illegal Goods: The Case of Drugs." *The Journal of Political Economy* 114: 38–60.

Bekker, Zsuzsa. 1999. "Bródy András 75 éves." *Közgazdasági Szemle* 46: 849–850.

Berend, Iván T. 1990. *The Hungarian Economic Reforms, 1953–1988*. Cambridge, UK: Cambridge University Press.

Berghahn, Volker. 2001. *America and the Intellectual Cold Wars in Europe*. Princeton, NJ: Princeton University Press.

Bergson, Abram. 1936. "Real Income, Expenditure Proportionality, and Frisch's 'New Methods of Measuring Marginal Utility.' " *Review of Economic Studies* 4(1): 33–52.

———. 1938. "A Reformulation of Certain Aspects of Welfare Economics." *The Quarterly Journal of Economics* 52(2): 310–333.

———. [1944] 1946. *The Structure of Soviet Wages: A Study in Socialist Economics*. Cambridge, MA: Harvard University Press.

———. 1948. "Socialist Economics." In *A Survey of Contemporary Economics*, edited by Howard S. Ellis, 412–448. Berkeley: University of California Press.

———. 1967. "Market Socialism Revisited." *The Journal of Political Economy* 75: 655–673.

———. 1992. "Recollections and Reflections of a Comparativist." In *Eminent Economists: Their Life Philosophies*, edited by Michael Szenberg, 60–68. Cambridge, UK: Cambridge University Press.

Bernstein, Michael. 1995. "American Economics and the National Security State, 1941–1953." *Radical History Review* 63: 8–26.

———. 2001. *A Perilous Progress: Economists, Their Discipline, and Public Purpose in Twentieth Century America*. Princeton, NJ: Princeton University Press.

Bhabha, Homi. 1994. *The Location of Culture*. London: Routledge.

Bianco, Gino. 1977. *Un socialista irregolare: Andrea Caffi, intellettuale e politico d'avanguardia*. Cosenza, Italy: Lerici.

Bieber, Ilona, József Fábián, and Emil Gulyás. 1957. "Megjegyzések a *Közgazdasági Szemle* 1956. 11-12. számának vezércikkéhez." *Közgazdasági Szemle* 4: 393–409.

Biglaiser, Glen. 2002. *Guardians of the Nation? Economists, Generals, and Economic Reform in Latin America*. Notre Dame, IN: University of Notre Dame Press.

Blackmer, Donald. 1975. "Continuity and Change in Postwar Italian Communism." In *Communism in Italy and France*, edited by Donald Blackmer and Sidney Tarrow, 21–68. Princeton, NJ: Princeton University Press.

Blanchard, Olivier. 1999. "An Interview with János Kornai," *Macroeconomic Dynamics* 3(3): 427–450.

Blaug, Mark. 1972. "Was there a Marginal Revolution?" *History of Political Economy* 4: 269–280.

Blinder, Alan. 1990. "Introduction." In *Paying for Productivity: A Look at the Evidence*, edited by Alan Blinder, 1–14. Washington, DC: Brookings Institution.

Block, Fred. 2003. "Karl Polanyi and the Writing of *The Great Transformation.*" *Theory and Society* 32: 275–306.

Blyth, Mark. 2002. *Great Transformations: Economic Ideas and Institutional Change in the Twentieth Century*. New York: Cambridge University Press.

Bobbio, Norberto. [1997] 1999. *Autobiografia*. Edited by Alberto Papuzzi. Rome: Laterza.

Bockman, Johanna K. 2000. "Economists and Social Change: Science, Professional Power, and Politics in Hungary, 1945–1995." PhD dissertation, Department of Sociology, University of California, San Diego.

———. 2007. "The Origins of Neoliberalism between Soviet Socialism and Western Capitalism: 'A Galaxy without Borders.'" *Theory and Society* 36: 343–371.

Bockman, Johanna K., and Michael Bernstein. 2008. "Scientific Community in a Divided World: Economists, Planning, and Research Priority during the Cold War." *Comparative Studies in Society and History* 50: 581–613.

Bockman, Johanna K., and Gil Eyal. 2002. "Eastern Europe as a Laboratory for Economic Knowledge: The Transnational Roots of Neoliberalism." *American Journal of Sociology* 108: 310–352.

Boettke, Peter J. 2004. "Hayek and Market Socialism: Science, Ideology, and Public Policy." Retrieved on November 6, 2009, from: http://mises.org/etexts/hayek2004.pdf.

Bogavac, Blagoje. 1968. "Yugoslavia and Technical Cooperation." *Review of International Affairs* 19(430): 24–27.

Bogetić, Željko. 1992. "Is There a Case for Employee Ownership?" In *The Transition from Socialism in Eastern Europe: Domestic Restructuring and Foreign Trade*, edited by Arye L. Hillman and Branko Milanovic, 83–104. Washington, DC: World Bank.

Böhm-Bawerk, Eugen von. [1889, 1891] 1971. *The Positive Theory of Capital*. London: Macmillan.

Boim, Leon, Glenn G. Morgan, and Aleksander W. Rudzinski. 1966. *Legal Controls in the Soviet Union*. Leyden: A. W. Sijthoff.

Boltanski, Luc, and Eve Chiapello. 2005. *The New Spirit of Capitalism*. New York: Verso.

Bornstein, Morris. 1974. *Comparative Economic Systems: Models and Cases*, 3rd ed. Homewood, IL: R. D. Irwin.

———. 1989. *Comparative Economic Systems: Models and Cases*, 6th ed. Homewood, IL: Irwin.

Bourdieu, Pierre, and Gunter Grass. 2002. "The 'Progressive' Restoration." *New Left Review* 14 (March–April): 63–77.

Bourdieu, Pierre, and Loïc Wacquant. 1999. "On the Cunning of Imperialist Reason." *Theory, Culture and Society* 16(1): 41–58.

Bozóki, András. 2002. "Introduction: The Significance of the Roundtable Talks." In *The Roundtable Talks of 1989: The Genesis of Hungarian Democracy, Analysis and* Documents, edited by András Bozóki, xv–xxxiv. Budapest: Central European University Press.

Bracke, Maud, and Thomas Ekman Jorgensen. 2002. "West European Communism after Stalinism: Comparative Approaches." EUI Working Paper HEC No. 2002/4. San Domenico, Italy: Badia Fiesolana.

Breslau, Daniel. 2003. "Economics Invents the Economy: Mathematics, Statistics, and Models in the Work of Irving Fisher and Wesley Mitchell." *Theory and Society* 32: 379–411.

Broad, Robin. 1988. *Unequal Alliance: The World Bank, the International Monetary Fund, and the Philippines*. Berkeley: University of California Press.

Bruno, Michael. 1989. "Econometrics and the Design of Economic Reform." *Econometrica* 57: 275–306.

Brus, Włodzimierz. 1972. *The Market in a Socialist Economy*. London: Routledge and K. Paul.

———. 1990. "Market Socialism." In *Problems of the Planned Economy*, edited by John Eatwell, Murray Milgate, and Peter Newman, 164–177. London: MacMillan.

———. 1992. "The Compatibility of Planning and Market Reconsidered." In *Market Socialism or the Restoration of Capitalism?* edited by Anders Åslund, 7–16. Cambridge, UK: Cambridge University Press.

Brus, Włodzimierz, and Kazimierz Laski. [1989] 1991. *From Marx to the Market: Socialism in Search of an Economic System*. Oxford, UK: Clarendon Press.

Brutzkus, Boris. [1922] 1935. *Economic Planning in Soviet Russia*. London: George Routledge & Sons.

Bryant, John. 1983. "A Simple Rational Expectations Keynes-Type Model." *The Quarterly Journal of Economics* 98: 525–528.

Bryant, Ralph, and Richard Portes, eds. 1987. *Global Macroeconomics*. New York: St. Martin's Press.

Buchanan, James M. 1959. "Positive Economics, Welfare Economics, and Political Economy." *Journal of Law and Economics* 2: 124–138.

Buckley, William F. 1951. *God and Man at Yale; the Superstitions of Academic Freedom*. Chicago: Regnery.

Budapesti Bizottság, A. 1952. *Marxizmus-Leninizmus Esti Egyetemének Munkaterve és Szervezeti Felépítése.*

Bukharin, Nikolai. [1919] 1927. "Preface to the Russian Edition." In *Economic Theory of the Leisure Class*. Retrieved on October 23, 2009, from: www.marxists.org/archive/bukharin/works/1927/leisure-economics/ preface1.htm.

Bukharin, Nikolai, and Evgeny Preobrazhensky. [1919] 1966. *The ABC of Communism*. Ann Arbor: The University of Michigan Press.

Burawoy, Michael. 1992. "The End of Sovietology and the Renaissance of Modernization Theory." *Contemporary Sociology* 21: 774–785.

———. 2001. "Review: Neoclassical Sociology: From the End of Communism to the End of Classes." *American Journal of Sociology* 106: 1099–1120.

Burawoy, Michael, and Katherine Verdery, eds. 1999. "Introduction." In *Uncertain Transition: Ethnographies of Change in the Postsocialist World*, edited by Michael Burawoy and Katherine Verdery, 1–18. Lanham, MD: Rowman & Littlefield.

Byrnes, Robert F. 1976. *Soviet–American Academic Exchanges, 1958–1975*. Bloomington: Indiana University Press.

Cairncross, Alec. 1952. "The Moscow Economic Conference." *Soviet Studies* 4: 113–132.

Caldwell, Bruce. 1997. "Hayek and Socialism." *Journal of Economic Literature* 35: 1856–1890.

Callinicos, Alex. 1991. *The Revenge of History: Marxism and the East European Revolutions*. University Park: Pennsylvania State University Press.

Callon, Michel. 1998. *The Laws of the Markets*. Malden, MA: Blackwell.

Campbell, John C. 1967. *Tito's Separate Road: America and Yugoslavia in World Politics*. New York: Harper & Row.

Campbell, John L. 1998. "Institutional Analysis and the Role of Ideas in Political Economy." *Theory and Society* 27: 377–409.

Campbell, John L., and Ove K. Pedersen. 2001. "Introduction." In *The Rise of Neoliberalism and Institutional Analysis*, edited by John L. Campbell and Ove K. Pedersen, 1–23. Princeton, NJ: Princeton University Press.

Campbell, Robert W. 1991. *The Socialist Economies in Transition: A Primer on Semi-Reformed Systems*. Bloomington: Indiana University Press.

Caplan, Bryan Douglas. 2007. *The Myth of the Rational Voter: Why Democracies Choose Bad Policies*. Princeton, NJ: Princeton University Press.

Carlton, Dennis W. 1978. "Market Behavior with Demand Uncertainty and Price Inflexibility." *The American Economic Review* 68: 571–587.

Cassel, Gustav. [1918] 1923. *The Theory of Social Economy*. London: T. Fisher Unwin.

Catanzaro, Raimondo. 2000. "La Fondazione Istituto Carlo Cattaneo." In *Le fondazioni culturali in Italia. Origini storiche e primi sviluppi istituzionali*, edited by Giuliana Gemelli, *Storia e Societa* 9: 707–724.

Caute, David. 1978. *The Great Fear: the Anti-Communist Purge under Truman and Eisenhower*. New York: Simon and Schuster.

Centeno, Miguel A. 1994. *Democracy within Reason: Technocratic Revolution in Mexico*. University Park: Pennsylvania State University Press.

———. 1998. "The Politics of Knowledge: Hayek and Technocracy." In *The Politics of Expertise in Latin America*, edited by Miguel A. Centeno and Patricio Silva, 36–51. New York: St. Martin's Press.

Centeno, Miguel A., and Patricio Silva, eds. 1998. *The Politics of Expertise in Latin America*. New York: St. Martin's Press.

Černe, France. 1966. *Tržište i cijene*. Zagreb: "Informator."

Chabot, Sean, and Jan Willem Duyvendak. 2002. "Globalization and Transnational Diffusion between Social Movements: Reconceptualizing the Dissemination of the Gandhian Repertoire and the 'Coming Out' Routine." *Theory and Society* 31: 697–740.

Chaloupek, Gunther K. 1990. "The Austrian Debate on Economic Calculation in a Socialist Economy." *History of Political Economy* 22: 659–675.

Charnes, Abraham. 1958. "Preface to L. Kantorovich's *On the Translocation of Masses*." *Management Science* 5(1): 1–4.

Chenery, Hollis. 1991. "Bela at the World Bank." In *Trade Theory and Economic Reform: North, South, and East: Essays in Honor of Bela Balassa*, edited by Jaime de Melo and Andre Sapir, xiv–xv. Cambridge, MA: Basil Blackwell.

Chomsky, Noam, Laura Nader, Immanuel Wallerstein, Richard C. Lewontin, and Richard Ohmann. 1997. *The Cold War & the University: Toward an Intellectual History of the Postwar Years*. New York: New Press.

Chossudowsky, E. M. 1939. "The Soviet Conception of Economic Equilibrium." *The Review of Economic Studies* 6(2): 127–146.

Cirillo, Renato. 1976. "The True Significance of Walras' General Equilibrium Theory." *Cahiers Vilfredo Pareto* 14(37): 5–13.

———. 1980. "The 'Socialism' of Leon Walras and His Economic Thinking." *American Journal of Economics and Sociology* 39(3): 295–303.

Coase, Ronald H. 1982. "Economics at LSE in the 1930's: A Personal View." *Atlantic Economic Journal* 10(1): 31–34.

———. 1988. "The Nature of the Firm: Origin." *Journal of Law, Economics, & Organization* 4(1): 3–17.

———. 1991. "The Nature of the Firm: Origin." In *The Nature of the Firm: Origins, Evolution, and Development*, edited by Oliver E. Williamson and Sidney G. Winter, 34–47. New York: Oxford University Press.

———. [1991] 1997a. "The Institutional Structure of Production," *Nobel Lectures, Economics 1991–1995*, edited by Torsten Perssen. Singapore: World Scientific Publishing Co. Available at: http://nobelprize.org/nobel_prizes/economics/laureates/1991/coase-lecture.html

———. [1991] 1997b. "Autobiography," *Nobel Lectures, Economics 1991–1995*, Torsten Perssen, ed. Singapore: World Scientific Publishing Co. Available at: http://nobelprize.org/nobel_prizes/economics/laureates/1991/coase-autobio.html

Coats, A. W. 1977. "The Current Crisis in Economics in Historical Perspective." *Nebraska Journal of Economics and Business* 16: 3–16.

———. 1981. *Economists in Government: An International Comparative Study*. Durham, NC: Duke University Press.

———. 1982. "The Distinctive LSE Ethos in the Inter-War Years." *Atlantic Economic Journal* 10(1): 18–30.

———, ed. 1986. *Economists in International Agencies, An Exploratory Study*. New York: Praeger.

———, ed. 1996. *The Post-1945 Internationalization of Economics*. Durham, NC: Duke University Press.

Cockett, Richard. 1995. *Thinking the Unthinkable: Think-Tanks and the Economic Counter-Revolution, 1931–1983*. London: Harper Collins.

Cohen, Stephen F. 1985. *Rethinking the Soviet Experience: Politics and History since 1917*. New York: Oxford University Press.

———. 2000. *Failed Crusade: America and the Tragedy of Post-Communist Russia*. New York: Norton.

Collins, Randall, and Sal Restivo. 1983. "Robber Barons and Politicians in Mathematics: A Conflict Model of Science." *Canadian Journal of Sociology/Cahiers canadiens de sociologie* 8(2): 199–227.

Comey, David Dinsmore. 1967. "Review: Soviet Ideology and the Osnovy." Book review of *Soviet Ideology Today* by Gustav A. Wetter. *Soviet Studies* 19(2): 278–281.

Comisso, Ellen T. 1979. *Workers' Control under Plan and Market: Implications of Yugoslav Self-Management.* New Haven, CT: Yale University Press.

———. 1981. "The Logic of Worker (Non)Participation in Yugoslav Self-Management." *Review of Radical Political Economics* 13(2): 11–22.

Corvinus University of Budapest, Faculty of Economics. 2009. "Tamás Szentes, Professor Emeritus, Member of the Hungarian Academy." Retrieved on July 16, 2009, from www.uni-corvinus.hu/index.php?id=24732.

Cotta, Maurizio. 1996. "Political Science in Italy." In *Report on the State of the Discipline in Western Europe*, 337–351. Available at www.epsnet.org/publications/sod/italy.pdf.

Cox, Terry. 2006. "1956: Discoveries, Legacies and Memory." *Europe-Asia Studies* 58: iii–xvi.

Cramer, Allan P. 1965. "International Copyright and the Soviet Union." *Duke Law Journal* 1965(3): 531–545.

Craver, Earlene. 1986. "The Emigration of the Austrian Economists." *History of Political Economy* 18: 1–32.

Creed, Gerald W. 1999. "Deconstructing Socialism in Bulgaria." In *Uncertain Transition: Ethnographies of Change in the Postsocialist World*, edited by Michael Burawoy and Katherine Verdery, 223–244. Lanham, MD: Rowman & Littlefield.

Csaba, László. 1995. "Hungary and the IMF: The Experience of a Cordial Discord." *Journal of Comparative Economics* 20: 211–234.

———. 2002. "Economics—Hungary." In *Three Social Science Disciplines in Central and Eastern Europe, Handbook on Economics, Political Science and Sociology (1989–2001)*, edited by Max Kaase, Vera Sparschuh, and Agnieszka Wenniger, 83–101. Berlin and Budapest: Social Science Information Centre (IZ)/Collegium Budapest.

Csikós-Nagy, Béla. 1989. "Personal Comments on the Socialist Market Economy." *Acta Oeconomica* 40(3–4): 216–219.

Cumings, Bruce. 1998. "Boundary Displacement: Area Studies and International Studies during and after the Cold War." In *Universities and Empire: Money and Politics in the Social Sciences during the Cold War*, edited by Christopher Simpson, 159–188. New York: New Press.

Curtis, Glenn E. 1990. "Yugoslavia: A Country Study." Federal Research Division, Library of Congress. Available at http://international.loc.gov/frd/cs/yutoc.html.

Cutler, David M., James M. Poterba, Louise M. Sheiner, and Lawrence H. Summers. 1990. "An Aging Society: Opportunity or Challenge?" *Brookings Papers on Economic Activity* 1: 1–74.

Dahrendorf, Ralf. [1990] 2005. *Reflections on the Revolution in Europe.* New Brunswick, NJ: Transaction.

Dale, Gareth. 2009. "Karl Polanyi in Budapest: On His Political and Intellectual Formation." *European Journal of Sociology* 50: 97–130.

Dallin, Alexander. 1973. "Bias and Blunders in American Studies on the USSR." *Slavic Review* 32: 560–576.

Darden, Keith A. 2009. *Economic Liberalism and Its Rivals: The Formation of International Institutions among the Post-Soviet States*. Cambridge, UK: Cambridge University Press.

Dasgupta, Partha, and Joseph Stiglitz. 1980a. "Industrial Structure and the Nature of Innovative Activity." *The Economic Journal* 90(358): 266–293.

———. 1980b. "Uncertainty, Industrial Structure, and the Speed of R&D." *The Bell Journal of Economics* 11: 1–28.

David-Fox, Michael. 2003. "The Fellow Travelers Revisited: The 'Cultured West' through Soviet Eyes." *The Journal of Modern History* 75: 300–335.

De Grand, Alexander. 1989. *The Italian Left in the Twentieth Century: A History of the Socialist and Communist Parties*. Bloomington: Indiana University Press.

Deutsch, Steven. 2005. "A Researcher's Guide to Worker Participation, Labor and Economic and Industrial Democracy." *Economic and Industrial Democracy* 26(4): 645–656.

Deutscher, Tamara. 1977. "USSR: Democratic Alternatives." *New Left Review* I/104: 114–120.

Devine, Pat. 1993. "Review: [untitled]." *The Economic Journal* 103: 243–245.

Dezalay, Yves, and Bryant G. Garth. 2002. *The Internationalization of Palace Wars: Lawyers, Economists, and the Contest to Transform Latin American States*. Chicago: University of Chicago Press.

Diamond, Peter A. 1982. "Aggregate Demand Management in Search Equilibrium." *The Journal of Political Economy* 90: 881–894.

Diamond, Sara. 1995. *Roads to Dominion: Right-Wing Movements and Political Power in the United States*. New York: The Guilford Press.

Diamond, Sigmund. 1992. *Compromised Campus: The Collaboration of Universities with the Intelligence Community, 1945–1955*. New York: Oxford University Press.

Dickinson, H. D. 1939. *Economics of Socialism*. London: Oxford University Press.

Djilas, Milovan. 1969. *The Unperfect Society: Beyond the New Class*. New York: Harcourt, Brace & World.

Dobb, Maurice. 1928. *Russian Economic Development since the Revolution*. London: G. Routledge & Sons.

Dobbin, Frank, Beth Simmons, and Geoffrey Garrett. 2007. "The Global Diffusion of Public Policies: Social Construction, Coercion, Competition, or Learning?" *Annual Review of Sociology* 33: 449–472.

Domar, Evsey. 1966. "The Soviet Collective Farm as a Producer Cooperative." *American Economic Review* 56: 734–757.

Douglas, Mary. 1966. *Purity and Danger: An Analysis of the Concepts of Pollution and Taboo*. London: Routledge & Kegan Paul.

Drèze, Jacques H. 1989. *Labour Management, Contracts, and Capital Markets: A General Equilibrium Approach*. Oxford, UK: Basil Blackwell.

Drutter, Izak. 1990. "Integralno Tržište." In *Socijalizam u reformi: iskustvo i problemi jugoslavenske privredne reforme*, edited by Zvonimir Baletić and Dragomir Vojnić, 36–42. Zagreb: Informator.

Dubey, Vinod, ed. 1975. *Yugoslavia: Development with Decentralization: Report of a Mission Sent to Yugoslavia by the World Bank*. Baltimore: Johns Hopkins University Press.

Dubravčić, Dinko. 1970. "Labour as Entrepreneurial Input: An Essay in the Theory of the Producer Co-operative Economy." *Economica* 37(147): 297–310.

Duggan, Lisa. 2003. *The Twilight of Equality? Neoliberalism, Cultural Politics, and the Attack on Democracy*. Boston: Beacon Press.

Dunayevskaya, Raya. 1944. "A New Revision of Marxian Economics." The *American Economic Review* 34(3): 531–537.

Dunlop, John Thomas, and Vasilii P. Diatchenko, eds. 1964. *Labor Productivity*. New York: McGraw-Hill.

Dunlop, John Thomas, and Nikolay P. Fedorenko, eds. 1969. *Planning and Markets: Modern Trends in Various Economic Systems*. New York: McGraw-Hill.

Dunn, W. N. 1978. Review of *Yugoslavia: Development with Decentralization*, by International Bank for Reconstruction and Development. *Economic Development and Cultural Change* 26(3): 625–633.

Durbin, E. F. M. 1936. "Economic Calculus in a Planned Economy." *Economic Journal* 46: 676–690.

———. 1949. *Problems of Economic Planning; Papers on Planning and Economics*. London: Routledge & Paul.

Easterly, William. 2008. "Hayek vs. The Development Experts." Hayek Lecture, Manhattan Institute for Policy Research, October 23, 2008. Retrieved on November 7, 2009, from www.manhattan-institute.org/html/hayek2008.htm.

"Egy játék színeváltozásai: Kapitalizz okosan!" 1997. *HVG*. Retrieved on July 3, 1997, from www.huvg.hu/lap/friss/972782.htm.

Ekelund, Robert B. Jr., and Robert F. Hébert. 1990. *A History of Economic Theory and Method*. New York: McGraw-Hill Publishing Company.

Ekonomski Fakultet, Universitet u Beogradu: 70 godina tradicija i razvoj. 2007. Belgrade: Čugura print.

Ekonomski Fakultet Zagreb, 1920–2005. 2005. Zagreb: Ekonomski fakultet.

Ellerman, David. 1990a. *The Democratic Worker-Owned Firm: A New Model for the East and West*. Boston: Unwin Hyman.

———. 1990b. "Report on a Socialist Reform Tour: Poland, Hungary, Soviet Union and Yugoslavia." *Economic and Industrial Democracy* 11(2): 205–215.

Ellerman, David P., Aleš Vahčič, and Tea Petrin. 1992. "Privatization Controversies in the East and West." In *Comrades Go Private: Strategies for Eastern European Privatization*, edited by Michael P. Claudon and Tamar L. Gutner, 117–144. New York: New York University Press.

Ellis, Howard S. 1948. "Preface." In *A Survey of Contemporary Economics*, edited by Howard S. Ellis, v–viii. Berkeley: University of California Press.

Ellman, Michael. 1973. *Planning Problems in the USSR: The Contribution of Mathematical Economics to Their Solution, 1960–1971*. Cambridge, UK: Cambridge University Press.

Engerman, David. 2009. *Know Your Enemy: The Rise and Fall of America's Soviet Experts*. Oxford, UK: Oxford University Press.

Estrin, Saul. 1982. "The Effects of Self-Management on Yugoslav Industrial Growth."
Soviet Studies 34: 69–85.

———. 1991. "Yugoslavia: The Case of Self-Managing Market Socialism." *The Journal of Economic Perspectives* 5: 187–194.

Estrin, Saul, and Milica Uvalić. 2008. "From Illyria towards Capitalism: Did Labour-Management Theory Teach Us Anything about Yugoslavia and Transition in Its Successor States?" *Comparative Economic Studies* 50: 663–696.

Eyal, Gil. 2000. "Anti-politics and the spirit of capitalism: Dissidents, monetarists, and the Czech transition to capitalism." *Theory and Society* 29(1): 49–92.

———. 2003. *The Origins of Postcommunist Elites: From Prague Spring to the Breakup of Czechoslovakia*. Minneapolis: University of Minnesota Press.

Eyal, Gil, Iván Szelényi, and Eleanor R. Townsley. 1998. *Making Capitalism without Capitalists: Class Formation and Elite Struggles in Post-Communist Central Europe.* London: Verso.

Falk, Barbara J. 2003. *The Dilemmas of Dissidence in East-Central Europe*. Budapest: Central European University Press.

Faucci, Riccardo, and Stefano Perri. 1995. "Socialism and Marginalism in Italy, 1880–1910." In *Socialism and Marginalism in Economics, 1870–1930*, edited by Ian Steedman, 116–169. London: Routledge.

Feiwel, George R. 1972. "On the Economic Theory of Socialism: Some Reflections on Lange's Contribution." *Kyklos* 25(3): 601–618.

———. 1982. "Samuelson and Contemporary Economics: An Introduction." In *Samuelson and Neoclassical Economics*, edited by George R. Feiwel, 1–28. Boston: Kluwer-Nijhoff Publishing.

Ferguson, James. 1994. *The Anti-Politics Machine: "Development," Depoliticization, and Bureaucratic Power in Lesotho*. Minneapolis: University of Minnesota Press.

Finetti, Ugo. 1978. *Il Dissenso Nel PCI*. Milano: SugarCo.

———. 1985. *La Partitocrazia Invisibile*. Milano: Mazzotta.

———. "Egemonia di sinistra, cultura del veleno?" *l'ircocervo* 3(2): 60–61. Available at: www.bietti.it/images/ircocervo/ircocervoarticoli-2-2004/pp60-61.pdf.

Fleron, Frederic J. Jr. 1969. "Introduction: Soviet Area Studies and the Social Sciences: Some Methodological Problems in Communist Studies." In *Communist Studies and the Social Sciences: Essays on Methodological and Empirical Theory*, edited by Frederic J. Fleron, 1–33. Chicago: Rand McNally and Company.

Foucault, Michel. [1978–1979] 2008. *The Birth of Biopolitics: Lectures at the Collège de France, 1978–79*. New York: Palgrave Macmillan.

Fourcade, Marion. 2006. "The Construction of a Global Profession: The Transnationalization of Economics." *American Journal of Sociology* 112: 145–194.

———. 2009. *Economists and Societies: Discipline and Profession in the United States, Britain, and France, 1890s to 1990s*. Princeton, NJ: Princeton University Press.

Fourcade, Marion, and Kieran Healy. 2007. "Moral Views of Market Society." *Annual Review of Sociology* 33: 285–311.

Fourcade-Gourinchas, Marion, and Sarah Babb. 2002. "The Rebirth of the Liberal Creed: Paths to Neoliberalism in Four Countries." *American Journal of Sociology* 108: 533–579.

Franičević, Vojmir. 1983. *Radikalna politička ekonomija u SAD*. PhD dissertation, Economics Faculty, University of Zagreb.

———. 1989. "Poduzetništvo kao politčki projekt." *Naša Tema* 33(11): 2773–2782.

———. 1999. "Privatization in Croatia: Legacies and Context." *Eastern European Economics* 37: 5–54.

Fraser, Nancy. 2009. "Feminism, Capitalism, and the Cunning of History." *New Left Review* 56 (March–April): 97–117.

Friedman, Milton. 1949. "The Marshallian Demand Curve." *The Journal of Political Economy* 57:463-495.

———. 1962a. *Capitalism and Freedom*. Chicago: University of Chicago Press.

———. 1962b. *Price Theory: A Provisional Text*. Chicago: Aldine Publishing Company.

———. 1970. *The Counter-Revolution in Monetary Theory*. London: Institute of Economic Affairs.

Friedman, Milton, and Rose D. Friedman. 1998. *Two Lucky People: Memoirs*. Chicago: University of Chicago Press.

Friss, István. 1969. *Reform of the Economic Mechanism in Hungary: Nine Studies*. Budapest: Akadémiai Kiadó.

Furner, Mary O. 1975. *Advocacy and Objectivity: A Crisis in the Professionalization of American Social Science, 1865–1905*. Lexington: The University Press of Kentucky.

Furubotn, Eirik. 1976. "The Long-Run Analysis of the Labor-Managed Firm: An Alternative Interpretation." *The American Economic Review* 66: 104–123.

Gaidar, Yegor. 1999. *Days of Defeat and Victory*. Seattle: University of Washington Press.

Galli, Giorgio. 2000. *Passato prossimo: Persone e incontri, 1949–1999*. Milan: Kaos edizioni.

Gardner, Roy. 1990. "L. V. Kantorovich: The Price Implications of Optimal Planning." *Journal of Economic Literature* 28(2): 638–648.

Garton Ash, Timothy. 1990. *The Magic Lantern: The Revolution of '89 Witnessed in Warsaw, Budapest, Berlin, and Prague*. New York: Random House.

Gelegonya, Judit. 1996. "Péter György szerepe a magyar közgazdasági reformgondolkodás fejlődésében." In *Ünnepi dolgozatok Mátyás Antal tanszékvezetöi kinevezésének 40. Evfordulójára*, edited by Géza Halász and István Mihalik, 119–133. Budapest: Aula Kiadó Kft.

Gemelli, Giuliana, and Thomas Row. 2003. "The Unexpected Effects of Institutional Fluidity: The Ford Foundation and the Shaping of the Johns Hopkins University Bologna Center." In *American Foundations in Europe: Grant-Giving Policies, Cultural Diplomacy and Trans-Atlantic Relations, 1920–1980*, edited by Guiliana Gemelli and Roy MacLeod, 181–197. Brussels: P. I. E. Peter Lang S.A.

George, Henry. 1879. *Progress and Poverty*. London: J. M. Dent and Sons.

Gerő, Ernő. 1948. "A haladó közgazdaságtudomány jelentősége a népi démokratikus Magyarországon." *Társadalmi Szemle* 3 (10–11): 652–657.

Gerovitch, Slava. 2002. *From Newspeak to Cyberspeak: A History of Soviet Cybernetics.* Cambridge, MA: The MIT Press.

Gide, Charles. 1904. *Principles of Political Economy.* Boston: D. C. Heath & Co.

Gill, Stephen. 1990. *American Hegemony and the Trilateral Commission.* Cambridge, UK: Cambridge University Press.

Gille, Zsuzsa. 2007. *From the Cult of Waste to the Trash Heap of History: The Politics of Waste in Socialist and Postsocialist Hungary.* Bloomington: Indiana University Press.

Giorello, Giulio. 2005. *Di nessuna chiesa: La liberta del laico.* Milan: Raffaelo Cortina Editore.

Gleason, Abbott. 1995. *Totalitarianism: The Inner History of the Cold War.* New York: Oxford University Press.

Gligorov, Vladimir. 1998. "Yugoslav Economics Facing Reform and Dissolution." In *Economic Thought in Communist and Post-Communist Europe,* edited by Hans-Jürgen Wagener, 329–361. London: Routledge.

Goldman, Marshall, Jeffrey Sachs, Paul Samuelson, and Martin Weitzman. 2005. "Testimonials." *Comparative Economic Studies* 47: 492–502.

Goodwin, Craufurd D. 1998. "The Patrons of Economics in a Time of Transformation." In *From Interwar Pluralism to Postwar Neoclassicism,* edited by Mary S. Morgan and Malcom Rutherford, 53–81. Durham, NC: Duke University Press.

Gorbachev, Mikhail Sergeevich. 1996. *Memoirs.* New York: Doubleday.

Gregory, Paul R., and Marshall Goldman. 2005. "Introduction." *Comparative Eocnmic Studies* 47: 239.

Greskovits, Béla. 1998. *The Political Economy of Protest and Patience: East European and Latin American Transformations Compared.* Budapest: Central European University Press.

———. 2002. "The Path-Dependence of Transitology." In *Postcommunist Transformation and the Social Sciences: Cross-Disciplinary Approaches,* edited by Frank Bönker, Klaus Müller, and Andreas Pickel, 219–246. Lanham, MD: Rowman & Littlefield Publishers.

Groppo, B., and G. Riccamboni, eds. 1987. *La Sinistra e il '56 in Italia e Francia.* Padova: Liviana Editrice.

Grosfeld, Irena. 1992. "Reform economics and western economic theory: Unexploited opportunities." In *Reform and Transformation in Eastern Europe: Soviet-Type Economics on the Threshold of Change,* edited by János Mátyás Kovács and Márton Tardos, 62–79. London and New York: Routledge.

Grossman, Gregory. 1963. Review of *Protiv burzhuaznykh ekonomicheskikh psevdoteorii sotsializma: Kriticheskii ocherk,* by S. A. Khavina. *The American Economic Review* 53(1): 211–213.

Grossman, Sanford J. 1977. "The Existence of Futures Markets, Noisy Rational Expectations and Informational Externalities." *The Review of Economic Studies* 44: 431–449.

Grzymala-Busse, Anna M. 2002. *Redeeming the Communist Past: The Regeneration of Communist Parties in East Central Europe.* Cambridge, UK: Cambridge University Press.

Haas, Peter M. 1992. "Introduction: Epistemic Communities and International Policy. Coordination." *International Organization* 46(1): 1–35.

Hahn, F. H. 1970. "Some Adjustment Problems." *Econometrica* 38: 1–17.

———. 1972. Review of *Economic Heresies: Some Old-Fashioned Questions in Economic Theory*, by Joan Robinson. *Economica* 39: 205–206.

Halabuk, L., Z. Kenessey, and E. Theiss. 1965. "An Econometric Model of Hungary." *Economics of Planning* 5(3): 30–43.

Hall, Stuart. 1988. "The Toad in the Garden: Thatcherism among the Theorists." In *Marxism and the Interpretation of Culture*, edited by Cary Nelson and Lawrence Grossberg, 35–57. Urbana: University of Illinois Press.

Halm, Georg. [1935] 1938. "Further Considerations on the Possibility of Adequate Calculation in a Socialist Community." In *Collectivist Economic Planning: Critical Studies on the Possibilities of Socialism*, edited by F. A. von Hayek, 131–200. London: George Routledge & Sons.

Haney, David Paul. 2008. *The Americanization of Social Science.* Philadelphia: Temple University Press.

Hannerz, Ulf. 1997. "Scenarios for Peripheral Cultures." In *Culture, Globalization and the World-System: Contemporary Conditions for the Representation of Identity*, edited by Anthony D. King, 107–128. Minneapolis: University of Minnesota Press.

Hansen, Alvin Harvey. 1953. *A Guide to Keynes.* New York: McGraw-Hill.

Hansen, Lars Peter, and Thomas J. Sargent. 1990. "Recursive Linear Models of Dynamic Economies," Working Paper no. 3479. New York: National Bureau of Economic Research.

———. [1994] 1996. "Recursive Linear Models of Dynamic Economies." In *Advances in Econometrics*, Sixth World Congress, vol. 1, edited by Christopher A. Sims, 97–139. Cambridge, UK: Cambridge University Press.

Hardt, John P. 2004. "Abram Bergson and the Development of Soviet Economic Studies." *Problems of Post-Communism* 51(4): 34–39.

Hardt, John P., and Richard F. Kaufman, eds. 1995. *East-Central European Economies in Transition.* Armonk, NY: M. E. Sharpe.

Hardt, Michael, and Antonio Negri. [2000] 2001. *Empire.* Cambridge, MA: Harvard University Press.

Hare, P. G., H. K. Radice, and N. Swain, eds. 1981. *Hungary: A Decade of Economic Reform.* London: George Allen and Unwin.

Hartley, James E. 1997. *The Representative Agent in Macroeconomics.* London: Routledge.

Hartwell, R. M. 1995. *A History of the Mont Pelerin Society.* Indianapolis: Liberty Fund.

Harvey, David. 2005. *A Brief History of Neoliberalism.* Oxford, UK: Oxford University Press.

Hayek, Friedrich A. von. [1935] 1938a. "The Nature and History of the Problem." In *Collectivist Economic Planning: Critical Studies on the Possibilities of Socialism*, edited by F. A. von Hayek, 1–40. London: George Routledge & Sons.

————. [1935] 1938b. "The Present State of the Debate." In *Collectivist Economic Planning: Critical Studies on the Possibilities of Socialism*, edited by F. A. von Hayek, 201–243. London: George Routledge & Sons.

————. 1944. *The Road to Serfdom*. London: G. Routledge & Sons.

————. 1978. *New Studies in Philosophy, Politics, Economics and the History of Ideas*. Abingdon, UK: Taylor & Francis.

Hedlund, Stefan. 2005. *Russian Path Dependence*. London: Routledge.

Hegedűs, A. 1989. "Merely a Beauty-Spot." *Acta Oeconomics* 40: 225–227.

Hegedűs, B. András, and János M. Rainer, eds. 1989. *A Petőfi Kör Vitái: Hiteles Jegyzőkönyvek alapján. I. Két Közgazdasági Vita*. Kelenföld, Hungary: ELTE.

Heimann, Eduard. 1932. *Sozialistische Wirtschafts- und Arbeitsordnung*. Potsdam: Alfred Protte.

————. 1934. "Planning and the Market System." *Social Research* 1(4): 486–504.

————. 1939. "Literature on the Theory of a Socialist Economy." *Social Research* 6(1): 88–113.

————. 1944. "Franz Oppenheimer's Economic Ideas." *Social Research* 11(1): 27–39.

Heller, Farkas. 1943. *A Közgazdasági Elmélet Története*. Budapest: Gergely R. Könyvkereskedése.

Heller, Walter W. 1975. "What's Right with Economics?" *The American Economic Review* 65: 1–26.

Hempel, Carl G. 1966. *Philosophy of Natural Science*. Englewood Cliffs, NJ: Prentice-Hall.

Henisz, Witold J., Bennet A. Zelner, and Mauro F. Guillén. 2005. "The Worldwide Diffusion of Market-Oriented Infrastructure Reform, 1977–1999." *American Sociological Review* 70: 871–897.

Herman, Ellen. 1998. "Project Camelot and the Career of Cold War Psychology." In *Universities and Empire: Money and Politics in the Social Sciences during the Cold War*, edited by Christopher Simpson, 97–133. New York: New Press.

Herzel, Leo. 1998. "My 1951 Color Television Article." *Journal of Law and Economics* 41(2, part 2): 523–527.

Hillman, Arye L., 1994. "The Transition from Socialism: An Overview from a Political Economy Perspective." *European Journal of Political Economy* 10(1): 191–225.

Hillman, Arye L., and Branko Milanović. 1992. "Introduction." In *The Transition from Socialism in Eastern Europe: Domestic Restructuring and Foreign Trade*, edited by Arye L. Hillman and Branko Milanovic, 1–10. Washington, DC: The World Bank.

Hodgson, Geoffrey M. 1999. *Economics and Utopia: Why the Learning Economy Is Not the End of History*. London: Routledge.

Hoffman, George W., and Fred Warner Neal. 1962. *Yugoslavia and the New Communism*. New York: Twentieth Century Fund.

Hollander, Paul. 1981. *Political Pilgrims: Travels of Western Intellectuals to the Soviet Union, China, and Cuba, 1928–1978*. New York: Oxford University Press.

Horvat, Branko. 1961. *Ekonomska Teorija Planske Privrede*. Belgrade: Kultura.

————. 1964. *Towards a Theory of Planned Economy*. Belgrade: Yugoslav Institute of Economic Research.

————. 1967. "A Contribution to the Theory of the Yugoslav Firm." *Ekonomska analiza* 1(1–2): 7–28.

————. 1968. *Ekonomska nauka i narodna privreda: Ogledi i studije.* Zagreb: Naprijed.

————. 1971. "Yugoslav Economic Policy in the Post-War Period: Problems, Ideas, Institutional Developments." *The American Economic Review* 61(3), Part 2: 71–169.

————. 1979. "Self-Management, Efficient and Neoclassical Economics." *Economic Analysis and Workers' Management (Ekonomska analiza)* 13(1–2): 167–174.

————. 1989. "What Is a Socialist Market Economy?" *Acta Oeconomica* 40: 233–235.

Horvath, Robert. 1963. "The Development and Present Status of Input-Output Methods in Hungary." *Economics of Planning* 3(3): 209–220.

Howard, Michael, and John King. 1995. "Value Theory and Russian Marxism before the Revolution." In *Socialism and Marginalism in Economics, 1870–1930*, edited by Ian Steedman, 224–257. London: Routledge.

Howey, Richard S. [1960] 1989. *The Rise of the Marginal Utility School, 1870–1889.* New York: Columbia University Press.

Hutt, W. H. 1940. "Economic Institutions and the New Socialism." *Economica* 7(28): 419–434.

Institut Ekonomskih Nauka, 1959–1969: Prvi decenij naucnog rada. 1969. Belgrade: Institut Ekonomskih Nauka.

Ives, Peter. 2006. "The Mammoth Task of Translating Gramsci." *Rethinking Marxism* 18: 15–22.

"Izveštaj Uprave Društva ekonomista Srbije—podnet na IX god. Skupštini u Nišu." 1953. *Ekonomist* 6(3): 59–70.

James, Émile. 1950. *Histoire Des Théories Économiques.* Paris: Flammarion.

Jasny, Naum. 1972. *Soviet Economists of the Twenties: Names to Be Remembered.* Cambridge, UK: Cambridge University Press.

Jasanoff, Sheila. 2004. "The Idiom of Co-production." In *States of Knowledge: The Co-Production of Science and Social Order*, edited by Sheila Jasanoff, 1–12. London: Routledge.

Johansen, Leif. 1976. "L. V. Kantorovich's Contribution to Economics." *The Scandinavian Journal of Economics* 78: 61–80.

Johnson, Harry G. 1971. "The Keynesian Revolution and the Monetarist Counter-Revolution." *The American Economic Review* 61: 1–14.

Johnson, Loch K. 1989. *America's Secret Power: The CIA in a Democratic Society.* New York: Oxford University Press.

Josephson, Paul R. 1997. *New Atlantis Revisited: Akademgorodok, the Siberian City of Science.* Princeton, NJ: Princeton University Press.

Jowitt, Kenneth. 1992. *New World Disorder: The Leninist Extinction.* Berkeley: University of California Press.

Judy, Richard W. 1971. "The Economists." In *Interest Groups in Soviet Politics*, edited by H. Gordon Skilling and Franklyn Griffiths, 209–251. Princeton, NJ: Princeton University Press.

Juhász, József. 2001. "A jugoszláv önigazgatási modell." *Múltunk* 46: 276–293.

Kaase, Max, Vera Sparschuh, and Agnieszka Wenniger, eds. 2002. *Three Social Science Disciplines in Central and Eastern Europe. Handbook on Economics, Political Science and Sociology (1989–2001).* Berlin and Budapest: Social Science Information Centre (IZ)/Collegium Budapest.

Káldor, Gyula. 1949. "Az állami ellenőrzés kérdései a népi demokráciában." *Társadalmi Szemle* 4: 470–474.

Kalogjera, Dražen. 1990. "Pluralizam vlasništva." In *Socijalizam u reformi: iskustvo i problemi jugoslavenske privredne reforme,* edited by Zvonimir Baletić and Dragomir Vojnić, 42–50. Zagreb: Informator.

Kantorovich, L. V. 1960. "Mathematical Methods of Organizing and Planning Production." *Management Science* 6: 366–422.

Karli, L. 1955. "Neka pitanja obrazovanja ekonomista." *Ekonomski Pregled* 6: 508–517.

Kaser, Michael. 1990. "The Technology of Decontrol: Some Macroeconomic Issues." *The Economic Journal* 100: 596–615.

Kaser, M. C., and E. A. G. Robinson, eds. 1992. *Early Steps in Comparing East–West Economies: The Bursa Conference of 1958.* New York: St. Martin's Press.

Katsenelinboigen, Aron. 1978–1979. "L. V. Kantorovich: The Political Dilemma in Scientific Creativity." *Journal of Post Keynesian Economics* 1(3): 129–147.

———. 1980. *Soviet Economic Thought and Political Power in the USSR.* New York: Pergamon Policy Studies.

Katz, Barry M. 1989. *Foreign Intelligence: Research and Analysis in the Office of Strategic Services 1942–1945.* Cambridge, MA: Harvard University Press.

Kelly, John L. 1997. *Bringing the Market Back In: The Political Revitalization of Market Liberalism.* New York: New York University Press.

Kemenes, Egon. 1981. "Hungary: Economists in a Socialist Planning System." *History of Political Economy* 13(3): 580–599.

Keren, Michael. 1993. "On the (Im)Possibility of Market Socialism." *Eastern Economic Journal* 19: 333–344.

Kestenbaum, David. "India's China Envy," NPR, May 20, 2010. Retrieved on June 2, 2010, from www.npr.org/templates/story/story.php?storyId=127014493.

Kestner, John W. 1999. "Through the Looking Glass: American Perceptions of the Soviet Economy, 1941–1964." PhD dissertation, Department of History, University of Wisconsin, Madison.

Keynes, John Maynard. [1925] 1963. "A Short View of Russia." In *Essays in Persuasion,* 297–311. New York: W. W. Norton & Co.

———. 1936. *The General Theory of Employment, Interest and Money.* London: Macmillan and Company.

Khalatbari, Firauzeh. 1977. "Market Imperfections and the Optimum Rate of Depletion of Natural Resources." *Economica* 44: 409–414.

Kidrič, Boris. [1950] 1979. "Teze o ekonomici prijelaznog perioda u nasoj zemlji." In *Socijalizem i ekonomija,* edited by Viljem Merhar, 79–100. Zagreb: Globus.

Kipnis, Andrew B. 2008. "Audit Cultures: Neoliberal Governmentality, Socialist Legacy, or Technologies of Governing?" *American Ethnologist* 35: 275–289.

Klatch, Rebecca E. 1998. *A Generation Divided: The New Right, the New Left, and the 1960s*. Berkeley: University of California Press.

Klaus, Václav. [1989] 1990. "The Imperatives of Long-Term Prognosis and the Dominant Characteristics of the Present Economy." *Eastern European Economics* 28: 39–52.

Klein, Lawrence Robert. 1947. *The Keynesian Revolution*. New York: Macmillan Co.

Klein, Lawrence R., and Marshall I. Pomer, eds. 2001. *The New Russia: Transition Gone Awry*. Stanford, CA: Stanford University Press.

Klein, Naomi. 2007. *The Shock Doctrine: The Rise of Disaster Capitalism*. New York: Metropolitan Books.

Knight, Peter T. 1975. *Peru: ¿Hacia la Autogestion?* Buenos Aires: Editorial proyección.

Knorr, Klaus. 1967. "Social Science Research Abroad: Problems and Remedies." *World Politics* 19: 465-485.

Kogut, Bruce, and J. Muir Macpherson. 2008. "The Decision to Privatize: Economists and the Construction of Ideas and Policies." In *The Global Diffusion of Markets and Democracy*, edited by Beth A. Simmons, Frank Dobbin, and Geoffrey Garrett, 104–140. Cambridge, UK: Cambridge University Press.

Konrád, György, and Iván Szelényi. 1979. *The Intellectuals on the Road to Class Power*. New York: Harcourt Brace Jovanovich.

Koopmans, Tjalling C. 1951. "Introduction." In *Activity Analysis of Production and Allocation*, edited by Tjalling C. Koopmans, 1–12. New York: John Wiley and Sons.

Kornai, János. [1957] 1959. *Overcentralization in Economic Administration*. London: Oxford University Press.

———. [1957] 1986. "A gazdasági vezetés túlzott központosítása." In *A Magyar Közgazdasági Gondolat Fejlődése, 1954–1978*, edited by László Szamuely, 127–153. Budapest: Közgazdasági és Jogi Könyvkiadó.

———. [1971] 1991. *Anti-Equilibrium: On Economic Systems Theory and the Tasks of Research*. Fairfield, NJ: A. M. Kelley, Publishers.

———. 1990a. "The Affinity between Ownership and Coordination Mechanisms: The Common Experience of Reform in Socialist Countries." *Journal of Economic Perspectives* 4(3): 131–147.

———. 1990b. "Comments and Discussion." In "Creating a Market Economy in Eastern Europe: The Case of Poland." *Brookings Papers on Economic Activity* 1990, by David Lipton and Jeffrey Sachs, 138–142.

———. 1992. *The Socialist System: The Political Economy of Communism*. Princeton, NJ: Princeton University Press.

———. 1994. "Péter György, a reformközgazdász." In *Péter György, 1903–1969: egy reformközgazdász emlékére*, edited by János Árvay and András B. Hegedűs, 75–89. Budapest: T-Twins Kiadó.

———. 2006. *By Force of Thought: Irregular Memoirs of an Intellectual Journey*. Cambridge, MA: MIT Press.

Kovács, Győző. 2008. "The Short History of M-3, the First Hungarian Electronic Digital Tube Computer." *IT Star Newsletter* 6(3): 4–6. Retrieved on November 5, 2009, from www.scholze-simmel.at/starbus/download/nl_3_08.pdf.

Kovács, János Mátyás. 1990. "Reform Economics: The Classification Gap." *Daedalus* 119(1): 215–248.

———. 1994. "Introduction." In *Transition to Capitalism? The Communist Legacy in Eastern Europe*, edited by János Mátyás Kovács, xi–xxiii. New Brunswick, NJ: Transaction Publishers.

Köves, Pál. 1994. "Theiss Ede." In *Magyar Közgazdászok a Két Viléghábóru Között*, edited by Antal Mátyás, 176–197. Budapest: Akadémiai Kiadó.

Kowalik, Tadeusz. 1965. "Biography of Oskar Lange." In *On Political Economy and Econometrics: Essays in Honour of Oskar Lange*, 1–13. Oxford, UK: Pergamon Press.

———. 1990. "Lange-Lerner Mechanism." In *Problems of the Planned Economy*, edited by John Eatwell, Murray Milgate, and Peter Newman, 147–150. London: Macmillan.

"A Közgazdaságtudomány Fellendítésének Szolgálatában." 1954. *Közgazdasági Szemle* 1: 1–5.

Krippner, Greta R., and Anthony S. Alvarez. 2007. "Embeddedness and the Intellectual Projects of Economic Sociology." *Annual Review of Sociology* 33: 219–240.

Krugman, Paul. 2007. "Who Was Milton Friedman?" *The New York Review of Books* 54(2).

Kuhn, Thomas S. 1962. *The Structure of Scientific Revolutions*. Chicago: University of Chicago Press.

Kumar, Krishan. 1992. "The Revolutions of 1989: Socialism, Capitalism, and Democracy." *Theory and Society* 21: 309–356.

Kurz, Heinz D. 1995. "Marginalism, Classicism and Socialism in German-Speaking Countries, 1871–1932." In *Socialism and Marginalism in Economics, 1870–1930*, edited by Ian Steedman, 7–86. London: Routledge.

Kydland, Finn, and Edward C. Prescott. 1982. "Time to Build and Aggregate Fluctuations." *Econometrica* 50: 1345–1370.

Laki, Mihály. 1989. "What Is the Solution?" *Acta Oeconomica* 40: 248–251.

———. 1996. Book Review of *Starting over in Eastern Europe* by S. Johnson and G. Loveman. *Acta Oeconomica* 48: 228–232.

Lampe, John R. 1996. *Yugoslavia as History: Twice There Was a Country*. Cambridge, UK: Cambridge University Press.

Lampe, John R., Russell O. Prickett, and Ljubiša S. Adamović. 1990. *Yugoslav-American Economic Relations since World War II*. Durham, NC: Duke University Press.

Lampert, Nicholas. 1985. *Whistleblowing in the Soviet Union: Complaints and Abuses under State Socialism*. London: MacMillan Press.

Lampland, Martha. 1995. *The Object of Labor: Commodification in Socialist Hungary*. Chicago: University of Chicago Press.

Landauer, Carl. 1931. *Planwirtschaft und Verkehrswirtschaft*. Munich and Leipzig: Verlag von Duncker & Humblot.

———. 1944. "From Marx to Menger: The Recent Development of Soviet Economics." *The American Economic Review* 34(2): 340–344.

———. 1959. *European Socialism: A History of Ideas and Movement, from the Industrial Revolution to Hitler's Seizure of Power*, vol. II. Berkeley and Los Angeles: University of California Press.

Lang, Rikard. 1955. *Međunarodna suradnja i ekonomski razvoj.* Zagreb: Kultura.

Lange, Oskar. 1934. "The Determinateness of the Utility Function." *The Review of Economic Studies* 1(3): 218–225.

———. 1935. "Marxian Economics and Modern Economic Theory." *The Review of Economic Studies* 2(3): 189–201.

———. 1936. "On the Economic Theory of Socialism: Part One." *The Review of Economic Studies* 4(1): 53–71.

———. 1937. "On the Economic Theory of Socialism: Part Two." *The Review of Economic Studies* 4(2): 123–142.

———. 1942. "The Foundations of Welfare Economics." *Econometrica* 10(3/4): 215–228.

———. 1945. "Marxian Economics in the Soviet Union." *The American Economic Review* 35(1): 127–133.

———. [1967] 1972. "The Computer and the Market." In *Socialist Economics*, edited by Alec Nove and D. M. Nuti, 401–405. London: Penguin Books.

Latour, Bruno. 1988. *The Pasteurization of France.* Cambridge, MA: Harvard University Press.

———. 1999. *Pandora's Hope: Essays on the Reality of Science Studies.* Cambridge, MA: Harvard University Press.

Lau, Lawrence J., Yingyi Qian, and Gérard Roland. 2000. "Reform without Losers: An Interpretation of China's Dual-Track Approach to Transition." *The Journal of Political Economy* 108: 120–143.

Lavigne, Marie. 1989. "A Note on Market Socialism." *Acta Oeconomica* 40: 251–253.

———. 1997. "The Political Economy of Socialism: What Is Left?" *Europe-Asia Studies* 49(3): 479–486.

Lavoie, Don. 1985. *Rivalry and Central Planning: The Socialist Calculation Debate Reconsidered.* Cambridge, UK: Cambridge University Press.

Lazarsfeld, Paul F., and Wagner Thielens Jr. 1958. *The Academic Mind: Social Scientists in a Time of Crisis.* Glencoe, IL: The Free Press.

Leff, Nathaniel H. 1979. "Entrepreneurship and Economic Development: The Problem Revisited." *Journal of Economic Literature* 17: 46–64.

Le Grand, Julian, and Saul Estrin, eds. 1989. *Market Socialism.* Oxford, UK: Clarendon Press.

Leontief, Wassily. 1938. "The Significance of Marxian Economics for Present-Day Economic Theory." *The American Economic Review* 28(1): 1–9.

———. 1971. "Theoretical Assumptions and Nonobservable Facts." *The American Economic Review* 61(1): 1–7.

Lerner, A. P. 1933. "The Diagrammatical Representation of Elasticity of Demand." *The Review of Economic Studies* 1(1): 39–44.

———. 1934a. "The Diagrammatical Representation of Demand Conditions in International Trade." *Economica* 1(3): 319–334.

———. 1934b. "Economic Theory and Socialist Economy." *The Review of Economic Studies* 2(1): 51–61.

———. 1944. *The Economics of Control: Principles of Welfare Economics.* New York: The Macmillan Company.

Lewin, Moshe. 1974. *Political Undercurrents in Soviet Economic Debates: From Bukharin to the Modern Reformers*. Princeton, NJ: Princeton University Press.

Lewis, Paul. 2001. "Dragoslav Avramovic, 81, Economist with the World Bank," *The New York Times*, April 23, 2001. Retrieved on January 13, 2011, from www.nytimes.com/2001/04/23/world/dragoslav-avramovic-81-economist-with-the-world-bank.html.

Lipsitz, George. 1988. Review of *The New York Intellectuals: The Rise and the Decline of the Anti-Stalinist Left from the 1950s to the 1980s* by Alan Wald. *The Oral History Review* 16(2): 161–163.

Lipton, David, and Jeffrey Sachs. 1990a. "Creating a Market Economy in Eastern Europe: The Case of Poland." *Brookings Papers on Economic Activity* 1990(1): 75–147.

———. 1990b. "Privatization in Eastern Europe: The Case of Poland." *Brookings Papers on Economic Activity* 1990(2): 293–341.

Litván, György, ed. 1996. *The Hungarian Revolution of 1956: Reform, Revolt, and Repression, 1953–1963*. London: Longman.

Ljungqvist, Lars, and Thomas J. Sargent. 2004. *Recursive Macroeconomic Theory*. Cambridge, MA: MIT Press.

Logue, John, Sergey Plekhanov, and John Simmons, eds. 1995. *Transforming Russian Enterprises: From State Control to Employee Ownership*. Westport, CT: Greenwood Press.

"The London School of Economics 1895–1945." 1946. *Economica* 13: 1–31.

Lotringer, Sylvère. 2004. "Foreword: We, the Multitude." In *A Grammar of the Multitude: For an Analysis of Contemporary Forms of Left*, by Paolo Virno, 7–19. Cambridge, MA: The MIT Press.

Lucas, Robert E. Jr. 1972. "Econometric Testing of the Natural Rate of Hypothesis." In *The Econometrics of Price Determination*, edited by Otto Eckstein, 50–59. Washington, DC: Board of Governors of the Federal Reserve System.

Lucas, Robert E. Jr., and Edward C. Prescott. 1971. "Investment under Uncertainty." *Econometrica* 39: 659–681.

Lupo, Salvatore. 2004. *Partito e Antipartito: Una storia politica della prima Repubblica (1946–78)*. Rome: Donzelli Editore.

Lydall, Harold. 1989. *Yugoslavia in Crisis*. Oxford, UK: Clarendon Press.

MacKenzie, Donald. 2006. *An Engine, Not a Camera: How Financial Models Shape Markets*. Cambridge, MA: MIT Press.

Mackenzie, Donald, and Yuval Millo. 2003. "Negotiating a Market, Performing Theory: The Historical Sociology of a Financial Derivatives Exchange." *American Journal of Sociology* 109: 107–145.

MacKenzie, Donald, Fabian Muniesa, and Lucia Siu, eds. 2007. *Do Economists Make Markets? On the Performativity of Economics*. Princeton, NJ: Princeton University Press.

Magyar Szocialista. 1964. *A Magyar Szocialista Munkáspárt határozatai és dokumentumai, 1956–62*. Budapest: Kossuth Könyvkiadó.

Magyar Szocialista. 1994. *A Magyar Szocialista Munkáspárt Határozatai és Dokumentumai, 1985–1989*. Edited by Henrik Vass. Budapest: Interart Stúdió.

Major, Iván. 1993. *Privatization in Eastern Europe: A Critical Approach*. Aldershot, UK: E. Elgar.

Maksimović, Ivan. 1958. *Teorija Socijalizma u Građanskoj Ekonomskoj Nauci*. Belgrade: Nolit.

———. 1965. "Professor Oskar Lange on Economic Theory of Socialism and Yugoslav Economic Thinking." In *On Political Economy and Econometrics: Essays in Honour of Oskar Lange*, 347–362. Oxford, UK: Pergamon Press.

Mankiw, N. Gregory. 2008. *Principles of Macroeconomics*, 5th ed. Mason, OH: Cengage South-Western.

Mankiw, N. Gregory, and Mark P. Taylor. 2006. *Economics*. London: Thomson Learning.

Marangos, John. 2004. *Alternative Economic Models of Transition*. Farnham, UK: Ashgate Publishing.

———. 2007. "Was Shock Therapy Consistent with the Washington Consensus?" *Comparative Economic Studies* 49: 32–58.

Margold, Stella. 1967. "Yugoslavia's New Economic Reforms." *American Journal of Economics and Sociology* 26(1): 65–77.

Máriás, A., S. Kovács, K. Balaton, E. Tari, and M. Dobak. 1981. "Organization of Large Industrial Enterprises in Hungary: A Comparative Analysis." *Acta Oeconomica* 27: 327–342.

Markoff, John, and Verónica Montecinos. 1993. "The Ubiquitous Rise of Economists." *Journal of Public Policy* 13: 37–68.

Marković, Dragan, and Savo Kržavac. 1978. *Liberalizam: Od Đilasa Do Danas*. Belgrade: Sloboda.

Márkus, Péter. 1996. "Tulajdon és hatalom (Közgazdaságtan es ideológia a rendszerváltás időszakában)." In *Ünnepi dolgozatok Mátyás Antal tanszékvezetői kinevezésének 40. Evfordulójára*, edited by Geza Halász and István Mihalik, 171–179. Budapest: Aula Kiadó Kft.

Marschak, Thomas. 1959. "Centralization and Decentralization in Economic Organizations." *Econometrica* 27(3): 399–430.

———. 1968. "Centralized versus Decentralized Resource Allocation: The Yugoslav 'Laboratory.'" *Quarterly Journal of Economics* 82(4): 561–587.

———. 1973. "Decentralizing the Command Economy: The Study of a Pragmatic Strategy for Reformers." In *Plan and Market: Economic Reform in Eastern Europe*, edited by Morris Bornstein, 23–63. New Haven, CT: Yale University Press.

Marx, Karl. [1867] 1990. *Capital: A Critique of Political Economy*, Volume 1. London: Penguin Classics.

———. [1885] 1992. *Capital: A Critique of Political Economy*, Volume 2. London: Penguin Classics.

———. [1894] 1991. *Capital: A Critique of Political Economy*, Volume 3. London: Penguin Classics.

Mason, John W. 1980. "Political Economy and the Response to Socialism in Britain, 1870–1914." *The Historical Journal* 23(3): 565–587.

Mason, Edward S., and Robert E. Asher. 1973. *The World Bank since Bretton Woods*. Washington, DC: The Brookings Institution.

Mátyás, Antal. 1960. *A Polgári Közgazdaságtan Főbb Irányzatai a Marxizmus Létrejötte Után*. n.p.: Közgazdaségi és Jogi Könyvkiadó.

Mayshar, Joram. 1977. "Should Government Subsidize Risky Private Projects?" *The American Economic Review* 67: 20–28.

McDonald, Jason. 1993. "Transition to Utopia: a Reinterpretation of Economics, Ideas, and Politics in Hungary, 1984 to 1990." *East European Politics and Societies* 7: 203–239.

McKenzie, Richard B. 1980. "The Neoclassicalists vs. the Austrians: A Partial Reconciliation of Competing Worldviews." *Southern Economic Journal* 47(1): 1–13.

Meade, J. E. 1972. "The Theory of Labour-Managed Firms and of Profit Sharing." *The Economic Journal* 82: 402–428.

———. 1974. "Labour-Managed Firms in Conditions of Imperfect Competition." *The Economic Journal* 84: 817–824.

———. 1989. *Agathotopia: The Economics of Partnership*. Aberdeen, UK: The Aberdeen University Press.

———. 1993. *Liberty, Equality, and Efficiency: Apologia Pro Agathotopia Mea*. New York: New York University Press.

Meier, Viktor. 1999. *Yugoslavia: A History of Its Demise*. London: Routledge.

Mencinger, Jože. 1992. "On the Privatization Dilemmas—The Experiences of Slovenia." Paper presented at the Second European Association for Comparative Economic Studies Conference, September 24–26.

———. 2002. "Economics—Slovenia." In *Three Social Science Disciplines in Central and Eastern Europe: Handbook on Economics, Political Science and Sociology*, edited by Max Kaase, Vera Sparschuh, and Agnieszka Wenninger, 187–194. Berlin and Budapest: Social Science Information Centre and Collegium Budapest.

———. 2004. "Transition to a National and a Market Economy: A Gradualist Approach." In *Slovenia: From Yugoslavia to the European Union*, edited by Mojmir Mrak, Matija Rojec, and Carlos Silva-Jáuregui, 67–82. Washington, DC: The International Bank for Reconstruction and Development/The World Bank.

Merritt, Richard L. 1972. "Effects of International Student Exchange." In *Communications in International Politics*, edited by Richard L. Merritt, 65–94. Urbana: University of Illinois Press.

Meyer, Alfred. 1993. "Politics and Methodology in Soviet Studies." In *Post-Communist Studies and Political Science*, edited by Frederic J. Fleron Jr. and Erik P. Hoffman, 163–175. Boulder, CO: Westview Press.

Michelini, Luca. 2001. "Marginalismo e socialismo nell'Italia liberale, 1870–1925." In *Marginalismo e Socialismo nell'Italia Liberale, 1870–1925*, edited by Marco E. L. Guidi and Luca Michelini, xli–cxxxi. Milan: Fondazione Giangiacomo Feltrinelli.

Mieli, Renato. 1984. "Il ritardo culturale della sinistra italiana." In *Riformismo e socialdemocrazia ieri e oggi*, 145–150. Naples: Edizioni scientifiche italiane.

———. [1964] 1988. *Togliatti 1937*. Milan: Biblioteca Universale Rizzoli.

———. 1996. *Deserto Rosso: Un decennio da comunista*. Bologna: il Mulino.

Milanovic, Branko. 1989. *Liberalization and Entrepreneurship: Dynamics of Reform in Socialism and Capitalism*. Armonk, NY: M. E. Sharpe.

———. 1992. "Privatization Options and Procedures." In *The Transition from Socialism in Eastern Europe: Domestic Restructuring and Foreign Trade*, edited by Arye L. Hillman and Branko Milanovic, 145–150. Washington, DC: The World Bank.

Milenkovitch, Deborah D. 1971. *Plan and Market in Yugoslav Economic Thought*. New Haven, CT: Yale University Press.

———. 1977. "The Case of Yugoslavia." *The American Economic Review* 67(1): 55–60.

———. 1984. "Is Market Socialism Efficient?" In *Comparative Economic Systems: An Assessment of Knowledge, Theory and Method*, edited by Andrew S. Zimbalist, 65–107. Boston: Kluwer-Nijhoff.

Mill, John Stuart. [1848] 1917. *Principles of Political Economy: With Some of Their Applications to Social Philosophy*. London: Longmans, Green, and Co.

Millar, James. 1980. "Where Are the Young Specialists on the Soviet Economy and What Are They Doing?" *Journal of Comparative Economics* 4: 317–329.

———. 1996. "From Utopian Socialism to Utopian Capitalism: The Failure of Revolution and Reform in Post-Soviet Russia." The George Washington Universty 175th Anniversary Papers. Washington, DC: The George Washington University.

———. 2005. "Bergson's Structure of Soviet Wages." *Comparative Economic Studies* 47: 289–295.

Mirowski, Philip. 1989. *More Heat Than Light: Economics as Social Physics, Physics as Nature's Economics*. Cambridge, UK: Cambridge University Press.

———. 2002. *Machine Dreams: Economics Becomes a Cyborg Science*. Cambridge, UK: Cambridge University Press.

———. 2004. Review of *From Newspeak to Cyberspeak: A History of Soviet Cybernetics* by Slava Gerovitch. *Journal of Economic Literature* 42(1): 214–215.

———. 2009. "Postface: Defining Neoliberalism." In *The Road from Mont Pélerin: The Making of the Neoliberal Thought Collective*, edited by Philip Mirowski and Dieter Plehwe, 417–456. Cambridge, MA: Harvard University Press.

Mirowski, Philip, and D. Wade Hands. 1998. "A Paradox of Budgets: The Postwar Stabilization of American Neoclassical Demand Theory." In *From Interwar Pluralism to Postwar Neoclassicism*. Annual Supplement to Volume 30, *History of Political Economy*, edited by Mary S. Morgan and Malcolm Rutherford, 260–292. Durham, NC: Duke University Press.

Mirowski, Philip, and Dieter Plehwe, eds. 2009. *The Road from Mont Pélerin: The Making of the Neoliberal Thought Collective*. Cambridge, MA: Harvard University Press.

Mirrlees, J. A. 1971. "An Exploration in the Theory of Optimum Income Taxation." *The Review of Economic Studies* 38: 175–208.

Mises, Ludwig von. [1920] 1938. "Economic Calculation in the Socialist Commonwealth." In *Collectivist Economic Planning: Critical Studies on the Possibilities of Socialism*, edited by F. A. von Hayek, 87–130. London: George Routledge & Sons.

———. 1922. *Die Gemeimwirtschaft: Untersuchungen über den Sozialismus*. Jena, Germany: Verlag von Gustav Fishcher.

———. 1923. "Neue Beiträge zum Problem der sozialistischen Wirtschaftsrechnung." *Archiv für Sozialwissenschaft und Sozialpolitik* 51(2): 488–500.

———. [1932] 1936. *Socialism: An Economic and Sociological Analysis.* Translated by J. Kahane. London: Jonathan Cape.

Mitchell, Allan. 1965. *Revolution in Bavaria, 1918–1919: The Eisner Regime and the Soviet Republic.* Princeton, NJ: Princeton University Press.

Mitchell, Timothy. 1990. "Everyday Metaphors of Power." *Theory and Society* 19(5): 545–577.

———. 1999. "Dreamland: The Neoliberalism of Your Desires." *Middle East Report* 210: 28–33.

———. 2002. *Rule of Experts: Egypt, Techno-Politics, Modernity.* Berkeley: University of California Press.

Moncada, Alberto, and Judith Blau. 2006. "Human Rights and the Roles of Social Scientists." *Societies without Borders* 1: 113–122.

Montenegrin Academy of Sciences and Arts. [n.d.]. "Dr. Branislav Šoškić." Retrieved on November 5, 2009, from www.canu.org.me/cms/dr_branislav_%C5%A0o%C5%A1ki%C4%87/

Monti-Bragadin, Stefano. 1971. Review of *Scritti politici* by Andrea Caffi. *Controcorrente: Verifica delle ipotesi di trasformazione delle societa* 3(4): 61–62.

Montias. 1959. "Economic Reform and Retreat in Jugoslavia." *Foreign Affairs* 37(2): 293–305.

Moore, John. 2003. "Remembering Warren Nutter." In *Looking Forward to the Past: The Influence of Communism after 1989,* edited by Richard Pipes, et al., 19–31. London: The Chameleon Press.

Morgenstern, Oskar. 1972. "Thirteen Critical Points in Contemporary Economic Theory: An Interpretation." *Journal of Economic Literature* 10: 1163–1189.

Morlino, Leonardo. 1991. "Political Science in Italy: Tradition and Empiricism." *European Journal of Political Research* 20: 341–358.

Mornati, Fiorenzo. 2001. "Pareto e il socialismo sino alla vigilia della pubblicazione dei *Systèmes socialistes*: una ricognizione dei testi." In *Marginalismo e Socialismo nell'Italia Liberale, 1870–1925,* edited by Marco E. L. Guidi and Luca Michelini, 1–34. Milan: Fondazione Giangiacomo Feltrinelli.

Morris, Bernard S. 1953. "The Cominform: A Five-Year Perspective." *World Politics* 5: 368–376.

Motyl, Alexander. 1993. "The Dilemmas of Sovietology and the Labyrinth of Theory." In *Post-Communist Studies and Political Science,* edited by Frederic J. Fleron Jr. and Erik P. Hoffman, 77–104. Boulder, CO: Westview Press.

Mudge, Stephanie. 2008. "What Is Neo-Liberalism?" *Socio-Economic Review* 6: 703–731.

Mujżel, Jan. 1988. "Democracy or Technocracy? Discussion: The Second Stage of the Reform." *Eastern European Economics* 26: 72–87.

Munck, Ronaldo. 2003. "Neoliberalism, Necessitarianism and Alternatives in Latin America: There Is No Alternative (TINA)?" *Third World Quarterly* 24: 495–511.

Murphy, Kevin M., Andrei Shleifer, and Robert W. Vishny. 1989. "Industrialization and the Big Push." *The Journal of Political Economy* 97: 1003–1026.

Murrell, Peter. 1983. "Did the Theory of Market Socialism Answer the Challenge of Ludwig von Mises? A Reinterpretation of the Socialist Controversy." *History of Political Economy* 15(1): 92–105.

———. 1995. "The Transition According to Cambridge, Mass." *Journal of Economic Literature* 33: 164–178.

Mussa, Michael. 1977. "External and Internal Adjustment Costs and the Theory of Aggregate and Firm Investment." *Economica* 44: 163–178.

Nagy, Imre. 1954. "A magyar tudomány elött álló feladatok." *Társadalmi Szemle* 9(6): 17–29.

Nagy, Tamás. [1964] 1986. "Az értéktörvény és az árak centruma a szocializmusban." In *A Magyar Közgazdasági Gondolat Fejlődése, 1954–1978*, edited by László Szamuely, 303–311. Budapest: Közgazdasági és Jogi Könyvkiadó.

———. 1989. "What makes a market economy socialist?" *Acta Oeconomica* 40: 259–264.

Naughton, Barry. 1995. *Growing Out of the Plan: Chinese Economic Reform, 1978–1993.* Cambridge, UK: Cambridge University Press.

Nee, Victor, and David Stark, eds. 1989. *Remaking the Economic Institutions of Socialism: China and Eastern Europe.* Stanford, CA: Stanford University Press.

Nelson, Lynn D., and Irina Y. Kuzes. 1994. *Property to the People: The Struggle for Radical Economic Reform in Russia.* Armonk, NY: M. E. Sharpe.

Nelson, Robert H. 1997. "In memoriam: On the death of the 'market mechanism.'" *Ecological Economics* 20: 187–197.

Neuberger, Egon. 1989. "Comparing Economic Systems." In *Comparative Economic Systems: Models and Cases*, 6th ed, edited by Morris Bernstein. Homewood, IL: Irwin.

Neuberger, Egon, and William J. Duffy. 1976. *Comparative Economic Systems: A Decision-Making Approach.* Boston: Allyn and Bacon.

Niehans, Jurg. [1990] 1994. *A History of Economic Theory: Classic Contributions, 1720–1980.* Baltimore: The Johns Hopkins University Press.

Nonini, Donald M. 2008. "Is China Becoming Neoliberal?" *Critique of Anthropology* 28: 145–176.

Nove, Alec. 1987. "Trotsky, Markets, and East European Reforms." *Comparative Economic Studies* 29(3): 30–40.

———. 1989. "The Role of Central Planning under Capitalism and Market Socialism." In *Alternatives to Capitalism*, edited by Jon Elster, and Karl Ove Moene, 98–109. Cambridge, UK: Cambridge University Press.

Nuti, D. Mario. 1988. "Perestroika: Transition from Central Planning to Market Socialism." *Economic Policy* 3(7): 353–389.

———. 1992. "Market Socialism: The Model That Might Have Been but Never Was." In *Market Socialism or the Restoration of Capitalism?* edited by Anders Åslund, 17–31. Cambridge, UK: Cambridge University Press.

———. 1996. "Efficiency, equality and enterprise democracy." In *Democracy and Efficiency in the Economic Enterprise*, edited by Ugo Pagano and Robert Rowthorn, 184–206. London: Routledge.

Obradović, Josip, and William N. Dunn. 1978. *Worker's Self-Management and Organizational Power in Yugoslavia*. Pittsburgh: University of Pittsburgh.

O'Connell, Charles Thomas. 1990. "Social Structure and Science: Soviet Studies at Harvard." PhD dissertation, Department of Sociology, University of California, Los Angeles.

O'Donnell, Guillermo A. 1973. *Modernization and Bureaucratic Authoritarianism. Studies in South American Politics*. Berkeley: Institute of International Studies, University of California.

O'Neil, Patrick H. 1998. *Revolution from Within: The Hungarian Socialist Workers' Party and the Collapse of Communism*. Cheltenham, UK: Edward Elgar.

Ong, Aihwa. 2006. *Neoliberalism as Exception: Mutations in Citizenship and Sovereignty*. Durham, NC: Duke University Press.

Orenstein, Mitchell A. 2001. *Out of the Red: Building Capitalism and Democracy in Postcommunist Europe*. Ann Arbor: The University of Michigan Press.

———. 2008. *Privatizing Pensions: The Transnational Campaign for Social Security Reform*. Princeton, NJ: Princeton University Press.

Oushakine, Serguei Alex. 2001. "The Terrifying Mimicry of Samizdat." *Public Culture* 13(2): 191–214.

Paczyńska, Agnieszka. 2009. *State, Labor, and the Transition to a Market Economy: Egypt, Poland, Mexico, and the Czech Republic*. University Park: Pennsylvania State University Press.

Pareto, Vilfredo. 1896. *Cours d'Economie Politique*, vol. 1. Lausanne: F. Rouge, Editeur.

———. 1897a. *Cours d'Economie Politique*, vol. 2. Lausanne: F. Rouge, Libraire-Editeur.

———. 1897b. "The New Theories of Economics." *The Journal of Political Economy* 5(4): 485–502.

———. [1927] 1971. *The Manual of Political Economy*. New York: A. M. Kelley.

Pease, Edward R. 1916. *The History of the Fabian Society*. London: A. C. Fifield.

Pels, Peter. 1999. "Professions of Duplexity: A Prehistory of Ethical Codes in Anthropology." *Current Anthropology* 40(2): 101–136.

Péter, György. [1954] 1986. "A gazdaságosság jelentőségéről és szerepéről a népgazdaság tervszerűirányításában." In *A Magyar Közgazdasági Gondolat Fejlődése, 1954–1978*, edited by László Szamuely, 74–91. Budapest: Közgazdasági és Jogi Könyvkiadó.

Péteri, György. 1991. "Academic Elite into Scientific Cadres: A Statistical Contribution to the History of the Hungarian Academy of Sciences, 1945–49." *Soviet Studies* 43: 281–299.

———. 1993. "The Politics of Statistical Information and Economic Research in Communist Hungary, 1949–56." *Contemporary European History* 2(2): 149–167.

———. 1996. "Controlling the Field of Academic Economics in Hungary, 1953–1976." *Minerva* 34: 367–380.

Pető, Iván. 2002. "A Rendszerváltás Naplója." *Buksz* 14(2): 114–125.

Petrin, Tea. 1991. "Is Entrepreneurship Possible in Public Enterprises." In *Entrepreneurship Development in Public Enterprises*, edited by Joseph Prokopenko and Igor Pavlin, 7–31. Ljubljana, Slovenia: International Center for Public Enterprises in Developing Countries.

Petrin, Tea and Alex Vahcic. 1988. "Entrepreneurial Management and Small-Scale Sector in Socialist Countries—the Case of Yugoslavia." *Development & South-South Cooperation* 3(6): 115–124.

Petrović, Pavle. 1988. "Price Distortion and Income Dispersion in a Labor-Managed Economy: Evidence from Yugoslavia." *Journal of Comparative Economics* 12(4): 592–603.

Phelps Brown, E. H. 1972. "The Underdevelopment of Economics." *The Economic Journal* 82: 1–10.

Pierson, Christopher. 1995. *Socialism after Communism: The New Market Socialism*. University Park: Pennsylvania State University Press.

Pierson, N. G. [1902] 1938. "The Problem of Value in the Socialist Community." In *Collectivist Economic Planning: Critical Studies on the Possibilities of Socialism*, edited by F. A. von Hayek, 41–85. London: George Routledge & Sons.

Pieterse, Jan Nederveen. 2001. *Development Theory*. Thousand Oaks, CA: Sage Publications.

Pistolese, Gennaro. 1996. "La Confindustria con il suo ieri." *Apulia* 2. Available at www.bpp.it/Content/Content.asp?idModulo=455#.

Plehwe, Dieter. 2009. "Introduction." In *The Road from Mont Pèlerin: The Making of the Neoliberal Thought Collective*, edited by Philip Mirowski and Dieter Plehwe, 1–44. Cambridge, MA: Harvard University Press.

Plehwe, Dieter, Bernhard Walpen, and Gisela Neunhöffer. 2005. "Reconsidering Neoliberal Hegemony." In *Neoliberal Hegemony: A Global Critique*, edited by Dieter Plehwe, Bernhard Walpen, and Gisela Neunhöffer, 1–24. New York: Routledge.

Porket, J. L. 1993. "Review: Socialism on the Retreat, but Not Dead." *The Slavonic and East European Review* 71: 133–136.

Polanyi, Karl. 1922. "Sozialistische Rechnungslegung." *Archiv für Sozialwissenschaft und Sozialpolitik* 49(2): 377–420.

———. [1944] 1957. *The Great Transformation: The Political and Economic Origins of Our Time*. Boston: Beacon Press.

Politikai Gazdaságtan: Tankönyv. [1954] 1956. Budapest: Szikra.

Pollock, Ethan. 2006. *Stalin and the Soviet Science Wars*. Princeton, NJ: Princeton University Press.

Popper, Karl R. [1945] 1950. *The Open Society and its Enemies*. Princeton, NJ: Princeton University Press.

———. 1959. *The Logic of Scientific Discovery*. New York: Basic Books.

Popov, Zoran. 1989. "Koliko su realistična očekivanja bliske reforme privrednog sistema." In *Ekonomisti O Krizi: Razgovor Ekonomista s Mandatorom Za SIV, Dipl. Ing. Antom Markovićem*, edited by Tomislav Popović, 139–143. Belgrade: Konzorcijum ekonomskih instituta Jugoslavije.

Portes, Richard D. 1972. "The Strategy and Tactics of Economic Decentralization." *Soviet Studies* 23: 629–658.

Prasad, Monica. 2006. *The Politics of Free Markets: The Rise of Neoliberal Economic Policies in Britain, France, Germany, and the United States.* Chicago: University of Chicago Press.

Prašnikar, Janez. 1980. "The Yugoslav Self-Managed Firm and Its Behaviour." *Economic Analysis and Workers' Management* 14(1): 1–32.

Prašnikar, Janez, Jan Svejnar, Dubravko Mihaljek, and Vesna Prašnikar. 1994. "Behavior of Participatory Firms in Yugoslavia: Lessons for Transforming Economies." *The Review of Economics and Statistics* 76(4): 728–741.

Prout, Christopher. 1985. *Market Socialism in Yugoslavia.* Oxford, UK: Oxford University Press.

Prychitko, David L. 2002. *Markets, Planning, and Democracy: Essays after the Collapse of Communism.* Cheltenham, UK: E. Elgar.

Račić, Gjuro. 1955. "II. Međunarodni Kongres Kolektivne Ekonomije." *Ekonomski Pregled* 6(10): 903–906.

Radičević, Rikard. 1957. *Osnove ekonomike poduzeća.* Zagreb: Tehnička knjiga.

Rainer, János. 1996. *Nagy Imre: Politikai Életrajz. Első Kötet: 1896–1953.* Budapest: 1956-os Intézet.

Raman, Parvathi, and Harry G. West. 2009. "Poetries of the Past in a Socialist World Remade." In *Enduring Socialism: Explorations of Revolution and Transformation, Restoration and Continuation*, edited by Harry G. West and Parvathi Raman, 1–28. New York: Berghahn Books.

Ramet, Pedro. 1985. "Factionalism in Church-State Interaction: The Croatian Catholic Church in the 1980s." *Slavic Review* 44(2): 298–315.

Ramet, Sabrina P. 2006. *The Three Yugoslavias: State-Building and Legitimation, 1918–2005.* Washington, DC: Woodrow Wilson Center Press.

Randall, Francis B. 1955. "Four Holes in the Iron Curtain." *Amherst Alumni News* 7(3): 2–5.

Raymond, Edward A. 1972. "Education of Foreign Nationals in the Soviet Union." In *Communications in International Politics*, edited by Richard L. Merritt, 120–145. Urbana: University of Illinois Press.

"Razgovor Redakcije 'Pitanja' s Brankom Horvatom." 1972. *Pitanja*, 1747–1763.

Reddaway, Peter. 2001. "Market Bolshevism Harmed Russia." Available at www .worldbank.org/html/prddr/trans/JulAugSep01/pgs16-19.htm.

Reddaway, Peter, and Dmitri Glinski. 2001. *The Tragedy of Russia's Reforms: Market Bolshevism against Democracy.* Washington, DC: U.S. Institute of Peace Press.

Rees, E. A. 1987. *State Control in Soviet Russia: The Rise and Fall of the Workers' and Peasants' Inspectorate, 1920–34.* London: MacMillan Press.

Reshetar, John S. Jr. 1955. *Problems of Analyzing and Predicting Soviet Behavior.* Garden City, NY: Doubleday and Company.

Révész, Gábor. 1979. "Enterprise and Plant Size Structure of the Hungarian Industry." *Acta Oeconomica* 22: 47–68.

————. [1988] 1989. "How the Economic Reforms Were Distorted." *Eastern European Economics* 27: 61–84.

Rezler, Julius. 1983. Review of *Hungary: A Decade of Economic Reform* by P. G. Hare, H. K. Radice, and N. Swain. *Slavic Review* 42: 143–144.

Richmond, Yale. 1987. *U.S.–Soviet Cultural Exchanges, 1958–1986: Who Wins?* Boulder, CO: Westview Press.

————. 2003. *Cultural Exchange and the Cold War: Raising the Iron Curtain.* University Park: Pennsylvania State University Press.

Ripa di Meana, Carlo. 2000. *Cane Sciolto.* Milan: Kaos.

Ripp, Zoltán. 2002. "Unity and Division: The Opposition Roundtable and its Relationship to the Communist Party." In *The Roundtable Talks of 1989: The Genesis of Hungarian Democracy, Analysis and Documents,* edited by András Bozóki, 3–39. Budapest: Central European University Press.

Robbins, Lionel. [1932] 1945. *An Essay on the Nature and Significance of Economic Science.* London: MacMillan.

Robin, Ron. 2001. *The Making of the Cold War Enemy: Culture and Politics in the Military–Intellectual Complex.* Princeton, NJ: Princeton University Press.

Roland, Gérard. 2000. *Transition and Economics: Politics, Markets, and Firms.* Cambridge, MA: The MIT Press.

Roman, Eric. 1996. *Hungary and the Victor Powers, 1945–1950.* New York: St. Martin's Press.

Róna-Tas, Ákos. 1997. *The Great Surprise of the Small Transformation: The Demise of Communism and the Rise of the Private Sector in Hungary.* Ann Arbor: University of Michigan Press.

Rose, Nikolas S. 1996. *Inventing Our Selves: Psychology, Power, and Personhood.* Cambridge, UK: Cambridge University Press.

————. 1999. *Powers of Freedom: Reframing Political Thought.* Cambridge, UK: Cambridge University Press.

Rosefielde, Steven. 1973. "Some Observations on the Concept of 'Socialism' in Contemporary Economic Theory." *Soviet Studies* 25: 229–243.

————. 1992. "Beyond Catastroika: Prospects for Market Transition in the Commonwealth of Independent States." *Atlantic Economic Journal* 20: 2–9.

Ross, Kristin. 2002. *May '68 and Its Afterlives.* Chicago: University of Chicago Press.

Rothschild, Michael, and Joseph Stiglitz. 1976. "Equilibrium in Competitive Insurance Markets: An Essay on the Economics of Imperfect Information." *The Quarterly Journal of Economics* 90: 629–649.

Rubinstein, Alvin Z. 1970. *Yugoslavia and the Nonaligned World.* Princeton, NJ: Princeton University Press.

Rudas, László. 1948. "Az új magyar Közgazdaságtudományi Egyetem feladatai." *Társadalmi Szemle* 3(10–11): 658–660.

Rusinow, Dennison I. 1977. *The Yugoslav Experiment, 1948–1974.* London: C. Hurst for the Royal Institute of International Affairs.

Sachs, Jeffrey. 1989. "Conditionality, Debt Relief, and the Developing Country Debt Crisis." In *Developing Country Debt and Economic Performance*, edited by Jeffrey Sachs, 255–298. Chicago: University of Chicago Press.

———. 1993. *Poland's Jump to the Market Economy*. Cambridge, MA: The MIT Press.

Sader, Emir. 2008. "The Weakest Link? Neoliberalism in Latin America." *New Left Review* 52 (July–August): 5–31.

Samuelson, Paul A. 1947. *Foundations of Economic Analysis*. Cambridge, MA: Harvard University Press.

———. [1948] 1951. *Economics: An Introductory Analysis*. New York: McGraw-Hill Book Company.

———. [1948] 1955. *Economics: An Introductory Analysis*. New York: McGraw-Hill Book Company.

———. [1949] 1966. "Market Mechanisms and Maximization." In *The Collected Scientific Papers of Paul A. Samuelson*, vol. 1, edited by Joseph E. Stiglitz, 425–492. Cambridge, MA: The MIT Press.

———. [1955] 1966. "Linear Programming and Economic Theory." In *The Collected Scientific Papers of Paul A. Samuelson*, vol. 1, edited by Joseph E. Stiglitz, 493–504. Cambridge, MA: The MIT Press.

———. 1972. "Liberalism at Bay." *Social Forces* 39: 16–31.

———. 1973. *Economics*. 9th ed. New York: McGraw-Hill.

———. 1983. "My Life Philosophy." *The American Economist* 27(2): 5–12.

———. 1997. "Credo of a Lucky Textbook Author." *The Journal of Economic Perspectives* 11(2): 153–160.

Sandmo, Agnar. 1971. "On the Theory of the Competitive Firm under Price Uncertainty." *The American Economic Review* 61: 65–73.

Santoro, Stefano. 2003. "The Cultural Penetration of Fascist Italy Abroad and in Eastern Europe." *Journal of Modern Italian Studies* 8(1): 36–66.

Sassoon, Donald. 1996. *One Hundred Years of Socialism: The West European Left in the Twentieth Century*. New York: The New Press.

Saunders, Frances Stonor. 2000. *The Cultural Cold War: The CIA and the World of Arts and Letters*. New York: New Press.

Scano, Luigi and Giampaolo Zucchini. 1969. "Avvertenza." *Controcorrente* 1(2): 5–6.

Schliwa, Rainer. 1997. "Enterprise Privatization and Employee Buy-Outs in Poland: An Analysis of the Process." Available at www.ilo.org/wcmsp5/groups/public/---ed_emp/---emp_ent/documents/publication/wcms_126666.pdf.

Schrecker, Ellen. 1986. *No Ivory Tower: McCarthyism and the Universities*. New York: Oxford University Press.

Schrenk, Martin. 1987. "The Bank's Analytical Approach to Socialist Countries and Economic Reform." Report no. CPD5, Departmental Working Paper. Washington, DC: World Bank.

Schrenk, Martin, Cyrus Ardalan, and Nawal A. El Tatawy, eds. 1979. *Yugoslavia: Self-Management Socialism and the Challenges of Development*. Baltimore: The Johns Hopkins University Press.

Schumpeter, Joseph [1954] 1966. *History of Economic Analysis*. New York: Oxford University Press.

Scott-Smith, Giles. 2002. *The Politics of Apolitical Culture: The Congress for Cultural Freedom, the CIA and Post-War American Hegemony*. London: Routledge.

Seleny, Anna. 1993. "The Long Transformation: Hungarian Socialism, 1949–1989." PhD dissertation, Department of Political Science, Massachusetts Institute of Technology.

Sen, Amartya. 1970. *Collective Choice and Social Welfare*. San Francisco: Holden-Day.

Sernau, Scott. 2011. *Social Inequalities in a Global Age*. Thousand Oaks, CA: Pine Forge Press.

Shapin, Steven. 1994. *A Social History of Truth: Civility and Science in Seventeenth-Century England*. Chicago: University of Chicago Press.

Shleifer, Andrei, Edward L. Glaeser, Florencio Lopez De Silanes, Rafael La Porta, and Simeon Djankov. 2003. "The New Comparative Economics." *SSRN eLibrary*. Retrieved on April 14, 2009, from: http://papers.ssrn.com/sol3/papers.cfm?abstract_id=390760.

Shleifer, Andrei, and Robert W. Vishny. 1994. "The Politics of Market Socialism." *The Journal of Economic Perspectives* 5(2): 165–176.

Sidgwick, Henry. 1887. *The Principles of Political Economy*. New York: MacMillan and Co.

———. 1895. "The Economic Lessons of Socialism." *The Economic Journal* 5(19): 336–346.

Šik, Ota. 1991. *Socialism Today? The Changing Meaning of Socialism*. New York: St. Martin's Press.

Simons, Henry Calvert. 1934. *A Positive Program for Laissez Faire; Some Proposals for a Liberal Economic Policy*. Chicago: University of Chicago Press.

Simpson, Christopher, ed. 1998. *Universities and Empire: Money and Politics in the Social Sciences during the Cold War*. New York: New Press.

Sirc, Ljubo. 1979. *The Yugoslav Economy under Self-Management*. New York: St. Martin's Press.

Sirotković, Jakov. 1959. "Input-output analiza i privredno planiranje." *Ekonomist* 1–2: 104–117.

Sivachev, Nikolai V., and Nikolai N. Yakovlev. 1979. *Russia and the United States*. Chicago: University of Chicago Press.

Sklair, Leslie. 2001. *The Transnational Capitalist Class*. Oxford, UK: Blackwell.

Skousen, Mark. 2005. *Vienna & Chicago, Friends or Foes? A Tale of Two Schools of Free-Market Economics*. Washington, DC: Capital Press/Regnery.

"Skupština Economskog Fakulteta u Zagrebu." 1955. *Ekonomski Pregled* 6: 1009–1029.

Smith, H. 1955. "The Economics of Socialism Reconsidered." *The Economic Journal* 65(259): 411–421.

Smith, James A. 1993. *The Idea Brokers: Think Tanks and the Rise of the New Policy Elite*. New York: The Free Press.

Smolinski, Leon. 1971. "The Origins of Soviet Mathematical Economics." *Jahrbuch der Wirtschaft Osteuropas* 2: 137–154.

Solberg, Winton U., and Robert W. Tomilson. 1997. "Academic McCarthyism and Keynesian Economics: The Bowen Controversy at the University of Illinois." *History of Political Economy* 29(1): 55–81.

Soltan, Karol E. 1984. Review of *The Political Economy of Socialism: A Marxist Social Theory* by Branko Horvat. *Ethics* 94: 333–335.

———. 2000. "1989 as Rebirth." In *Between Past and Future: The Revolutions of 1989 and Their Aftermath*, edited by Sorin Antohi and Vladimir Tismaneanu, 25–38. New York: Central European University Press.

Soós, Károly Attila. [1989] 1990. "Privatization, Dogma-Free Self-Management, and Ownership Reform." *Eastern European Economics* 28: 53–70.

Šoškić, Branislav. 1952. "Emile James: Istorija ekonomskih teorija." *Ekonomist* 5(1): 89–94.

———. 1959. "Opšti pogled na stanje naše ekonomske nauke." *Naša Stvarnost* 12: 607–620.

Spence, A. Michael. 1973. "Time and Communication in Economic and Social Interaction." *The Quarterly Journal of Economics* 87: 651–660.

Spiegel, Henry William. 1991. *The Growth of Economic Thought*. Durham, NC: Duke University Press.

Spriano, Paolo. 1967. *Storia del Partito Comunista Italiano*. Torino, Italy: G. Einaudi.

Staffa, Dario. 1975. "Spunti per un'analisi del rapporto tra regime totalitario e letteratura." In *Totalitarismo nelle societa moderne*, Special issue of *L'Est*, edited by Dario Staffa, 7: 7–28.

Stark, David 1989. "Coexisting Organizational Forms in Hungary's Emerging Mixed Economy." In *Remaking the Economic Institutions of Socialism: China and Eastern Europe*, edited by Victor Nee and David Stark, 137–168. Stanford, CA: Stanford University Press.

———. 1992. "From System Identity to Organizational Diversity: Analyzing Social Change in Eastern Europe." *Contemporary Sociology* 21: 299–304.

Stark, David and László Bruszt. 1998. *Postsocialist Pathways: Transforming Politics and Property in East Central Europe*. Cambridge, UK: Cambridge University Press.

Stark, David, and Victor Nee. 1989. "Toward an Institutional Analysis of State Socialism." In *Remaking the Economic Institutions of Socialism: China and Eastern Europe*, edited by Victor Nee and David Stark, 1–31. Stanford, CA: Stanford University Press.

Steedman, Ian, ed. 1995. *Socialism and Marginalism in Economics, 1870–1930*. London: Routledge.

Steele, David Ramsay. 1992. *From Marx to Mises: Post-Capitalist Society and the Challenge of Economic Calculation*. La Salle, IL: Open Court.

Stephanson, Anders. 1984. "Feasible Socialism: A Conversation with Alec Nove." *Social Text* 11(Winter, 1984–1985): 96–109.

Stigler, George. 1965. "The Economist and the State." *The American Economic Review* 55 (1–2): 1–18.

Stiglitz, Joseph E. 1994. *Whither Socialism?* Cambridge, MA: The MIT Press.

———. 1999. "Whither Reform? Ten Years of the Transition," Keynote address at the annual bank conference on development economics, World Bank, Washington, DC.

———. [2002] 2003. *Globalization and Its Discontents*. New York: W. W. Norton.

Stojanović, Radmila. 1956. "Prikaz Kongresa u Rimu." *Ekonomist* 4: 594–604.

Strada, Vittorio. 1988. "Lo Stalinismo come fenomeno europeo." In *Lo stalinismo nella sinistra italiana*. Supplement of *Argomenti socialisti* 4(April): 21–36.

Summers, Lawrence, Jonathan Gruber, and Rodrigo Vergara. 1993. "Taxation and the Structure of Labor Markets: The Case of Corporatism." *The Quarterly Journal of Economics* 108(2): 385–411.

Sumner, Gregory D. 1996. *Dwight Macdonald and the* politics *Circle.* Ithaca, NY: Cornell University Press.

Sutela, Pekka. 1991. *Economic Thought and Economic Reform in the Soviet Union.* Cambridge, UK: Cambridge University Press.

————. 1992. "Rationalizing the Centrally Managed Economy: The Market." In *Market Socialism or the Restoration of Capitalism?* edited by Anders Åslund, 67–91. Cambridge, UK: Cambridge University Press.

Šuvaković, Đorđe. 1977. *Samoupravno i kapitalisticko preduzeće.* Belgrade: Savremena administracija.

Swain, Nigel. 1992. *Hungary: The Rise and Fall of Feasible Socialism.* London and New York: Verso.

Swain, Geoffrey, and Nigel Swain. 1993. *Eastern Europe since 1945.* London: The Macmillan Press.

Sweezy, P. M. 1935. "Economics and the Crisis of Capitalism." *Economic Forum* 3.

Szabó, Béla. 1989. Preface to *Szent barmunk a politika alaprendje* by Tibor Liska. Budapest: Betűvető Kisszövetkezet.

Szabó, Kálmán. 1954. "A közgazdaságtudomány fellendítéséért." *Közgazdasági Szemle* 9(4): 55–74.

Szalai, Erzsébet. 2005. *Socialism: An Analysis of Its Past and Future.* Budapest: Central European University Press.

Szamuely, László. 1982. "The First Wave of the Mechanism Debate (1954–1957)." *Acta Oeconomica* 29(1–2): 1–24.

————. 1984. "The Second Wave of the Mechanism Debate in Hungary and the 1968 Reform in Hungary." *Acta Oeconomica* 33(1–2): 43–67.

————, ed. 1986. *A Magyar Közgazdasági Gondolat Fejlődése, 1954–1978.* Budapest: Közgazdasági és Jogi Könyvkiadó.

Szamuely, László, and László Csaba. 1998. "Economics and Systemic Changes in Hungary, 1945–96." In *Economic Thought in Communist and Post-Communist Europe*, edited by Hans-Jürgen Wagener, 158–212. London and New York: Routledge.

Szentes, Tamás, 1996. "Mátyás Antal." In *Ünnepi dolgozatok Mátyás Antal tanszékvezetői kinevezésének 40. Evfordulójára*, edited by Geza Halász and István Mihalik, 7–13. Budapest: Aula Kiadó Kft.

Tajnikar, Maks. 1977. "The Coexistence of Market and Plan in the Development of Yugoslav Economic Thought." *Eastern European Economics* 16(1): 74–101.

Tardos, Márton. 1982. "Development Program for Economic Control and Organization in Hungary." *Acta Oeconomica* 28(3–4).

Tarshis, Lorie. 1947. *The Elements of Economics, an Introduction to the Theory of Price and Employment.* Boston: Houghton Mifflin Co.

Taussig, Frank William. 1911. *Principles of Economics.* New York: MacMillan and Co.

Taylor, Fred M. 1929. "The Guidance of Production in a Socialist State." *The American Economic Review* 19(1): 1–8.

Teodori, Massimo, ed. 1998. *L'anticomunismo democratico in Italia: Liberali e socialisti che non tacquero su Stalin e Togliatti*. Florence: Liberal Libri.

Tinbergen, Jan. [1956] 1967. *Economic Policy: Principles and Design*. Amsterdam: North-Holland Publishing Company.

———. 1961. "Do Communist and Free Economies Show a Converging Pattern?" *Soviet Studies* 12: 333–341.

Tőkés, Rudolph. 1996. *Hungary's Negotiated Revolution: Economic Reform, Social Change, and Political Succession, 1957–1990*. Cambridge, UK: Cambridge University Press.

Toma, Péter A., and Iván Völgyes. 1977. *Politics in Hungary*. San Francisco: W. H. Freeman and Company.

Tomaš, Rajko. 1989. "Preduzetništvo i privredna reforma." *Naše Teme* 33(11): 2879–2884.

Tomlinson, John. 1999. *Globalization and Culture*. Chicago: University of Chicago Press.

Tranfaglia, Nicola. 2005. *Ma esiste il quarto potere in Italia? Stampa e potere politico nella storia dell'Italia unita*. Milan: Baldini Castoldi Dalai editore.

Treanor, Paul. [n.d.] "Neoliberalism: Origins, Theory, Definition." Retrieved on May 4, 2009, from http://web.inter.nl.net/users/Paul.Treanor/neoliberalism.html.

Tsing, Anna. 2001. "Inside the Economy of Appearances." In *Globalization*, edited by Arjun Appadurai, 155–188. Durham, NC: Duke University Press.

Turner, Victor. 1967. *The Forest of Symbols: Aspects of Ndembu Ritual*. Ithaca, NY: Cornell University Press.

———. [1969] 1995. *The Ritual Process: Structure and Anti-Structure*. Chicago: Aldine Publishing Co.

Tyson, Laura D'Andrea. 1980. *The Yugoslav Economic System and its Performance in the 1970s*. Berkeley: University of California Press.

Uebel, Thomas Ernst. 2004. "Introduction: Neurath's Economics in Critical Context." In *Economic Writings, Sections 1904–1945*, by Otto Neurath, 1–108. Dordrecht: Kluwer Academic Publishers.

UNESCO. 1960. "Candidate for Election to the Executive Board, Curriculum Vitae, Professor Radivoj Uvalic (Yugoslavia)." Retrieved on July 2, 2009, from http://unesdoc.unesco.org/images/0016/001631/163145eb.pdf.

University of Belgrade, Faculty of Law. [n.d]. "In Memoriam, Ivan Maksimović." Retrieved on January 23, 2006, from www.ius.bg.ac.yu/informacije/in_memoriam%20Ivan%20Maksimovic.htm.

University of Zagreb, Faculty of Law. [n.d.]. "Rikard Lang (1913–1994)." Retrieved on November 5, 2009, from www.pravo.hr/PE/onkp/rikard_lang.

Urbinati, Nadia. 1994. Preface to *Liberal Socialism* by Carlo Rosselli. Princeton, NJ: Princeton University Press.

———. 2000. Preface to *On Liberal Revolution* by Piero Gobetti. New Haven, CT: Yale University Press.

Urbinati, Nadia, and Monique Canto-Sperber, eds. [2003] 2004. *Liberal-socialisti: Il futuro di una tradizione*. Venice: Marsilio Editori.

Uvalić, Milica. 1989. "Shareholding Schemes in the Yugoslav Economy." In *Financial Reform in Socialist Economies*, edited by Christine Kessides, Timothy King, Mario Nuti, and Catherine Sokil, 106–125. Washington, DC: The World Bank.

———. 1992. *Investment and Property Rights in Yugoslavia: The Long Transition to a Market Economy.* Cambridge, UK: Cambridge University Press.

Uvalić, Milica, and Vojmir Franičević. 2000. "Introduction: Branko Horvat—Beyond the Mainstream." In *Equality, Participation, Transition: Essays in Honour of Branko Horvat*, edited by Milica Uvalić and Vojmir Franičević, xx–xxxi. New York: St. Martin's Press.

Uvalić, Radivoj. 1952. "Stanje i razvoj ekonomske misli i prakse i njihov medjsobni odnos u našoj zemlji." *Ekonomist* 9–30.

———. 1954. "The Teaching of Economics in Yugoslavia." In *The University Teaching of Social Sciences: Economics*, edited by C. W. Guillebaud et al., 262–282. Amsterdam: UNESCO.

Vahčič, Aleš, and Tea Petrin. 1989. "Financial System for Restructuing the Yugoslav Economy." In *Financial Reform in Socialist Economies*, edited by Christine Kessides, Timothy King, Mario Nuti, and Catherine Sokil, 154–161. Washington, DC: The World Bank.

Valdés, Juan Gabriel. 1995. *Pinochet's Economists: The Chicago School in Chile.* Cambridge, UK: Cambridge University Press.

van der Zweerde, Evert. 2003. "Soviet Philosophy Revisited—Why Joseph Bocheński Was Right while Being Wrong." *Studies in East European Thought* 55(4): 315–342.

Vanek, Jaroslav. 1969. "Decentralization under Workers' Management: A Theoretical Appraisal." *The American Economic Review* 59(1969): 1006–1014.

———. 1970. *The General Theory of Labor-Managed Market Economies.* Ithaca, NY: Cornell University Press.

Varga, György. 1978. "Enterprise Size Pattern in the Hungarian Industry." *Acta Oeconomica* 20: 229–246.

Vas, Zoltán. 1990. *Betiltott Könyvem, Életem III.* Budapest: Szabad Tér Kiadó.

Verdery, Katherine. 1999. "Fuzzy Property: Rights, Power, and Identity in Transylvania's Decollectivization." In *Uncertain Transition: Ethnographies of Change in the Postsocialist World*, edited by Michael Burawoy and Katherine Verdery, 53–81. Lanham, MD: Rowman & Littlefield.

"Vilfredo Pareto, 1848–1923," The History of Economic Thought website. Retrieved May 12, 2009, from: http://homepage.newschool.edu/het//profiles/pareto.htm.

Virno, Paolo. 2004. *A Grammar of the Multitude: For an Analysis of Contemporary Forms of Left.* Cambridge, MA: MIT Press.

Vojnić, Dragomir. 1989. *Ekonomska kriza i reforma socijalizma.* Zagreb: Globus.

Voszka, Éva. 1991. "Ownership Reforms or Privatization?" *Eastern European Economics* 30: 57–91.

———. 1992. "Chances and Dilemmas of Privatization in Hungary." *Annals of Public and Cooperative Economics* 63(2): 317–323.

Wachtel, Howard M. 1973. *Workers' Management and Workers' Wages in Yugoslavia: The Theory and Practice of Participatory Socialism.* Ithaca, NY: Cornell University Press.

Wagener, Hans-Jürgen, ed. 1998. *Economic Thought in Communist and Post-Communist Europe.* London: Routledge.

Wald, Alan M. 1987. *The New York Intellectuals: The Rise and Decline of the Anti-Stalinist Left from the 1930s to the 1980s*. Chapel Hill: University of North Carolina Press.

Walras, Léon. [1874] 1984. *Elements of Pure Economics or the Theory of Social Wealth*. William Jaffé, trans. Philadelphia: Orion Editions.

———. [1896] 1969. *Études d'économie sociale*. Rome: Bizzarri.

Ward, Benjamin Needham. 1956a. "From Marx to Barone: Socialism and the Postwar Yugoslav Industrial Firm." PhD dissertation, University of California, Berkeley.

———. 1956b. "What Is Welfare Economics?" *Ethics* 66(3): 209–213.

———. 1958. "The Firm in Illyria." *The American Economic Review* 48(4): 566–589.

———. 1972. *What's Wrong with Economics?* New York: Basic Books.

"Wassily Leontief—Autobiography." Nobelprize.org. Retrieved on August 18, 2010, from http://nobelprize.org/nobel_prizes/economics/laureates/1973/leontief.html.

Wedel, Janine. 2001. *Collision and Collusion*. New York: St. Martin's Press.

Weintraub, E. Roy. 1985. *General Equilibrium Analysis: Studies in Appraisal*. Cambridge, UK: Cambridge University Press.

Wieser, Friedrich von. [1893] 1989. *Natural Value*. Fairfield, NJ: Augustus M. Kelley, Publishers.

Willetts, Peter. 1978. *The Non-Aligned Movement: The Origins of a Third World Alliance*. London: Frances Pinter.

Williamson, John 1990. "What Washington Means by Policy Reform." Available at www.iie.com/publications/papers/paper.cfm?ResearchID=486.

Winks, Robin. 1987. *Cloak & Gown: Scholars in the Secret War, 1939–1961*. New York: Morrow.

Wolfe, Alan. 1988. Review of *The New York Intellectuals: The Rise and Decline of the Anti-Stalinist Left from the 1930s to the 1980s* by Alan M. Wald. *American Journal of Sociology* 93(4): 974–975.

Woodward, Susan Lampland. 1977. "From Revolution to Post-Revolution: How Much Do We Really Know about Yugoslav Politics?" *World Politics* 30(1): 141–166.

———. 1987. "Symposium on Trotsky's Revolution Betrayed: Fifty Years After." *Comparative Economic Studies* 29(3): 1–3.

———. 1995. *Balkan Tragedy: Chaos and Dissolution after the Cold War*. Washington, DC: Brookings Institution.

Worswick, G. D. N. 1972. "Is Progress in Economic Science Possible?" *The Economic Journal* 82: 73–86.

Wright, Steve. 2002. *Storming Heaven: Class Composition and Struggle in Italian Autonomist Marxism*. London: Pluto Press.

Yergin, Daniel, and Joseph Stanislaw. 1998. *The Commanding Heights: The Battle between Government and the Marketplace That Is Remaking the Modern World*. New York: Simon and Schuster.

Yonay, Yuval P. 1998. *The Struggle over the Soul of Economics: Institutionalist and Neoclassical Economists in America between the Wars*. Princeton, NJ: Princeton University Press.

Young, Cristobal. 2005. "The Politics, Mathematics and Morality of Economics: A Review Essay on Robert Nelson's *Economics as Religion*." *Socio-Economic Review* 3: 161–172.

Yugoslavia: Economic Co-operation with Developing Countries. 1983. Ljubljana: RCCDC.

Yurchak, Alexei. 2006. *Everything Was Forever, Until It Was No More.* Princeton, NJ: Princeton University Press.

Zaccaria, Guelfo. 1964. *200 Comunisti italiani tra le vittime dello stalinismo. Appello del Comitato per la verità sui misfatti dello stalinismo.* Milan: Edizioni Azione Comune.

Zhelitski, Bela. 1997. "Postwar Hungary, 1944–1946." In *The Establishment of Communist Regimes in Eastern Europe, 1944–1949,* edited by Norman Naimark and Leonid Gibianskii, 73–92. Boulder, CO: Westview Press.

Zimmerman, Andrew. 2005. "A German Alabama in Africa: The Tuskeegee Expedition to German Togo and the Transnational Origins of West African Cotton Growers." *American Historical Review* 110(5): 1362–1398.

———. 2010. *Alabama in Africa: Booker T. Washington, the German Empire, and the Globalization of the New South.* Princeton, NJ: Princeton University Press.

Žižek, Slavoj. 1999. "Attempts to Escape the Logic of Capitalism." *London Review of Books* 21(21): [1–13]. Available at www.bard.edu/hrp/resource_pdfs/Žižek.havel.pdf.

———. 2001. *Did Somebody Say Totalitarianism? Five Interventions in the (Mis)use of a Notion.* London and New York: Verso.

Zubek, Voytek. 1994. "The Reassertion of the Left in Post-Communist Poland." *Europe-Asia Studies* 46: 801–837.

Zucchini, Giampaolo. 1970. Review of *Filosofia delle scienze sociali* by R. S. Rudner. *Controcorrente* 2(1–2): 134–136.

Zukin, Sharon. 1975. *Beyond Marx and Tito: Theory and Practice in Yugoslav Socialism.* London: Cambridge University Press.

Županov, Josip. 1969. *Samoupravljanje i društvena moć.* Zagreb: Naše teme, Zagreb.

———. 1990. "Samoupravni socijalizam: Konac jedne utopije." In *Socijalizam u reformi: iskustvo i problemi jugoslavenske privredne reforme,* edited by Zvonimir Baletić and Dragomir Vojnić, 22–36. Zagreb: Informator.

Index

Abbott, Andrew, 226n14
Ács, Lajos, 250n66
Adam, Jan, 260n15
Adamović, Ljubiša S., 82, 92–93
Akerlof, George A., 172
Albania, 191
Alessio, Silvano, 154
Aligica, Paul Dragos, 2, 13, 210, 225n4
Alvarez, Anthony S., 229n24
Amadae, S. M., 234n24
American Council of Learned Societies, 255n43
American Economic Association, 17, 48, 159, 170; *A Survey of Contemporary Economics,* 45
American Economic Review, 41, 95, 97, 166
American Political Science Association, 255n43
American Statistical Association, 128
anarchism, 137, 138, 139, 153
Antal, I., 162
anthropology, 53, 72, 233n10
Antos, István, 247n25
Appel, Hilary, 208
Ardalan, Cyrus, 178
Arendt, Hannah, 254n37
Armstrong, John A., 235n26

Arnott, Richard, 220
Arnsperger, Christian, 226n12
Arrow, Kenneth, 52, 172, 220, 230n40, 232n6, 250n63; Arrow-Debreu model, 47–48, 57, 123, 161, 195–96; "Existence of an Equilibrium for a Competitive Economy," 47–48, 57, 123, 161, 265n11; *Social Choice and Individual Values,* 47–48, 57; on socialism, 33
Asher, Robert E., 243n63
Åslund, Anders, 191, 192, 220, 262n48
Association for Slavic, East European, and Eurasian Studies (ASEEES), 232n2
auction design, 267n2
Augusztinovics, Mária, 114
Austrian School of economics, 114, 168, 261n34, 267n37; and neoclassical economics, 6, 12, 23–24, 30, 34, 84, 116, 159, 170–71, 220, 226n17, 229n23, 242n44, 259n5, 262n39; after Second World War, 6, 83, 159, 170–71, 210, 259n5; and shock therapy, 210; and socialist calculation debate, 17–18, 28–29, 31–32, 87. *See also* Böhm-Bawerk, Eugen von; Hayek, Friedrich A. von; Mises, Ludwig von
Austrian socialism, 25–26, 27, 34
Autonomia movement, 219, 253n24